Research in Critical Theory Since 1965

Research in Critical Theory Since 1965

A Classified Bibliography

Compiled by Leonard Orr

Bibliographies and Indexes in World Literature, Number 21

GREENWOOD PRESS
New York • Westport, Connecticut • London

Library of Congress Cataloging-in-Publication Data

Orr, Leonard.
  Research in critical theory since 1965 : a classified bibliography
/ compiled by Leonard Orr.
    p. cm. — (Bibliographies and indexes in world literature.
ISSN 0742-6801 : no. 21)
  Includes indexes.
  ISBN 0-313-26388-4 (lib. bdg. : alk. paper)
  1. Criticism—Bibliography. I. Title. II. Series.
Z6514.C97077 1989
(PN81]
016.801'95—dc20   89-16863

British Library Cataloguing in Publication Data is available.

Library of Congress Catalog Card Number: 89-16863
ISBN: 0-313-26388-4
ISSN: 0742-6801

First published in 1989

Greenwood Press, Inc.
88 Post Road West, Westport, Connecticut 06881

Printed in the United States of America

The paper used in this book complies with the
Permanent Paper Standard issued by the National
Information Standards Organization (Z39.48-1984).

10 9 8 7 6 5 4 3 2 1

Contents

Preface

Again and again, critics involved in any sort of survey of literary studies since 1965 observe the sudden and sustained importance of critical theory. In his introduction to the valuable 1987 collection <u>Tracing Literary Theory</u>, Joseph Natoli uses the Bakhtinian terms "carnival," "dialogic," "heteroglossia," and "grotesque body," attempting to set forth a ground or space for contemporary critical theories. In this grotesque body of theory, according to Natoli, "continuity and closure are replaced with disruption and openness. Interpenetration here is between the grotesque body and the world in its carnivalesque guise; the world of the carnival itself is a world of openings, of holes and tears in the fabric of the social order. The polyphony of the grotesque theory body attends to the voices of the carnivalesque world" (Natoli, xviii). W. J. T. Mitchell, editor of the journal *Critical Inquiry*, introduced a 1985 collection entitled <u>Against Theory</u> by asking, "What is the importance of all this fuss over theory in literary studies? A gross oversimplification of the controversy might go this way: in the last twenty years, theory has, for a variety of reasons, become one of the 'glamour' fields in academic literary study. . . . Any literature department that does not have a 'theorist' of some sort on its faculty is clearly out of step. More important, any specialist trained in one of the traditional historical fields in literary history is likely to be asked what sort of theory he or she subscribes to. The general assumption is that everyone has a theory that governs his or her practice, and the only issue is whether one is self-conscious about that theory. Not to be aware of one's theoretical assumptions is to be a mere practitioner, slogging along in the routines of scholarship and interpretation" (Mitchell, 1-2).

By the late seventies, a common theme for books of criticism or literary theory was the astonishing increase of interest in criticism on every level of literary studies and in the interdisciplinary excitement literary critical theory had generated. Jonathan Culler, analyzing the success of contemporary theory that is, the appeal it has had within the academy, the way in which it has become a major element of the institutions of literary study treats theory collectively as a genre: "What distinguishes members of this genre is their ability to function not as demonstrations within the parameters of a discipline but as redescriptions that challenge disciplinary boundaries. The works we allude to as 'theory' are those that have had the power to make readers conceive of their own thinking, behavior, and institutions in new ways" (Culler, 9).

This is not, of course, to say that the popularity of critical theory was received wholly as a welcome thing, even from those who are considered to be theorists. Focus on critical theory or metatheory certainly took attention away from the close analysis of literary texts or the historical and textual scholarship that had been the mainstays of literary study prior to 1965. Many critics are concerned about the insularity of critical theory, the isolation of the major theorists, the concentration on terminology, "newness," the exotic, and the lack of connection between literary theory and practical criticism or, more importantly and obviously, the barriers between theory as an advanced intellectual discourse to which people outside the academy have no access and which seems outside of their concerns. While agreeing with Stanley Fish's analysis of "interpretive communities," Edward Said finds that, once again, "we are back to the quandary suggested by the three thousand advanced critics reading each other to everyone else's unconcern. Is it the inevitable conclusion to the formation of an interpretive community that its constituency, its specialized language, and its concerns tend to get tighter, more airtight, more self-enclosed as its own self-confirming authority acquires more power, the solid status of orthodoxy, and a stable constituency?" (Said 15).

The reaction against theory, by the beginning of the 1980s was such that a number of established and respected voices announced that theory was dead, just as critics of an earlier period had announced the death of the novel. For example, Stanley Fish, after almost twenty years of theoretical work, declared the imminent end of theory because of its inconsequentiality for practice. "The fading away of theory is signaled not by silence but by more and more talk, more journals, more symposia, and more entries in the contest for the right to sum up theory's story," according to Fish. His article ends with a suitable flourish: "theory's day is dying; the hour is late; and the only thing left for a theorist to do is to say so, which is what I have been saying here, and, I think, not a moment too soon." (Fish, "Consequences," 128).

The conservative anti-theorists, or those who have come out against the variety of critical theories that became prominent after1967 and are influenced by continental European theorists and philosophers (that is, all of the theoretical approaches or schools that are the subject of this volume), include Gerald Graff, E. D. Hirsch, Howard Felperin, Walter Jackson Bate, William Cain, and Laurence Lerner. Many of these critics seek a return to some perceived simpler and more clearly defined critical moment, less contentious, less scattered and polyphonic, less confusing and forbidding for those who are outside of literary studies, within the universities and without.

Daniel O'Hara, in a strong response to those who are "against theory," specifically Steven Knapp and Walter Benn Michaels, notes that the "effect of their polemic is that it leaves the field open to the long-established and well-heeled, native American, fly-by-the-seat-of-one's-pants critical pragmatists and know-nothings, who have been waiting in the wings ever since the later sixties for such boring annoyances as critical theory, feminism, affirmative action programs, and so forth to disappear; we then can go back to doing business as usual, waging our polite and sensible battles over the sources and significances of some line in Pound's Pisan Cantos or Joyce's Finnegans Wake" (O'Hara 37).

The present critical environment has much to commend it, but the same arguments given in behalf of theory can be used by those who believe in a "crisis-in-criticism" to argue against theory:

(1) critical theory is now diverse and much more highly specialized than it was prior to 1965 so as better to reflect the diversity and complexity of the texts, societies, and institutions which it confronts.

(2) critical theory and literary study generally are now self-conscious in all acts, writings, and phases. Everything is subjected to reinterpretations (always plural), and criticism is understood as being in process or in action, rather than as a closed critical act.

(3) there is a focus now on the institutions relative to the writing and production of criticism, critical theory, and the critic; on the discourses or rhetoric in which criticism takes place; and on the idea of empowerment and persuasion. Criticism is seen as communal, highly intertextual and with both overt and covert agendas and subtexts.

(4) the introduction and development of a critical theory does not mean that the themes, techniques, images, and ideas developed through any other particular critical theory is somehow erased and made only into a relic of the past. William Cain, for example, has pointed out that New Criticism survived in different forms long after it was considered dead and the periods of structuralism and poststructuralism were in force. Similarly,

poststructuralism is unimaginable without the earlier theoretical work in semiotics and structuralism. But this activity of critical theories, their growth and development, their movement into the center and then to the periphery of the academic canon of criticism is something that is continuous; the competitive and careerist aspects of theory are not necessarily related to the values and importance of the concepts or ideas of the theories. The recent flood of theoretical writing has demonstrated the impossibility of sequestering any form of criticism or any critical work. The new environment of theory crosses disciplinary boundaries, drawing upon linguistics, psychoanalysis, philosophy, political analysis, and so on. The wider range of disciplines (and their vocabularies and assumptions) and the use of texts or genres previously considered beyond the purview of the literary critic increase the complexity of theory and practice and the likelihood of dissension. The appearance of fragmentation and chaos also increases the likelihood of attacks upon critical theory and literary studies.

Research in Critical Theory since 1965: A Classified Bibliography is the first of three closely related books that will be published in the next two years by Greenwood Press, the other volumes being A Dictionary of Critical Theory and A Handbook of Critical Theory. Together, these three volumes should form a coherent and substantial starting point for scholars interested in studying either a number of different critical theorists or critical methods or those interested in just one particular theorist or school of criticism. Although the volumes may be used independently, they complement one another. Someone researching, for example, hermeneutics or narratology, may read the appropriate chapters in the Handbook, look up terms from those theories in the Dictionary, and then find substantial, representative, and indexed bibliographies in Research in Critical Theory since 1965.

This classified bibliography is meant to assist anyone researching topics in critical theory or seeking works by major theorists. Coverage is near comprehensive from 1965 through 1987, although a number of works through August 1988 are included. Because I perceive the audience for this work to be a varied one, with different backgrounds and interests in critical theory, I have not excluded works because they were either introductory or too advanced. Instead, I have tried to guide readers to appropriate works through the section-by-section bibliographies. There are 5,523 works listed here (books, articles, dissertations), of which about 350 are repeated in more than one section for the convenience of the researcher. I have limited my listings to works available in English, French, or German. I realize that this is a traditional and biased selection of languages and that there are excellent arguments for including items available only in other languages, especially

Spanish, Italian, and Russian, however, this work is already far longer than expected and sources in other languages must be left to other researchers.

I should say something about the problems of deciding what sections to include, what types of criticism to focus on, and even the order of the sections of the bibliography. Virgil Lokke has recently published an essay titled "Taxonomies Are Never Innocent," in introducing a classification of contemporary critical theories into an "Author-Text-Reader and World" model. Probably the best-known general classification of critical theories is that of M. H. Abrams' The Mirror and the Lamp (1953), which divides theories into the mimetic, the pragmatic, the expressive, and the objective. Many other such classifications have been attempted, but all seemed too broad and slippery to serve the purposes of a reference book such as this. I decided, after trying and abandoning several classification schemes, to use the generally accepted names of current critical approaches, to extensively index each approach, and then to have a general index of the indexes so that works that cover more than one theory or that have not by consensus been classified into one of the theories can still be conveniently located.

There remained a need to organize the approaches and theories in some way. It made sense, for a work which covers criticism since 1965, to begin with structuralism and to end with deconstruction and poststructuralism. Although this may give a possibly false illusion of chronology and teleology to the categories, various plots may be presented within this classification: we begin with formalism or formalistic approaches largely derived from French, Saussurean linguistics, and Czech structuralism; we thus begin with fairly firm disciplinary boundaries and with a focus on particular texts or a corpus of texts, as structuralism seeks a stable grammar or system of rules that regulate the literary texts. Sections A through C (Structuralism; Semiotics [excluding narrative semiotics]; and Narratology) have in common this formalist and linguistic foundation, an interest in norms, rules, systems of signs, and particular techniques, and a tendency towards positivism.

Section A focuses on works about structuralist theories and methods, especially French structuralism, Czech structuralism, and works by Claude Lévi-Strauss, Vladimir Propp, Roland Barthes, and Jan Mukarovsky, or works about or based upon these theorists. Section B focuses on works about semiotic theories and methods, in particular works by and about such theorists as Umberto Eco, Charles Pierce, Juri Lotman, Julia Kristeva, and Ferdinand de Saussure. Section C includes narratology, narrative text-grammars, and narrative semiotics. This section brings together a number of different narrative theories and focuses on those formal elements and techniques that are associated with narrative: characterization, description, repetition, closure, embedded and framed narratives, fictionality and theories of the referent, focalization, intertextuality, narrators and narratees, reflexivity, representation, space, time, and speech. The major theorists for this section include Gérard Genette, A. J. Greimas, Philippe Hamon, Julia Kristeva, Mieke Bal, Juri Lotman, and Mikhail Bakhtin.

After C, we move away from the formalist approaches. Section D, Psychological Criticism, includes, of course, Freudian and Lacanian criticism, but also lists representative works of "Third Force" psychological criticism, Jungian criticism, feminist psychoanalytic criticism, and poststructuralist psychoanalytic criticism and feminist and poststructuralist critiques of psychoanalysis (i.e., Jacques Derrida, Gilles Deleuze and Félix Guattari, Luce Irigaray, Jean-François Lyotard). For the purposes of this bibliography, I have been especially interested in those works which link psychoanalytic approaches with other theories or approaches: psychoanalytic criticism and reader-response, narrative theory and psychoanalytic criticism, semiotics and psychoanalytic criticism, ideological criticism or deconstruction and psychoanalytic criticism, and so on.

The next three sections, E through G, are the more social, political, and ideologically based approaches. Section E concentrates on the works that explicitly are linked to sociological theory and methods, those that provide models for sociological studies of authors and readers, and also non-Marxist theories of the relationship between literary production or consumption and society. Section F focuses on Marxist and ideological theories of literature and literary production and consumption, the relationships between culture and politics, literature and politics, and the ideological bases of theories and theorists. The major theorists for this section include Theodor Adorno, Walter Benjamin, Louis Althusser, Raymond Williams, Terry Eagleton, Fredric Jameson, and, in particular, Gyorgy Lukacs. Section G is devoted to feminist criticism and gender studies.

Sections H through K focus on the activity of reading and interpreting, the activity of understanding a text, and the interrelationships of reader, texts, and world (world in a philosophical or existential sense). Section H is devoted to reader-response criticism. The major theorists include Stanley Fish, Norman Holland, David Bleich, and Wolfgang Iser. Section I deals with reception aesthetics, reception-histories, and the study of collective reading experiences of a text or type of text; the major theorist for this section is Hans-Robert Jauss. Section J lists works of phenomenological criticism and theory, especially those based upon the Geneva School (Georges Poulet, Jean Starobinski, Jean Rousset, Jean-Pierre Richard) and the writings of Jean-Paul Sartre, Maurice Blanchot, Roman Ingarden, Gaston Bachelard, and Maurice Merleau-Ponty. Section K lists works in literary hermeneutics, especially works by and about Martin Heidegger, Hans-Georg Gadamer, Peter Szondi, and Paul Ricoeur.

"Deconstructionist and Poststructuralist Criticism," section L, is probably the most problematic classification, in part because of the ubiquity of terms involved and in part because of the resistance of these theorists to such classification and definitions. In addition, many poststructuralists would place themselves in opposition to deconstruction, as well as structuralism and formalist approaches. I include in this section theorists who attempt to place themselves beyond, outside of, or against a traditional cultural form of thinking that believes in ground, presence, direction, empiricism, and authority. The list of theorists included in this section indicates the diversity and lack of consensus within the rubric of the section: here are included works by and about Jacques Derrida, Harold Bloom, Gilles Deleuze, Jean Baudrillard, Philippe Lacoue-Labarthe and Jean-Luc Nancy, Paul de Man, J. Hillis Miller, Geoffrey Hartman, Jean-François Lyotard, and Michel Foucault. Many of the works in this section are devoted to defining the characteristics of poststructuralism, postmodernism, or post-Derridean philosophy or criticism.

Each section has its own index and thus may be used independently of the other sections, if one is interested just in one particular theoretical field or approach. These section indexes are grouped together following the Classified Bibliography as "Classified Indexes of Subjects and Major Theorists," their organization paralleling that of the bibliography proper. Following the classified indexes is a General Index which will guide the researcher to the appropriate sections of the bibliography. The General Index usually should be checked first for specific theorists or topics. The final Author Index applies to the entire bibliography, accessing every item. Every item in the bibliography has a letter, indicating the section, and a number indicating its place within the section, and these entry codes are used in the indexing. One can check a topic such as *intertextuality* in the General Index and find "B, C, D, G, H." Checking these individual section indexes will lead to items on intertextuality classified by approach or critical theory. Not included in the General Index are listings of anthologies, applications of theories, bibliographies, and introductions and methodological surveys: these categories appear in every section index. Journal title abbreviations follow the abbreviations established by the Modern Language Association (these appear in every annual MLA Bibliography).

It was not possible to make this bibliography either complete in the various sections or exactly current with the moment of publication. I have tried to make up for this by listing the many introductions and methodological surveys (the largest item in each section index) and any bibliographies on the theories or individual theorists. I have also listed, for each section, a number of representative applications of the theory to various literatures, periods, and genres so that the researcher new to that theory can read some examples of the practice and results. I have used many sources in compiling this bibliography. Besides the obvious sources, such as the annual bibliographies of the MLA, the MHRA, and such works as <u>Dissertations Abstracts International</u> and <u>Language and Language Behavior Abstracts</u>, I have also made a number of database searches for topics, keywords, and theorists.

There are many advantages to having this information gathered in a single volume, classified, and indexed. While my ideal reader will of course begin with the first item of section A and read straight through until the end of the General Index, noting down, along the way, any items that seem to be of interest, I expect that most readers will be researching a specific topic or theorist, using the indexes, or else learning about a single critical theory by consulting an entire section and its section index.

WORKS CITED

Cain, William E. <u>The Crisis in Criticism: Theory, Literature, and Reform in English Studies</u> (Baltimore: Johns Hopkins UP, 1984).

Culler, Jonathan. <u>On Deconstruction</u> (Ithaca: Cornell UP, 1982).

Fish, Stanley. "Consequences," in Mitchell, ed., <u>Against Theory</u> (Chicago: U of Chicago P, 1985), 106-31.

Lokke, Virgil. "Introduction: *Taxonomies are Never Innocent,*" in Clayton Koelb and Virgil Lokke, eds. <u>The Current in Criticism: Essays on the Present and Future of Literary Theory</u> (West Lafayette IN: Purdue UP, 1987), 1-25.

Mitchell, W. J. T., ed. <u>Against Theory: Literary Studies and the New Pragmatism</u> (Chicago: U of Chicago P, 1985).

Natoli, Joseph, ed. <u>Tracing Literary Theory</u> (Urbana: U of Illinois P, 1987).

O'Hara, Daniel. "Revisionary Madness: The Prospects of American Literary Theory at the Present Time," in Mitchell, ed., <u>Against Theory</u> (Chicago: U of Chicago P, 1985), 31-47.

Said, Edward W. "Opponents, Audiences, Constituencies, and Community," in W. J. T. Mitchell, ed. <u>The Politics of Interpretation</u> (Chicago: U of Chicago P, 1983), 7-32.

ADDITIONAL REFERENCES

Adams, Hazard and Leroy Searle, eds. <u>Critical Theory since 1965</u> (Tallahassee: UP of Florida/Florida State UP, 1986).

Arac, Jonathan. <u>Critical Genealogies: Historical Situations for Postmodern Literary Studies</u> (NY: Columbia UP, 1987).

Eagleton, Terry. <u>Literary Theory: An Introduction</u> (Minneapolis: U of Minnesota P, 1983).

Graff, Gerald and Reginald Gibbons, eds. <u>Criticism in the University</u> (Evanston: Northwestern UP, 1985).

Jay, Gregory S. and David L. Miller, eds. <u>After Strange Texts: The Role of Theory in the Study of Literature</u> (University AL: U of Alabama P, 1985).

Nelson, Cary, ed. <u>Theory in the Classroom</u> (Urbana: U of Illinois P, 1986).

Smith, Barbara Herrnstein. <u>Contingencies of Value: Alternative Perspectives for Critical Theory</u> (Cambridge: Harvard UP, 1988).

Weber, Samuel. <u>Institution and Interpretation</u> (Minneapolis: U of Minnesota P, 1987).

Acknowledgments

While researching the materials for this book, I have been assisted by many individuals and institutions. I received a one-semester research leave from the University of Notre Dame which gave me time to complete the first draft of the manuscript. I would like to thank Michael Loux and Nathan Hatch, Dean and Associate Dean of the College of Arts and Letters, for their support of my work. My colleagues in the Department of English have been helpful in many ways: they have made helpful suggestions, read sections of manuscript, discussed critical ideas with me, introduced me to theoretical works which proved to be very valuable, and lent me books and articles. I wish to thank, in particular, the chair of the department, Joseph Buttigieg, Charlene Avallone, Gerald Bruns, Stephen Fredman, and Chris Vanden Bossche. I have received much help from the professional staff of the University library, especially Laura Fuderer and Linda Gregory. Margaret Jasiewicz and Cheryl Reed prepared the manuscript for publication and assisted my work in many ways.

This book began as the bibliography to my handbook of critical theory, still in preparation. My editor at Greenwood Press, Marilyn Brownstein, suggested that we make the unwieldy bibliography a separate book, and she made suggestions about the classifications and indexes. I am very grateful to her for her encouragement, her support for these projects, and for her patience. Finally, I would like to thank my wife, Sarah, and my daughter, Leah, for their patience with my projects.

Research in Critical
Theory Since 1965

A. Structuralism

a1. Abel, Lionel. "Sartre vs. Lévi-Strauss." <u>Commonweal</u> 84 (1966), 364-68.

a2. Ackerman, Robert. "Frazer on Myth and Ritual." <u>JHI</u> 36 (1975), 115-34.

a3. Alberes, R.-M. "Qu-est-ce que le 'structuralisme' dans la littérature? <u>RdP</u> 74 (July-Aug., 1967), 8-15.

a4. Ames, Sanford S. "Structuralism, Language, and Literature." <u>JAAC</u> 32 (1973), 89-94.

a5. Anozie, Sunday O. <u>Structural Models and African Poetics: Towards a Pragmatic Theory of Literature</u> (Boston: Routledge & Kegan Paul, 1981).

a 6. <u>L'Analyse structurale du récit</u> (Paris: Seuil, 1981) [rpt. of <u>Communications</u> 8 (1966)].

a7. Antoine, Gerald. "La nouvelle critique: How Far Has It Got?" <u>Style</u> 8 (1974), 18-33.

a8. Armstrong, Nancy. "Domesticating a Foreign Devil: Structuralism in English Letters a Decade Later." <u>Semiotica</u> 42 (1982), 247-77.

a9. Auzias, Jean-Marie. <u>Clefs pour le structuralisme</u> (Paris: Seghers, 1967).

a10. Badcock, C. R. <u>Lévi-Strauss: Structuralism and Sociological Theory</u> (NY: Holmes & Meier, 1976).

a11. Bader, Wolfgang. "Der genetische Strukturalismus Lucien Goldmanns: Untersuchung uber den Zusammenhang seiner Begriffe." <u>Neohelicon</u> 8 (1981), 63-109.

a12. Baran, Henryk, ed. <u>Semiotics and Structuralism: Readings from the Soviet Union</u> (White Plains NY: International Arts and Sciences Press, 1976).

a13. Barthes, Roland. <u>Le Degré zéro de l'écriture/Elements de sémiologie</u> (Paris: Gonthier, 1965 [<u>Elements of Semiology</u> (London: Cape; NY: Hill & Wang, 1967) and <u>Writing Degree Zero</u> (London: Cape; NY: Hill & Wang, 1972)].
a14. ----------. <u>Critique et vérité</u> (Paris: Seuil, 1966) [<u>Criticism and Truth</u> (Minneapolis: U of Minnesota P, 1987)].
a15. ----------. <u>Systeme de la mode</u> (Paris: Seuil, 1967) [<u>The Fashion System</u> (NY: Hill & Wang, 1983)].
a16. ----------. <u>L'Empire des signes</u> (Geneva: Skira, 1970) [<u>Empire of Signs</u> (NY: Hill & Wang, 1982)].
a17. ----------. <u>S/Z</u> (Paris: Seuil, 1970) [Eng. trans., <u>S/Z</u> (NY: Hill & Wang, 1974)].
a18. ----------. <u>Sade, Fourier, Loyola</u> (Paris: Seuil, 1971) [Eng. trans., NY: Hill & Wang, 1977].
a19. ----------, *et al* . <u>Exégese et herméneutique</u> (Paris: Seuil, 1971).
a20. ----------. <u>Critical Essays</u> (Evanston: Northwestern UP, 1972) [orig. pubd. 1964].
a21. ----------. <u>Mythologies</u> (London: Cape; NY: Hill & Wang, 1972) [orig. pubd. 1957].
----------. <u>Le plaisir du texte</u> (Paris: Seuil, 1973) [<u>The Pleasure of the Text</u> (NY: Hill & Wang, 1975)].
a22. ----------, *et al* . <u>Structural Analysis and Biblical Exegesis: Interpretational Essays</u> (Pittsburgh: Pickwick P, 1974).
a23. ----------. <u>Roland Barthes par Roland Barthes</u> (Paris: Seuil, 1975) [Eng. trans. (NY: Hill & Wang, 1977)].
a24. ----------, *et al* . <u>Poétique du récit</u> (Paris: Seuil, 1977).
a25. ----------. <u>Fragments d'un discours amoureux</u> (Paris: Seuil, 1977) [<u>A Lover's Discourse: Fragments</u> (NY: Hill & Wang, 1978)].
a26. ----------. <u>Image-Music-Text</u> (London: Fontana/Collins; NY: Hill & Wang, 1977).
a27. ----------. <u>Leçon: Leçon inaugurale de la chaire de sémiologie littéraire du College de France</u> (Paris: Seuil, 1978).
a28. ----------. <u>Sollers écrivain</u> (Paris: Seuil, 1979) [<u>Writer Sollers</u> (Minneapolis: U of Minnesota P, 1987).
a29. ----------. <u>The Eiffel Tower and Other Mythologies</u> (NY: Hill & Wang, 1979).

a30. ----------. La Chambre claire: Note sur la photographie (Paris: Gallimard, Seuil, 1980) [Camera Lucida (NY: Hill & Wang, 1982)].

a31. ----------. Sur la litterature (Grenoble: Presses de l'université de Grenoble, 1980).

a32. ----------. New Critical Essays (NY: Hill & Wang, 1980).

a33. ----------. La Grain de la voix. Entretiens 1962-1980 (Paris: Seuil, 1981) [The Grain of the Voice: Interviews 1962-1980 (NY: Hill & Wang, 1985)].

a34. ----------. L'obvie et l'obtus: essais critiques III (Paris: Seuil, 1982) [The Responsibility of Forms: Critical Essays on Music, Art, and Representation (NY: Hill & Wang, 1985)].

a35. ----------. Le bruissement de la langue: essai critiques IV (Paris: Seuil, 1984) [The Rustle of Language (NY: Hill & Wang, 1986)].

a36. ----------. L'aventure sémiologique (Paris: Seuil, 1985).

a37. ----------. Incidents (Paris: Seuil, 1987).

a38. Bayley, John. "Formalist Games and Real Life." EIC 31.4 (1981), 271-81.

a39. Beauchamp, William. "From Structuralism to Semiotics." RR 67 (1976), 226-36.

a40. Belic, Oldrich. "Les principes méthodologiques du structuralisme esthétique tschéchoslavique." La pensée 154 (1970), 52-61.

a41. Bellour, Raymond and Catherine Clément, eds. Claude Lévi-Strauss (Paris: Gallimard, 1979).

a42. Bennett, James R. "Todorov and the Structuralist Science of Poetics," in H. R. Garvin, ed. Phenomenology, Structuralism, Semiology (Lewisburg: Bucknell UP, 1976), 127-39.

a43. Benoist, Jean Marie. La Révolution structurale (Paris: Grasset, 1975).

a44. Bensmaia, Reda. The Barthes Effect: The Essay as Reflective Text (Minneapolis: U of Minnesota P, 1987).

a45. Bierwisch, Manfred. "Strukturalismus, Geschichte, Probleme und Methoden." Kursbuch 5 (1966), 77-152.

a46. Boon, James A. From Symbolism to Structuralism: Lévi-Strauss in a Literary Tradition (NY: Harper and Row, 1972).

a47. ----------. "An Endogamy of Poets and Vice Versa: Exotic Ideals in Romanticism/Structuralism." SIR 18 (1979), 333-61.

a48. Boudon, Raymond. The Uses of Structuralism (London: Heinemann, 1971).
a49. ----------. Structuralism (Cambridge: Schenkman, 1977).

a50. Bourdieu, P. "Structuralism and Theory of Social Knowledge." Social Research 35 (1968), 681-706.

a51. Bovon, François, ed. Analyse structurale et exégese biblique (Neuchatel: Delachaux & Niestlé, 1971).

a52. Bowers, Fred. "Content, Form and Meaning in Literary Texts." ESC 7.2 (1981), 225-33.

a53. Brady, Patrick. Structuralist Perspectives in Criticism of Fiction: Essays on Manon Lescaut and La Vie de Marianne (Bern: Lang, 1978).

a54. Bremond, Claude. Logique du récit (Paris: Seuil, 1973).

a55. Broekman, Jan. Structuralism: Moscow, Prague, Paris (Dordrecht, Holland, and Boston: D. Reidl, 1974).

a56. Bruss, Elizabeth W. "Signs and Practices: An Expanded Poetics." Poetics 7 (1978), 263-72.
a57. ----------. "Roland Barthes," in Beautiful Theories: The Spectacle of Discourse in Contemporary Criticism (Baltimore: Johns Hopkins UP, 1982), 363-461.

a58. Brutting, Richard. "Zur Situation des franzosischen Strukturalismus: Ein Literaturbericht." LiLi 14 (1974), 111-35.

a59. Cabanes, Jean-Louis. Critique littéraire et sciences humaines (Toulouse: Privat, 1974).

a60. Calinescu, Alexandru. "La Poétique structurale de Roland Barthes." Synthesis 7 (1980), 83-91.

a61. Calloud, Jean. Structral Analysis of Narrative (Philadelphia: Fortress P, 1976).

a62. Caws, Peter. "What Is Structuralism?" PR 35 (1968), 75-91.
a63. ----------. "Structuralism," in Philip P. Wiener, ed., Dictionary of the History of Ideas: Studies of Selected Pivotal Ideas (NY: Scribner's, 1973), 4: 322-40.
a64. ----------. "The Recent Literature of Structuralism, 1965-1970." Philosophische Rundschau 18 (1971), 63-78.

a65. Cervenka, Miroslav. "Die Grundkatagorien des Prager literaturwissenschaft-lichen Strukturalismus," in V. Zmegac and Z. Skreb, eds. Zur Kritik literatur-wissenschaftlicher Methodologie (Frankfurt: Athenaum, 1973), 137-68.

a66. ----------. Der Bedeutungsaufbau der literarischen Werks (Munchen: Fink, 1978).

a67. ----------. "New Perspectives on Czech Structuralism." PTL 4 (1979), 359-70.

a68. ----------. "The Literary Work as Sign," in J. Odmark, ed., Language, Literature and Meaning II: Current Trends in Literary Research (Amsterdam: Benjamins, 1980), 1-25.

a69. ----------. "The Literary Artifact," in W. Steiner, ed. The Sign in Music and Literature (Austin: U of Texas P, 1981), 86-102.

a70. Champagne, Roland A. "Between Orpheus and Eurydice: Roland Barthes and the Historicity of Reading." ClioI 8 (1979), 229-38.

a71. ----------. "The Dialectics of Style: Insights from the Semiology of Roland Barthes." Style 13 (1979), 279-91.

a72. ----------. Literary History in the Wake of Roland Barthes: Re-Defining the Myths of Reading (Birmingham AL: Summa, 1984).

a73. Chatman, Seymour. "On the Formalist-Structuralist Theory of Character." JLS 1 (1972), 57-79.

a74. ----------. Story and Discourse: Narrative Structure in Fiction and Film (Ithaca: Cornell UP, 1978).

a75. Chvatik, Kvetoslav. Strukturalismus und Avantgarde (Munchen: Hanser, 1970).

a76. ----------. Tschechoslowakischer Strukturalismus: Theorie und Geschichte (Munchen: Fink, 1981).

a77. ----------. "Semiotics of a Literary Work of Art: Dedicated to the 90th Birthday of Jan Mukarovsky (1891-1975)." Semiotica 37 (1981), 193-214.

a78. Civikov, G. "Das aesthetische Zeichen der Prager Strukturalismus und das Peircesche Zeichenmodel." Neophilologus 65 (1981), 321-42.

a79. Clément, Catherine. Lévi-Strauss, ou la structure et le malheur (Paris: Seghers, 1974).

a80. Clifford, Gay. "The Benefits of Wilderness: Structuralist Criticism." Encounter 57.1 (July, 1981), 53-59.

a81. Collinder, Bjorn. "Les origines du structuralisme," in Acta Societatis Linguisticae Upsaliensis, N. S. I. (Uppsala: Almqvist & Wiksell, 1968), 1-15.

a82. Conley, Tom. "Barthes *Exces* : The Silent Apostrophe of S/Z." VLang 11 (1977), 355-84.

a83. Coquet, Jean-Claude. "Questions de sémantique structurale." Critique 24 (1968), 70-85.

a84. Corvez, Maurice. "Les nouveaux structuralistes." RPL 67 (1969), 582-605.
a85. ----------. Les structuralistes: les linguistes, Michel Foucault, Claude Lévi-Strauss, Jacques Lacan, Louis Althusser, les critiques littéraires (Paris: Aubier Montaigne, 1969).

a86. Courtes, Joseph. Lévi-Strauss et les contraintes de la pensée mythique (Paris: Mame, 1973).

a87. Cressant, Pierre. Lévi-Strauss (Paris: Editions Universitaires, 1970).

a88. Culler, Jonathan. "Structure of Ideology and Ideology of Structure." NLH 4 (1973), 471-82.
a89. ----------. Structuralist Poetics: Structuralism, Linguistics, and the Study of Literature (Ithaca: Cornell UP, 1975).
a90. ----------. Roland Barthes (NY: Oxford UP, 1983).

a91. Curtis, James M. "Marshall McLuhan and French Structuralism." Boundary 1 (1972), 134-46.

a92. Dahl, Rex C. "Structural Literary Analysis in Prose Literature: A Morphological Approach." LangQ 12.3-4 (1974), 47-49.

a93. D'Amico, Robert. "The Contours and Coupures of Structuralist Theory." Telos 17 (1977), 70-97.

a94. Davidson, Hugh M. "The Critical Position of Roland Barthes." ConL 9 (1968), 367-76.
a95. ----------. "Sign, Sense, and Roland Barthes," in W. K. Wimsatt, ed., Literary Criticism: Idea and Act (Berkeley: U of California P, 1974), 228-41.

a96. Deak, Frantisek. "Structuralism in Theatre: The Prague School Contribution." Drama Review 20 (1976), 83-94.

a97. Dee, James H. "Lévi-Strauss at the Theban Gates." Classical World 72 (1979), 257-61.

a98. DeGeorge, Fernande. "From Russian Formalism to French Structuralism." Comparative Literature Studies 14 (1977), 20-30.

a99. DeGeorge, Richard T. and Fernande M. DeGeorge, eds. The Structuralists: From Marx to Lévi-Strauss (NY: Doubleday/Anchor, 1972).

a100. DeJean, Joan. "In Search of the Artistic Text: Recent Works by Lotman and Uspensky." Sub-Stance 17 (1977), 149-58.

a101. De Lauretis, Teresa. "The Shape of the World: Report on Structuralism and Semiotics in Italy." BA 49 (1975), 227-32.

a102. Dessaix, Robert. "Yuri Lotmann: Theories of a Soviet Structuralist." NLRev 5 (1978), 38-44.

a103. Detweiler, Robert. Story, Sign, and Self: Phenomenology and Structuralism as Literary-Critical Methods (Philadelphia: Fortress, 1978),

a104. Dijk, Teun A. van., ed. "The Future of Structural Poetics." Poetics 8.6 (1979) [special issue].

a105. Dolezel, Lubomir. "The Prague School and the Statistical Theory of Poetic Language." Prague Studies in Mathematical Linguistics 2 (1967), 97-104.
a106. ----------. "Russian and Prague School Functional Stylistics." Style 2 (1968), 143-58.
a107. ----------. "Prague School Stylistics," in B. B. Kachru and H. F. W. Stahlke, eds. Current Trends in Stylistics (Edmonton: Linguistic Research, 1972), 37-48.
a108. ----------. "From Motifemes to Motifs." Poetics 4 (1972), 55-90.
a109. ----------. "Narrative Composition: A Link Between German and Russian Poetics," in S. Bann and J. E. Bowlt, eds. Russian Formalism (Edinburgh: Scottish Academic P, 1973), 73-84.
a110. ----------. "Extensional and Intensional Narrative Worlds." Poetics 8 (1979), 193-211.
a111. ----------. "In Defence of Structural Poetics." Poetics 8 (1979), 521-30.
a112. ----------. Essays in Structural Poetics and Narrative Semantics (Toronto: Prepub. of Toronto Semiotic Circle, Victoria U, 1979).
a113. ----------. "Mukarovsky and the Idea of Poetic Truth." Russian Literature 12 (1982), 283-97.
a114. ----------. "The Conceptual System of Prague School Poetics: Mukarovsky and Vodicka," in P. Steiner, M. Cervenka, and R. Vroon, eds. The Structure of the Literary Process: Studies Dedicated to the Memory of Felix Vodicka (Amsterdam: John Benjamins, 1982), 109-26.

a115. Donato, Eugenio. "On Structuralism and Literature." <u>MLN</u> 82 (1967), 549-74.
a116. ----------. "Structuralism: The Aftermath." <u>Sub-Stance</u> 7 (1973), 9-26.

a117. Donoghue, Denis, Peter Brooks, and Edith Kurzweil. "French Structuralist Theories." <u>PR</u> 47 (1980), 397-425.

a118. Dorfman, Eugene. <u>The Narreme in the Medieval Epic and Romance: An Introduction to Narrative Structure</u> (Toronto: U of Toronto P, 1969).

a119. Doubrovsky, Serge. <u>The New Criticism in France</u> (Chicago: U of Chicago P, 1973).

a120. Ducrot, Oswald, *et al* . <u>Qu'est-ce que le structuralisme?</u> (Paris: Seuil, 1968).

a121. Durand, Gilbert. "'Les chats, les rats, et les structuralistes.' Symbole et structuralisme figuratif." <u>CIS</u> 17-18 (1969), 13-38.

a122. Eagle, Herbert. "The Czech Structuralist Debate on the Role of Intonation in Verse Structure," in L. Matejka, ed. <u>Sound, Sign, and Meaning: Quinquagenary of the Prague Linguistic Circle</u> (Ann Arbor: Michigan Slavic Contributions, 1976), 521-41.
a123. ----------. "The Semiotics of Art: A Dynamic View." <u>Semiotica</u> 19 (1977), 367-96.
a124. ----------. "Verse as a Semiotic System: Tynjanov, Jakobson, Mukarovsky, Lotman Extended." <u>SEEJ</u> 25 (1981), 47-61.

a125. Ehrmann, Jacques, ed. <u>Structuralism</u> (NY: Doubleday/Anchor, 1970) [rpt. of special issue of <u>YFS</u>, 36-37 (1966)].

a126. Eimermacher, Karl. "Zum Verhaltnis von formalisitscher, strukturalistischer und semiotischer Analyse," in D. Kimpel and B. Pinkerneil, eds. <u>Methodische Praxis der Literaturwissenschaft: Modelle der Interpretation</u> (Kronberg: Scriptor, 1975), 259-83.

a127. Elevich, Bernard. "Structuralism: The Name of the Game." <u>BForum</u> 1 (1974), 99-110.

a128. Ellis, David. "roland BARTHES par roland barthes." <u>Cambridge Quarterly</u> 7.3 (1977), 252-66.

a129. Elstein, Yoav. "Structuralism in Literary Criticism: A Method and Application in Two Representative Hasidic Tales." <u>DAI</u> 35 (1975), 5397A.

a130. Erickson, John D. "Structuralism and the Missing Third Term." ECr 16.1 (1976), 68-75.

a131. Fages, Jean-Baptiste. Comprendre le structuralisme (Toulouse: Eduard Privat, 1967).
a132. ----------. Le Structuralisme en proces (Toulouse: Privat, 1968).

a133. Felperin, Howard. "Structuralism in Retrospect," in Beyond Deconstruction: The Uses and Abuses of Literary Theory (Oxford: Clarendon, 1985), 74-103.

a134. Ferrara, Fernando. "Theory and Model for the Structural Analysis of Fiction." NLH 5 (1974), 245-68.

a135. Filho, Leodegario A. de Azevedo. "Strukturalismus und Prosadichtung." GRM 20 (1971), 213-20.

a136. Finas, Lucette. "La pirogue et la spirale." Critique 27 (1971), 998-1008.

a137. Finney, Kathe Davis. "Crazy Janes Talks with Jonathan Culler: Using Structuralism to Teach Lyric Poetry." CEA 43.3 (1981), 29-36.

a138. Fish, Stanley. "Structuralist Homiletics," in Is There a Text in this Class? The Authority of Interpretive Communities (Cambridge: Harvard UP, 1980), 181-96.

a139. Fizer, John. "Ingarden's and Mukarovsky's Binominal Definition of the Literary Work of Art: A Comparative View of their Respective Onotologies." Russian Literature 13 (1983), 269-90.

a140. Flaschka, Horst. "Von der Mytheanalyse zur strukturalen Analyse literarischer Werke: Strukturalismus am Beispiel von Lévi-Strauss." WW 27 (1977), 402-13.

a141. Fokkema, Douwe Wessel. "Continuity and Change in Russian Formalism, Structuralism, and Soviet Semiotics." PTL 1 (1976), 153-96.
---------- and Elrud Kunne-Ibsch. Theories of Literature in the Twentieth Century: Structuralism, Marxism, Aesthetics of Reception (NY: St. Martin's Press, 1978).

a142. Francq, H. "Polemique de la critique universitaire et de la nouvelle critique." Culture 29 (1968), 150-67.

a143. Freedman, Sanford and Carole Taylor. Roland Barthes: A Bibliographical Reader's Guide (NY: Garland, 1983).

a144. Funt, David. "Roland Barthes and the *Nouvelle Critique* ." JAAC 26.3 (1968), 329-40.
a145. ----------. "Piaget and Structuralism." Diacritics 1.2 (1971), 15-20.

a146. Galan, F. W. "Literary System and Literary Change: The Prague School Theory of Literary History." PMLA 94 (1979), 275-85.
a147. ----------. Historic Structures: The Prague School Project, 1928-1946 (Austin: U of Texas P, 1985).

a148. Gardner, Howard. The Quest for Mind: Piaget, Lévi-Strauss, and the Structuralist Movement (NY: Vintage, 1974).

a149. Geertz, Clifford. "The Cerebral Savage: On the Work of Claude Lévi-Strauss." Encounter 28 (1967), 25-32.

a150. Gellner, Ernest. "What Is Structuralism?" TLS (July 31, 1981), 881-83.

a151. Genette, Gérard. Figures (Paris: Seuil, 1966).
a152. ----------. Figures II (Paris: Seuil, 1969).
a153. ----------. Figures III (Paris: Seuil, 1972).
a154. ----------. Mimologiques, Voyage en Cratylie (Paris: Seuil, 1976).
a155. ----------. Introduction a l'architexte (Paris: Seuil, 1979).
a156. ----------. Narrative Discourse: An Essay in Method (Ithaca: Cornell UP, 1980).
a157. ----------. Figures of Literary Discourse (NY: Columbia UP, 1982).
a158. ----------. Palimpsestes: La littérature au second degré (Paris: Seuil, 1982).

a159. Girard, René. "Differentiation and Undifferentiation in Lévi-Strauss and Current Critical Theory." ConL 17 (1976), 404-29.

a160. Glowinski, Michael. "Polish Structuralism." BA 49 (1975), 239-43.

a161. Glucksmann, Miriam. Structuralist Analysis in Contemporary Social Thought: A Comparison of the Theories of Claude Lévi-Strauss and Louis Althusser (London: Routledge, 1974).

a162. Gonseth, Ferdinand. "La philosophie ouverte, terrain d'accueil du structuralisme." CIS 17-18 (1969), 39-71.

a163. Goodheart, Eugene. "The Myths of Roland." PR 47 (1980), 199-212 [on Barthes].

a164. Goodson, A. C. "Oedipus Anthropologicus." MLN 94 (1979), 688-701.

a165. Gras, Vernon W., ed. European Literary Theory and Practice. From Existential Phenomenology to Structuralism (NY: Delta, 1973).

a166. Greenblatt, Daniel L. "Structuralism and Literary Studies." Centrum 2.2 (1974), 73-83.

a167. Greenwood, David. Structuralism and the Biblical Text (Berlin and NY: Mouton, 1985).

a168. Grigsby, John L. "Sign, Symbol and Metaphor: Todorov and Chretien de Troyes." ECr 18.3 (1978), 28-40.

a169. Grivel, Ch. "Analytiques du discourse littéraire: Prenant argument de Figures par Gérard Genette." Neophil 52 (1968), 12-21, 129-38.

a170.Grygar, Mojmir. "The Possibilities of a Structural Analysis of the Literary Process." Russian Literature 12 (1982), 331-400.

a171. Gunther, Hans. "Zur Strukturalismus-Diskussion in der sowjetischen Literaturwissenschaft." WSI 14 (1969), 1-21.
a172. ----------. Struktur als Prozess: Studien zur Asthetik und Literaturtheorie des tschechischen Strukturalismus (Munchen: Fink, 1973).
a173. ----------. "Exakte Literaturwissenschaft und Kultursemiotik: Zwei Tendenzen im sowjetischen Strukturalismus." LiLi 4 (1974), 137-46.
a174. ----------. "Literarische Evolution und Literaturgeschichte: Zum Beitrag des russischen Formalismus," in B. Cerquiglini and H. U. Gumbrecht, eds. Der Diskurs der Literatur- und Sprachgeschichte (Frankfurt: Suhrkamp, 1983), 265-79.

a175. Hamon, Philippe. "Rhetorical Status of the Descriptive." YFS 61 (1981), 1-26.

a176. Harari, Josué V. Structuralists and Structuralism: A Selected Bibliography of French Contemporary Thought 1960-1970 (Ithaca: Diacritics, 1971).
a177. ----------. "The Maximum Narrative: An Introduction to Barthes' Recent Criticism." Style 8 (1974), 56-77.
a178. ----------. "Changing the Object of Criticism: 1965-1978." MLN 94 (1979), 784-96.

a179. ----------, ed. Textual Strategies: Perspectives in Post-Structuralist Criticism (Ithaca: Cornell UP, 1979).

a180. Harland, Richard. Superstructuralism: The Philosophy of Structuralism and Post-Structuralism (London and NY: Methuen, 1987).

a181. Harris, Marvin. The Rise of Anthropological Theory: A History of Theories of Culture (NY: Crowell, 1968) [chap. on "French Structuralism"].

a182. Hartman, Geoffrey H. "Structuralism: The Anglo-American Adventure," in Beyond Formalism: Literary Essays 1958-1970 (New Haven: Yale UP, 1970), 3-23.

a183. Hawkes, Terence. Structuralism and Semiotics (Berkeley: U of California P, 1977).

a184. Heath, Stephen. Vertige du déplacement. Lecture de Barthes (Paris: Fayard, 1974).

a185. Heller, L. G. and James Macris. Toward a Structural Theory of Literary Analysis (Worcester MA: Institute of Systems Analysis, 1970).

a186. Hendricks, William O. "The Structural Study of Narration: Sample Analyses." Poetics 3 (1972), 100-23.
a187. ----------. "Linguistic Models and the Study of Narration: A Critique of Todorov's Grammaire du Décameron." Semiotica 5 (1972), 263-89.
a188. ----------. "Methodology of Narrative Structural Analysis." Semiotica 7 (1973), 163-84.
a189. ----------. Essays on Semiolinguistics and Verbal Art (The Hague: Mouton, 1973).

a190. Hermand, Jost. "French Structuralism from a German Point of View." BA 49 (1975), 213-21.

a191. Holenstein, Elmar. Roman Jakobson's Approach to Language: Phenomeno-logical Structuralism (Bloomington: Indiana UP, 1976).
a192. ----------. "The Structure of Understanding: Structuralismn versus Hermeneutics." PTL 1 (1976), 223-38.
a193. ----------. "Prague Structuralism: A Branch of the Phenomenological Movement," in J. Odmark, ed. Language, Literature and Meaning I: Problems of Literary Theory (Amsterdam: Benjamins, 1979), 71-97.

a194. Holloway, John. "Supposition and Supersession: A Model of Analysis for Narrative Structure." CritI 3 (1976), 39-55.

a195. Hopkins, Mary Frances. "Structuralism: Its Implications for the Performance of Prose Fiction." ComM 44 (1977), 93-105.

a196. Huckle, John J. "Without Man: Some Aspects of the Structuralism of Claude Lévi-Strauss." Thought 56 (Dec., 1981), 387-401.

a197. Hund, Wulf D., ed. Strukturalismus: Ideologie und Dogmengeschichte (Darmstadt: Luchterhand, 1973).

a198. Iverson, Niels Johs. "La notion de structure et son emploi chez Lévi-Strauss, Piaget et Eco." Prepub 38 (1978), 19-45.

a199. Jaeggi, Urs J. V. Ordnung und Chaos: der Strukturalismus als Methode und Mode (Frankfurt am Main: Suhrkamp, 1968).

a200. Jagric, Janez and Henrietta Beese. Russischer Strukturalismus 1962-1972 (Berlin: Ullstein-Taschenbuch-Verlag, 1978).

a201. Jakobson, Roman. Questions de poétique (Paris: Seuil, 1973).
a202.----------. "Structuralisme et teleologie." L'Arc 60 (1974), 50-54.
a203. ----------. "A Few Remarks on Structuralism." MLN 91 (1976), 1534-39.
a204. ----------. Verbal Art, Verbal Sign, Verbal Time (Minneapolis: U of Minnesota P, 1985).

a205. Jameson, Frederic. The Prison House of Language: A Critical Account of Structuralism and Russian Formalism (Princeton: Princeton UP, 1972).

a206. Johnson, Alfred M., ed. The New Testament and Structuralism (Pittsburgh: Pickwick P, 1976).
a207. ----------. Structural Analysis and Biblical Exegesis (Pittsburgh: Pickwick P, 1976).

a208. Johnson, Barbara. "The Critical Difference: BartheS/BalZac," in The Critical Difference: Essays in the Contemporary Rhetoric of Reading (Baltimore: Johns Hopkins UP, 1980), 3-12.

a209. Johnson, Nancy S. and Jean M. Mandler. "A Tale of Two Structures: Underlying and Surface Forms in Stories." Poetics 9 (1980), 51-86.

a210. Johnson, R. E. "Structuralism and the Reading of Contemporary Fiction." Soundings 58.2 (1975), 281-306.

a211. Jones, Robert Emmett. Panorama de la nouvelle critique en France: de Gaston Bachelard a Jean-Paul Weber (Paris: Sedes, 1968), chap. 4.

a212. Jolles, André. Einfache Formen: Legende, Sage, Mythe, Ratsel, Spruch, Kasus, Memorabile, Marchen, Witz, 3rd ed. (Tubingen: Niemeyer, 1965).

a213. Kacer, Miroslav. "Der Prager Strukturalismus in der Asthetik und Literaturwissenschaft." Welt der Slaven 13 (1968), 64-86.

a214. Karbusicky, Vladimir. Widerspiegelungstheorie und Strukturalimus (Munchen: Hauser, 1973).

a215. Kermode, Frank. "The Use of the Codes," in The Art of Telling: Essays on Fiction (Cambridge: Harvard UP, 1983), 72-91.

a216. Kevelson, Roberta. "A Restructure of Barthes's Readerly Text." Semiotica 3 (1976), 253-67.

a217. Kress, Gunther R. "Structuralism and Popular Culture," in C. W. E. Bigsby, ed. Approaches to Popular Culture (Bowling Green OH: Bowling Green U Popular P, 1977), 85-106.

a218. Krieger, Murray and L. S. Dembo, eds. Directions for Criticism: Structuralism and Its Alternatives (Madison: U of Wisconsin P, 1977).

a219. Kristeva, Julia. "Le Sens et la mode." Critique 20 (Dec., 1967), 1005-1031 [on Barthes, esp. Systeme de la mode].

a220. Kurzweil, Edith. "The Mythology of Structuralism." PR 42 (1975), 416-30.
a221. ----------. The Age of Structuralism: Lévi-Strauss to Foucault (NY: Columbia UP, 1980).

a222. Lane, Michael, ed. Structuralism: A Reader (London: Jonathan Cape, 1970) [pubd. as Introduction to Structuralism (NY: Basic Books, 1970)].

a223. Larivaille, Paul. "L'analyse (morpho) logique du récit." Poétique 19 (1974), 368-88.

a224. Lavers, Annette. Roland Barthes: Structuralism and After (Cambridge: Harvard UP, 1982).

a225. Leach, Edmund, ed. The Structural Study of Myth and Totemism (London: Tavistock, 1967).
a226. ----------. Genesis as Myth: And Other Essays (London: Jonathan Cape, 1969).
a227. ----------. Claude Lévi-Strauss (NY: Viking; London: Fontana, 1970).

a228. ---------- and D. Alan Aycock. Structuralist Interpretations of Biblical Myth (Cambridge: Cambridge UP, 1983).

a229. Lefebvre, Henri. Au-dela du structuralisme (Paris: Anthropos, 1971).
a230. ---------. L'Idéologie structuraliste (Paris: Seuil, 1975).

a231. Leiber, Justin. Structuralism (Boston: Twayne, 1973).

a232. Le Sage, Laurent. The French New Criticism: An Introduction and a Sampler (University Park: Pennsylvania State UP, 1967).

a233. Levin, Isidor. "Vladimir Propp: An Evaluation on his Seventieth Birthday." JFI 4 (1967), 32-49.

a234. Levin, Samuel R. "On the Progress of Structural Poetics." Poetics 8 (1979), 513-15.

a235. Lévi-Strauss, Claude. Mythologiques, 4 vols. (Paris: Plon, 1964-71) [Eng.: The Raw and the Cooked (1969), From Honey to Ashes (1973), The Origin of Table Manners (1973), all NY: Harper & Row].
a236. ----------. La Voie des masques Geneva: Skira, 1975).
a237. ----------, ed. L'Identité (Paris: Grasset, 1977).
a238. ----------. Le Regard éloigné (Paris: Plon, 1984).

a239. Lewis, T. J., ed. "With and Beyond Structuralism." BA 49 (1975), 199-243 [special issue].

a240. Leyvraz, Jean-Pierre. Uber den Strukturalismus (Basel: Verlag fur Recht und Gesellschaft, 1972).

a241. Link, Jurgen. Literaturwissenschaftliche Grundbegriffe: Einne programmierte Einfuhrung auf strukturalistischer Basis (Munchen: Fink, 1974).

a242. Lodge, David. Working with Structuralism: Essays and Reviews on Nineteenth and Twentieth-Century Literature (Boston: Routledge, 1981).

a243. Lotman, Jurij M. "The Discrete Text and the Iconic Text: Remarks on the Structure of Narrative." NLH 6 (1975), 333-38.
a244. ----------. "Point of View in a Text." NLH 6 (1975), 339-52.
a245. ----------. Analysis of the Poetic Text (Ann Arbor: Ardis, 1976).
a246. ----------. The Structure of the Artistic Text (Ann Arbor: Michigan Slavic Contributions, 1977).
a247. ----------. "The Future of Structural Poetics." Poetics 8 (1979), 501-07.

a248. Lund, Steffen Nordahl. L'aventure du signifiant: une lecture de Barthes (Paris: PUF, 1981).

a249. Macksey, Richard and Eugenio Donato, eds. The Languages of Criticism and the Sciences of Man: The Structuralist Controversy (Baltimore: Johns Hopkins UP, 1970) [pubd. with title and subtitle reversed, 1972].

a250. Marc-Lipiansky, Mireille. Le Structuralisme de Lévi-Strauss (Paris: Payot, 1973).

a251. Martens, Gunter. "Textstrukturen aus rezeptionsasthetischer Sicht: Perspektiven einer Textasthetik auf der Grundlage des Prager Strukturalismus." Wirkendes Wort 23 (1973), 359-79.

a252. Martin, Wallace. "Formal Analysis of Traditional Fictions." PLL 17.1 (1981), 3-22.

a253. Matejka, Ladislav and Krystyna Pomorska, eds. Readings in Russian Poetics: Formalist and Structuralist Views (Cambridge MA: M.I.T. P, 1971).
a254. ----------, ed. Sound, Sign, and Meaning: Quinquagenary of the Prague Linguistic Circle (Ann Arbor: Michigan Slavic Pub., 1976).

a255. Mautner, Renata R. "Literary Structuralism--An Exposition." DAI 34 (1974), 4272A-73A.

a256. McKnight, Edgar. Meaning in Texts (Philadelphia: Fortess P, 1978).

a257. McNicholl, Ambrose. Structuralism (Rome: Herder, 1975).

a258. Meletinsky, E. and D. Segal. "Structuralism and Semiotics in the USSR." Diogenes 73 (1971), 88-116.

a259. Mellac, Guy de and Margaret Eberbach. Barthes (Paris: Universitaires/ Delarge, 1972).

a260. Merquior, José G. "Analyse structurale des mythes et analyse des oeuvres d'art." RE 23 (1970), 365-82.

a261. Mest'an, Antonin. "Der literaturwissenschaftliche Strukturalismus der Gegenwart in der Sowjetunion und der Tschechoslowakei. . . ." WSl 17 (1972), 418-36.

a262. Miller, Joan M. French Structuralism: A Multidisciplinary Bibliography (NY: Garland, 1981).

a263. Millet, Louis and M. D'Ainvelle. Le Structuralisme (Paris: Editions Universitaires, 1970).

a264. Mitchell, Bonner. "The French Quarrel over Structuralism and a Parallel of Sixty Years Ago." BA 49 (1975), 199-204.

a265. Mitra, Ranadhir. "Literary Criticism as Science: Problems and Possibilities in Structuralist and Marxist Endeavors." DAI 33 (1973), 3596A-97A.

a266. Morris, Wesley. Friday's Footprint: Structuralism and the Articulated Text (Columbus: Ohio State UP, 1979).

a267. Mosher, Harold F., Jr. "A Contemporary Russian Structuralist." JLS 5 (1976), 31-37 [on Uspenskij].
a268. ----------. "A Reply to Some Remarks on Genette's Structuralism." Poetics 7 (1978), 283-88.

a269. Motschmann, Jochen. "Zum Strukturbegriff im russischen Formalismus und Prager Strukturalismus," in W. Hund, ed. Strukturalismus: Ideologie und Dogmengeschichte (Darmstadt: Luchterhand, 1973), 349-77.

a270. Mukarovsky, Jan. The Word and Verbal Art (New Haven: Yale UP, 1977).
a271. ----------. Structure, Sign, and Function (New Haven: Yale UP, 1978).

a272. Mullen, Judith M. "Some Readings on Reading with a Brief Introductory Initiation into Structuralism." RLSt 9 (1978), 77-87.

a273. Nathhorst, Bertil. Formal or Structural Studies of Traditional Tales: The Usefulness of Some Methodological Proposals Advanced by Vladimir Propp, Alan Dundes, Claude Lévi-Strauss, and Edmund Leach (Stockholm: Amqvist & Wiksell, 1969).

a274. Neilson, Frank P. "The Philosophical Pressures in Structuralist Criticism." L&I 17 (1974), 31-38.

a275. Nemoianu, Virgil. "Structuralist Theory: Maturity and Failure." SFR 1 (1977), 415-34.

a276. Neschke-Hentschke, Ada. "Griechischer Mythos und Strukturale Anthropologie: Kritische Bemerkungen zu Claude Lévi-Strauss' Methode der Mythendeutung." Poetica 10 (1978), 135-53.

a277. Newman, Lawrence W. "Towards a Prague School Theory of Semantics." Semiotica 19 (1977), 341-54.

a278. Nobis, Helmut. "Literarische Evolution, Historizitat und Geschichte." LiLi 4 (1974), 91-110 [Prague School].

a279. Norris, Christopher. "Les plaisirs des clercs: Barthes's Latest Writings." BJA 14.3 (1974), 250-57.
a280. ----------. "Roland Barthes: The View from Here." Critical Quarterly 20 (1978), 27-43.

a281. Nutini, Hugo. "Some Considerations of Social Structure and Model Building: A Critique of Claude Lévi-Strauss and Edmund Leach." American Anthropologist 67 (1965), 707-31.
a282. ---------- and Ira R. Buchler, eds. Essays in Structural Anthropology: In Honor of Claude Lévi-Strauss (NY: Appleton-Century-Crofts, 1970).
a283. ----------. "The Ideological Bases of Lévi-Strauss' Structuralism." American Anthropologist 73 (1971), 537-44.

a284. O'Donnell, Thomas J. "'Une Exploration des deserts de ma mémoire': Pastoral Aspects of Lévi-Strauss' Tristes Tropiques," in R. F. Hardin, ed. Survivals of the Pastoral (Lawrence: U of Kansas P, 1979), 86-102.

a285. Orr, Leonard. Semiotic and Structuralist Analyses of Fiction: An Introduction and a Survey of Applications (Troy NY: Whitston, 1987).

a286. Osolsobe, Ivo. "Czechoslovak Semiotics Past and Present." Semiotica 9 (1973), 140-56.

a287. Palomo, Dolores. "Scholes, Barthes, and Structuralist Criticism." MLQ 36 (1975), 193-206.

a288. Parain-Vial, Jeanne. Analyses structurale et idéologies structuralistes (Toulouse: Privat, 1969).

a289. Patocka, Jan. "Roman Jakobsons phanomenologischer Strukturalismus." Tydschrift voor Filosofie 38 (1976), 129-35.

a290. Patte, Daniel. What Is Structural Analysis? (Philadelphia: Fortress P, 1976).

a291. ---------- and Aline Patte. Structural Exegesis: From Theory to Practice (Philadelphia: Fortress P, 1978).

a292. Patzig, Gunther. "Der Strukturalismus und seine Grenzen." NDH 146 (1975), 247-66.

a293. Paz, Octavio. Claude Lévi-Strauss: An Introduction (Ithaca: Cornell UP, 1970).

a294. Pettit, Philip. The Concept of Structuralism: A Critical Analysis (Berkeley: U of California P, 1975).

a295. Philippi, Klaus-Peter. "Formalismus-Strukturalismus," in J. Hauff, ed. Methodendiskussion (Frankfurt: Athenaum, 1971), 101-26.

a296. Piaget, Jean. Structuralism (NY: Harper & Row, 1970).

a297. Picard, Raymond. Nouvelle critique ou nouvelle imposture (Paris: Pauvert, 1965) [New Criticism or New Fraud? (Pullman: Washington State UP, 1969)].

a298. Pierssens, Michel. "Le S/Z de Roland Barthes: l'avenir du 'texte.'" Sub-Stance 1 (1971), 37-48.

a299. Polzin, Robert. Biblical Structuralism (Philadelphia: Fortress P, 1977).

a300. Pouillon, J. "[Structuralism] Présentation: un essai de définition." Les Temps Modernes 22 (1966), 769-90.
a301. ---------- and P. Maranda, eds. Exchanges et Communications, 2 vols. (The Hague: Mouton, 1970).

a302. Prince, Gerald. "Practical Poetics." Diacritics 5.2 (1975), 19-23.

a303. Riccomini, Domald R. "Northrop Frye and Structuralism: Identity and Difference." UTQ 49 (1979), 33-47.

a304. Rimmon, Shlomith. "Barthes' 'Hermeneutic Code' and Henry James' Literary Detective: Plot-Composition in 'The Figure in the Carpet.'" HUSL 1.2 (1973), 183-207.
a305. ----------. "A Comprehensive Theory of Narrative: Genette's Figures III and the Structuralist Study of Fiction." PTL 1 (1976), 33-62.

a306. Robey, David, ed. Structuralism: An Introduction (London and NY: Oxford UP, 1973).

a307. "Roland Barthes." L'Arc 56 (1974) [special issue].

a308. Rosenthal, Peggy. "Deciphering S/Z." CE 37.2 (1975), 125-44.

a309. Rossi, Ino, ed. The Unconscious in Culture: The Structuralism of Claude Lévi-Strauss in Perspective (NY: Dutton, 1974).

a310. Roudiez, Leon. "With and Beyond Literary Structuralism." BA 49 (1975), 204-12.

a311. Rudy, Stephen. "Jakobson's Inquiry into Verse and the Emergence of Structural Poetics," in L. Matejka, ed. Sound, Sign, and Meaning: Quinquagenary of the Prague Linguistic Circle (Ann Arbor: Michigan Slavic Contributions, 1976), 477-520.

a312. Ruegg, Maria. "The End(s) of French Style: Structuralism and Post-Structuralism in the American Context." Criticism 21 (1979), 189-216.
a313. ----------. "Metaphor and Metonymy: The Logic of Structuralist Rhetoric." Glyph 6 (1979), 141-57.

a314. Runciman, W. G. "What Is Structuralism?" British Journal of Sociology 20 (1969), 253-65.

a315. Said, Edward. Beginnings: Intention and Method (Baltimore: Johns Hopkins UP, 1975), chap. 5.

a316. Sabri, Mohammed Arjamand. "Structure of Literary Texts: Structuralist Analysis and the Poetics of Narrative." DAI 37 (1976), 2841A.

a317. Schiwy, Gunther. Der franzosische Strukturalismus. Mode, Methode, Ideologie, 5th rev. ed. (Hamburg: Rowohlt, 1971).
a318. ----------. Neue Aspekte des Strukturalismus (Munich: Deutscher Taschenbuch-Verlag, 1973).
a319. ----------. Strukturalismus und Zeichensysteme (Munich: Beck, 1973).

a320. Schlegov, Yu. K. "Towards a Description of Detective Story Structure." Russ. Poetics in Tr. 1 (1975), 51-77.

a321. Schmid, Herta. "Zum Begriff der asthetischer Konkretisation im tschechischen Strukturalismus." Sprache im technischen Zeitalter 36 (1970), 290-318.
a322. ----------. "Entwicklungsschritte zu einer modernen Dramentheorie im russischen Formalismus und im tschechischen Strukturalismus," in A. van Kestern and H. Schmid, eds. Moderne Dramentheorie (Kronberg: Scriptor, 1975), 7-40.

a323. ----------. "Aspekte und Probleme der asthetischen Funktion im tschechischen Strukturalismus," in L. Matejka, ed. Sound, Sign, and Meaning: Quinquagenary of the Prague Linguistic Circle (Ann Arbor: Michigan Slavic Contributions, 1976), 386-424.

a324. Schmid, Wolf. Der asthetische Inhalt: Zur semantischen Funktion poetischer Verfahren (Lisse: Peter de Ridder, 1976).

a325. Scholes, Robert. Structuralism in Literature: An Introduction (New Haven: Yale UP, 1974).

a326. Schwarz, Ulrich. Rittende Kritik und antizipierte Utopie: Zum geschichtlichen Gehalt asthetischer Erfahrung in den Theorien von Jan Mukarovsky, Walter Benjamin und Theodor W. Adorno (Munchen: Fink, 1981).

a327. Schwimmer, Erik. "Myth and the Ethnograher: A Critique of Lévi-Strauss," in H. R. Garvin, ed. Phenomenology, Structuralism, Semiology (Lewisburg: Bucknell UP, 1976), 162-85.

a328. Sedmidubsky, M. and W. Kroll. "Bibliographie zum Tschechischen und Slovakischen Literaturwissenschaftlichen Strukturalismus," in J. Odmark, ed. Language, Literature & Meaning II: Current Trends in Literary Research (Amsterdam: Benjamins, 1980), 457-524.

a329. Segre, C. "Structuralism in Italy." Semiotica 4.3 (1971), 215-39.

a330. Selz, Dorothy B. "Structuralism for the Non-Specialist: A Glossary and a Bibliography." CE 37 (1975), 160-66.

a331. Seung, T. K. Structuralism and Hermeneutics (NY: Columbia UP, 1982).

a332. Short, M. H. "Some Thoughts on Foregrounding and Interpretation." Lang&S 6 (1973), 97-108.

a333. Simmons, Sarah. "Mukarovsky, Structuralism, and the Essay." Semiotica 19 (1977), 335-40.

a334. Slawinski, Jan. Literatur als System und Prozeß, ed. R. Fieguth (Munchen: Hanser, 1975).

a335. Smithson, Isaiah. "Structuralism as a Method of Literary Criticism." CE 37 (1975), 145-59.

a336. Sosnoski, James J. "On the Anvil of Theoretical Debate: Story and Discourse as Literary Theory." JJQ 18.3 (1981), 267-76.

a337. Sperber, Dan. "Claude Lévi-Strauss," in J. Sturrock, ed. Structuralism and Since: From Lévi-Strauss to Derrida (NY: Oxford UP, 1979), 19-51.

a338. Stadtke, Klaus. "Mimesis oder poetisches Regelsystem: Zur Frage des Struklturalismus in der Literaturwissenschaft." WB (1968), 555-86.

a339. Stankiewicz, Edward. "Structural Poetics and Linguistics." Current Trends in Linguistics 12.1 (1974), 629-60.
a340. ----------. "Poetics and Verbal Art," in T. Sebeok, ed. A Perfusion of Signs (Bloomington: Indiana UP, 1977), 54-76.
a341. ----------. "Roman Jakobson (A Commemorative Essay)." Semiotica 44 (1983), 1-20.

a342. St. Armand, Barton Levi. "A Superior Abstraction: Todorov on the Fantastic." Novel 8 (1975), 260-67.

a343. Steiner, George. "Orpheus with His Myths: Claude Lévi-Strauss," in Language and Silence: Essays on Language, Literature, and the Inhuman (NY: Atheneum, 1974), 239-50.

a344. Steiner, Peter. "The Conceptual Basis of Prague Structuralism," in L. Matejka, ed. Sound, Sign, and Meaning: Quinquagenary Essays of the Prague Linguistic Circle (Ann Arbor: Michigan Slavic Contributions, 1976), 351-85.
a345. ----------. "Jan Mukarovsky and Charles W. Morris: Two Pioneers of the Semiotics of Art." Semiotica 19 (1977), 321-34.
a346. ---------- and Sergej Davydov. "The Biological Metaphor in Russian Formalism: The Concept of Morphology." Sub-Stance 17 (1977), 149-58.
a347. ----------. "Jan Mukarovsky's Structural Aesthetics," in J. Mukarovsky, Structure, Sign, and Function, tr. and ed. J. Burbank and P. Steiner (New Haven: Yale UP, 1978), ix-xxxiv.
a348. ---------- and Wendy Steiner. "The Axes of Poetic Language," in J. Odmark, ed. Language, Literature and Meaning I: Current Trends in Literary Research (Amsterdam: John Benjamins, 1979), 35-70.
a349. ----------. "'Formalism' and 'Structuralism': An Exercise in Metahistory." Russian Literature 12 (1982), 290-330.
a350. ----------. "In Defense of Semiotics: The Dual Asymmetry of Cultural Signs." NLH 12 (1982), 415-35.
a351. ----------, ed. The Prague School: Selected Writings, 1929-1946 (Austin: U of Texas P, 1982) [inc. "The Roots of Structuralist Aesthetics," 174-219].

a352. ----------, Miroslav Cervenka, and Ronald Vroon, eds. The Structures of Literary Process: Studies Dedicated to the Memory of Felix Vodicka (Amsterdam: John Benjamins, 1982).

a353. Strickland, Geoffrey. Structuralism or Criticism? Thoughts on How We Read (Cambridge: Cambridge UP, 1981).

a354. Strohmaier, Eckart. Theorie des Strukturalismus: Zur Kritik der strukturalistischen Literaturanalyse (Bonn: Bouvier, 1977).

a355. Strohschneider-Kors, Ingrid. Literarische Struktur und geschichtlicher Wandel (Munchen: Fink, 1971).

a356. Sturm-Maddox, Sara. "Lévi-Strauss in the Waste Forest." ECr 18.3 (1978), 82-94.

a357. Sturrock, John. "Roland Barthes," in J. Sturrock, ed. Structuralism and Since: From Lévi-Strauss to Derrida (NY: Oxford UP, 1979), 52-80.

a358. Suleiman, Susan. "Structural Analysis of Narrative: A Method and Its Application." NTLTL 14.2 (1975), 11-32.
a359. ----------. "Redundancy and the 'Readable' Text." PoT 1.3 (1980), 119-42.
a360. ----------. "What Can Structuralism Do for Us?" in Paul Hernadi, ed. What Is Criticism? (Bloomington: Indiana UP, 1981).

a361. Sus, Oleg. "Les traditions de l'esthétique tchéque moderne et du structuralisme de Jan Mukarovsky: Du 'formisme' au structuralisme." Revue d'esthétique 24 (1971), 29-38.
a362. ----------. "Die Wege der tschechischen wissenschaftlichen Asthetik (J. Mukarovsky)." Welt der Slaven 17 (1972), 155-74.
a363. ----------. "Die Genese der semantischen Kunstauffassung in der modernen tschechischen Asthetik." Welt der Slaven 17 (1972), 201-24.
a364. ----------. "On the Genetic Preconditions of Czech Structuralist Semiology and Semantics: An Essay on Czech and German Thought." Poetics 4 (1972), 28-54.
a365. ----------. "On the Origin of the Czech Semantics of Art: The Theory of Music and Poetry in the Psychological Semantics of Otakar Zich." Semiotica 9 (1973), 117-39.
a366. ----------. "On Some Structural-Semantic Problems in Mukarovsky's Theory of Aesthetic Norm." Zagadnienia rodzajow literackich 19 (1976), 35-52.
a367. ----------. "Zwischen 'Formalismus' und 'Strukturalismus': Zur Kritik am sog. slavischen Formalismus und zu den Problemen des Ubergangs von

der 'Prager asthetischer Schule' zur strukturalen Literatur- und Kunsttheorie." Welt der Slaven 22 (1977), 401-31.
a368. ----------. "From the Pre-history of Czech Structuralism: F. X. Salda, T. G. Masaryk and the Genesis of Symbolist Aesthetics and Poetics in Bohemia," in P. Steiner, M. Cervenka, and R. Vroon, eds. The Structure of the Literary Process (Amsterdam: John Benjamins, 1982), 547-80.

a369. Szaboleski, Miklos. "Possibilité d'une unité des methodes génétique et structuralistes dans l'interprétation des textes." ALitASH 10 (1968), 165-73.

a370. Sziklay, Laszlo. "The Prague School," in L. Nyiros, ed. Literature and Its Interpretation (The Hague: Mouton, 1979), 69-111.

a371. Thody, Philip. Roland Barthes: A Conservative Estimate (London: Macmillan, 1977).

a372. Thompson, Ewa. "Structuralism: Some Possibilities and Implications." SHR 7 (1973), 247-60.
a373. ----------. "Russian Structuralist Theory." BA 49 (1975), 232-38.
a374. ----------. "Jurij Lotman's Literary Theory and Its Context." SEEJ 21 (1977), 225-38.

a375. Timpanaro, Sebastiano. "Structuralism and Its Successors." ConL 22.4 (1981), 600-22.

a376. Todorov, Tzvetan. Littérature et signification (Paris: Larousse, 1967).
a377. ----------. Grammaire du Décaméron (The Hague: Mouton, 1969).
a378. ----------. Introduction a la littérature fantastique (Paris: Seuil, 1970) [Eng. Cleveland: Case Western Reserve UP, 1973)].
a379. ----------. Poétique de la Prose (Paris: Seuil 1971) [The Poetics of Prose (Ithaca: Cornell UP, 1977)].
a380. ----------. Introduction to Poetics (Minneapolis: U of Minnesota P, 1981).
a381. ----------. "Jakobson's Poetics," in Theories of the Symbol (Ithaca: Cornell UP, 1982), 271-84.

a382. Turner, Terence. "Piaget's Structuralism: Review Article." American Anthropologist 75 (1973), 351-73.
a383. ----------. "Narrative Structure and Mythopoesis: A Critique and Reformulation of Structuralist Concepts of Myth, Narrative and Poetics." Arethusa 10 (1977), 103-63.

a384. Ungar, Steven. "From Writing to the Letter: Barthes and Alphabetese." VLang 11 (1977), 390-428.

a385. ----------. "Doing and Not Doing Things with Barthes." Enclitic 2.2 (1978), 86-109.
a386. ----------. Roland Barthes, the Professor of Desire (Lincoln: U of Nebraska P, 1983).

a387. Uspensky, B. A. "Structural Isomorphism of Verbal and Visual Art." Poetics 5 (1972), 5-39.

a388. Vachek, Josef. The Linguistic School of Prague: An Introduction to Its Theory and Practice (Bloomington: Indiana UP, 1966).
a389. ----------. "Prague Linguistic School: Its Origins and Present-Day Heritage." Wiener Slawistischer Almanach 7 (1981), 217-41.

a390. Velan, Yves. "Barthes," in John Simon, ed. Modern French Criticism: From Proust to Structuralism (Chicago: U of Chicago P, 1972), 311-39.

a391. Veltrusky, Jiri. Drama as Literature (Atlanatic Highlands NJ: Humanities Press, 1977).
a392. ----------. "Jan Mukarovsky's Structural Poetics and Esthetics." PoT 2.1b (1980-81), 117-57.
a393. ----------. "The Prague School Theory of Theater." PoT 2 (1981), 225-35.

a394. Volek, Emil. "Die Begriffe 'Fabel' und 'Sujet' in der modernen Literaturwissenschaft: Zur Struktur der 'Erzahlstruktur.'" Poetica 9 (1977), 141-66.

a395. Wahl, François, ed. Qu'est-ce que le structuralisme? (Paris: Seuil, 1968).

a396. Wasserman, George R. Roland Barthes (Boston: Twayne, 1981).

a397. Waugh, Butler. "Structural Analysis in Literature and Folklore." WF 25 (1966), 153-64.

a398. Waugh, Linda R. Roman Jakobson's Science of Language (Lisse: Peter de Ridder, 1976).
a399. ----------. "The Poetic Function and the Nature of Language." PoT 2.1a (1980), 57-82.

a400. Weimann, Robert. "French Structuralism and Literary History: Some Critiques and Reconsiderations." NLH 4 (1973), 437-69.

a401. Weinrich, Harald. "Structures narratives du mythe." Poétique 1 (1970), 25-34.

a402. Wellek, René. The Literary Theory and Aesthetics of the Prague School (Ann Arbor: Michigan Slavic Contributions, 1969).

a403. White, Hayden. "Structuralism and Popular Culture." JPC 7 (1974), 759-75.
a404. ----------. "Michel Foucault," in J. Sturrock, ed. Structuralism and Since: From Lévi-Strauss to Derrida (NY: Oxford UP, 1979), 81-115.

a405. Wilden, Anthony. System and Structure: Essays in Communication and Exchange (London: Tavistock, 1972).
a406. ----------. "Structuralism, Communication, and Evolution." Semiotica 6.3 (1972), 244-56.

a407. Winner, Thomas G. "The Aesthetics and Poetics of the Prague Linguistic Circle." Poetics 8 (1973), 77-96.
a408. ----------. "Genre Theory in the Light of Structural Poetics and Semiotics," in J. Strelka, ed. Theories of Literary Genres (University Park: Pennsylvania State UP, 1976), 254-68.
a409. ----------. "Grande themes de la poétique jakobsonienne." L'Arc 60 (1976), 55-63.
a410. ----------. "Jan Mukarovsky: The Beginnings of Structural and Semiotic Aesthetics," in L. Matejka, ed. Sound, Sign, and Meaning: Quinquagenary of the Prague Linguistic Circle (Ann Arbor: Michigan Slavic Contributions, 1976), 433-55.
a411. ----------. "On the Relation of the Verbal and the Nonverbal Arts in Early Prague Semiotics: Jan Mukarovsky," in R. W. Bailey, et al , eds. The Sign: Semiotics Around the World (Ann Arbor: Michigan Slavic, 1978), 227-37.

a412. Wittig, Susan, ed. "Structuralism: An Interdisciplinary Study." Soundings 58.2 (1975) [special issue].
a413. ----------. "The Historical Development of Structuralism." Soundings 58.2 (1975), 145-66.
a414. ----------. Stylistic and Narrative Structures in the Middle English Romances (Austin: U of Texas P, 1978).

a415. Zimmerman, Marc Jay. "Genetic Structuralism: Lucien Goldmann's Answer to the Advent of Structuralism." DAI 36 (1975), 1489A-90A.
a416. ----------. "Lucien Goldmann and the Science of Mental Structures." Gradiva 1 (1978), 273-94.

B. Semiotics
(Excluding Narrative Semiotics)

b1. Adams, Jean-Michel. Linguistique et discours littéraire: théorie et pratique des textes (Paris: Larousse, 1976).

b2. Adriaens, Mark. "Ideology and Literary Production: Kristeva's Poetics," in P. V. Zima, ed. Semiotics and Dialectics: Ideology and the Text (Amsterdam: Benjamins, 1981).

b3. Angenot, Marc. "L'Intertextualité: Enquete sur l'émergence d'un champ notionnel." RSH 1.189 (1983), 121-35.

b4. "Applied Semiotics." Diogenes 113-14 (1981), 127-251 [special section].

b5. Armstrong, Nancy. "Inside Greimas's Square: Literary Characters and Cultural Constraints," in W. Steiner, ed. The Sign in Music and Literature (Austin: U of Texas P, 1981), 52-66.

b6. Arrivé, Michel. "Postulats pour la description linguistique des textes littéraires." Langue Française 3 (1969), 3-13.

b7. Arroyabe, Estanislao. Semiotik und Literatur (Bonn: Bouvier, 1984).

b8. Baer, Eugen. "Thomas A. Sebeok's Doctrine of Signs," in Martin Krampen, et al , eds. Classics of Semiotics (NY and London: Plenum Press, 1987), 181-210.

b9. Bailey, Richard, *et al* , eds. The Sign: Semiotics Around the World (Ann Arbor: Michigan Slavic Pub., 1978).

b10. Bal, Mieke. "Why I? Discussing the Subject in/of Semiotics." PoT 5.4 (1984), 857-65.

b11. Ballon, Enrique. "Semiotics in Peru," in T. A. Sebeok and J. Umiker-Sebeok, eds. The Semiotic Sphere (NY and London: Plenum, 1986), 387-405.

b12. Baran, Henryk, ed. Semiotics and Structuralism: Readings from the Soviet Union (NY: International Arts and Sciences P, 1976).

b13. Baron, Naomi S. "Linguistics and Semiotics: Two Disciplines in Search of a Subject." Semiotica 29.3-4 (1979), 289-310.
b14. ----------. Speech, Writing, and Sign: A Functional View of Linguistic Representation (Bloomington: Indiana UP, 1981).

b15. Barry, Jackson G. "Semiotics and the Meaning of Form," in J. Deely, ed. Semiotics 1984 (Lanham MD: UP of America, 1985), 119-26.

b16. Barthes, Roland. Systeme de la mode (Paris: Seuil, 1967).
b17. ----------. Writing Degree Zero and Elements of Semiology (Boston: Beacon, 1970).
b18. ----------. S/Z (Paris: Seuil, 1970).
b19. ----------. Mythologies (NY: Hill & Wang, 1972).
b20. ----------. Le plaisir du texte (Paris: Seuil, 1973).
b21. ----------. Le grain de la voix (Paris: Seuil, 1981).
b22. ----------. L'aventure sémiologique (Paris: Seuil, 1985).

b23. Beauchamp, William. "From Structuralism to Semiotics." Romanic Review 67.3 (1976), 226-36.

b24. Bense, Max. "Die semiotik Konzeption der Asthetik." LiLi 27-28 (1977), 188-201.
b25. ----------. Axiomatik und Semiotik (Baden-Baden: Agis, 1981).
b26. ----------. Das Universum der Zeichen: Essays uber die Expansionen der Semiotik (Baden-Baden: Agis, 1983).

b27. Benveniste, Emile. Problemes de linguistique générale (Paris: Gallimard, 1966).
b28. ----------. "Sémiologie de la langue." Semiotica 1 (1969), 1-12, 127-35.

b29. Benzon, William. "Cognitive Networks and Literary Semantics." MLN 91 (1976), 952-82.

b30. Berger, Arthur Asa. Signs in Contemporary Culture: An Introduction to Semiotics (NY and London: Longman, 1984).

b31. Bettetini, Gianfranco and Francesco Casetti. "Semiotics in Italy," in T. A. Sebeok and J. Umiker-Sebeok, eds. The Semiotic Sphere (NY and London: Plenum, 1986), 293-321.

b32. Blanchard, Marc Eli. "Up Against the Text." Diacritics 11.3 (1981), 13-26 [on Riffaterre].

b33. Blonsky, Marshall, ed. On Signs (Baltimore: Johns Hopkins UP, 1985).

b34. Boelhower, William. Through a Glass Darkly: Ethnic Semiosis in American Literature (NY: Oxford UP, 1987).

b35. Boklund-Lagopoulou, Karin and A.-Ph. Lagopoulos. "Semiotics in Greece," in T. A. Sebeok and J. Umiker-Sebeok, eds. The Semiotic Sphere (NY and London: Plenum, 1986), 253-78.

b36. Borbe, Tasso, et al. Semiotics Unfolding, 3 vols. (Berlin & NY: Mouton, 1983).

b37. Boussiac, Paul. "Semiotics in Canada," in T. A. Sebeok and J. Umiker-Sebeok, eds. The Semiotic Sphere (NY and London: Plenum, 1986), 59-98.

b38. Braga, Maria Lucia Santaella, ed. "Semiotics and Poetics in Brazil." Dispositio 6 (1981) [special issue].
b39. ----------. "Semiotics: Science or Method?" Dispositio 6 (1981), 109-17.

b40. Brandt, Per Aage. "Aléthique et déontique: Esquisse d'une nouvelle analyse sémiotique des modalités," in H. Parret and H.-G. Ruprecht, eds. Exigences et perspectives de la sémiotique: Receuil d'hommages pour Algirdas Julien Greimas (Amsterdam: Benjamins, 1985), 123-32.

b41. Brind'Amour, Lucie and Eugene Vance, eds. Archéologie du signe (Toronto: Pontifical Institute of Medieval Studies, 1983) [medieval semiotics].

b42. Broden, Thomas F. III. "The Development of A. J. Greimas: Lexicology, Structural Semantics, Semiotics." Diss.: Indiana Univ., 1986.

b43. Browne, Robert M. "The Typology of Literary Signs." CE 33 (1971), 1-17.

b44. Burks, Arthur W. "Man: Sign, or Algorithm? A Rhetorical Analysis of Peirce's Semiotics," in W. Steiner, ed. Image and Code (Ann Arbor: U of Michigan, 1981), 57-70.

b45. Carlson, Marvin. "Semiotics and Nonsemiotics in Performance." MD 28.4 (1985), 670-76.

b46. Carontini, E. and D. Peraya. Le projet sémiotique (Paris: Jean-Pierre Delarge, 1975).

b47. Cervenka, Miroslav. "The Literary Work as Sign," in John Odmark, ed. Language, Literature & Meaning II: Current Trends in Literary Research (Amsterdam: Benjamins 1980), 1-25.
b48. ----------. "The Literary Artifact," in W. Steiner, ed. The Sign in Music and Literature (Austin: U of Texas P, 1981), 86-102.

b49. Champagne, Roland A. "The Dialectics of Style: Insights from the Semiology of Roland Barthes." Style 13 (1979), 279-91.

b50. Cherwitz, Richard. "Charles Morris' Conception of Semiotic: Implication for Rhetorical Criticism." Communication Quarterly 29 (1981), 218-27.

b51. Chumbley, Robert. "For a Prelude to Semiotics of the Literary Text," in B. Kopeczi and G. M. Vajda, eds. Actes du VIIIe Congres de l'Association Internationale de Littérature Comparée (Stuttgart: Bieber, 1980), 781-84.

b52. Clarke, D. S. Principles of Semiotic (London & NY: Routledge & Kegan Paul, 1987).

b53. Coletti, Theresa. Naming the Rose: Eco, Medieval Signs, and Modern Theory (Ithaca: Cornell UP, 1988).

b54. Colish, Marcia L. The Mirror of Language: A Study in the Medieval Theory of Knowledge (Lincoln: U of Nebraska P, 1983) [on medieval semiotics].

b55. Colomb, Gregory. "Semiotics Since Eco: Part 1, Semiotic Texts." PLL (1981), 329-48; "Part Two, Semiotic Readers." PLL (1981), 443-59.
b56. ----------. "The Semiotic Study of Literary Works," in Joseph Natoli, ed., Tracing Literary Theory (Urbana: U of Illinois P, 1987), 306-49.

b57. Copeland, James E., ed. New Directions in Linguistics and Semiotics (Houston TX: Rice UP, 1984).

b58. Coquet, Jean-Claude. Sémiotique littéraire (Tours: Mame, 1973).

b59. Corti, Maria. Introduction to Literary Semiotics (Bloomington: Indiana UP, 1978).

b60. Courtes, Joseph. Introduction a la sémiotique narrative et discursive (Paris: Hachette, 1976).

b61. Coward, Rosalind, and John Ellis. Language and Materialism: Developments in Semiology and the Theory of the Subject (London: Routledge & Kegan Paul, 1977).

b62. Crowder, Diane Griffin. "The Semiotic Functions of Ideology in Literary Discourse." BuR 27.1 (1982), 157-68.

b63. Culler, Jonathan. Structuralist Poetics: Structuralism, Linguistics and the Study of Literature (Ithaca: Cornell UP, 1975).
b64. ----------. The Pursuit of Signs: Semiotics, Literature, Deconstruction (Ithaca: Cornell UP, 1981).
b65. ----------. "Semiotics: Communication and Signification," in W. Steiner, ed. Image and Code (Ann Arbor: U of Michigan, 1981), 78-84.
b66. ----------. "Semiotic Consequences." StTCL 6.1-2 (1981-82), 5-15.
b67. ----------. "Junk and Rubbish: A Semiotic Approach." Diacritics 15.3 (1985), 2-13.
b68. ----------. Ferdinand de Saussure, rev. ed. (Ithaca: Cornell UP, 1986).

b69. Daddesio, Thomas C. "Critique of Pure Semiotics," in J. Deely, ed. Semiotics 1984 (Lanham MD: UP of America, 1985), 373-79.

b70. Dascal, Marcelo. La Sémiologie de Leibniz (Paris: Aubier Montaigne, 1978).
b71. ----------. Leibniz, Language, Signs and Thought: A Collection of Essays (Amsterdam and Philadelphia: Benjamins, 1987).

b72. Deely, John. Introducing Semiotic: Its History and Doctrine (Bloomington: Indiana UP, 1982).
b73. ----------, ed. Semiotics 1984 (Lanham MD: UP of America, 1985).
b74. ----------, Brooke Williams, and Felicia E, Kruse, eds. Frontiers in Semiotics (Bloomington: Indiana UP, 1986).

b75. DeGeorge, Richard, ed. Semiotic Themes (Lawrence: U of Kansas, 1981).

b76. Dénes, Imrich. "Textual Features of Adapted Texts," in B. Kopeczi and G. M. Vajda, eds. Actes du VIIIe Congres de l'Association Internationale de Littérature Comparée (Stuttgart: Bieber, 1980), 961-63.

b77. Diggory, Terence. "Painting the Speaking Subject." Diacritics 15.3 (1985), 15-23.

b78. Dubois, Jacques. "Codes, textes, métatextes." Lit 12 (1973), 3-11.

b79. Dutz, Klaus D. Glossar der semiotischen Terminologie Charles W. Morris'. Zur Terminologie der Semiotik Munster: MAks, 1979).
b80. ---------- and H. J. Wulff, eds. Kommunikation, Funktion und Zeichentheorie (Munster: MAKS, 1983).
b81. ---------- and Peter Schmitter, eds. Historiographia semioticae: Studien zur Rekonstruktion der Theorie und Geschichte der Semiotik (Munster: MAKS, 1985).

b82. Eagle, Herbert J. "Verse as a Semiotic System: Tynjanov, Jakobson, Mukarovsky, Lotman Extended." SEEJ 25.4 (1981), 47-61.

b83. Eco, Umberto. "Peirce's Notion of Interpretant." MLN 91 (1976), 1457-72.
b84. ----------. A Theory of Semiotics (Bloomington: Indiana UP, 1976).
b85. ----------. "Semiotics: A Discipline and an Interdisciplinary Method," in T. Sebeok, ed., Sight, Sound and Sense (Bloomington: Indiana UP, 1978), 73-97.
b86. ----------. The Role of the Reader: Explorations in the Semiotics of Texts (Bloomington: Indiana UP, 1979).
b87. ----------, et al. "The Theory of Signs and the Role of the Reader." BMMLA 14.1 (1981), 33-55.
b88. ---------- and Thomas Sebeok, eds. The Sign of Three: Dupin, Holmes, Peirce (Bloomington: Indiana UP, 1983).
b89. ----------. Semiotics and the Philosophy of Language (Bloomington: Indiana UP, 1984).
b90. ----------. "Metaphor, Dictionary, and Encyclopedia." NLH 15.2 (1984), 255-71.
b91. ----------. "Sémiotique générale et philosophie du langage." Critique 41 (1985), 35-36.
b92. ----------. "On Symbols," in J. Deely, B. Williams, and F. E. Kruse, eds. Frontiers in Semiotics (Bloomington: Indiana UP, 1986), 153-80.
b93. ----------. "The Influence of Roman Jakobson on the Development of Semiotics," in Martin Krampen, et al , eds. Classics of Semiotics (NY and London: Plenum Press, 1987), 109-27.

b94. Eimermacher, K. Arbeiten sowjetischer Semiotiker der Moskauer und Tartuer Schule (Auswahlbibliographie) (Kronberg Ts.: Scriptor, 1974).
b95. ---------- and S. Shishkoff. Subject Bibliography of Soviet Semiotics: The Moscow-Tartu School (Ann Arbor: Michigan Slavic Publications, 1977).

b96. Elam, Keir. The Semiotics of Theatre and Drama (London: Methuen, 1980).

b97. Emanuele, Pietro. "Semiotik und Heuristik." Semiosis 11.3 (1986), 28-39.

b98. Eschbach, Achim. Zeichen, Text, Bedeutung: Bibliographie zu Theorie und Praxis der Semiotik (Munchen: Fink, 1974).
b99. ----------, ed. Charles W. Morris: Zeichen, Wert, Asthetik (Frankfurt: Suhrkamp, 1975).
b100. ----------, ed. Zeichen uber Zeichen uber Zeichen. 15 Studien uber Charles W. Morris (Tubingen: Narr, 1981).
b101. ---------- and Jurgen Trabant, eds. History of Semiotics (Amsterdam and Philadelphia: Benjamins, 1983).

b102. Evans, Jonathan. "Medieval Studies and Semiotics: Perspectives on Research," in J. Deely, ed. Semiotics 1984 (Lanham MD: UP of America, 1985), 511-21.
b103. ---------- and André Helbo, eds. Semiotics and International Scholarship: Towards a Language of Theory (Dordrecht & Boston: Martinus Nijhoff, 1986).

b104. Even-Zohar, Itamar. Papers in Historical Poetics (Tel Aviv: Porter Inst. for Poetics and Semiotics, Tel Aviv U, 1978) [cultural semiotics, polysystem theory].
b105. ----------. "Polysystem Theory." PoT 1.1-2 (1979), 287-310.

b106. Faur, Jose. Golden Doves with Silver Dots: Semiotics and Textuality in Rabbinic Tradition (Bloomington: Indiana UP, 1986).

b107. Fawcett, Robin P., et al. The Semiotics of Culture and Language, 3 vols. (London and Dover NH: F. Pinter, 1984).

b108. Fiordo, Richard A. Charles Morris and the Criticism of Discourse (Lisse: Ridder; Bloomington: Indiana UP, 1977).

b109. Fisch, Max. "Peirce's General Theory of Signs," in T. Sebeok, ed., Sight, Sound, and Sense (Bloomington: Indiana UP, 1978), 31-70.

b110. ----------. "Just *How* General is Peirce's General Theory of Signs?" American Journal of Semiotics 2.1-2 (1983), 55-60.
b111. ----------. Peirce, Semiotic, and Pragmatism (Bloomington: Indiana UP, 1986).

b112. Fitzgerald, J. J. Peirce's Theory of Signs as Foundation for Pragmatism (The Hague: Mouton, 1966).

b113. Fizer, John. "Indeterminacies as Structural Components in Semiotically Meaningful Wholes," in B. Kopeczi and G. M. Vajda, eds. Actes du VIIIe Congres de l'Association Internationale de Littérature Comparée (Stuttgart: Bieber, 1980), 767-73.

b114. Fokkema, Douwe W. "Continuity and Change in Russian Formalism, Czech Structuralism, and Soviet Semiotics." PTL 1.1 (1976), 154-96.
b115. ---------- and Elrud Kunne-Ibsch. Theories of Literature in the Twentieth Century: Structuralism, Marxism, Aesthetics of Reception, Semiotics (NY: St. Martin's Press, 1977).
b116. ----------. "The Concept of Code in the Study of Literature." PoT 6.4 (1985), 643-56.

b117. Freadman, Anne. "*Riffaterra Cognita:* A Late Contribution to the Formalism Debate." SubStance 13.1 (1984), 31-45 [on Riffaterre].
b118. ---------- and Meaghan Morris. "Semiotics in Australia," in T. A. Sebeok and J. Umiker-Sebeok, eds. The Semiotic Sphere (NY and London: Plenum, 1986), 1-17.

b119. Gaillard, Françoise. "Code(s) littéraire(s) et idéologie." Lit 12 (1973), 21-35.

b120. Gallardo, Andrés and Jorge Sanchez. "Semiotics in Chile," in T. A. Sebeok and J. Umiker-Sebeok, eds. The Semiotic Sphere (NY and London: Plenum, 1986), 99-114.

b121. Genette, Gérard. "L'homme et les signes." Critique 21 (1965), 99-114.
b122. ----------. Figures (Paris: Seuil, 1966).
b123. ----------. Figures II (Paris: Seuil, 1969).
b124. ----------. "The Reverse Side of the Sign." Social Science Information 8.4 (1969), 69-82.
b125. ----------. Figures III (Paris: Seuil, 1972).

b126. Geppert, Hans Vilmar. "Peirce und Bahtin: Zur Asthetik der Prosa." Semiosis 11.2 (1986), 23-45.

b127. Gillian, Garth. From Sign to Symbol (Brighton, Sussex: Harvester; Atlantic Highlands NJ: Humanities, 1982).

b128. Godel, Robert. "F. de Saussure's Theory of Language." Current Trends in Linguistics 3 (1966), 479-93.
b129. ----------. Les Sources manuscrites du Cours de linguistique générale de F. de Saussure (Geneve: Librairie Droz, 1969).

b130. Goldschlager, Alain. "Towards a Semiotics of Authoritarian Discourse." PoT 3.1 (1982), 11-20.

b131. Golopentia-Eretescu, Sanda. "Semiotics in Romania," in T. A. Sebeok and J. Umiker-Sebeok, eds. The Semiotic Sphere (NY and London: Plenum, 1986), 417-72.

b132. Gonzalez, Cristina. "Semiotics in Spain," in T. A. Sebeok and J. Umiker-Sebeok, eds. The Semiotic Sphere (NY and London: Plenum, 1986), 473-84.

b133. Gowa, Ferdinand. "New German Criticism: Max Bense." CLAJ 9 (1965), 51-60.

b134. Greenlee, Douglas. Peirce's Concept of Sign (The Hague: Mouton, 1973).

b135. Greimas, A. J. "The Relationship Between Structural Linguistics and Poetics." ISSJ 19 (1967), 8-16.
b136. ----------. Du sens (Paris: Seuil, 1970).
b137. ----------. Essais de la sémiotique poétique (Paris: Larousse, 1972).
b138. ---------- and J. Courtes, Sémiotique: dictionnaire raisonée de la théorie du langage (Paris: Hachette, 1979).

b139. Grivel, Charles. "Pour une sémiotique des produits d'expression, I: Le Texte." Semiotica 10 (1974), 101-15.
b140. ----------. "L'Histoire dans le visage," in J. Decottignies, ed. Les Sujets de l'écriture (Lille: PU de Lille, 1981), 175-221.

b141. Grossberg, Lawrence. "Experience, Signification, and Reality: The Boundaries of Cultural Semiotics." Semiotica 41 (1982), 73-106.

b142. Guiraud, Pierre. Semiology. Tr. George Gross. (London: Routledge, 1975).

b143. Gunther, Hans. "'Exakte' Literaturwissenschaft und Kultursemiotik--zwei Tendenzen im sowjetischen Strukturalismus." LiLi 14 (1974), 137-46.

b144. Guttgemanns, Erhardt. "Elementare semiotische Texttheorie." LBib 49 (1981), 85-112.

b145. Haidu, Peter. "Considérations théoriques sur la sémiotique socio-historique," in H. Parret and H.-G. Ruprecht, eds. Exigences et perspectives de la sémiotique: Receuil d'hommages pour Algirdas Julien Greimas (Amsterdam: Benjamins, 1985), 215-28.

b146. Hall, Dennis R. "Semiotics: An Approach to Interdisciplinary Studies." HS 49 (1979), 5-6.

b147. Halliday, M. A. K. Language as a Social Semiotic (University Park: Pennsylvania State UP, 1977).

b148. Hamilton, Ruth, ed. "Medieval Semiotics." Style 20.2 (1986) [special issue].

b149. Hardwick, C. S., ed. Semiotic and Significs: The Correspondence Between Charles S. Peirce and Victoria Lady Welby (Bloomington: Indiana UP, 1977).

b150. Hawkes, Terence. Structuralism and Semiotics (Berkeley: U of California P, 1977).

b151. Helbo, André, ed. Le champ sémiologique: perspectives internationales (Paris: Editions Complexe, 1979).

b152. Henault, Anne. Les Enjeux de la sémiotique (Paris: PUF, 1979).
b153. ----------. "Semiotics in France," in T. A. Sebeok and J. Umiker-Sebeok, eds. The Semiotic Sphere (NY and London: Plenum, 1986), 153-75.

b154. Hervey, Sandor G. J. Semiotic Perspectives (London: Allen & Unwin, 1982).

b155. Herzfeld, Michael and Margot Lenhart, eds. Semiotics 1980 (NY: Plenum, 1982).

b156. Hodge, Robert and Gunther Kress. "Functional Semiotics: Key Concepts for the Analysis of Media, Culture and Society." AJCS 1.1 (1983), 1-17.

b157. Holenstein, Elmar. Roman Jakobson's Approach to Language: Phenomenological Structuralism (Bloomington: Indiana UP, 1976).

b158. Hookway, Christopher. Peirce (London: Routledge & Kegan Paul, 1985).

b159. Innis, Robert E. Karl Buhler: Semiotic Foundations of Language Theory (NY: Plenum, 1982).
b160. ----------, ed. Semiotics: An Introductory Anthology (Bloomington: Indiana UP, 1985).

b161. "Intertextuality." AJS 3.4 (1985) [special issue].

b162. Jakobson, Roman. Selected Writings, 8 vols. (S'Gravenhage: Mouton, 1962--).
b163. ----------. Roman Jakobson: A Bibliography of His Writings (The Hague: Mouton, 1971).
b164. ----------. Questions de poétique (Paris: Seuil, 1973).
b165. ----------. Coup d'oeil sur le développement de la sémiotique (Bloomington: Research Center for Language and Semiotic Studies, 1975).
b166. ----------. "A Few Remarks on Peirce, Pathfinder in the Science of Language." MLN 92 (1977), 1026-32.
b167. ----------. The Framework of Language (Ann Arbor: Grad. School, U of Michigan, 1980).
b168. ---------- and Krystyna Pomorska. Dialogues (Cambridge MA: MIT P, 1983).
b169. ---------- and Linda R. Waugh. The Sound Shape of Language, 2nd ed. (Berlin & NY: Mouton de Gruyter, 1987).
b170. ----------. Language in Literature (Cambridge MA: Belknap P, 1987).

b171. Janik, Dieter. "Contribution a une théorie sémiologique des signifiants littéraires," in B. Kopeczi and G. M. Vajda, eds. Actes du VIIIe Congres de l'Association Internationale de Littérature Comparée (Stuttgart: Bieber, 1980), 751-55.

b172. Jiménez-Ottalengo, Regina. "Semiotics in Mexico," in T. A. Sebeok and J. Umiker-Sebeok, eds. The Semiotic Sphere (NY and London: Plenum, 1986), 359-67.

b173. Johansen, Jorgen Dines. "Sign Concepts/Semiosis/Meaning." OL supp. 4 (1979), 123-76.
b174. ----------. "Semiotics and the Study of Literature." Neohelicon 8 (1981), 269-83.
b175. ----------. "The Place of Semiotics in the Study of Literature," in J. D. Evans and A. Helbo, eds. Semiotics and International Scholarship: Towards a Language of Theory (Dordrecht: Nijhoff, 1986), 101-26.

b176. ----------. "Sign, Concept, Meaning, and the Study of Literature," in J.
D. Johansen and H. Sonne, eds. Pragmatics and Linguistics (Odense: Odense
UP, 1986), 95-102.
b177. ----------. "Semiotics in Denmark," in T. A. Sebeok and J. Umiker-
Sebeok, eds. The Semiotic Sphere (NY and London: Plenum, 1986), 115-43.

b178. Johnson, Anthony L. "Signifier and Signified in Verbal Art," in A
Vitalist Seminar (Salzburg: Inst. fur Anglistik und Amerikanistik, U of
Salzburg, 1984), 22-53.

b179. Jusdanis, Gregory. "The Poetics of Roman Jakobson: Aesthetics or
Semiotics?" in J. Deely, ed. Semiotics 1984 (Lanham MD: UP of America,
1985), 267-75.

b180. Kalinowski, Georges. "Concepts et distinctions pour une sémiotique
réaliste," in H. Parret and H.-G. Ruprecht, eds. Exigences et perspectives de
la sémiotique: Receuil d'hommages pour Algirdas Julien Greimas
(Amsterdam: Benjamins, 1985), 25-39.

b181. Kaufman, Chana. A Selective Bibliography of Semiotics and Related
Fields in Israel in Recent Years (Tel Aviv: Dept. of Poetics & Comp. Lit.,
Tel Aviv U, 1978).

b182. Kevelson, Roberta. "Semiotics in the United States," in T. A. Sebeok
and J. Umiker-Sebeok, eds. The Semiotic Sphere (NY and London: Plenum,
1986), 519-54.
b183. ----------. Charles S. Peirce's Method of Methods (Amsterdam and
Philadelphia: Benjamins, 1987).

b184. Koch, Walter A., ed. Semiotische Versuche zu literarischen
Strukturen (Hildesheim: Olms, 1979).
b185. ----------, ed. Semiogenesis: Essays on the Analysis of the Genesis of
Language, Art, and Literature (Frankfurt am Main: Lang, 1982).
b186. ----------. Evolutionare Kultursemiotik (Bochum: Brockmeyer,
1986).
b187. ----------. Philosophie der Philologie und Semiotik: Literatur und
Welt: Versuche zur Interdiziplinaritat der Philologie (Bochum:
Brockmeyer, 1986).

b188. Koller, Wilhelm. Semiotik und Metapher: Untersuchungen zur
grammatischen Struuktur und kommunikativen Funktion von Metaphern
(Stuttgart: Metzler, 1975).

b189. Kowzan, Tadeusz. Analyse sémiolgique du spectacle théatrale (Lyon:
Université de Lyon, 1976).

b190. Krampen, Martin, *et al,* eds. Classics of Semiotics (NY and London: Plenum Press, 1987).
b191. ----------. "Ferdinand de Saussure and the Development of Semiology," in Martin Krampen, *et al* , eds. Classics of Semiotics (NY and London: Plenum Press, 1987), 59-88.

b192. Kristeva, Julia. "La linguistique et sémiologie aujord'hui en U.R.S.S." Tel Quel 35 (1968), 3-8.
b193. ----------. [Semiotike]: Recherches pour une sémanalyse (Paris: Seuil, 1969).
b194. ----------. "La sémiologie comme science des idéologies." Semiotica 1 (1969), 196-204.
b195. ----------. Le texte du roman: approache sémiologique d'une structure discursive transformationnelle (The Hague: Mouton, 1970).
b196. ----------. "La mutation sémiotique." Annales 25 (1970), 1497-1522.
b197. ----------. La révolution du langage poétique (Paris: Seuil, 1974).
b198. ----------. Polylogue (Paris: Seuil, 1977).
b199. ----------, *et al* , eds. Essays in Semiotics/Essais de sémiotique (The Hague: Mouton, 1971).

b200. Kuper, Christoph. "Roman Jakobson und Jurij Lotman: Die Entwicklung einer semiotischer Asthetik," in Arbeiten zur Sprachentwicklung und Sprachbeschreibung (Berlin: Inst. fur Ling., Technische U Berlin, 1979), 30-62.

b201. Lachmann, Renate. "Zwei Konzepte der Textbedeutung bei Jurij Lotman." Russian Literature 5.1 (1977), 1-36.
b202. ----------. "Wertaspekte in Jurij Lotmans Textbedeutungstheorie," in B. Lenz and B. Schulte-Middelich, eds. Beschreiben, Interpretieren, Werten: Das Wertungsproblem in der Literatur aus der Sicht unterschiedlicher Methoden (Munich: Fink, 1982), 134-55.

b203. Laferriere, Daniel. Sign and Subject: Semiotic and Psychoanalytic Investigations into Poetry (Lisse: De Ridder, 1978).

b204. Lamy, Marie-Noelle. "In Defence of A. J. Greimas' Theory of Discourse." JLS 13.3 (1984), 205-25.

b205. Lange-Seidl, Annemarie. "Semiotics in East and West Germany and Austria," in T. A. Sebeok and J. Umiker-Sebeok, eds. The Semiotic Sphere (NY and London: Plenum, 1986), 177-227.

b206. Lauretis, Teresa de. "The Discreet Charm of Semiotics, or Esthetics in the Emperor's New Clothes." Diacritics 5.3 (1975), 16-23.

b207. Legrand, Jacques. "Max Bense et le groups de Stuttgart." <u>Critique</u> 218 (1965), 619-28.

b208. Lieb, J. "On Peirce's Classification of Signs," in C. S. Hardwick, ed., <u>Semiotic and Significs</u> (Bloomington: Indiana UP, 1977), Appendix B.

b209. Ljung, Per Erik. "Semiotics in Sweden," in T. A. Sebeok and J. Umiker-Sebeok, eds. <u>The Semiotic Sphere</u> (NY and London: Plenum, 1986), 485-504.

b210. Lotman, Jurij and A. M. Pjatigorskij. "Le texte et la fonction." <u>Semiotica</u> 1 (1969), 205-17.
b211. ----------. "Different Cultures, Different Codes." <u>TLS</u> (Oct. 12, 1973), 1213-15.
b212. ----------. <u>Aufsatze zur Theorie und Methodologie der Literatur und Kultur</u> (Kronberg Ts.: Scriptor, 1974).
b213. ----------, <i>et al</i>. "Theses on the Semiotic Study of Cultures (as Applied to Slavic Texts)," in T. Sebeok, ed. <u>The Tell-Tale Sign: A Survey of Semiotics</u> (Lisse: Peter de Ridder, 1975), 57-83.
b214. ----------. "On the Metalanguage of a Typ[ological Description of Culture." <u>Semiotica</u> 14 (1975), 97-123.
b215. ----------. "Point of View in a Text." <u>NLH</u> 6.2 (1975), 339-52.
b216. ----------. <u>Analysis of the Poetic Text</u> (Ann Arbor: Ardis, 1976).
b217. ----------. "The Content and Structure of the Concept of 'Literature.'" <u>PTL</u> 1.2 (1976), 339-56.
b218. ---------- and B. Ouspenski, eds. <u>Travaux sur les systemes de signes: Ecole de Tartu</u> (Brussells: Editions Complexe, 1976).
b219. ----------. <u>The Structure of the Artistic Text</u> (Ann Arbor: Michigan Slavic, 1977).

b220. Lucid, Daniel P., ed. <u>Soviet Semiotics</u> (Baltimore: Johns Hopkins UP, 1977).

b221. Lyne, John. "Semiotics Self-Signifying: The Ongoing Constitution of Sign Studies." <u>QJS</u> 70.1 (1984), 80-110.

b222. MacCannell, Dean and Juliet Flower MacCannell. <u>The Time of the Sign: a Semiotic Interpretation of Modern Culture</u> (Bloomington: Indiana UP, 1982).

b223. MacCannell, Juliet Flower. "The Semiotic of Modern Culture." <u>Semiotica</u> 35.3-4 (1981), 287-301.

b224. Macksey, Richard A., Henry Sussman, and Samuel Weber, eds. "The Charles Sanders Peirce Symposium on Semiotics and the Arts." MLN 91.6 (1976), 1427-1571 [special issue].

b225. Madsen, Peter. "Semiotics and Dialectics." Poetics 6 (1972), 29-49.

b226. Margolin, Uri. "Juri Lotman on the Creation of Meaning in Literature." Canadian Review of Comparative Literature (1975), 262-82.

b227. Marin, Louis. Etudes sémiologiques: écritures, peintures (Paris: Klincksieck, 1972).
b228. ----------. La critique du discours: Etudes sur la 'Logique de Port Royal' et des Pensées de Pascal (Paris: Minuit, 1975).
b229. ----------. Détruire la peinture (Paris: Editions Galilée, 1977).

b230. Markiewicz, Henryk. "Die Literatur aus semiotischer Sicht: Randbemerkungen zu den Arbeiten J. Lotmans," in P. V. Zima, ed. Semiotics and Dialectics: Ideology and the Text (Amsterdam: Benjamins, 1981), 331-59.

b231. Martin, Richard. "Semiotics in Belgium," in T. A. Sebeok and J. Umiker-Sebeok, eds. The Semiotic Sphere (NY and London: Plenum, 1986), 19-45.

b232. Martinet, Jeanne. Clefs pour une sémiologie (Paris: Seghers, 1973).

b233. Matejka, Ladislav, et al, eds. "Soviet Semiotics of Culture." Dispositio 1.3 (1976) [special issue].
b234. ----------. "Literary History in a Semiotic Framework: Prague School Contributions," in P. Steiner, et al, eds. The Structure of the Literary Process (Amsterdam: 1982), 341-70.

b235. Mayenowa, Maria Renata. "Lotman as Historian of Literature." Russian Literature 5.1 (1977), 81-90.
b236. ----------. "Verbal Texts and Iconic-Visual Texts," in W. Steiner, ed. Image and Code (Ann Arbor: U of Michigan, 1981), 133-37.

b237. McCormick, Hugo. "Semiotics in Venezuela: Critical Revision of the Notion of the Unconscious and Its Effects in the Second Semiology Field," in T. A. Sebeok and J. Umiker-Sebeok, eds. The Semiotic Sphere (NY and London: Plenum, 1986), 599-611.

b238. McMahon, Edward. "René Girard and the Project of a General Semiotic Theory," in J. Deely, ed. Semiotics 1984 (Lanham MD: UP of America, 1985), 401-07.

b239. Meletinsky, E. and D. Segal. "Structuralism and Semiotics in the USSR." Diogenes 73 (1971), 88-115.

b240. Merrell, Floyd. Semiotic Foundations: Steps Toward an Epistemology of Written Texts (Bloomington: Indiana UP, 1982).
b241. ----------. A Semiotic Theory of Texts (Berlin & NY: de Gruyter, 1985).

b242. Meyers, Walter E. "Literary Terms and Jakobson's Theory of Communication." CE 30 (1969), 518-26.

b243. Miers, Paul. "A Cognitive Program for Semiotic Functions." MLN 97.5 (1982), 1129-46.

b244. Morgan, Thais E. "Is There an Intertext in this Text? Literary and Interdisciplinary Approaches to Intertextuality." AJS 3.4 (1985), 1-40.

b245. Morris, Charles. Writings on the General Theory of Signs (The Hague: Mouton, 1971).

b246. Mouloud, Noel. Langage et structure: essai de logique et de semeiology (Paris: Payot, 1969).

b247. Mounin, Georges. Introduction a la sémiologie (Paris: Minuit, 1970).
b248. ----------. "The Semiologies of Literary Texts," in R. Posner and J. N. Green, eds. Trends in Romance Linguistics and Philology, 3: Language and Philology in Romance (The Hague: Mouton, 1982), 79-96.
b249. ----------. Semiotic Praxis (NY: Plenum, 1985).

b250. Mueller, Lauren E. "Semiotics in Italy: Cesare Segre, Gianfranco Bettetini, Pier Paolo Pasolini, Emilio Garroni" (Ph.D. diss., Purdue U, 1982).

b251. Mukarovsky, Jan. Structure, Sign, and Function (New Haven: Yale UP, 1978).

b252. Nagy, Gregory. "Sema and Noesis: Some Illustrations." Arethusa 16.1-2 (1983), 35-55.

b253. Nakhimovsky, Alexander D. and Alice Stone Nakhimovsky, eds. The Semiotics of Russian Cultural History: Essays by Iurii M. Lotman, Lidiia Ia. Ginsburg, Boris A. Uspenskii (Ithaca: Cornell UP, 1985).

b254. Net, Mariana. "Towards a Pragmatics of Poetic Intertextuality." RRL 28 (1983), 159-62.

b255. ----------. "Types of the Referents of the Artistic Text." RRL 28 (1983), 55-58.

b256. Noakes, Susan. "Literary Semiotics and Hermeneutics: Towards a Taxonomy of the Interpretant." American Journal of Semiotics 3.3 (1985), 109-19.

b257. Norrick, Neal R. Semiotic Principles in Semantic Theory (Amsterdam: John Benjamins, 1981).

b258. Norris, Christopher. "Semiotics in Great Britain," in T. A. Sebeok and J. Umiker-Sebeok, eds. The Semiotic Sphere (NY and London: Plenum, 1986), 229-51.

b259. Noth, Winfried. Handbuch der Semiotik (Stuttgart: Metzler, 1985).

b260. Odmark, John. "Style in Narrative Structures: A Semiotic Approach," in B. Kopeczi and G. M. Vajda, eds. Actes du VIIIe Congres de l'Association Internationale de Littérature Comparée (Stuttgart: Bieber, 1980), 905-09.

b261. Oehler, Klaus. "An Outline of Peirce's Semiotics," in Martin Krampen, et al , eds. Classics of Semiotics (NY and London: Plenum Press, 1987), 1-21.

b262. Oguibenine, Boris. "The Semiotic Approach to Human Culture," in W. Steiner, ed. Image and Code (Ann Arbor: U of Michigan, 1981), 85-95.

b263. Oldani, Louis. "Literary Language and Postmodern Theories of Semiotics," in R. T. DeGeorge, ed. Semiotic Themes (Lawrence: U of Kansas, 1981), 95-108.

b264. Ormiston, G. L. "Peirce's Categories" Structure of Semiotic." Semiotica 19 (1977), 202-32.

b265. Orr, Leonard. "Intertextuality and the Cultural Text in Recent Semiotics." CE 48.8 (Dec., 1986), 32-44.
b266. ----------. Semiotic and Structuralist Analyses of Fiction: An Introduction and a Survey of Applications (Troy NY: Whitston, 1987).

b267. Pagnini, Marcello. The Pragmatics of Literature (Bloomington: Indiana UP, 1987).

b268. Parret, Herman. Semiotics and Pragmatics (Amsterdam and Philadelphia: Benjamins, 1983).

b269. Paruolo, Silvana. "Semiotics and Its Range." Diogenes 113-14 (1981), 127-56.

b270. Pavis, Patrice. Problemes de la sémiologie théatrale (Montreal: Presses de Quebec, 1976).
b271. ----------. Languages of the Stage: Essays in the Semiology of the Theatre (NY: Performing Arts Journal Publications, 1982).

b272. Pearson, C. "A Theory of Sign Structure." Semiotic Scene 1.2 (1977), 1-22.

b273. Peckham, Morse. "Perceptual and Semiotic Discontinuity in Art." Poetics 7 (1980), 217-30.

b274. Peirce, Charles. Complete Published Works including Secondary Materials, ed. K. Ketner, et al , microfiche ed. (Greenwich, CT: Johnson, 1977).
b275. ----------. A Comprehensive Bibliography and Index of the Published Works with a Bibliography of Secondary Studies ed. K. Ketner, et al , microfiche ed. (Greenwich, CT: Johnson, 1977).
b276. ----------. Writings of Charles S. Peirce: A Chronological Edition ed. Max Fisch et al (Indianapolis: Indiana U-Purdue U at Indianapolis, and Bloomington: Indiana UP, 1982---).

b277. Peradotto, John. "Texts and Unrefracted Facts: Philology, Hermeneutics and Semiotics." Arethusa 16.1-2 (1983), 15-33.

b278. Pharies, David A. Charles S. Peirce and the Linguistic Sign (Amsterdam and Philadelphia: Benjamins, 1985).

b279. Pittelkow, Ralf. "On Literature as a Social Phenomenon (Semiological Notes)." Poetics 6 (1972), 7-28.

b280. Popovic, Anton. "Communication Aspect in Slovak Literary Scholarship," in John Odmark, ed., Language, Literature & Meaning, II: Current Trends in Literary Research (Amsterdam: Benjamins, 1980), 55-108.
b281. ----------. "Inter-Semiotic, Inter-Literary Translation," in B. Kopeczi and G. M. Vajda, eds. Actes du VIIIe Congres de l'Association Internationale de Littérature Comparée (Stuttgart: Bieber, 1980), 763-65.

b282. Posner, Roland and H.-P. Reinecke, eds. Zeichenprozesse--Semiotische Forschung in den Einzelwissenschaften (Wiesbaden: Athenaion, 1977).

b283. ----------. Rational Discourse and Poetic Communication. Methods of Linguistic, Literary, and Philosophical Analysis (Berlin and NY: Mouton, 1982).
b284. ----------. "Charles Morris and the Behavioral Foundations of Semiotics," in Martin Krampen, et al , eds. Classics of Semiotics (NY and London: Plenum Press, 1987), 23-57.

b285. Poster, Mark. "Semiology and Critical Theory: From Marx to Baudrillard." Boundary 8.1 (1979), 275-87.

b286. Prince, Gerald. "On Metanarrative Signs," in B. Kopeczi and G. M. Vajda, eds. Actes du VIIIe Congres de l'Association Internationale de Littérature Comparée (Stuttgart: Bieber, 1980), 911-15.

b287. Ransdell, Joseph. "On the Paradigm of Experience Appropriate for Semiotics," in M. Herzfeld and M. D. Lenhart, eds. Semiotics 1980 (NY: Plenum, 1982), 427-37.

b288. Rauch, Irmengard and Gerald F. Carr, eds. The Signifying Animal: The Grammar of Language and Experience (Bloomington: Indiana UP, 1980).

b289. Rector, Monica. "Semiotics in Brazil," in T. A. Sebeok and J. Umiker-Sebeok, eds. The Semiotic Sphere (NY and London: Plenum, 1986), 47-58.

b290. Reeves, Charles Eric. "Convention and Literary Behavior," in P. Steiner, et al, eds. The Structure of the Literary Process (Amsterdam: Benjamins, 1982), 431-54.

b291. Reichler, Claude. "On the Notion of Intertextuality: The Example of the Libertine Novel." Diogenes 113-14 (1981), 205-15 [discusses Lotman].

b292. Réthoré, Joelle. "Lecture et interprétation: Une Partition sémiotique des savoirs." Semiosis 27.3 (1982), 32-38.

b293. Revzina, O. G. "The Fourth Summer School on Secondary Modelling Systems." Semiotica 6 (1972), 222-43.

b294. Rewar, Walter. "Semiotics and Literature." DAI 33 (1973), 3600A.
b295. ----------. "Notes for a Typology of Culture." Semiotica 18.4 (1976), 361-78.
b296. ----------. "Semiotics and Communication in Soviet Criticism." Lang&S 9 (1976), 3-16.
b297. ----------. "Tartu Semiotics." Bulletin of Literary Semiotics 3 (1976), 1-16.

b298. ----------. "Cybernetics and Poetics: The Semiotic Information of Poetry." Semiotica 25.3-4 (1979), 273-305 [on Lotman].

b299. Rey, Alain. "Lecture du 'signe,'" in L. Brind'Amour and E. Vance, eds. Archéologie du signe (Toronto: Pontifical Inst. of Medieval Studies, 1983), 1-16 [medieval semiotics].

b300. Riffaterre, Michael. Semiotics of Poetry (Bloomington: Indiana UP, 1978).
b301. ----------. "Descriptive Imagery." YFS 61 (1981), 107-25.
b302. ----------. "Interpretation and Undecidability." NLH 12.2 (1981), 227-42.
b303. ----------. Text Production (NY: Columbia UP, 1983).
b304. ----------. "The Interpretant in Literary Semiotics." AJS 3.4 (1985), 41-55.

b305. Robey, David. "Umberto Eco," in M. Caesar and P. Hainsworth, eds. Writers & Society in Contemporary Italy (NY: St. Martin's, 1984), 63-87.

b306. Rochberg-Halton, Eugene. and K. McMurtrey. "The Foundations of Modern Semiotic: Charles Peirce and Charles Morris." American Journal of Semiotics 2 (1983), 129-56.
b307. ----------. "The Fetishism of Signs," in J. Deely, ed. Semiotics 1984 (Lanham MD: UP of America, 1985), 409-18.

b308. "Roland Barthes." Poétique 12.47 (1981) [special issue].

b309. Rose, Marilyn Gaddis. "Decadent Language Strategies: A Semiotic Survey." ALitASH 21.1-2 (1979), 69-77.

b310. Rubin, Nancy Felson, ed. "Semiotics and Classicial Studies." Arethusa 16.1-2 (1983) [special issue].

b311. Rudy, Stephen. "Semiotics in the U. S. S. R.," in T. A. Sebeok and J. Umiker-Sebeok, eds. The Semiotic Sphere (NY and London: Plenum, 1986), 555-82.

b312. Ruprecht, Hans-George. "Ouvertures métasémiotiques: Entretien avec Algirdas Julien Greimas." CJRS 4.1 (1984), 1-23.

b313. Sangster, Rodney B. Roman Jakobson and Beyond: Language as a System of Signs (Berlin & NY: Mouton, 1982).

b314. Saussure, Ferdinand de. Course in General Linguistics, tr. W. Baskin (NY: McGraw-Hill, 1966).

b315. ----------. Cours de linguistique générale, ed. Rudolf Engler, 2 vols. (Wiesbaden: O. Harrassowitz, 1967-74).
b316. ----------. Cours de linguistique générale, ed. Tullio de Mauro (Paris: Payot, 1973).

b317. Schmid, Herta and Aloysius Van Kesteren, eds. Semiotics of Drama and Theatre (Amsterdam and Philadelphia: Benjamins, 1984).

b318. Schnaiderman, Boris. "Semiotics in the U.S.S.R.: A Search for 'Missing Links.'" Dispositio 6 (1981), 93-107.

b319. Scholes, Robert. "Toward a Semiotics of Literature." CritI 4 (1977), 105-20.
b320. ----------. Semiotics and Interpretation (New Haven: Yale UP, 1982).

b321. Seabra, José Augusto. "Semiotics in Portugal," in T. A. Sebeok and J. Umiker-Sebeok, eds. The Semiotic Sphere (NY and London: Plenum, 1986), 407-15.

b322. Sebeok, Thomas. "Semiotics: A Survey of the State of the Art." Current Trends in Linguistics, 12 (1974), 211-64.
b323. ----------, ed. The Tell-Tale Sign: A Survey of Semiotics (Lisse: Peter de Ridder Press, 1975).
b324. ----------. "Iconicity." MLN 91.6 (1976), 1427-56.
b325. ----------, ed. A Perfusion of Signs (Bloomington: Indiana UP, 1977).
b326. ----------, ed. Sight, Sound, and Sense (Bloomington: Indiana UP, 1978).
b327. ----------. The Sign & Its Masters (Austin: U of Texas P, 1979).
b328. ----------. The Play of Musement (Bloomington: Indiana UP, 1981).
b329. ----------, ed. Carnival! (Berlin & NY: Mouton, 1984).
b330. ---------- and Jean Umiker-Sebeok, eds. The Semiotic Sphere (NY and London: Plenum, 1986).
b331. ----------, et al, eds. Encyclopedic Dictionary of Semiotics, 3 vols. (Berlin & NY: de Gruyter, 1986).
b332. ----------. I Think I am a Verb: More Contributions to the Doctrine of Signs (NY: Plenum, 1986).
b333. ----------. "Karl Buhler," in Martin Krampen, et al , eds. Classics of Semiotics (NY and London: Plenum Press, 1987), 129-45.
b334. ---------- and Jean Umiker-Sebeok, eds. The Semiotic Web 1986 (Berlin and NY: de Gruyter, 1987).

b335. See, Fred G. Desire and the Sign: Nineteenth-Century American Fiction (Baton Rouge: Louisiana State UP, 1987).

b336. Segal, D. M. Aspects of Structuralism in Soviet Philology (Tel Aviv: Porter Inst. for Poetics and Semiotics, 1974).

b337. Segre, Cesare. Semiotics and Literary Criticism (The Hague: Mouton, 1973).
b338. ----------. Introduction to the Analysis of the Literary Text (Bloomington: Indiana UP, 1988).

b339. Seung, T. K. Semiotics and Thematics in Hermeneutics (Ithaca: Cornell UP, 1982).

b340. Seyffert, Peter. Soviet Literary Structuralism: Background, Debate, Issues (Columbus OH: Slavica, 1985).

b341. Shapiro, Michael. "Sémiotique de la rime." Poétique 20 (1974), 501-19.
b342. ---------- and Marianne Shapiro. Figuration in Verbal Art (Princeton NJ: Princeton UP, 1988).

b343. Shaumyan, Sebastian. A Semiotic Theory of Language (Bloomington: Indiana UP, 1987).

b344. Sherriff, John K. "Charles S. Peirce and the Semiotics of Literature," in Richard T. DeGeorge, ed., Semiotic Themes (Lawrence: U of Kansas, 1981), 51-74.

b345. Shukman, Ann. "The Canonization of the Real: Jurij Lotman's Theory of Literature and the Analysis of Poetry." PTL 1.2 (1976), 317-38.
b346. ----------. "Jurij Lotman and the Semiotics of Culture." Russian Literature 5.1 (1977), 41-54.
b347. ----------. Literature and Semiotics: A Study of the Writings of Juri Lotman (Amsterdam: North-Holland, 1977).
b348. ----------. "The Moscow--Tartu Semiotics School: A Bibliography of Works and Comments in English." PTL 3 (1978), 593-601.
b349. ----------. "The Dialectics of Change: Culture, Codes, and the Individual," in P. V. Zima, ed. Semiotics and Dialectics: Ideology and the Text (Amsterdam: Benajmins, 1981), 311-29.
b350. ----------, ed. The Semiotics of Russian Culture (Ann Arbor: Dept. of Slavic Langs. & Lits., U of Michigan, 1984).

b351. Silverman, Kaja. "The Site of Reading." Semiotica 25.3-4 (1979), 257-72 [on Soviet semiotics].
b352. ----------. The Subject of Semiotics (NY: Oxford UP, 1983).

b353. Skulsky, Harold. "On the Pursuit of Signs." JAAC 41.3 (1983), 289-99 [on Culler].

b354. Sless, David. In Search of Semiotics (Totowa NJ: Barnes & Noble, 1986).

b355. Spa, Jaap J. Sémiologie et linguistique: Réflexions préparadigmatiques (Amsterdam: Rodopi, 1985).

b356. Spinner, Kaspar H. "Totalitatsanspruch des poetischen Zeichens? Semiotische Klarung und didaktische Konsequenzen." Lit 27-28 (1977), 137-53.

b357. Steiner, Peter. "Jan Mukarovsky and Charles W. Morris: Two Pioneers of the Semiotics of Art." Semiotica 19 (1977), 321-34.
b358. ----------. "In Defense of Semiotics: The Dual Asymmetry of Cultural Signs." NLH 12.3 (1981), 415-35.
b359. ----------. "The Semiotics of Literary Reception," in P. Steiner, et al, eds. The Structure of the Literary Process (Amsterdam: Benjamins, 1982), 503-20.

b360. Steiner, Wendy, ed. Image and Code (Ann Arbor: U of Michigan, 1981).
b361. ----------, ed. The Sign in Music and Literature (Austin: U of Texas P, 1981).

b362. Stewart, Susan. On Longing: Narratives of the Miniature, the Gigantic, the Souvenir, the Collection (Baltimore: Johns Hopkins UP, 1984).

b363. Stockinger, Peter. "Fur eine Text- und Kultursemiotik." JIG 17.1 (1985), 25-46.

b364. Storelv, Sven. "Semiotics in Norway," in T. A. Sebeok and J. Umiker-Sebeok, eds. The Semiotic Sphere (NY and London: Plenum, 1986), 369-85.

b365. Strickland, Geoffrey. "Benveniste and Semiology." Cambridge Quarterly 7.2 (1977), 113-28.

b366. Swiggers, Pierre. "Semiotics in the Low Countries," in T. A. Sebeok and J. Umiker-Sebeok, eds. The Semiotic Sphere (NY and London: Plenum, 1986), 343-57.

b367. Talens, Jenaro and Juan M. Company. "The Textual Space: On the Notion of Text." JMMLA 17.2 (1984), 24-36.

b368. Tamir-Ghez, Nomi, ed. "Getting the Message: On the Semiotics of Literary Signification." StTCL 6.1-2 (1981-82) [special issue].

b369. Taranto, Robert E. "Sign, Data, and Information: An Introduction to a Semiotic Understanding of Information." Semiosis 32 (1983), 17-24.

b370. Tarasti, Eero. "Semiotics in Finland," in T. A. Sebeok and J. Umiker-Sebeok, eds. The Semiotic Sphere (NY and London: Plenum, 1986), 145-52.

b371. Thérien, Gilles. "Petite sémiologie de l'écrire." EF 18.1 (1982), 5-19.
b372. ----------. Sémiologies (Montreal: U du Quebec, 1985).

b373. Thompson, Clive. "The Semiotics of M. M. Bakhtin." RUO 53.1 (1983), 11-21.

b374. Thompson, Ewa M. "Jurij Lotman's Literary Theory and Its Context." SEEJ 21.2 (1977), 225-38.

b375. Tiefenbrun, Susan. "The State of Literary Semiotics: 1983." Semiotica 51.1-3 (1984), 7-44.

b376. Titunik. I. R. "Bachtin's and Soviet Semiotics: A Case Study." RusL 10.1 (1981), 1-16.

b377. Todorov, Tzvetan. "Saussure's Semiotics," in Theories of the Symbol (Ithaca: Cornell UP, 1982), 256-70.

b378. Toyama, Tomonori. "Semiotics in Japan," in T. A. Sebeok and J. Umiker-Sebeok, eds. The Semiotic Sphere (NY and London: Plenum, 1986), 323-42.

b379. Trabant, Jurgen. Zur Semiologie des Literarischen Kunstwerks (Munich: Fink, 1970).
b380. ----------. "Zeichen," in K. Kanzog, D. Kanzog, and A. Masser, eds. Reallexikon der deutschen Literatur, IV: 9, 10)Berlin: de Gruyter, 1984), 965-76.
b381. ----------. "Louis Hjelmslev: Glossematics as General Semiotics," in Martin Krampen, et al , eds. Classics of Semiotics (NY and London: Plenum Press, 1987), 89-108.

b382. Uexkull, Thure von. "The Sign Theory of Jakob von Uexkull," in Martin Krampen, et al , eds. Classics of Semiotics (NY and London: Plenum Press, 1987), 147-79.

b383. Uspenskij, Boris A. Principles of Structural Typology (The Hague: Mouton, 1968).

b384. ----------. "A Structural Isomorphism of Verbal and Visual Art." Poetics 5 (1972), 5-39.

b385. ----------. A Poetics of Composition (Berkeley: U of California P, 1973).

Vance, Eugene. Mervelous Signals: Poetics and Sign Theory in the Middle Ages (Lincoln: U of Nebraska P, 1986).

b386. Veltrusky, Jiri. "Comparative Semiotics of Art," in W. Steiner, ed. Image and Code (Ann Arbor: U of Michigan, 1981), 109-32.

b387. Venclova, Tomas. "The Unstable Equilibrium: Eight Russian Poetic Texts." DAI 46 (1986), 3371A [Soviet semiotics].

b388. Vlad, Carmen. "Le Statut sémiotique de la critique littéraire." Degrés 28 (1981), o1-04,

b389. Voigt, Vilmos. "Semantics and Semiotics of Works of Art in High and Folk Literature," in B. Kopeczi and G. M. Vajda, eds. Actes du VIIIe Congres de l'Association Internationale de Littérature Comparée (Stuttgart: Bieber, 1980), 757-61.

b390. ----------. "Semiotics in Hungary," in T. A. Sebeok and J. Umiker-Sebeok, eds. The Semiotic Sphere (NY and London: Plenum, 1986), 279-92.

b391. Waugh, Linda R. Roman Jakobson's Science of Language (Lisse: Peter de Ridder P, 1976).

b392. Weber, Samuel. "Saussure and the Apparition of Language: The Critical Perspective." MLN 91 (1976), 913-38.

b393. Wellbery, David E. Lessing's Laocoon: Semiotics and Aesthetics in the Age of Reason (Cambridge and NY: Cambridge UP, 1984).

b394. Wells, R. "Criteria for Semiosis," in T. Sebeok, ed., A Perfusion of Signs (Bloomington: Indiana UP, 1977), 1-21.

b395. Wienold, Gotz. Semiotik der Literatur (Frankfurt: Athenaum, 1972).

b396. Wing, Nathaniel. "Semiotics of Poetry: The Meaning of Form." Diacritics 4.3 (1974), 20-27.

b397. Winner, Irene Portis. "The Semiotics of Cultural Texts." Semiotica 18.2 (1976), 101-56.

b398. ----------. "The Semiotic Character of the Aesthetic Function as Defined by the Prague Linguistic Circle," in W. C. McCormack and S. A. Wurms, ed. Language and Thought: Anthropological Issues (The Hague: Mouton, 1977), 407-40.
b399. ----------. "Ethnicity, Modernity, and Theory of Cultural Texts." Semiotica 27 (1979), 103-47 [Soviet semiotics, cultural semiotics].

b400. Wittig, Susan. "Toward a Semiotic Theory of the Drama." ETJ 26 (1974), 441-54.
b401. ----------. "Semiology and Literary Theory." BuR 22.1 (1976), 140-50.

b402. Zeman, J. J. "The Esthetic Sign in Peirce's Semiotic." Semiotica 19 (1977), 241-58.
b403. ----------. "Peirce's Theory of Signs," in T. Sebeok, ed., A Perfusion of Signs (Bloomington: Indiana UP, 1977), 22-39.

b404. Zepp, Evelyn H. "The Criticism of Julia Kristeva: A New Mode of Critical Thought." RR 73.1 (1982), 80-97.

b405. Zima, Peter V., ed. Semiotics and Dialectics: Ideology and the Text (Amsterdam: Benjamins, 1981).

b406. Zolkiewski, S. "Poétique de la composition." Semiotica 3 (1972), 205-24.
b407. ----------. "Des principes de classement des textes de culture." Semiotica 1 (1973), 1-17.

C. Narratology, Narrative Text-Grammar, Narrative Semiotics

c1. Adams, Jean-Michel. "The Macro-Structure of the Conventional Narrative." <u>PoT</u> 3.4 (1982), 135-68.

c2. ----------. <u>Le Récit</u> (Paris: PUF, 1984).

c3. ----------. <u>Le Texte narratif</u> (Paris: Fernand Nathan, 1985).

c4. Alexandrescu, Sorin. <u>Logique du personnage</u> (Tours: Mame, 1974).

c5. Amossy, Ruth. "Stereotypes and Representation in Fiction." <u>PoT</u> 5.4 (1984), 689-700.

c6. Anderegg, Johannes. <u>Fiktion und Kommunikation</u> (Gottingen: Vandenhoeck und Ruprecht, 1973).

c7. Armstrong, Nancy. "Inside Greimas's Square: Literary Characters and Cultural Constraints," in W. Steiner, ed. <u>The Sign in Music and Literature</u> (Austin: U of Texas P, 1981), 52-66.

c8. Arrathoon, Leigh, ed. <u>The Craft of Fiction: Essays in Medieval Poetics</u> (Rochester MI: Soalris, 1984).

c9. Arrivé, Michel. "Pour une théorie des textes poly-isotopiques." <u>Langages</u> 31 (1973), 53-63.

c10. Bagby, Lewis. "Narrative Double-Voicing in Lermontov's *A Hero of Our Time* ." <u>SEEJ</u> 22 (1978), 265-86 [re: Bakhtin].

c11. ----------. "Mikhail Bakhtin's Discourse Typologies: Theoretical and Practical Considerations." Slavic Rev 41 (1982), 35-58.

c12. Baguley, David. "Reluctant Thematologists: Some Recent French Genre Theories." EiP 9.2 (1984), 1-23 [discusses Genette, Lejeune, Todorov].

c13. Baker, John Ross. "From Imitation to Rhetoric: The Chicago Critics, Wayne C. Booth, and *Tom Jones*," in M. Spilka, ed. Towards a Poetics of Fiction (Bloomington: Indiana UP, 1977), 136-56.

c14. Bakhtin, Mikhail. Rabelais and His World (Cambridge: MIT P, 1968).
c15. ----------. "Discourse Typology in Prose," in L. Matejka and K. Pomorska, eds. Readings in Russian Poetics: Formalist and Structuralist Views (Cambridge: MIT P, 1971), 176-96.
c16. ----------. Problems of Dostoevsky's Poetics (Ann Arbor: Ardis, 1973).
c17. ----------. "The Word in the Novel." Comparative Criticism 2 (1980), 213-20.
c18. ----------. The Dialogic Imagination: Four Essays (Austin: U of Texas P, 1981).
c19. ----------. Problems of Dostoevsky's Poetics (Minneapolis: U of Minnesota P, 1984).
c20. ----------. Speech Genres and Other Late Essays (Austin: U of Texas P, 1986).

c21. Bal, Mieke. "Mise en abyme et iconicité." Lit 29 (1978), 116-28.
c22. ----------. "Descriptions: Etude du discours descriptif dans le texte narratif," in J. Perrot and J. Lallot, eds. LALIES: Actes des sessions de linguistique et de littérature, I (Paris: Ecole Normale Superieur, 1980), 99-129.
c23. ----------. "Narrativité et manipulation." Degrés 24-25 (1980-81), c1-c24.
c24. ----------. "Notes on Narrative Embedding." PoT 2 (1981), 41-59.
c25. ----------. "The Laughing Mice; or, On Focalization." PoT 2 (1981), 203-10.
c26. ----------. "On Meanings and Descriptions." StTCL 6.1-2 (1981-82), 100-48.
c27. ----------. "The Narrating and the Focalizing: A Theory of the Agents in Narrative." Style 17 (1983), 234-69.
c28. ----------. "Réfléchir la réflexion: Du nom propre a la mise en abyme." AION-SR 26.1 (1984), 7-47 [mise-en-abyme, Dallenbach].
c29. ----------. Narratology: Introduction to the Theory of Narrative (Toronto: U of Toronto P, 1985).
c30. ----------. "Tell-Tale Theories." PoT 7.3 (1986), 555-64 [rev.-essay on Brooks, Genette, Stanzel].

c31. Banfield, Ann. "Narrative Style and the Grammar of Direct and Indirect Speech." Foundations of Language 10 (1973), 1-39.

c32. ----------. "The Formal Coherence of Represented Speech and Thought." PTL 3 (1978), 289-314.

c33. ----------. "Where Epistemology, Style, and Grammar Meet Literary History: The Development of Represented Speech and Thought." NLH 9 (1978), 415-54.

c34. ----------. "Reflective and Non-Reflective Consciousness in the Language of Fiction." PoT 2.2 (1981), 61-76.

c35. ----------. Unspeakable Sentences: Narration and Representation in the Language of Fiction (Boston: Routledge & Kegan Paul, 1982).

c36. ----------. "*Ecriture,* Narration, and the Grammar of French," in J. Hawthorn, ed. Narrative: From Malory to Motion Pictures (London: Edward Arnold, 1985), 1-22.

c37. Barthoud, J. A. "Narrative and Ideology: A Critique of Fredric Jameson's *The Political Unconscious,*" in J. Hawthorn, ed. Narrative: From Malory to Motion Pictures (London: Edward Arnold, 1985), 100-15.

c38. Basic, Sonja. "From James's Figures to Genette's *Figures* : Point of View and Narratology." RFEA 8 (1983), 201-15.

c39. Bayer, Udo. "Erzahltext und epische Fiktion als semiotischer Zusammenhang." Semiosis 34 (1984), 49-60.

c40. Beaugrande, Robert de. Text, Discourse, and Process: Towards a Multidisciplinary Science of Texts (Norwood NJ: Ablex, 1980).

c41. Beaujour, Michel. "Some Paradoxes of Description." YFS 61 (1981), 27-59.

c42. Beiner, Ronald. "Philosophical and Narrative Truth: The Theorist as Storyteller." QQ 19.3 (1984), 549-59.

c43. Bennett, James R. "Plot Repetition: Theme and Variation of Narrative Micro-Episodes." PLL 17.4 (1981), 405-20.

c44. Benoist, Jean Marie. "The Fictional Subject." Twentieth-Century Studies 6 (1971), 88-97.

c45. Ben-Porat, Ziva. "The Poetics of Literary Allusion." PTL 1 (1976), 105-28.

c46. Berendsen, Marjet. "Formal Criteria of Narrative Embedding." JLS 10 (1981), 79-94.

c47. ----------. "The Teller and the Observer: Narration and Focalization in Narrative Texts." Style 18.2 (1984), 140-58 [discusses Bal, Genette].

c48. Bialostosky, Don H. "Bakhtin versus Chatman on Narrative: The Habilitation of the Hero." RUO 53.1 (1983), 109-16.
c49. ----------. "Booth's Rhetoric, Bakhtin's Dialogics and the Future of Novel Criticism." Novel 18 (1985), 209-16.
c50. ----------. "Dialogics as an Art of Discourse in Literary Criticism." PMLA 101 (1986), 788-97.

c51. Bickerton, Derek. "Modes of Interior Monologue: A Formal Definition." MLQ 28 (1967), 229-39.

c52. Bilan, R. P. "The Basic Concepts and Criteria of F. R. Leavis's Novel Criticism," in M. Spilka, ed. Towards a Poetics of Fiction (Bloomington: Indiana UP, 1977), 157-76.

c53. Blanchard, Jean-Marc. "The Pleasures of Description." Diacritics 7.2 (1977), 22-34 [on Louis Marin].

c54. Blanchard, Marc-Eli. Description: Sign, Self, Desire: Critical Theory in the Wake of Semiotics (The Hague: Mouton, 1980).
c55. ----------. "Up Against the Text." Diacritics 11.3 (1981), 13-26 [on Riffaterre].

c56. Blumenberg, Hans. "The Concept of Reality and the Possibility of the Novel," in R. E. Amacher and V. Lange, eds. New Perspectives in German Literary Criticism (Princeton: Princeton UP, 1979), 29-48.

c57. Boheemen, Christine van. "The Semiotics of Plot: Toward a Typology of Fictions." PoT 3.4 (1982), 89-96.

c58. Bonheim, Helmut. The Narrative Modes: Techniques of the Short Story (Cambridge: D. S. Brewer, 1982).

c59. Booth, Wayne. "*The Rhetoric of Fiction* and the Poetics of Fiction." Novel 1.2 (1968), 105-13.
c60. ----------. The Rhetoric of Fiction, 2nd ed. (Chicago: U of Chicago P, 1983).

c61. Boudon, Pierre. "Le Logos greimassien: Narrativité et discursivité, I." CJRS 3.4 (1983), 376-408 [on Greimas].

c62. Bové, Carol Mastrangelo. "The Text as Dialogue in Bakhtin and Kristeva." Revue de L'Université d'Ottawa 53.1 (1983), 117-24.

c63. Bowditch, Livia Polanyi. "The Role of Redunancy in Cohesion and Evaluative Functioning in Narrative--A Grab for the Referential Hierarchy." Rackham LitS 7 (1976), 19-37.
c64. ----------. "Why the Whats are When: Mutually Contextualizing Realms of Narrative." Proceedings of the Second Annual Meeting of the Berkeley Linguistics Society (1976), 59-77.

c65. Boyd, Michael. The Reflexive Novel: Fiction as Critique (Lewisburg: Buckenll UP, 1983).

c66. Bradbury, Malcolm. "An Approach through Structure," in M. Spilka, ed. Towards a Poetics of Fiction (Bloomington: Indiana UP, 1977), 3-10.

c67. Bredin, Hugh. "The Displacement of Character in Narrative Theory." BJA 22.4 (1982), 291-300.

c68. Bremond, Claude. Logique du récit (Paris: Seuil, 1973).
c69. ----------. "The Logic of Narrative Possibilities." NLH 11 (1980), 398-411.
c70. ----------. "A Critique of the Motif," in T. Todorov, ed. French Literary Theory Today (Cambridge: Cambridge UP; Paris: Editions de la Maison des Sciences de l'Homme, 1982), 125-46.
c71. ----------. "Concept et theme." Poétique 64 (1985), 415-23.

c72. Brewer, Maria Minich. "A Loosening of Tongues: From Narrative Economy to Women Writing." MLN 99.5 (1984), 1141-61.

c73. Brinker, Menakhem. "Verisimilitude, Conventions, and Beliefs." NLH 14 (1983), 253-67.

c74. Brinton, Laurel. "'Represented Perception': A Study in Narrative Style." Poetics 10 (1980), 363-81.

c75. Broich, Ulrich. "Gibt es eine 'neutrale Erzahlsituation'?" GRM 33.2 (1983), 129-45 [on Stanzel].
c76. ----------, Manfred Pfister, and Bernd Schulte-Middelich, eds. Intertextualitat: Formen, Funktionen, anglistische Fallstudien (Tubingen: Niemeyer, 1985).

c77. Bronzwaer, W. Tense in the Novel: An Investigation of Some Potentialities of Linguistic Criticism (Groningen: Wolters-Noordhoff, 1970).
c78. ----------. "Implied Author, Extradiegetic Narrator, and Public Reader: Gérard Genette's Narratological Model and the Reading Version of Great Expectations ." Neophilologus 52 (1978), 1-18.

c79. ----------. "Mieke Bal's Concept of Focalization: A Critical Note." PoT 2.2 (1981), 193-201.

c80. Brooke-Rose, Christine. A Rhetoric of the Unreal: Studies in Narrative and Structure, especially of the Fantastic (Cambridge: Cambridge UP, 1981).

c81. Brooks, Peter. "Fictions of the Wolfman: Freud and Narrative Understanding." Diacritics 9 (1979), 72-81.
c82. ----------. Reading for the Plot: Design and Intention in Narrative (NY: Knopf, 1984).

c83. Brown, Richard Harvey. "Narrative, Literary Theory, and the Self in Contemporary Society." PoT 6.4 (1985), 573-90.

c84. Bruss, Elizabeth W. "Models and Metaphors for Narrative Analysis." Centrum 2.1 (1974), 14-42.

c85. Budniakiewicz, Therese. "A Conceptual Survey of Narrative Semiotics." Dispositio 3 (1978), 189-217.

c86. Carrier, David. "On Narratology." P&L 8.1 (1984), 32-42.

c87. Carroll, David. "The Alterity of Discourse: Form, History, and the Question of the Political in M. M. Bakhtin." Diacritics 13.2 (1983), 65-83.
c88. ----------. "Narrative, Heterogeneity, and the Question of the Political: Bakhtin and Lyotard," in M. Krieger, ed. The Aims of Representation: Subject/Text/History (NY: Columbia UP, 1987), 69-106.

c89. Caserio, Robert L. Plot, Story, and the Novel: From Dickens to the Modern Period (Princeton: Princeton UP, 1979).

c90. Casey, Edward S. "Literary Description and Phenomenological Method." YFS 61 (1981), 176-201.

c91. Caws, Mary Ann. Reading Frames in Modern Fiction (Princeton: Princeton UP, 1985).

c92. Cebik. L. B. Fictional Narrative and Truth And Truth: An Epistemic Analysis (Lanham MD: UP of America, 1984).

c93. Chabrol, Claude, ed. Sémiotique narrative et textuelle (Paris: Larousse, 1973) [includes Chabrol's "De quelques problemes de grammaire narrative et textuelle," 7-28].

c94. Chambers, Ross. Story and Situation: Narrative Seduction and the Power of Fiction (Minneapolis: U of Minnesota P, 1984).

c95. Champagne, Roland A. "The Spiralling *Discours* : Todorov's Model for a Narratology in *Les Liaisons dangereuses* ." ECr 14 (1974), 342-52.
c96. ----------. A Grammar of the Languages of Culture: Literary Theory and Yury M. Lotman's Semiotics." NLH 9 (1978), 205-10.

c97. Chatelain, Daniele. "Récit itératif et concrétisation." RR 72.3 (1981), 304-16 [discusses Genette].
c98. ----------. "Frontieres de l'itératif." Poétique 17 (1986), 111-24.

c99. Chatman, Seymour. "On the Formalist-Structuralist Theory of Character." JLS 1 (1972), 57-79.
c100. ----------. "Genette's Analysis of Narrative Time Relations." L'Esprit Créateur 14 (1974), 353-68.
c101. ----------. "Toward a Theory of Narrative." NLH 6 (1975), 295-318.
c102. ----------. Story and Discourse: Narrative Structure in Fiction and Film (Ithaca: Cornell UP, 1978).
c103. ----------. "The Rhetoric of Difficult Fiction: Cortazar's 'Blow-Up.'" PoT 1.4 (1980), 23-66.
c104. ----------. "How Do We Establish New Codes of Verisimilitude?" in W. Steiner, ed. The Sign in Music and Literature (Austin: U of Texas P, 1981), 26-38.
c105. ----------. "What Novels Can Do That Films Can't (and Vice Versa)," in W. J. T. Mitchell, ed. On Narrative (Chicago: U of Chicago P, 1981), 117-36.
c106. ----------. "On the Notion of Theme in Narrative," in J. Fisher, ed. Essays in Aesthetics (Philadelphia: Temple UP, 1983), 161-79.
c107. ----------. "Characters and Narrators: Filter, Center, Slant, and Interest-Focus." PoT 7.2 (1986), 189-204.
c108. ----------. "On Deconstructing Narratology." Style 22.1 (1988), 9-17.

c109. Ci, Jiwei. "An Alternative to Genette's Theory of Order." Style 22.1 (1988), 18-38 [followed by a reply by Genette, 39-41].

c110. Cixous, Hélene. "The Character of 'Character.'" NLH 5 (1974), 383-402.

c111. Clark, Katerina and Michael Holquist. Mikhail Bakhtin (Cambridge: Harvard UP, 1984).

c112. Cobley, Evelyn. "Sameness and Difference in Literary Repetition." CJRS 3.3 (1983), 248-61.

c113. Cohn, Dorrit. "Narrated Monologue: Definition of a Fictional Style." CL 18 (1966), 97-112.

c114. ----------. Transparent Minds: Narrative Modes for Presenting Consciousness in Fiction (Princeton: Princeton UP, 1978).

c115. ----------. "The Encirclement of Narrative: On Franz Stanzel's Theorie des Erzahlens ." PoT 2 (1981), 157-82 [also discusses Genette].

c116. ---------- and Gérard Genette. "Nouveaux nouveaux discours du récit." Poétique 61 (1985), 101-09.

c117. Columb, Gregory. "Semiotics Since Eco." PLL 16 (1980), 329-48, 443-59.

c118. Corn, Peggy Ward. "Functions of the Story within a Story in Twentieth-Century Literature." DAI 44 (1984), 3380A.

c119. Costello, Edward Thomas. "Modality and Narration: A Linguistic Theory of Plotting." DAI 36 (1976), 6654A-55A.

c120. Courtes, J. Introduction a la sémiotique narrative et discursive (Paris: Hachette, 1976).

c121. Coward, Rosalind and John Ellis. Language and Materialism: Developments in Semiology and the Theory of the Subject (London: Routledge & Kegan Paul, 1977).

c122. Culler, Jonathan. "Defining Narrative Units," in R. Fowler, ed. Style and Structure in Literature: Essays in the New Stylistics (Ithaca: Cornell UP, 1975), 123-42.

c123. ----------. "Fabula and Sjuzhet in the Analysis of Narrative." PoT 1.3 (1980), 27-37.

c124. ----------. The Pursuit of Signs: Semiotics, Literature, Deconstruction (Ithaca: Cornell UP, 1981).

c125. ----------. "Problems in the Theory of Fiction." Diacritics 14.1 (1984), 2-11.

c126. Currie, Gregory. "Fictional Truth." PhS 50.2 (1986), 195-212.

c127. Curtis, James M. "Spatial Form in the Context of Modernist Aesthetics," in J. R. Smitten and A. Daghistany, eds. Spatial Form in Narrative (Ithaca: Cornell UP, 1981), 161-78.

c128. Dallenbach, Lucien. "Intertexte et autotexte." Poétique 27 (1976), 282-96.

c129. ----------. Le récit spéculaire: Essai sur la mise en abyme (Paris: Seuil, 1977).

c130. Dameron, Charles Franklin, Jr. "The Fictional Narratee: A Rhetorical Study." DAI 46 (1985), 977A.

c131. Danow, David K. "M. M. Bakhtin's Concept of the Word." American Journal of Semiotics 3.1 (1984), 79-97.
c132. ----------. "M. M. Bakhtin in Life and Art." American Journal of Semiotics 3.3 (1984), 131-41.

c133. Davis, Robert Con, ed. Lacan and Narration: The Psychoanalytic Difference in Narrative Theory (Baltimore: Johns Hopkins UP, 1984).

c134. Debray-Genette, Raymonde. "La Pierre descriptive." Poétique 43 (1980), 293-304.
c135. ----------. "Traversées de l'espace descriptif." Poétique 51 (1982), 359-68.
c136. ----------. "Some Functions of Figures in Novelistic Descriptions." PoT 5.4 (1984), 677-88.

c137. Demetz, Peter. "Lauter erfundene Geschichten: Uber den Erzahler in der Fiktion." DASDJ 1 (1982), 9-23.

c138. Derrida, Jacques. "Economimesis." Diacritics 11.2 (1981), 3-25.
c139. ----------. "The Law of Genre," in W. J. T. Mitchell, ed. On Narrative (Chicago: U of Chicago P, 1981), 51-77.

c140. Diengott, Nilli. "Narratology and Feminism." Style 22.1 (1988), 42-51.

c141. Dijk, Teun A. van. Some Aspects of Text Grammars: A Study in Theoretical Linguistics and Poetics (The Hague: Mouton, 1972).
c142. ----------, et al . Zur Bestimmung narrativer Strukturen auf der Grundlage von Textgrammatiken (Hamburg: Buske, 1972).
c143. ----------. "Action, Action Description, and Narrative." NLH 6 (1975), 273-94.
c144. ----------. "Philosophy of Action and Theory of Narrative." Poetics 5 (1976), 287-338.
c145. ----------. "Narrative Macro-Structures: Logical and Cognitive Foundations." PTL 1 (1976), 547-68.
c146. ----------. "Story Comprehension: An Introduction." Poetics 9 (1980), 1-21.
c147. ----------. Macrostructures (Hillsale NJ: Erlbaum, 1980).

c148. Dillon, George and Frederick Kirchhoff. "On the Form and Function of Free Indirect Style." PTL 1 (1976), 431-40.

c149. Docherty, Thomas. Reading (Absent) Character: Towards a Theory of Characterization in Fiction (Oxford: Clarendon, 1983).

c150. Dolezel, Lubomir. "The Typology of the Narrator: Point of View in Fiction," in To Honor Roman Jakobson (The Hague: Mouton, 1967), 541-52.
c151. ----------. "From Motifemes to Motifs." Poetics 4 (1972), 55-90.
c152. ----------. Narrative Modes in Czech Literature (Toronto: U of Toronto P, 1973).
c153. ----------. "Narrative Modalities." JLS 5.1 (1976), 5-14.
c154. ----------. "Narrative Worlds," in L. Matejka, ed. Sound, Sign and Meaning (Ann Arbor: Michigan Slavic Contributions, 1976), 542-52.
c155. ----------. "Narrative Semantics." PTL 1 (1976), 129-51.
c156. ----------. "A Scheme of Narrative Time," in L. Matejka and I. Titunik, eds. Semiotics of Art: Prague School Contributions (Cambridge: M.I.T. Press, 1976), 209-17.
c157. ----------. Essays in Structural Poetics and Narrative Semantics [Prepublication] (Toronto: Victoria U, Toronto Semiotic Circle, 1979).
c158. ----------. "Truth and Authenticity in Narrative." PoT 1 (1980), 7-25.
c159. ----------. "Intensional Function, Invisible Worlds, and Franz Kafka." Style 17.2 (1983), 120-41.
c160. ----------. "Literary Text, Its World and Its Style," in M. J. Valdes and O Miller, eds. Identity of the Literary Text (Toronto: U of Toronto P, 1985), 189-203.

c161. Donato, Eugenio. "The Shape of Fiction: Notes Toward a Possible Classification of Narrative Discourse." MLN 86 (1973), 6-26.

c162. Donoghue, Denis. "Reading Bakhtin." Raritan 5.2 (1985), 107-19.

c163. Dorfman, Eugene. The Narreme in the Medieval Romance Epic: An Introduction to Narrative Structures (Toronto: U of Toronto P, 1969).

c164. Drake, Sara Matson. "Spacetime Aspects of the Literary Work." DAI 45 (1984), 1391A-92A.

c165. Dry, Helen Aristar. "The Movement of Narrative Time." JLS 12.2 (1983), 19-53.
c166. ----------. "Approaches to Coherence in Natural and Literary Narrative," in E. Sozer, ed. Text Connectivity, Text Coherence: Aspects, Methods, Results (Hamburg: Buske, 1985), 484-99.

c167. Dubois, J., et al . A General Rhetoric (Baltimore: Johns Hopkins UP, 1981) [esp. chaps. 7 & 8].

c168. Duyfhuizen, Bernard Boyd. "Difficult Transmissions: The Narrator's Contact with the Reader." DAI 44 (1983), 483A.

c169. Eckhard, Michel. "Fonction narrative et champ positionnel de la narrativité." Neohelicon 8 (1981), 111-18.

c170. Eco, Umberto. The Role of the Reader: Explorations in the Semiotics of Texts (Bloomington: Indiana UP, 1979).
c171. ----------. "Two Problems in Textual Interpretation." PoT 2.1a (1980), 145-61.
c172. ----------. Semiotics and the Theory of Language (Bloomington: Indiana UP, 1984).

c173. Egan, Kieran. "What Is Plot?" NLH 9 (1978), 455-73.

c174. Eng, Jan van der and Mojmir Grygar, eds. Structure of Texts and Semiotics of Culture (The Hague: Mouton, 1973).

c175. Ermath, Elizabeth Deeds. Realism and Consensus in the English Novel (Princeton: Princeton UP, 1983).

c176. Even-Zohar, Itamar. "Constraints of Realeme Insertability in Narrative." PoT 1.3 (1980), 65-74.

c177. Farrell, Thomas B. "Narrative in Natural Discourse: On Conversation and Rhetoric." JC 35.4 (1985), 109-27.

c178. Fellinger, Raimund. "Zur Struktur von Erzahltexten," in H. Brackert and J. Stuckrath, eds. Literaturwissenschaft: Grundkurs I (Reinbeck bei Hamburg: Rowohlt, 1981), 338-52.

c179. Fisette, Jean. Le Texte automatiste: Essai de théorie/pratique de sémiotique textuelle (Montreal: U du Quebec, 1977).

c180. Fisher, Walter R. "The Narrative Paradigm: An Elaboration." ComM 52.4 (1985), 347-67.

c181. Fowler, Roger. "Referential Code and Narrative Authority." Language and Style 10 (1977), 129-61.
c182. ----------. "Anti-Language in Fiction," in his Language as Social Discourse: The Practice of Linguistic Criticism (Bloomington: Indiana UP, 1981), 142-61 [on Bakhtin].
c183. ----------. "How to See Through Language: Perspective in Fiction." Poetics 11.3 (1982), 213-35 [discusses Uspensky, Halliday].

c184. Francoeur, Louis. "Le Monologue intérieur narratif." Etudes Littéraires 9 (1976), 341-65.
c185. ----------. "The Dialogical Semiosis of Culture." American Journal of Semiotics 3.3 (1985), 121-30.

c186. Freedman, Ralph. "The Possibility of a Theory of the Novel," in P. Demetz, et al , eds. The Disciplines of Criticism (New Haven: Yale UP, 1968), 57-77.

c187. Fricke, Harald. "Semantics of Pragmatics of Fictionality: A Modest Proposal." Poetics 11.4-6 (1982), 439-52.

c188. Frow, John. "Intertextuality," in his Marxism and Literary History (Cambridge: Harvard UP, 1986), 125-69.
c189. ----------. "Spectacle Binding: On Character." PoT 7.2 (1986), 227-50.

c190. Fuger, Wilhelm. "Zur Tiefenstruktur des Narrativen: Prolegomena zu einer generativen 'Grammatik' des Erzahlens." Poetica 5 (1972), 268-92.
c191. ----------. "Mikronarrativik: Zur Syntax und Semantik elementarer Erzahanssagen." GRM 33.2 (1983), 179-98.

c192. Gaillard, Françoise. "The Great Illusion of Realism, or the Real as Representation." PoT 5.4 (1984), 753-66.

c193. Galloway, Patricia. "Narrative Theories as Computational Models: Reader-Oriented Theory and Artificial Intelligence." CHum 17.4 (1983), 169-74.

c194. Garvey, James. "Characterization in Narrative." Poetics 7 (1978), 63-78.

c195. Gasparov, Boris. "The Narrative Text as an Act of Transmission." NLH 9 (1978), 245-61.

c196. Gelley, Alexander. Narrative Crossings: Theory and Pragmatics of Prose Fiction (Baltimore: Johns Hopkins UP, 1987).

c197. Genette, Gérard. Figures (Paris: Seuil, 1966).
c198. ----------. Figures II (Paris: Seuil, 1969).
c199. ----------. Figures III (Paris: Seuil, 1972).
c200. ----------. Mimologiques, Voyage en Cratylie (Paris: Seuil, 1976).
c201. ----------. Introduction a l'architexte (Paris: Seuil, 1979).
c202. ----------. Narrative Discourse: An Essay in Method (Ithaca: Cornell UP, 1980).

c203. ----------. Figures of Literary Discourse (NY: Columbia UP, 1982).
c204. ----------. Palimpsestes: La littérature au second degré (Paris: Seuil, 1982).
c205. ----------. Nouveau discours du récit (Paris: Seuil, 1983).

c206. Genot, Gérard. Problemes de calcul du récit, 2 vols. (Université Pars X--Nanterre, 1976-77).
c207. ----------. Elements of Narrativics: Grammar in Narrative, Narrative in Grammar (Hamburg: Helmut Buske, 1979).
c208. ----------. "Narrativity and Text Grammar," in J. S. Petofi, ed. Text vs. Sentence: Basic Questions of Text Linguistics (Hamburg: Buske, 1979), 524-39.
c209. ----------. "From Meaning Postulates to Narrative Motifs." Italianist 1 (1981), 89-114.
c210. ----------. Grammaire et récit: Essai de linguistique textuelle (Université Paris X--Nanterre, 1984).

c211. Girard, René. Deceit, Desire, and the Novel: Self and Other in Literary Structure (Baltimore: Johns Hopkins UP, 1965).
c212. ----------. "French Theories of Fiction: 1947-1974." Bucknell Rev 22.1 (1976), 117-26.

c213. Glowinski, Michal. "Der Dialog im Roman." Poetica 8.1 (1974), 1-16.
c214. ----------. "On the First-Person Novel." NLH 9 (1977), 103-14.

c215. Goetsch, Paul. "Leserfiguren in der Erzahlkunst." GRM 33.2 (1983), 199-215.

c216. Goodman, Nelson. "Twisted Tales; or, Story, Study, and Symphony," in W. J. T. Mitchell, ed. On Narrative (Chicago: U of Chicago P, 1981), 99-115.

c217. Greimas, Algirdas Julien. Sémantique structurale (Paris: Larousse, 1966) [Structural Semantics: An Attempt at a Method (Lincoln: U of Nebraska P, 1983)].
c218. ----------. Du sens: Essais sémiotiques (Paris: Seuil, 1970).
c219. ----------. "Narrative Grammar: Units and Levels." MLN 86 (1971), 793-806.
c220. ----------. Maupassant: La sémiotique du texte: excercices pratiques (Paris: Seuil, 1976).
c221. ---------- and Joseph Courtes. "The Cognitive Dimension of Narrative Discourse." NLH 7 (1976), 433-47.
c222. ----------. Sémiotiques et Sciences Sociales (Paris: Seuil, 1976).
c223. ---------- and Joseph Courtes. Semiotics and Language: An Analytical Dictionary (Bloomington: Indiana UP, 1982; rev. French edition, 1986).

c224. ----------. Du sens II: Essais sémiotiques (Paris: Seuil, 1983).
c225. ----------. On Meaning: Selected Writings in Semiotic Theory (Minneapolis: U of Minnesota P, 1987).

c226. Grimaud, Michel. "Critical Notes: Narratology and Discourse Processing." Sub-Stance 28 (1980), 86-89.

c227. Grivel, Charles. "L'Histoire dans le visage," in J. Decottignes, ed. Les Sujets de l'écriture (Lille: PU de Lille, 1981), 175-221.

c228. Grosse, Ernst Ulrich. "French Structuralist Views on Narrative Grammar," in W. U. Dressler, ed. Current Trends in Textlinguistics (Berlin and NY: Walter de Gruyter, 1977), 155-73.
c229. ----------. "Von den Satzgrammatik zum Erzahltextmodell: Linguistische Grundlagen und Defizienzen bei Greimas und Bremond," in J. S. Petofi, ed. Text vs. Sentence: Basic Questions of Text Linguistics (Hamburg: Buske, 1979), 595-617.

c230. Haezewindt, B. P. R. "The Concept of 'Narrative Mass' and the Construction of Narrative Texts." JLS 14.2 (1985), 121-29 [on Barthes, Genette, Prince].

c231. Hall, John. "Mikhail Bakhtin and the Critique of Systematicity," in Literary Theory Today (Hong Kong: Hong Kong UP, 1981), 109-36.
c232. ----------. "Towards a Dialogic History of Narrative," in Rewriting Literary History (Hong Kong: Hong Kong UP, 1984), 234-76 [on Bakhtin].

c233. Halperin, John, ed. The Theory of the Novel: New Essays (NY: Oxford UP, 1974).

c234. Hamburger, Kate. The Logic of Literature (Bloomington: Indiana UP, 1973).

c235. Hamon, Philippe. "Pour un statut sémiologique de personnage." Lit 6 (1972), 86-110.
c236. ----------. "Mise au point sur les problemes de l'analyse du récit." Le Française moderne 40 (1972), 200-21.
c237. ----------. "Un discours contraint." Poétique 16 (1973), 411-45.
c238. ----------. "Narrative Semiotics in France." Style 8 (1974), 34-45.
c239. ----------. "Clausules." Poétique 24 (1975), 495-526.
c240. ----------. "Texte littéraire et métalanguage." Poétique 31 (1977), 261-84.
c241. ----------. "Sur quelques concepts narratologiques." LR 33 (1979), 51-59.

c242. ----------. Introduction a l'analyse du descriptif (Paris: Hachette, 1981).

c243. ----------. "What Is a Description?" in T. Todorov, ed. French Literary Theory Today (Cambridge: Cambridge UP; Paris: Editions de la Maison des Sciences de l'Homme, 1982), 147-78.

c244. ----------. Le personnel du roman (Geneva: Droz, 1983).

c245. Haney, William Stanley, II. "The Theory of the Referent." DAI 46 (1985), 144A.

c246. Hardy, Barbara. "An Approach through Narrative," in M. Spilka, ed. Towards a Poetics of Fiction (Bloomington: Indiana UP, 1977), 31-40.

[Harshaw, Benjamin. See Hrushovski, Benjamin].

c247. Hawthorn, Jeremy, ed. Narrative: From Malory to Motion Pictures (London: Arnold, 1985).

c248. ----------. Unlocking the Text: Fundamental Issues in Literary Theory (London: Edward Arnold, 1987) [chap. 5: "Reference and Fictionality"].

c249. Hayman, David. Re-Forming the Narrative: Towards a Mechanics of Modernist Fiction (Ithaca: Cornell UP, 1987).

c250. Heath, Stephen. "Narrative Space." Screen 17.3 (1976), 68-112.

c251. Hénault, Anne. Les enjeux de la sémiotique (Paris: P.U.F., 1979) [on Greimas].

c252. Hendricks, William O. "Methodology of Narrative Structural Analysis." Semiotica 7 (1973), 163-84.

c253. Hernadi, Paul. "Dual Perspective: Free Indirect Discourse and Related Techniques." CL 24 (1972), 32-43.

c254. Heuvel, Pierre van den. "Le Narrateur narrataire ou le narrateur lecteur de son propore discours." Agora 14-15 (1977), 53-77.

c255. ----------. "Le discours rapporté." Neophilologus 62.1 (1978), 19-38.

c256. Hirschkop, Ken. "The Domestication of M. M. Bakhtin." EiP 11.1 (1986), 76-87.

c257. Hochman, Baruch. Character in Literature (Ithaca: Cornell UP, 1985).

c258. Hoffman, Gerhard. Raum, Situation, erzahlte Wirklichkeit (Stuttgart: Metzler, 1978).

c259. Holloway, John. "Supposition and Supersession: A Model of Analysis for Narrative Structure." CritI 3 (1976), 39-56.
c260. ----------. Narrative and Structure (Cambridge: Cambridge UP, 1979).

c261. Holquist, Michael and Walter Reed. "Six Theses on the Novel and Some Metaphors." NLH 11 (1979-80), 413-23.

c262. Horner, Winifred Bryan. "Text Act Theory: A Study of Nonfiction Texts." DAI 36 (1976), 6649A.

c263. Hrushovski, Benjamin. Segmentation and Motivation in the Text Continuum of Literary Prose. The First Episode of War and Peace (Tel Aviv: Porter Inst. for Poetics and Semiotics, 1976).
c264. ----------. "The Structure of Semiotic Objects: A Three-Dimensional Model." PoT 1.1-2 (1979), 363-76.
c265. ----------. "Fictionality and Fields of Reference: Remarks on a Theoretical Framework." PoT 5.2 (1984), 227-51.

c266. Hulanicki, Leo S. "Spatial Depictor in Literary Art." Lang&S 16.4 (1983), 391-410.

c267. Hult, David, ed. "Concepts of Closure." YFS 67 (1984) [special issue].

c268. Hunt, Peter. "Narrative Theory and Children's Literature." CLAQ 9.4 (1985), 191-94.
c269. ----------. "Necessary Misreadings: Directions in Narrative Theory for Children's Literature." SLitI 18.2 (1985), 107-21.

c270. Hutchens, Eleanor N. "An Approach through Time," in M. Spilka, ed. Towards a Poetics of Fiction (Bloomington: Indiana UP, 1977), 52-61.

c271. Hutcheon, Linda. Narcissistic Narrative: The Metafictional Paradox (London: Methuen, 1980).
c272. ----------. "The Carnivalesque and Contemporary Narrative: Popular Culture and the Erotic." Revue de l'Université d'Ottawa 53 (1983), 82-94 [discusses Bakhtin].
c273. ----------. A Theory of Parody: The Teachings of Twentieth-Century Art Forms (London: Methuen, 1985).
c274. ----------. "Metafictional Implications for Novelistic Reference," in A. Whiteside and M. Issacharoff, eds. On Referring in Literature (Bloomington: Indiana UP, 1987), 1-13.

c275. Hutchinson, Peter. Games Authors Play (London and NY: Methuen, 1985).

c276. Hutchison, Chris. "The Act of Narration: A Critical Survey of Some Speech-Act Theories of Narrative Discourse." JLS 13 (1984), 3-35.

c277. Ibsch, Elrud. "Historical Changes of the Function of Spatial Description in Literary Texts." PoT 3.4 (1982), 97-113.

c278. Idt, Genevieve. "Intertextualité, 'transposition,' critique des sources." Nova Renascença 4 (1984), 5-20 [discusses Bakhtin, Kristeva, Riffaterre].

c279. Ihwe, Jens. "On the Foundations of a General Theory of Narrative Structure." Poetics 3 (1972), 5-14.

c280. "Intertexualité." StCL 36.1 (1985) [special issue].

c281. Ionescu-Muresanu, Marina. "Pour une lecture pragmatique de la narration." Degrés 28 (1981), k1-k5.

c282. Ireland, K. R. "Towards a Grammar of Narrative Sequence: The Model of *The French Lieutenant's Woman.*" PoT 7.3 (1986), 397-420.

c283. Issacharoff, Michael. "Qu'est-ce que l'espace littéraire?" L'Information Littéraire 3 (1978), 117-22.

c284. Jameson, Fredric. The Political Unconscious: Narrative as a Socially Symbolic Act (Ithaca: Cornell UP, 1981).

c285. Janik, Dieter. Die Kommunikationsstruktur des Erzahlwerks: Ein semiologisches Modell (Bebenhausen: Rotsch, 1973).

c286. Jefferson, Ann. "Intertextuality and the Poetics of Fiction." Comparative Criticism 2 (1980), 235-50.
c287. ----------. The Nouveau Roman and the Poetics of Fiction (Cambridge: Cambridge UP, 1980).
c288. ----------. "*Mise en abyme* and the Prophetic in Narrative." Style 17.2 (1983), 196-208.

c289. Jenny, Laurent. "The Strategy of Form," in T. Todorov, ed. French Literary Theory Today (Cambridge: Cambridge UP; Paris: Editions de la Maison des Sciences de l'Homme, 1982), 34-63.

c290. Johnson, Nancy S. and Jean M. Mandler. "A Tale of Two Structures: Underlying and Surface Forms in Stories." Poetics 9 (1980), 87-98.

c291. Kavanagh, Thomas M. "Uneasy Theories: The Ethics of Narration in Contemporary French Criticism." Criticism 28.4 (1986), 445-58.

c292. Kellman, Steven G. The Self-Begetting Novel (NY: Columbia UP, 1980).

c293. Kellner, Hans. "The Inflatable Trope as Narrative Theory: Structure or Allegory?" Diacritics 11.1 (1981), 14-28.

c294. Kenshur, Oscar. "Fragments and Order: Two Modern Theories of Discontinuous Form." PLL 17.3 (1981), 227-44.

c295. Kermode, Frank. The Sense of an Ending: Studies in the Theory of Fiction (NY: Oxford UP, 1967).
c296. ----------. "An Approach through History," in M. Spilka, ed. Towards a Poetics of Fiction (Bloomington: Indiana UP, 1977), 23-30.
c297. ----------. The Genesis of Secrecy: On the Interpretation of Narrative (Cambridge: Harvard UP, 1979).
c298. ----------. "Figures in the Carpet: On Recent Theories of Narrative Discourse." CCrit 2 (1980), 291-301.
c299. ----------. The Art of Telling: Essays on Fiction (Cambridge: Harvard UP, 1983).

c300. Kestner, Joseph A. The Spatiality of the Novel (Detroit: Wayne State UP, 1978).

c301. Kittay, Jeffrey. "Descriptive Limits." YFS 61 (1981), 225-43.

c302. Klaus, Peter. "Description and Event in Narrative." Orbis Litterarum 37 (1982), 211-16.

c303. Kloepfer, Rolf. "Zum Problem des 'narrativen Kode.'" LiLi 27-28 (1977), 69-90.
c304. ----------. "Trends in West German Literary Semiotics: Preliminary Sketch." PoT 1.1-2 (1979), 377-96.
c305. ----------. "Dynamic Structures in Narrative Literature: 'The Dialogical Principle.'" PoT 1 (1980), 115-34 [on Bakhtin].

c306. Kloesel, Lynn Franken. "The Rogue's Eye: Epistemology and Ontology in Subversive Narration." DAI 44 (1984), 2759A-60A [first-person narration].

c307. Knight, Diana. "Structuralism I: Narratology: Joseph Conrad, Heart of Darkness ," in D. Tallack, ed. Literary Theory at Work: Three Texts (Totowa NJ: Barnes and Noble, 1987), 9-28.

c308. Kock, Christian. "Narrative Tropes: A Study of Points in Plots," in G. D. Caie, *et al* , eds. Occasional Papers 1976-1977 (Copenhagen: Univ.-forl. i Kobenhavn, 1978), 202-52.

c309. Krieger, Murray. "Fiction, History, and Empirical Reality." CritI 1 (1974), 335-60.

c310. Kristeva, Julia. Semeiotike: Recherches pour une sémanalyse (Paris: Seuil, 1969).
c311. ----------. Le Texte du roman: approche sémiologique d'une structure discursive transformationnelle (The Hague: Mouton, 1970).
c312. ----------. "Une Poétique ruinée," preface to Bakhtin's La Poétique de Dostoevski (Paris: Seuil, 1970), 5-27.
c313. ----------. "The System and the Speaking Subject," in T. Sebeok, ed. The Tell-Tale Sign: A Survey of Semiotics (Lisse: Peter de Ridder, 1975), 47-55 [orig. pubd. TLS 12 Oct., 1973), 1249-52].
c314. ----------. La Révolution du langage poétique (Paris: Seuil, 1974) [Revolution in Poetic Language (NY: Columbia UP, 1984)].
c315. ----------. Polylogue (Paris: Seuil, 1977).
c316. ----------. Pouvoirs de l'horreur (Paris: Seuil, 1980) [Powers of Horror (NY: Columbia UP, 1982).
c317. ----------. Desire in Language: A Semiotic Approach to Literature and Art (Oxford: Blackwell; NY: Columbia UP, 1980).
c318. ----------. Histoires d'amour (Paris: Denoel, 1983).

c319. Kuiper, Koenraad and Vernon Small. "Constraints on Fiction." PoT 7.3 (1986), 495-426 [on "possible world" theory].

c320. LaCapra, Dominick. "Bakhtin, Marxism, and the Carnivalesque," in Rethinking Intellectual History: Texts, Contexts, Language (Ithaca: Cornell UP, 1983), 291-324.

c321. Lanser, Susan Sniader. The Narrative Act: Point of View in Prose Fiction (Princeton: Princeton UP, 1981).
c322. ----------. "Shifting the Paradigm: Feminism and Narratology." Style 22.1 (1988), 52-60.

c323. Larivaille, Paul. "L'Analyse (morpho) logique du récit." Poétique 19 (1974), 368-88.

c324. Laruccia, Victory A. "Progress, Perrault and Fairy Tales: Ideology and Semiotics." DAI 35 (1975), 3655A-56A.
c325. ----------. "Little Red Riding Hood's Metacommentary: Paradoxical Injunction, Semiotics & Behavior." MLN 90 (1975), 517-34.

c326. Lee, David. "Modality, Perspective and the Concept of Objective Narration." JLS 11.2 (1982), 104-11 [discusses Halliday].

c327. Leech, Thomas Hale. "Approaches to Narrative in German: The Critical Theories of Ernst Hirt, Robert Petsch, Eberhard Lammert, and Franz Stanzel." DAI 47 (1986), 539A.

c328. Le Huenen, Roland and Paul Perron. "Reflections on Balzacian Models of Representation." PoT 5.4 (1984), 711-28.

c329. Leitch, Thomas M. What Stories Are: Narrative Theory and Interpretation (University Park: Pennsylvania State UP, 1986).

c330. Levine, George. The Realistic Imagination: English Fiction from Frankenstein to Lady Chatterly (Chicago: U of Chicago P, 1981).

c331. Lewis, Philip E. "Revolutionary Semiotics." Diacritics 4.3 (1974), 28-32 [on Kristeva].

c332. Lewis, Thomas E. "Notes Toward a Theory of the Referent." PMLA 94 (1979), 459-75.
c333. ----------. "The Referential Act," in A. Whiteside and M. Issacharoff, eds. On Referring in Literature (Bloomington: Indiana UP, 1987), 158-74.

c334. Lindner, Monika. "Integrationsformen der Intertextualitat," in U. Broich, M. Pfister, and B. Schulte-Middelich, eds. Intertextualitat: Formen, Funktionen, anglistische Fallstudien (Tubingen: Niemeyer, 1985), 116-34.

c335. Lintvelt, Jaap. Essai de typologie narrative: Le 'point de vue.' (Paris: Corti, 1981).

c336. Lipski, John M. "From Text to Narrative: Spanning the Gap." Poetics 5 (1976), 191-205.

c337. Lodge, David. The Modes of Modern Writing: Metaphor, Metonymy, and the Typology of Literature (Ithaca: Cornell UP, 1977).
c338. ----------. "An Approach through Language," in M. Spilka, ed. Towards a Poetics of Fiction (Bloomington: Indiana UP, 1977), 11-22.

c339. Lotman, Jurij M. "The Discrete Text and the Iconic Text: Remarks on the Structure of Narrative." NLH 6 (1975), 333-38.
c340. ----------. "Point of View in a Text." NLH 6 (1975), 339-52.
c341. ----------. The Structure of the Artistic Text (Ann Arbor: Michigan Slavic Contributions, 1977).

c342. ----------. "The Origin of Plot in the Light of Typology." PoT 1.1-2 (1979), 161-84.

c343. Lucaites, John Louis and Celeste Michelle Condit. "Re-Constructing Narrative Theory: A Functional Perspective." JC 35.4 (1985), 90-108.

c344. Luhr, William. "The Function of Narrative in Literature and Film," in P. Ruppert, et al, eds. Ideas of Order in Literature and Film (Tallahassee: UP of Florida, 1980), 32-38.

c345. Malcuzynski, M.-Pierrette. "Mikhail Bakhtin and Contemporary Narrative Theory." Revue de l'Université d'Ottawa 53 (1983), 51-65.
c346. ----------. "Polyphonic Theory and Contemporary Literary Practices." StTCL 9 (1984), 75-87.

c347. Malmgren, Carl Darryl. Fictional Space in the Modernist and Postmodernist Novel (Lewisburg PA: Bucknell UP, 1985).
c348. ----------. "Reading Authorial Narration: The Example of The Mill on the Floss ." PoT 7.3 (1986), 471-94.

c349. Margolin, Uri. "Juri Lotman on the Creation of Meaning in Literature." CRCL 2 (1975), 262-82.
c350. ----------. "Narrative as System: Seymour Chatman's Story and Discourse." CRCL 9.1 (1982), 207-15.
c351. ----------. "Characterization in Narrative: Some Theoretical Prolegomena." Neophilologus 67 (1983), 1-14.
c352. ----------. "Narrative and Indexicality: A Tentative Framework." JLS 13.3 (1984), 181-284.
c353. ----------. "The Doer and the Deed: Action as a Basis for Chracterization in Narrative." PoT 7.2 (1986), 205-25.

c354. Margolis, Joseph. "The Logic and Structures of Fictional Narrative." Philosophy and Literature 7 (1983), 162-81.

c355. Markiewicz, Henryk. "Die Literatur aus semiotischer Sicht: Randbemerkungen zu den Arbeiten J. Lotmans," in P. V. Zima, ed. Semiotics and Dialectics: Ideology and the Text (Amsterdam: John Benjamins, 1981), 331-59.

c356. Martin, Wallace. Recent Theories of Narrative (Ithaca: Cornell UP, 1986).

c357. Martinez-Bonati, Felix. Fictive Discourse and the Structure of Literature: A Phenomenological Approach (Ithaca: Cornell UP, 1981).

c358. ----------. "Towards a Formal Ontology of Fictional Worlds."
Philosophy and Literature 7 (1983), 182-95.

c359. Mathieu[-Colas], Michel. "Les Acteurs du récit." Poétique 19 (1974),
357-67.
c360. ----------. "Analyse du récit." Poétique 30 (1977), 226-59 [an
annotated bibliography].
c361. ----------. "Frontieres de la narratologie." Poétique 65 (1986), 91-110.

c362. McCormick, Peter. "Feelings and Fictions." RUO 55.4 (1985), 19-32
[on fictionality].

c363. McGuirk, Bernard. "Structuralism II: Character Theory. Henry
James, In the Cage ," in D. Tallack, ed. Literary Theory at Work: Three
Texts (Totowa NJ: Barnes & Noble, 1987), 29-48.

c364. McHale, Brian. "Free Indirect Discourse: A Survey of Recent
Accounts." PTL 3 (1978), 249-87.
c365. ----------. "Islands in the Stream of Consciousness: Dorrit Cohn's
Transparent Minds ." PoT 2.2 (1981), 183-91.
c366. ----------. "Unspeakable Sentences, Unnatural Acts: Linguistics and
Poetics Revisited." PoT 1 (1983), 17-45.
c367. ----------. Postmodernist Fiction (NY and London: Methuen,1987).

c368. Meiger, Jan M. "Literature as Information: Some Notes on Lotman's
Book: Struktura xudozestvennogo teksta ," in J. van der Eng and M. Grygar,
eds. Structure of Texts and Semiotics of Culture (The Hague: Mouton,
1973), 209-24.

c369. Meltzer, Françoise. "Renaming in Literature: Faces of the Moon," in
A. Whiteside and M. Issacharoff, eds. On Referring in Literature
(Bloomington: Indiana UP, 1987), 70-83.

c370. Mickelson, David. "Types of Spatial Structure in Narrative," in J. R.
Smitten and A. Daghistany, eds. Spatial Form in Narrative (Ithaca: Cornell
UP, 1981), 63-78.

c371. Miel, Jan. "Temporal Form in the Novel." MLN 84 (1969), 916-30.

c372. Miller, D. A. Narrative and Its Discontents: Problems of Closure in
the Traditional Novel (Princeton: Princeton UP, 1981).

c373. Miller, J. Hillis. The Form of Victorian Fiction (Notre Dame IN: U of
Notre Dame P, 1968).
c374. ----------, ed. Aspects of Narrative (NY: Columbia UP, 1971).

c375. ----------. "Narrative and History." ELH 41 (1974), 455-73.
c376. ----------. "Ariadne's Thread: Repetition and the Narrative Line."
CritI 3 (1976), 57-78.
c377. ----------. "Ariachne's Broken Woof." GeorgiaR 31 (1977), 44-60.
c378. ----------. "The Figure in the Carpet." PoT 1.3 (1980), 107-18.
c379. ----------. Fiction and Repetition: Seven English Novels (Cambridge:
Harbard UP, 1982).

c380. Miller, Owen. "Intertextual Identity," in M. J. Valdes and O. Miller,
eds. Identity of the Literary Text (Toronto: U of Toronto P, 1985), 19-40.

c381. Mink, Louis O. "History and Fiction as Modes of Comprehension."
NLH 1 (1969-70), 541-58.
c382. ----------. "Narrative Form as a Cognitive Instrument," in R. Canary
and H. Kozicki, eds. The Writing of History: Literary Form and Historical
Understanding (Madison: U of Wisconsin P, 1978), 129-49.

c383. Mitchell, W. J. T., ed. On Narrative (Chicago: U of Chicago P, 1981).

c384. Morgan, Thais E. "Is There an Intertext in this Text? Literary and
Interdisciplinary Approaches to Intertextuality." American Journal of
Semiotics 3 (1985), 1-40.

c385. Morrissette, Bruce. "Narrative 'You' in Contemporary Literature."
CLS 2 (1965), 1-24.
c386. ----------. "Referential Intertextuality: Pre-Code, Code, and Post-
Code," in A. Whiteside and M. Issacharoff, eds. On Referring in Literature
(Bloomington: Indiana UP, 1987), 111-21.

c387. Morson, Gary Saul. The Boundaries of Genre: Dostoevsky;s Diary of
a Writer and the Traditions of Literary Utopia (Austin: U of Texas P,
1981).
c388. ----------, ed. Bakhtin: Essays and Dialogues on His Work (Chicago: U
of Chicago P, 1986).

c389. Mortimer, Anthony, ed. Contemporary Approaches to Narrative
(Tubingen: Narr, 1984).

c390. Mosher, Harold F., Jr. "A New Synthesis of Narratology." PoT 1
(1980), 171-86.
c391. ----------. "Review Essay: Recent Studies in Narratology." PLL 17.1
(1981), 88-110.

c392. Murray, David. "Dialogics. Joseph Conrad, *Heart of Darkness* ," in D. Tallack, ed. Literary Theory at Work: Three Texts (Totowa NJ: Barnes & Noble, 1987), 115-34.

c393. Nanny, Max. "Narrative and Modes of Communication," in A. Mortimer, ed. Contemporary Approaches to Narrative (Tubingen: Narr, 1984), 51-62.

c394. Nash, Christopher. World-Games: The Tradition of Anti-Realist Revolt (London & NY: Methuen, 1987).

c395. Nef, Frédéric. "Case Grammar vs. Actantial Grammar: Some Remarks on Semantic Roles," in J. S. Petofi, ed. Text vs. Sentence: Basic Questions of Text Linguistics (Hamburg: Buske, 1979), 634-53.

c396. Novitz, David. "Pictures, Fiction, and Resemblance." BJA 22.3 (1982), 222-32.

c397. Omanson, Richard C. "An Analysis of Narratives: Identifying Central, Supportive, and Distracting Content." DPr 5.3-4 (1982), 195-224.

c398. Orr, Leonard. "Digression and Nonsequential Interpolation: The Example of Melville." JNT 9.2 (1979), 93-108.
c399. ----------. "Vraisemblance and Alienation Technique: The Basis for Reflexivity in Fiction." JNT 11 (1981), 199-215.
c400. ----------. "Varieties of Time in the Nonlinear, Nonteleological Novel," in De-Structing the Novel: Essays in Applied Postmodern Hermeneutics (Troy NY: Whitston, 1982), 155-83.
c401. ----------. "Teun van Dijk's Textgrammar Model: A Critique." Neophilologus 68 (1984), 1-8.
c402. ----------. "Random Verbal Generators and Verbal Constraints in Experimental Fiction." MFS 30.2 (1984), 203-15.
c403. ----------. "Intertextuality and the Cultural Text in Recent Semiotics." College English 48.8 (1986), 811-23.
c404. ----------. "The Semiotics of Description in Conrad's *Nostromo* ," in Ted Billy, ed. Critical Essays on Joseph Conrad (Boston: G. K. Hall, 1987), 113-28.
c405. ----------. Semiotic and Structuralist Analyses of Fiction: An Introduction and a Survey of Applications (Troy NY: Whitston, 1987).

c406. O'Toole, Lawrence M. "Dimensions of Semiotic Space in Narrative Structure." PoT 1.4 (1980), 135-49.

c407. Palumbo-Liou, Ernestina. "Le Narrateur: Expérience, médiation et vetement." RE 1 (1981), 163-69.

c408. Parret, Herman and Hans-George Ruprecht, eds. Aims and Prospects of Semiotics: Essays in Honor of Algirdas Julien Greimas, 2 vols. (Amsterdam: John Benjamins, 1985).

c409. Pascal, Roy. The Dual Voice: Free Indirect Speech and Its Functioning in the Nineteenth-Century European Novel (Manchester: Manchester UP, 1977).

c410. Patte, Daniel. Carré sémiotique et syntaxe narrative (Paris: CNRS, 1981).
c411. ----------. "Greimas' Model for the Generative Trajectory of Meaning in Discourses," in Paris School Semiotics: Texts and Documents. 1. Theory (Toronto: Victoria U, Toronto Semiotic Circle, 1983), 75-90.
c412. ----------. "The Semantic Function in Narrative Semiotics," in J. Pelc, et al, eds. Sign, System and Function (Berlin: Mouton, 1984), 281-96 [on Greimas].

c413. Pavel, Thomas. "Remarks on Narrative Grammars." Poetics 8 (1973), 5-30.
c414. ----------. La Syntaxe narrative des tragedies de Corneille (Paris: Klincksieck, 1976).
c415. ----------. "'Possible Worlds' in Literary Semantics." JAAC 34 (1976), 165-76.
c416. ----------. "Fiction and the Causal Theory of Names." Poetics 8.1-2 (1979), 179-91.
c417. ----------. "Narrative Domains." PoT 1 (1980), 105-14.
c418. ----------. "Ontological Items in Poetics: Speech Acts and Fictional Worlds." JAAC 40 (1981), 167-78.
c419. ----------. "Fiction and the Ontological Landscape." STCL 6 (1981-82), 149-63.
c420. ----------. "Incomplete Worlds, Ritual Emotions." Philosophy and Literature 7 (1983), 48-57.
c421. ----------. "Literary Narratives," in T. van Dijk, ed. Discourse and Literature (Amsterdam: Benjamins, 1985), 85-103.
c422. ----------. "Convention et représentation." Lit. 57 (1985), 31-47.
c423. ----------. The Poetics of Plot: The Case of English Renaissance Drama (Minneapolis: U of Minnesota P, 1985).

c424. Pelc, Jerzy. "On the Concept of Narration." Semiotica 2.3 (1971), 1-19.

c425. Perlina, Nina. "Mikhail Bakhtin and Martin Buber: Problems of Dialogic Imagination." STCL 9 (1984), 13-27.
c426. ----------. Varieties of Poetic Utterance: Quotation in The Brothers Karamazov (Lanham MD: UP of America, 1985).

c427. Perri, Carmela. "On Alluding." Poetics 7 (1978), 289-307.

c428. Perry, Menakhem. "Literary Dynamics: How the Order of a Text Creates Its Meanings." PoT 1.1 (1979), 35-64, 311-61.

c429. Petitot, Jean. "Topologie du carré sémiotique." ELit 10 (1977), 347-428.

c430. Petofi, Janos S. "Text Grammars, Text-Theory and the Theory of Literature." Poetics 7 (1973), 36-76.

c431. Pier, John. "Concerning the Subject of the Narrative Text." ArsS 4.1 (1981), 1-28.
c432. ----------. "Narrative Discourse: An Essay in Method ." CLS 19.1 (1982), 83-86 [on Genette].
c433. ----------. "Towards a Triadic Theory of Narrative," in T. Barbé, ed. Semiotic Unfolding (Berlin: Mouton, 1984), 969-75 [discusses Genette].

c434. Pimentel-Anduiza, Luz Aurora. "Metaphoric Narration: The Role of Metaphor in Narrative Discourse." DAI 46 (1986), 1933A.

c435. Piwowarczyk, Mary Ann. "The Narratee and the Situation of Enunciation: A Reconsideration of Prince's Theory." Genre 9 (1976), 161-77.

c436. Polet, Jean-Claude. "A travers 'Semeiotike' de J. Kristeva, ou l'illusion sémiotique." LR 28 (1974), 361-99.

c437. Pollard, D. E. B. "Fictions and Resemblances." BJA 24.2 (1984), 156-59.

c438. Polletta, Gregory T. "The Author's Place in Contemporary Narratology," in A. Mortimer, ed. Contemporary Approaches to Narrative (Tubingen: Narr, 1984),109-23.

c439. Polzin, Robert. "Dialogic Imagination in the Book of Deuteronomy." StTCL 9.1 (1984), 135-43 [uses Bakhtin].

c440. Pomorska, Krystyna. "Mixhail Baxtin and His Verbal Universe." PTL 3 (1978), 379-86.

c441. Prado, C. G. Making Believe: Philosophical Reflections on Fiction (Westport CT: Greenwood P, 1984).

c442. Prince, Gerald. "Notes Toward a Preliminary Categorization of Fictional 'Narratees.'" Genre 9 (1971), 100-06.

c443. ----------. A Grammar of Stories: An Introduction (The Hague: Mouton, 1973).

c444. ----------. "Introduction a l'étude du narrataire." Poétique 14 (1973), 178-96.

c445. ----------. "On Presupposition and Narrative Strategy." Centrum 1.1 (1973), 23-31.

c446. ----------. "Narrative Signs and Tangents." Diacritics 4.3 (1974), 2-8.

c447. ----------. "Remarques sur les signes métanarratifs." Degrés 11-12 (1977), e1-e10.

c448. ----------. "Le Discours attributif et le récit." Poétique 35 (1978), 305-13.

c449. ----------. "Questions, Answers, and Narrative Legibility," in T. S. Kobler, W. E. Tanner, and J. D. Bishop, eds. Retrospectives and Perspectives: A Symposium in Rhetoric (Denton TX: Texas Woman's UP, 1978), 75-90.

c450. ----------. "Aspects of a Grammar of Narrative." PoT 1.3 (1980), 49-63.

c451. ----------. "Introduction to the Study of the Narratee," in J. P. Tompkins, ed. Reader-Response Criticism (Baltimore: Johns Hopkins UP, 1980), 7-25.

c452. ----------. "Reading and Narrative Competence." L'Esprit Créateur 21 (1981), 81-88.

c453. ----------. Narratology: The Form and Function of Narrative (The Hague: Mouton, 1982).

c454. ----------. "Understanding Narrative." StTCL 6.1-2 (1981-82), 37-50.

c455. ----------. "Narrative Analysis and Narratology." NLH 13.2 (1982), 179-88.

c456. ----------. "Narrative Pragmatics, Message, and Point." Poetics 12 (1983), 527-36.

c457. ----------. "Thématiser." Poétique 64 (1985), 425-33.

c458. ----------. "The Narratee Revisited." Style 19.3 (1985), 299-303.

c459. ----------. A Dictionary of Narratology (Lincoln: U of Nebraska P, 1987).

c460. ----------. "Bad References," in A. Whiteside and M. Issacharoff, eds. On Referring in Literature (Bloomington: Indiana UP, 1987), 33-41.

c461. ----------. "The Disnarrated." Style 22.1 (1988), 1-8.

c462. Rabinowitz, Peter J. "Assertion and Assumption: Fictional Patterns and the External World." PMLA 96.3 (1981), 408-19.

c463. ----------. Before Reading: Narrative Conventions and the Politics of Interpretation (Ithaca: Cornell UP, 1987).

c464. Rabkin, Eric S. Narrative Suspense: "When Slim Turned Sideways. . ." (Ann Arbor: U of Michigan P, 1973).

c465. Radar, Edmond. "Pour une science de la littérature: La Structure du texte artistique de Iouri Lotman." Lang. et l'Homme 24 (1974), 64-68.

c466. Raoul, Valerie. The French Fictional Journal: Fictional Narcissicism/ Narcissistic Fiction (Toronto: U of Toronto P, 1980).

c467. Rastier, François. Essai de sémiotique discursive (Tours: Mame, 1973).
c468. ----------. "The Concept of Isotopy and Its Development," in Paris School Semiotics: Texts and Documents. 1. Theory (Toronto: Victoria U, Toronto Semiotic Circle, 1983), 51-73.

c469. Reed, Walter L. "The Problem with a Poetics of the Novel," in M. Spilka, ed. Towards a Poetics of Fiction (Bloomington: Indiana UP, 1977), 62-74.

c470. Reid, Ian. "Storypower: A Renewed Narratology?" SoRA 18.2 (1985), 215-31.

c471. Reiser, Brian J., John B. Black, and Wendy G. Lehnert. "Thematic Knowledge Structures in the Understanding and Generation of Narratives." DPr 8.3 (1985), 357-89.

c472. Ricardou, Jean. Problemes du nouveau roman (Paris: Seuil, 1967).
c473. ----------. Pour une théorie du nouveau roman (Paris: Seuil, 1971).
c474. ----------. Le Nouveau roman (Paris: Seuil, 1973).
c475. ----------. Nouveaux problemes du roman (Paris: Seuil, 1978).
c476. ----------. "The Story within the Story." JJQ 18.3 (1981), 323-38 [mise-en-abyme, reflexivity].

c477. Ricoeur, Paul. "The Narrative Function." Semeia 13 (1978), 177-202.
c478. ----------. "Narrative Time," in W. J. T. Mitchell, ed. On Narrative (Chicago: U of Chicago P, 1981), 165-86.
c479. ----------. "Greimas' Narrative Grammar," in Paris School Semiotics: Texts and Documents. 1. Theory (Toronto: Victoria U, Toronto Semiotic Circle, 1983), 91-114.
c480. ----------. Time and Narrative, 3 vols. (Chicago: U of Chicago P, 1984-88).

c481. Rieser, Hannes. "On the Development of Text Grammar," in W. U. Dressler, ed. Current Trends in Textlinguistics (Berlin and NY: Walter de Gruyter, 1977), 6-20.

c482. Riffaterre, Michael. "Systeme d'un genre descriptif." Poétique 9 (1972), 15-30.
c483. ----------. "La Trace de l'intertexte." La Pensée 215 (1980), 4-18.
c484. ----------. "L'Intertexte inconnu." Lit 41 (Feb. 1981), 4-7.
c485. ----------. Text Production (NY: Columbia UP, 1983).

c486. Rimmon-Kenan, Shlomith. "Barthes 'Hermeneutic Code' and Henry James's Literary Detective: Plot-Composition in 'The Figure in the Carpet.'" HUSL 1 (1973), 183-207.
c487. ----------. "A Comprehensive Theory of Narrative: Genette's *Figures III* and the Structuralist Study of Fiction." PTL 1 (1976), 33-62.
c488. ----------. The Concept of Ambiguity: The Example of James (Chicago: U of Chicago P, 1977).
c489. ----------. "From Reproduction to Production: The Status of Narration in Faulkner's *Absalom, Absalom!* " Degrés 16 (1978), f-f19.
c490. ----------. "The Paradoxical Status of Repetition." PoT 1.4 (1980), 151-59.
c491. ----------. "Ambiguity and Narrative Levels: Christine Brooke-Rose's *Thru* ." PoT 3 (1982), 21-32.
c492. ----------. Narrative Fiction: Contemporary Poetics (London: Methuen, 1983).

c493. Ringler, Susan Jane. "Narrators and Narrative Contexts in Fiction." DAI 42 (1982), 4821A.

c494. Ron, Moshe. "Free Indirect Discourse, Mimetic Language Games and the Subject of Fiction." PoT 2.2 (1981), 17-39.
c495. ----------. "The Restricted Abyss: Nine Problems in the Theory of Mise en Abyme." PoT 8.2 (1987), 417-38.

c496. Ronen, Ruth. "Space in Fiction." PoT 7.3 (1986), 421-38.

c497. Rorty, Richard. "Is There a Problem about Fictional Discourse?" in Consequences of Pragmatism (Essays 1972-1980) (Minneapolis: U of Minnesota P, 1982), 110-38.

c498. Rose, Margaret. Parody/Meta-fiction: An Analysis of Parody as a Critical Mirror to the Writing and Reception of Fiction (London: Croom Helm, 1979).

c499. Rosenberg, Bruce. "Lineality and Simultaneity in Narrative." SFQ 43.1-2 (1979), 121-31.

c500. Rosler, Wolfgang. "Die Entdeckung der Fiktionalitat in der Antike." Poetica 12.3-4 (1980), 283-319.

c501. Rossum-Guyon, Françoise van. "Point de vue ou perspective narrative." Poétique 4 (1970), 476-97.

c502. Rousset, Jean. Narcisse romancier: Essai sur la premiere personne dans le roman (Paris: Corti, 1973).

c503. Roy, Ashish. "*Fabula* of the *Sjuzet* : Criticism and the Value of the Literary Lie." DAI 45 (1985), 3130A.

c504. Rudinow, Joel. "Representation, Voyeurism, and the Vacant Point of View." P&L 3.2 (1979), 173-86.

c505. Ruppert, Peter. "Recent Ideas of Narrative Order," in P. Ruppert, *et al*. Ideas of Order in Literature and Film (Tallahassee: UP of Florida, 1980), 1-11.

c506. Rusinko, Elaine. "Intertextuality: The Soviet Approach to Subtext." Dispositio 4 (1979), 213-35.

c507. Ryan, Marie-Laure. "Growing Texts on a Tree." Diacritics 7.4 (1977), 34-46 [on van Dijk].
c508. ----------. "Linguistic Models in Narratology." Semiotica 28 (1979), 127-55.
c509. ----------. "The Pragmatics of Personal and Impersonal Fiction." Poetics 10 (1981), 517-39.
c510. ----------. "Fiction as a Logical, Ontological, and Illocutionary Issue." Style 18 (1984), 121-39.
c511. ----------. "The Modal Structure of Narrative Universes." PoT 6 (1985), 717-55.
c512. ----------. "Embedded Narratives and Tellability." Style 20.3 (1986), 319-40.

c513. Said, Edward. Beginnings: Intention and Method (NY: Basic Books, 1975).

c514. Savran, George. "The Character as Narrator in Biblical Narrative." Prooftexts 5.1 (1985), 1-17.

c515. Sceglov, Ju. K. and A. K. Zolkovskij. "Poetics as a Theory of Expressiveness: Towards a 'Theme--Expressiveness Devices--Text' Model of Literary Structure." Poetics 5 (1976), 207-46.

c516. Schafer, Roy. "Narration in the Psychoanalytic Dialogue," in W. J. T. Mitchell, ed. On Narrative (Chicago: U of Chicago P, 1981), 25-49.

c517. ----------. Narrative Actions in Psychoanalysis (Worcester MA: Clark UP, 1981).

c518. Schleifer, Ronald. "The Space and Dialogue of Desire: Lacan, Greimas, and Narrative Temporality," in R. C. Davis, ed. Lacan and Narration: The Psychoanalytic Difference in Narrative Theory (Baltimore: Johns Hopkins UP, 1984), 871-90.
c519. ----------. A. J. Greimas and the Nature of Meaning: Linguistics, Semiotics and Discourse Theory (Lincoln: U of Nebraska P, 1987).

c520. Schmid, Wolf. Der Textaufbau in der Erzahlungen Dostoievskijs (Munich: Wilhelm Fink, 1973).

c521. Scholes, Robert and Robert Kellogg. The Nature of Narrative (NY: Oxford UP, 1966).
c522. ----------. Structuralism in Literature: An Introduction (New Haven: Yale UP, 1974).
c523. ----------. "An Approach through Genre," in M. Spilka, ed. Towards a Poetics of Fiction (Bloomington: Indiana UP, 1977), 41-51.
c524. ----------. "The Contributions of Formalism and Structuralism to the Theory of Fiction," in M. Spilka, ed. Towards a Poetics of Fiction (Bloomington: Indiana UP, 1977), 107-24.
c525. ----------. Semiotics and Interpretation (New Haven: Yale UP, 1982).
c526. ----------. "Interpretation and Narrative: Kermode and Jameson." Novel 17.3 (1984), 266-78.

c527. Schulze, Joachim. "Histoire, Discours, Ersetzungsregeln: Zu einer 'Tiefenstruktur des Narrativen.'" Poetica 9 (1977), 106-216.

c528. Schwarz, Daniel R. The Humanistic Heritage: Critical Theories of the English Novel from James to Hillis Miller (Philadelphia: U of Pennsylvania P, 1986).

c529. Searle, John. "The Logical Status of Fictional Discourse," in Expression and Meaning: Studies in the Theory of Speech Acts (Cambridge: Cambridge UP, 1979), 58-75.

c530. Segre, Cesare. Semiotics and Literary Criticism (The Hague: Mouton, 1973).
c531. ----------. Structure and Time: Narration, Poetry, Models (Chicago: U of Chicago P, 1979).
c532. ----------. Introduction to the Analysis of the Literary Text (Bloomington: Indiana UP, 1988).

c533. Shapiro, Marianne. "How Narrators Report Speech." Lang&S 17 (1984), 67-78.

c534. Shen, Yeshayahu. "On Importance Hierarchy and Evaluation Devices in Narrative Texts." PoT 6.4 (1985), 681-98.

c535. Sherzer, Dina. Representation in Contemporary French Fiction (Lincoln: U of Nebraska P, 1986).

c536. Shukman, Ann. "The Canonization of the Real: Jurij Lotman's Theory of Literature and Analysis of Poetry." PTL 1 (1976), 317-38.
c537. ----------. "Between Marxism and Formalism: The Stylistics of Mikhail Bakhtin." Comparative Criticism 2 (1980), 221-34.
c538. ----------. "The Dialectics of Change: Culture, Codes, and the Individual," in P. V. Zima, ed. Semiotics and Dialectics: Ideology and the Text (Amsterdam: John Benjamins, 1981), 311-29.

c539. Singer, Alan. "The Methods of Form: On Narrativity and Social Consciousness." Sub-Stance 12.4 (1983), 64-77.

c540. Slusser, Daniele Chatelain. "Le Récit itératif et Flaubert." DAI 43 (1983), 3333A [on Genette].

c541. Smith, Barbara Herrnstein. On the Margins of Discourse: The Relation of Literature to Language (Chicago: U of Chicago P, 1978).
c542. ----------. "Narrative Versions, Narrative Theories," in W. J. T. Mitchell, ed. On Narrative (Chicago: U of Chicago P, 1981), 209-32.

c543. Smitten, Jeffrey and Ann Daghistany, ed. Spatial Form in Narrative (Ithaca: Cornell UP, 1982).

c544. Sosnoski, James J. "On the Anvil of Theoretical Debate: Story and Discourse as Literary Theory." JJQ 18.3 (1981), 267-76.

c545. Spence, Donald. Narrative Truth and Historical Truth: Meaning and Interpretation in Psychoanalysis (NY: Norton, 1982).

c546. Spilka, Mark, ed. Towards a Poetics of Fiction (Bloomington: Indiana UP, 1977).

c547. Stanzel, Franz. Narrative Situations in the Novel (Bloomington: Indiana UP, 1971).
c548. ----------. "Second Thoughts on Narrative Situations in the Novel : Towards a 'Grammar of Fiction.'" Novel 11 (1978), 247-64.

c549. ----------. "Teller-Characters and Reflector-Characters in Narrative Theory." PoT 2 (1981), 5-15.

c550. ----------. Linguistische und literarische Aspekte der erzahlenden Diskurses (Vienna: Osterreichische Akad. der Wissenschaften, 1984) [speech act theory, text linguistics].

c551. ----------. A Theory of Narrative (Cambridge: Cambridge UP, 1984).

c552. Stein, Nancy L. "The Definition of a Story." Journal of Pragmatics 6 (1982), 487-507.

c553. Steinberg, Gunter. Erlebte Rede: Ihre Eigenart und ihre Formen in neurer deutscher, franzosischer und englischer Erzahlliteratur, 2 vols. (Gottingen: Kummerle, 1971).

c554. Steinley, Gary. "Introductory Remarks on Narratology." CE 38 (1976), 311-15.

c555. Sternberg, Meir. Expositional Modes and Temporal Ordering in Fiction (Baltimore: Johns Hopkins UP, 1978).

c556. ----------. "Ordering the Unordered: Time, Space, and Descriptive Coherence." YFS 61 (1981), 60-88.

c557. ----------. "Mimesis and Motivation: The Two Faces of Fictional Coherence," in J. Strelka, ed. Literary Criticism and Philosophy (University Park PA: Pennsylvania State UP, 1983), 145-88.

c558. ----------. "Spatiotemporal Art and the Other Henry James: The Case of The Tragic Muse ." PoT 5.4 (1984), 775-830.

c559. ----------. "The World from the Addressee's Viewpoint: Reception as Representation, Dialogue as Monologue." Style 20.3 (1986), 295-318.

c560. Stevick, Philip. The Chapter in Fiction: Theories of Narrative Division (Syracuse NY: Syracuse UP, 1970).

c561. Stewart, Susan. Nonsense: Aspects of Intertextuality in Folklore and Literature (Baltimore: Johns Hopkins UP, 1978).

c562. Stierle, Karl-Heinz. "Story as Exemplum--Exumplum as Story: On the Pragmatics and Poetics of Narrative Texts," in R. E. Amacher and V. Lange, eds. New Perspectives in German Literary Criticism: A Collection of Essays (Princeton NJ: Princeton UP, 1979), 389-417.

c563. Strauch, Gérard. "De quelques interprétations récentes du style indirect libre." Recherches Anglaises et Américaines 7 (1974), 40-73.

c564. Suleiman, Susan R. "Redundancy and the 'Readable' Text." PoT 1 (1980), 119-42.

c565. ----------. Authoritarian Fictions: The Ideological Novel as a Literary Genre (NY: Columbia UP, 1983).

c566. Tamir-Ghez, Nomi. "Personal Narrative and Its Linguistic Foundation." PTL 1.3 (1976), 403-30.

c567. Thibault, Paul. "Narrative Discourse as a Multi-level System of Communication: Some Theoretical Proposals Concerning Bakhtin's Dialogic Principle." STCL 9 (1984), 89-117.

c568. Thorndyke, Perry W. "Cognitive Structures in Comprehension and Memory of Narrative Discourse." Cognitive Psychology 9 (1977), 77-110.

c569. Titzmann, Michael. Strukturale Textanalyse: Theorie und Praxis der Interpretation (Munich: Fink, 1977).

c570. Tobin, Patricia. Time in the Novel: The Genealogical Imperative (Princeton: Princeton UP, 1978).

c571. Todorov, Tzvetan. Mikhail Bakhtin: The Dialogical Principle (Minneapolis: U of Minnesota P, 1984).

c572. Toker, Leona. "Self-Conconscious Paralepsis in Vladimir Nabokov's Pnin and 'Recruiting.'" PoT 7.3 (1986), 459-69 [discusses Genette].

c573. Toolan, Michael. "Analyzing Conversation in Fiction." PoT 8.2 (1987), 393-416.

c574. Torgovnik, Marianna. Closure in the Novel (Princeton: Princeton UP, 1981).

c575. Uspenskij, Boris A. A Poetics of Composition: The Structure of the Artistic Text and Typology of a Compositional Form (Berkeley: U of California P, 1973).

c576. Verrier, Jean. "Temporal Structuring in the Novel." Renaissance and Modern Studies 27 (1983), 30-46 [on Genette].

c577. Vitoux, Pierre. "Le jeu de la focalisation." Poétique 51 (1982), 359-68.

c578. Volek, Emil. "Colloquial Language in Narrative Structure: Towards a Nomothetic Typology of Styles and of Narrative Discourse." Dispositio 5-6 (1980-81), 57-84.

c579. Wall, Anthony. "Characters in Bakhtin's Theory." StTCL 9.1 (1984), 41-56.

c580. Walther, Elisabeth. "Zur Sprache des modernen Romans." Lang&S 2 (1968), 109-14.

c581. Warning, Rainer. "Irony and the 'Order of Discourse' in Flaubert." NLH 13.2 (1982), 253-86.

c582. Watt, Ian. "Serious Reflections on *The Rise of the Novel*," in M. Spilka, ed. Towards a Poetics of Fiction (Bloomington: Indiana UP, 1977), 90-103.

c583. Waugh, Patricia. Metafiction: The Theory and Practice of Self-Conscious Fiction (London: Methuen, 1984).

c584. Weimann, Robert. "History, Appropriation, and the Uses of Representation in Modern Narrative," in M. Krieger, ed. The Aims of Representation: Subject/Text/History (NY: Columbia UP, 1987), 175-215.

c585. Weinberg, Henry H. "Centers of Consciousness Reconsidered." PoT 5.4 (1984), 767-73.

c586. Weinold, Gotz. "Probleme der linguistischen Analyse des Romans." JIG 1.1. (1969), 108-28.
c587. ----------. "On Deriving Models of Narrative Analysis from Models of Discourse Analysis." Poetics 3 (1972), 15-28.
c588. ----------. "Das Konzept der Textverarbeitung und die Semiotik der Literatur." LiLi 27-28 (1977), 46-54.
c589. ----------. "Textlinguistic Approaches to Written Works of Art," in W. U. Dressler, ed. Current Trends in Textlinguistics (Berlin and NY: Walter de Gruyter, 1977), 133-54.

c590. Weinsheimer, Joel. "Theory of Character: *Emma* ." PoT 1.1-2 (1979), 185-211.

c591. Wellek, René. "Bakhtin's View of Dostoevsky: 'Polyphony' and the 'Carnivalesque,'" in R. L. Jackson and S. Rudy, eds. Russian Formalism: A Retrospective Glance (New Haven: Yale Center for International and Area Studies, 1985), 231-41.

c592. White, Allon. "Bakhtin, Sociolinguistics, and Deconstruction," in F. Gloversmith, ed. The Theory of Reading (Sussex: Harvester; Totowa NJ: Barnes & Noble, 1984), 123-46.

c593. White, Hayden. "The Value of Narrativity in the Representation of Reality," in W. J. T. Mitchell, ed. On Narrative (Chicago: U of Chicago P, 1981), 1-23.
c594. ----------. "The Question of Narrative in Contemporary Historical Theory." History and Theory 23 (1984), 1-33.

c595. Whiteside, Anna and Michael Issacharoff, eds. On Referring in Literature (Bloomington: Indiana UP, 1987) [includes Whiteside's "Theories of Reference," 175-208].

c596. Wiegmann, Hermann. "Typologie und Systematik in der Erzahltheorie: Bemerkungen zu den Voraussetzungen einer Typologie mit kritischen Anmerkungen zu Stanzels *Theorie des Erzahlens* ." LWU 14.3 (1981), 176-84.

c597. Wittig, Susan. Stylistic and Narrative Structures in the Middle English Romances (Austin: U of Texas P, 1978).

c598. Wittmann, Henri. "Théorie des narremes et algorithmes narratifs." Poetics 4 (1975), 19-28.

c599. Wright, Austin. The Formal Principle in the Novel (Ithaca: Cornell UP, 1982).

c600. Wright, Terence. "Rhythm in the Novel." MLR 80 (1985), 1-15.

c601. Yacobi, Tamar. "Fictional Reliability as a Communicative Problem." PoT 2.2 (1981), 113-26.
c602. ----------. "Narrative Structure and Fictional Mediation." PoT 8.2 (1987), 335-72.

c603. Young, Katherine. "Ontological Puzzles About Narrative." Poetics 13.3 (1984), 213-59.

c604. Zavarzadeh, Mas'ud. "The Semiotics of the Foreseen: Modes of Narrative Intelligibility in (Contemporary) Fiction." PoT 6.4 (1985), 607-26.

c605. Zeraffa, Michel. Personne et personnage (Paris: Klincksieck, 1969).

c606. Zholkovsky, Alexander. Themes and Texts: Towards a Poetics of Expressiveness (Ithaca: Cornell UP, 1984).

c607. Zoran, Gabriel. "Towards a Theory of Space in Narrative." PoT 5.2 (1984), 309-35.

D. Psychological Criticism

d1. Abdulla, Adnan K. Catharsis in Literature (Bloomington: Indiana UP, 1985).

d2. Agosti, Stefano. "Modeles psychoanalytiques et théorie du texte," in H. Parret and H.-G. Ruprecht, eds. Exigences et perspectives de la sémiotique: Recueil d'hommages pour Algirdas Julien Greimas/Aims and Prospects of Semiotics: Essays in Honor of Algirdas Julien Greimas (Amsterdam: Benjamins, 1985), 383-96.

d3. Alexander, Anne. Thomas Hardy: The 'Dream Country' of His Fiction (Totowa NJ: Barnes & Noble, 1987) [Jungian].

d4. Althusser, Louis. "Freud and Lacan," in Lenin and Philosophy (NY: Monthly Review P, 1971).

d5. Amalric, Jean-Claude. "Psychological and Structuralist Polarities in Recent French Criticism of Victorian and Edwardian Literature: A Review-Essay." TSLL 25.3 (1983), 495-502.

d6. André, Robert. Ecriture et pulsions dans le roman stendhalien (Paris: Klincksieck, 1977).

d7. "Anti-Oedipus: From Psychoanalysis to Schizopolitics." Semiotext(e) 2.3 (1977) [special issue: Kristeva, Lacan, Deleuze and Guattari].

d8. Anzieu, Didier. "Oedipe avant le complexe." Temps Modernes 22 (1966), 675-715.

d9. ----------, ed. Psychanalyse du génie créateur (Paris: Dunod, 1974).

d10. Apter, T. E. Fantasy Literature: An Approach to Reality (Bloomington: Indiana UP, 1982).

d11. Aronson, Alex. Psyche and Symbol in Shakespeare (Bloomington: Indiana UP, 1972).

d12. Arrivé, Michel. "Notes sur le métalangage et sa dénégation lacanienne," in H. Parret and H.-G. Ruprecht, eds. Exigences et perspectives de la sémiotique: Recueil d'hommages pour Algirdas Julien Greimas/Aims and Prospects of Semiotics: Essays in Honor of Algirdas Julien Greimas (Amsterdam: Benjamins, 1985), 99-112.

d13. Astle, Richard. "Dracula as Totemic Monster: Lacan, Freud, Oedipus, and History." Sub-Stance 25 (1980), 98-105.

d14. Baker, Christopher P. "Comments on the Relationship Between Psychoanalysis and Literary Criticism." LJHum 3.1 (1977), 41-44.

d15. Bal, Mieke, ed. "Psychopoetics." Style 18.3 (1984) [special issue].

d16. ----------, ed. "Psychopoetics." Poetics 13.4-5 (1984) [special issue].

d17. ----------. "Myth a la lettre : Freud, Mann, Genesis and Rembrandt, and the Story of the Son,"in S. Rimmon-Kenan, ed. Discourse in Psychoanalysis and Literature (London and NY: Methuen, 1987), 57-89.

d18. ----------. "Force and Meaning: The Interdisciplinary Struggle of Psychoanalysis, Semiotics, and Esthetics." Semiotica 63.3-4 (1987), 317-44.

d19. Bar, Eugen. "The Language of the Unconscious According to Jacques Lacan." Semiotica 3 (1971), 241-68.

d20. ----------. "Understanding Lacan," in L. Goldberger and V. H. Rosen, eds. Psychoanalysis and Contemporary Science, vol. 3 (NY: International Universities P, 1974).

d21. Barrish, Phil. "Rehearsing a Reading." Diacritics 16.4 (1986), 15-30 [on Gallop, Lacan].

d22. Bartels, Martin. "Traum und Witz bei Freud: Die Paradigmen psychoanalytischer Dichtungstheorie." T&K 10 (supp., 1981), 10-29.

d23. Bass, Alan. "The Double Game: An Introduction," in J. H. Smith and W. Kerrigan, eds. Taking Chances: Derrida, Psychoanalysis, and Literature (Baltimore: Johns Hopkins UP, 1984), 66-85.

d24. Bassett, Sharon. "Freudian Psychoanalysis: A Rhetorical Situation?" Pre/Text 1.1-2 (1980), 115-22.

d25. Baudouin, Charles. Psychanalyse de Victor Hugo (Paris: Colin, 1972).

d26. Baudry, Jean-Louis. "Freud et la création littéraire." TelQ 32 (1968), 63-85.

d27. Begley, Carl E. and Dell Lebo. "A Two Factor Theory of Psychoanalytic Symbolism: In Prose and Verse." IJSym 2.2 (1971), 1-6.

d28. Beharriell, Frederik J. "Freud und die Literatur." LuK 1.4 (1966), 53-59.

d29. Beirnaert, Louis. Aux frontieres de l'acte analytique: la Bible, Saint Ignace, Freud et Lacan (Paris: Seuil, 1987).

d30. Bellemin-Noel, Jean. Psychanalyse et littérature (Paris: PUF, 1978).
d31. -----------. Vers l'inconscient du texte (Paris: PUF, 1979).

d32. Bem, Jeanne. "Psychanalyse et poétique baudelairienne." Poétique 25 (1976), 31-35.

d33. Benveniste, Emile. "Remarks on the Function of Language in Freudian Theory," in Problems in General Linguistics, vol. 1 (Coral Gables FL: U of Miami P, 1971).

d34. Benvenuto, Bice and Roger Kennedy. The Works of Jacques Lacan (NY: St. Martin's P, 1986).

d35. Bercovitch, Sacvan. "Literature and the Repetition Compulsion." CE 29 (1968), 607-15.

d36. Beresford, Thomas. "Playing and the Two Traditions: Clinical Psychiatry and Literary Criticism." SoR 18.2 (1982), 259-79.

d37. Berg, William J., Michel Grimaud, and George Moskos. Saint/Oedipus: Psychocritical Approaches to Flaubert's Art (Ithaca: Cornell UP, 1982).

d38. Berge, André, et al . Entrétiens sur l'art et la psychanalyse (Paris: Mouton, 1968).

d39. Bernheimer, Charles. Flaubert and Kafka: Studies in Psychopoetic Structure (New Haven: Yale UP, 1982).

d40. Bersani, Leo. "From Bachelard to Barthes." Partisan Rev 2 (1967), 215-32.
d41. ----------. A Future for Asyntax: Character and Desire in Literature (Boston: Little, Brown, 1976).
d42. ----------. Baudelaire and Freud (Berkeley: U of California P, 1977).
d43. ----------. "Representation and Its Discontents." Raritan 1.1 (1981), 3-17.
d44. ----------. The Freudian Body: Psychoanalysis and Art (NY: Columbia UP, 1986).

d45. Bessette, Gérard. "La Psychocritique." V&I 1.1 (1975), 72-79.
d46. ----------. "Psychoanalytic Criticism," in L. Shouldice, ed. Contemporary Quebec Criticism (Toronto: U of Toronto P, 1979), 162-70.

d47. Bettelheim, Bruno. The Uses of Enchantment: The Meaning and Importance of Fairy Tales (London: Thames & Hudson, 1976).

d48. Beutin, Wolfgang, ed. Literatur und Psychoanalyse: Ansatze zu einer psychoanalytischen Textinterpretation Dreisehn Aufsatze (Munchen: Nymphenburger, 1972).

d49. Bickman, Martin. The Unsounded Centre: Jungian Studies in American Romanticism (Chapel Hill: U of North Carolina P, 1980).

d50. Binstock, William A. "Purgation through Pity and Terror." International Journal of Psychoanalysis 54 (1973), 499-504 and 56 (1975), 225-27.

d51. Bleikasten, André. "Fathers in Freud," in R. C. Davis, ed. The Fictional Father: Lacanian Readings of the Text (Amherst: U of Massachusetts P, 1981), 115-46.

d52. Bloom, Harold. The Anxiety of Influence: A Theory of Poetry (London: Oxford UP, 1975).
d53. ----------. Poetry and Repression (New Haven: Yale UP, 1976).
d54. ----------. "Freud and the Poetic Sublime: A Catastrophe Theory of Creativity." Antaeus 30-31 (1978), 355-77.
d55. ----------. A Map of Misreading (Oxford and NY: Oxford UP, 1980).
d56. ----------. "Freud's Concepts of Defense and the Poetic Will." Psychiatry and the Humanities 4 (1980) 1-28.
d57. ----------. Agon: Towards a Theory of Revisionism (Oxford and NY: Oxford UP, 1981).
d58. ----------, ed. Sigmund Freud's "The Interpretation of Dreams" (NY: Chelsea House, 1987).

d59. Boheemen-Saaf, Christine van. "'The Universe Makes an Indifferent Parent': *Bleak House* and the Victorian Family Romance." <u>Psychiatry and the Humanities</u> 6 (1983), 225-58.
d60. ----------. <u>The Novel as Family Romance: Language, Gender, and Authority from Fielding to Joyce</u> (Ithaca: Cornell UP, 1987).

d61. Bonnat, J. L. "Freud et l'écriture," in <u>Littérature et psychanalyse: Une Clinique de l'écriture</u> (Nantes: Dept. of Psych. U of Nantes, 1986), 1-25.

d62. Borch-Jacobsen, Mikkel. <u>The Freudian Subject</u> (Stanford CA: Stanford UP, 1988).

d63. Bowie, Malcolm. "Jacques Lacan," in J. Sturrock, ed. <u>Structuralism and Since: From Lévi-Strauss to Derrida</u> (Oxford: Oxford UP, 1979), 116-53.
d64. ----------. <u>Freud, Proust, and Lacan: Theory as Fiction</u> (Cambridge: Cambridge UP, 1987).

d65. Brantlinger, Patrick. "Romances, Novels, and Psychoanalysis." <u>Criticism</u> 17 (1975), 15-40.

d66. Brenkman, John. "The Other and the One: Psychoanalysis, Reading, *The Symposium* ," in S. Felman, ed. <u>Literature and Psychoanalysis: The Question of Reading: Otherwise</u> (Baltimore: Johns Hopkins UP, 1982), 396-456.

d67. Brink, Andrew. "On the Psychological Sources of Creative Imagination." <u>QQ</u> 81 (1974), 1-19.
d68. ----------. "Aggression in the Psychology of Art." <u>Sphinx</u> 3 (1975), 41-50.

d69. Brisman, Susan Hawk and Leslie Brisman. "Lies Against Solitude: Symbolic, Imaginary, and Real." <u>Psychiatry and the Humanities</u> 4 (1980), 29-66.

d70. Brivic, Sheldon. <u>Joyce Between Freud and Jung</u> (Port Washington NY: Kennikat P, 1980).

d71. Broca, Roland. "La Fonction de l'écrit dans la psychose," in <u>Littérature et psychanalyse: Une Clinique de l'écriture</u> (Nantes: Dept. of Psych. U of Nantes, 1986), 102-33.

d72. Brooke-Rose, Christine. "Id is, is Id?"in S. Rimmon-Kenan, ed. <u>Discourse in Psychoanalysis and Literature</u> (London and NY: Methuen, 1987), 19-37.

d73. Brooks, Peter. "Fictions of the Wolfman: Freud and Narrative Understanding." Diacritics 9.1 (1979), 72-81.
d74. ----------. "Freud's Masterplot: Questions of Narrative," in S. Felman, ed. Literature and Psychoanalysis: The Question of Reading: Otherwise (Baltimore: Johns Hopkins UP, 1982), 280-300.
d75. ----------. Reading for the Plot: Design and Intention in Narrative (NY: Knopf, 1984).
d76. ----------. "Constructions psychoanalytiques et narratives." Poétique 61 (1985), 63-73.
d77. ----------. "Psychoanalytic Constructions and Narrative Meanings." Paragraph 7 (1986), 53-76.
d78. ----------. "The Idea of a Psychoanalytic Literary Criticism," in S. Rimmon-Kenan, ed. Discourse in Psychoanalysis and Literature (London and NY: Methuen, 1987), 1-18.

d79. Brownstein, Marilyn. "Postmodern Language and the Perpetuation of Desire." TCL 31.1 (1985), 73-88 [applies M. Klein and D. W. Winnicott].

d80. Bruss, Neal H. "Re-Stirring the Waters, or the Voice that Sees the World as Patients." MR 20 (1979), 337-54.
d81. ----------. "Lacan and Literature: Imaginary Objects and Social Order." MR 221.1 (1981), 62-92.

d82. Burke, Carolyn. "Irigaray through the Looking Glass." FSt 7.2 (1981), 288-306 [Irigaray, Derrida, and Lacan].

d83. Butery, Karen Ann. "The Contributions of Horneyan Psychology to the Study of Literature." Amer. Jour. of Psychoanalysis 42.1 (1982), 39-50.

d84. Byrd, Charles. "Freud's Influence on Bakhtin: Traces of Psychoanalytic Theory in Rabelais and His World ." Germano-Slavica 5.5-6 (1987), 223-30.

d85. Calogeras, Roy C. "Lévi-Strauss and Freud: Their 'Structural' Approaches to Myths." AI 30 (1973), 57-79.

d86. Caramagno, Thomas C. "The Psychoanalytic Aesthetics of Eneas Sweetland Dallas." Literature and Psychology 33.2 (1987), 21-33.
d87. ----------. "Manic-Depressive Psychosis and Critical Approaches to Virginia Woolf's Life and Work." PMLA 103 (1988), 10-23.

d88. Carroll, David. "Freud and the Myth of Origin." NLH 6 (1975), 513-28.
d89. ----------. "For Example: Psychoanalysis and Fiction or the Conflict of Generation(s)." Sub-Stance 21 (1978), 49-67.

d90. ----------. The Subject in Question: The Languages of Theory and the Strategies of Fiction (Chicago: U of Chicago P, 1982).
d91. ----------. "Institutional Authority vs. Critical Power, or the Uneasy Relations of Psychoanalysis and Literature," in J. H. Smith and W. Kerrigan, eds. Taking Chances: Derrida, Psychoanalysis, and Literature (Baltimore: Johns Hopkins UP, 1984), 107-34.

d92. Caruth, Cathy. "Speculative Returns: Bloom's Recent Work." MLN 98.5 (1983), 1286-96.

d93. Casey, Edward S. and J. Melvin Woody. "Hegel, Heidegger, Lacan: The Dialectic of Desire." Psychiatry and the Humanities 6 (1983), 75-112.

d94. Cazenave, Michel. La subversion de l'ame: mythanalyse de l'histoire de Tristan et Iseut (Paris: Seghers, 1981) [Jungian].

d95. Certeau, Michel de. "The Freudian Novel: History and Literature." HIS 4.2-3 (1981), 121-41.
d96. ----------. "Lacan: une éthique de la parole." Débat 22 (1982), 54-69.
d97. ----------. Heterologies: Discourse on the Other (Minneapolis: U of Minnesota P, 1986) [pt. 1 on Freud and Lacan].

d98. Chabot, C. Barry. Freud on Schreber: Psychoanalytic Theory and the Critical Act (Amherst: U of Massachusetts P, 1982).

d99. Chaitin, Gilbert D. The Unhappy Few: The Psychological Novels of Stendhal (Bloomington: Indiana UP, 1972).
d100. ----------. "The Voices of the Dead: Love, Death, and Politics in Zola's Fortune des Rougon ." L&P 26 (1976), 131-44, 148-58.
d101. ----------. "Psychoanalysis and Literary Interpretation." L&P 27 (1977), 174-82.
d102. ----------. "De l'autobiographie au roman: Quelques remarques sur la création chez Stendhal." Stendhal Club 21 (1979), 99-108.
d103. ----------. "Chatiment et scene primitive: Le contre-sens de l'"Expiation.'" Revue des lettres modernes: Série Victor Hugo 1 (1982).
d104. ----------. "Psychoanalysis and Narrative Action: The Primal Scene of the French Novel." Style 18.3 (1984), 284-311.

d105. Charney, Hanna. "Oedipal Patterns in the Detective Novel," in M. Charney and J. Reppen, eds. Psychoanalytic Approaches to Literature and Film (Rutherford NJ: Fairleigh Dickinson UP, 1987), 238-48.

d106. Charney, Maurice and Joseph Reppen, eds. Psychoanalytic Approaches to Literature and Film (Rutherford NJ: Fairleigh Dickinson UP,

1987) [includes Charney's "Analogy and Infinite Regress in *Hamlet* ," 156-70].

d107. Chase, Cynthia. "'Transference' as Trope and Persuasion,"in S. Rimmon-Kenan, ed. Discourse in Psychoanalysis and Literature (London and NY: Methuen, 1987), 211-32.
d108. ----------. "The Witty Butcher's Wife: Freud, Lacan, and the Conversion of Resistance to Theory." MLN 102.5 (1987), 989-1013.

d109. Chasseguet-Smirgel, Janine, *et al* . Female Sexuality (Ann Arbor: U of Michigan P, 1970).
d110. ----------. Pour une psychanalyse de l'art et de la créativité (Paris: Payot, 1971).
d111. ----------, ed. Les Chemins de l'Anti-Oedipe (Toulouse: Privat, 1974).

d112. Chessick, Richard D. "The Search for the Authentic Self in Bergson and Proust," in M. Charney and J. Reppen, eds. Psychoanalytic Approaches to Literature and Film (Rutherford NJ: Fairleigh Dickinson UP, 1987), 19-36.

d113. Cixous, Hélene. "La fiction et ses fantomes: Un lecture de l'*Unheimliche* de Freud." Poétique 3 (1972), 199-216.

d114. Clancier, Anne. Psychanalyse et critique littéraire (Toulouse: Privat, 1973).

d115. Clancier, Georges-Emmanuel. "Psychanalyse, littérature et critique." Nef 24 (juillet-oct 1967), 101-10.

d116. Clark, Michael. Jacques Lacan: An Annotated Bibliography, 2 vols. (NY: Garland, 1988).

d117. Clément, Catherine, *et al* . Pour une critique marxiste de la théorie psychanalytique (Paris: Editions Sociales, 1973).
d118. ----------. Le pouvoir des mots: Symbolique et idéologique (Paris: Mame, 1974).
d119. ----------. Miroirs du sujet (Paris: Plon, 1975).
d120. ----------. Vies et Légendes de Jacques Lacan (Paris: Grasset, 1981) [The Lives and Legends of Jacques Lacan (NY: Columbia UP, 1983)].
d121. ----------. The Weary Sons of Freud (London: Verso, 1987).

d122. Collas, Ion K. Madame Bovary: A Psychoanalytic Reading (Geneve: Librairie Droz, 1985).

d123. Collins, Jerre, *et al* . "Questioning the Unconscious: The Dora Archive." Diacritics 13.1 (1983), 37-42 [Freud].

d124. Cooper, David Dale. "The Paradox of Spirit and Instinct: A Comparative Examination of the Psychologies of C. G. Jung and Sigmund Freud." DAI 38 (1978), 7330A-31A.
d125. ----------. "The Poet as Elaborator: Analytical Psychology as a Critical Paradigm." CritI 6 (1979), 51-63.

d126. Corngold, Stanley. The Fate of the Self: German Writers and French Theory (NU: Columbia UP, 1986).

d127. Corvez, Maurice. "Le structuralisme de Jacques Lacan." Revue philosophique de Louvain 66 (1968), 282-308.

d128. Coste, Didier. "Conscience de la lettre et lettre d'inconscient." Lit 54 (1984), 20-38.

d129. Coursen, Herbert R. The Compensatory Psyche: A Jungian Approach to Shakespeare (Lanham MD: UP of America, 1986).

d130. Cousineau, Thomas. "*Molloy* and the Paternal Metaphor." MFS 29.1 (1983), 81-91.
d131. ----------. "Descartes, Lacan, and *Murphy* ." College Lit 11.3 (1984), 223-32.

d132. Coward, Rosalind and John Ellis. Language and Materialism: Developments in Semiology and the Theory of the Subject (Boston: Routledge & Kegan Paul, 1977).

d133. Crecelius, Kathryn J. Family Romances: George Sand's Early Novels (Bloomington: Indiana UP, 1987).

d134. Crews, Frederick. The Sins of the Fathers: Hawthorne's Psychological Themes (London: Oxford UP, 1966).
d135. ----------. "Literature and Psychology," in J. Thorpe, ed. Relations of Literary Study: Essays on Interdisciplinary Contributions (NY: MLA, 1967), 73-87.
d136. ----------, ed. Psychoanalysis and Literary Process (Cambridge MA: Winthrop, 1970) [includes Crews' "Anesthetic Criticism," 1-24].
d137. ----------. Out of My System: Psychoanalysis, Ideology, and Critical Method (NY: Oxford UP, 1975).
d138. ----------. "Reductionism and Its Discontents." CritI 1 (1975), 543-58 [Freudian criticism].

d139. Crouzet, Michel. "Psychanalyse et culture littéraire." RHL 70 (1970), 884-917.

d140. Dalton, Elizabeth. Unconscious Structure in The Idiot : A Study in Literature and Psychoanalysis (Princeton: Princeton UP, 1979).

d141. Danto, Arthur C. "Freudian Explanations and the Language of the Unconscious." Psychiatry and the Humanities 3 (1978), 325-53.

d142. David-Menard, Monique. "Lacanians Against Lacan." Social Text 6 (1982), 86-111.

d143. Davis, Robert Con, ed. The Fictional Father: Lacanian Readings of the Text (Amherst: U of Massachusetts P, 1981) [includes Davis' "Critical Introduction: The Discourse of the Father," 1-26; "Post-Modern Paternity: Donald Barthelme's The Dead Father ," 169-82; and "The Discourse of Jacques Lacan," 183-89].
d144. ----------, ed. Lacan and Narration: The Psychoanalytic Difference in Narrative Theory (Baltimore: Johns Hopkins UP, 1983) [includes Davis' "Introduction: Lacan and Narration," 848-59, and "Lacan, Poe, and Narrative Repression," 983-1005].
d145. ----------. "Freud's Resistance to Reading and Teaching." CE 49.6 (1987), 621-27.

d146. Deleuze, Gilles. "Le schizophrene et le mot." Critique 24 (1968), 731-46.
d147. ----------. Logique du sens (Paris: Minuit, 1969).
d148. ---------- and Félix Guattari. L'Anti-Oedipe (Paris: Minuit, 1972 [Anti-Oedipus: Capitalism and Schizophrenia (Minneapolis: U of Minnesota P, 1983)].
d149. ----------. "The Schizophrenic and Language: Surface and Depth in Lewis Carroll and Antonin Artaud," in J. V. Harari, ed. Textual Strategies: Perspectives in Post-Structuralist Criticism (Ithaca: Cornell UP, 1979), 277-95.
d150. ----------. Différence et répétition (Paris: PUF, 1979).

d151. Denham, Robert D. "Anti-Aesthetics; or, the Turn of the Freudian Crews." Centrum 1 (1973), 105-22.

d152. Den Hartog, Dirk. Dickens and Romantic Psychology: The Self in Time in Nineteenth-Century Literature (NY: St. Martin's P, 1987).

d153. Derrida, Jacques. "The Purveyor of Truth." YFS 52 (1975), 30-113.
d154. ----------. "Freud and the Scene of Writing," in Writing and Difference (Chicago: U of Chicago P, 1978), 196-231.

d155. ----------. "Coming Into One's Own," in G. Hartman, ed.
Psychoanalysis and the Question of the Text (Baltimore: Johns Hopkins UP,
1978), 114-48.
d156. ----------. La carte postale: de Socrate a Freud et au-dela (Paris:
Flammarion, 1980) [The Post Card: From Socrates to Freud and Beyond
(Chicago: U of Chicago P, 1987)].
d157. ----------. Dissemination (Chicago: U of Chicago P, 1981).
d158. ----------. Géopsychanalyse: Les souterains de l'institution (Paris:
Confrontation, 1981).
d159. ----------. "My Chance/Mes Chances : A Rendezvous with Some
Epicurean Stereophonies," in J. H. Smith and W. Kerrigan, eds. Taking
Chances: Derrida, Psychoanalysis, and Literature (Baltimore: Johns Hopkins
UP, 1984), 1-32.

d160. Dervin, Daniel, ed. "Special Section: Psychoanalysis & Creativity."
PsyculR 3.3-4 (1979), 227-98.

d161. Descombes, Vincent. L'Inconscient malgré lui (Paris: Minuit, 1977).

d162. Dettmering, Peter. Dichtung und Psychoanalyse (Munich: Wilhelm
Fink, 1969).
d163. ----------. Dichtung und Psychoanalyse II: Shakespeare, Goethe, Jean
Paul, Doderer (Munich: Nymphenburger, 1974).
d164. ----------. Psychoanalyse als Instrument der Literaturwissenschaft
(Frankfurt am Main: Fachbuchhandlung fur Psychologie, 1981).

d165. Deutelbaum, Wendy. "Two Psychoanalytic Approaches to Reading
Literature." BuR 26.1 (1981), 89-101 [on Charles Mauron and Norman
Holland, reader-response and psychoanalysis].

d166. De Waelhens, Alphonse. Schizophrenia: A Philosophical Reflection on
Lacan's Structuralist Interpretation (Pittsburgh: Duquesne UP, 1978).

d167. Dickstein, Morris. "The Price of Experience: Blake's Reading of
Freud." Psychiatry and the Humanities 4 (1980), 67-112.

d168. Dijkstra, Bram. Idols of Perversity: Fantasies of Feminine Evil in Fin-
de-Siecle Germany (Oxford: Oxford UP, 1987).

d169. Donahue, Patricia and Ellen Quandahl. "Freud and the Teaching of
Interpretation." CE 49.6 (1987), 641-49.

d170. Dor, Joel. Bibliographie des travaux de Jacques Lacan (Paris:
InterEditions, 1983).

d171. Doubrovsky, Serge. La Place de la Madeleine (Paris: Mercure de France, 1974).

d172. ----------. Parcours critique (Paris: Galilée, 1980).

d173. ----------. "Statements on *Amour-propre* : From Lacan to La Rochefoucauld." NYLF 8-9 (1981), 141-61.

d174. ----------. "'The Nine of Hearts': Fragments of a Psychoreading of *La Nausée*," in E. Kurzweil and W. Phillips, eds. Literature and Psychoanalysis (NY: Columbia UP, 1983), 378-88.

d175. ----------. Writing and Fantasy in Proust (Lincoln: U of Nebraska P, 1986).

d176. Driscoll, James P. Identity in Shakespearean Drama (Lewisburg PA: Bucknell UP, 1983) [Jungian].

d177. Driscoll, Kerry. Wiliam Carlos Williams and the Maternal Muse (Ann Arbor: UMI Research P, 1987).

d178. DuBois, Page. "Sexual Differences: Ancient and Modern." PCP 19.1-2 (1984), 43-49.

d179. Dumouchel, Paul. Violence and Truth: On the Work of René Girard (Stanford: Stanford UP, 1987).

d180. Durand, Régis. Melville: Signes et Métaphores (Lausanne: L'Age d'homme, 1980) [Lacanian].

d181. ----------. "'The Captive King': The Absent Father in Melville's Text," in R. C. Davis, ed. The Fictional Father: Lacanian Readings of the Text (Amherst: U of Massachusetts P, 1981), 48-72.

d182. ----------. "On *Aphanisis* : A Note on the Dramaturgy of the Subject in Narrative Analysis," in R. C. Davis, ed. Lacan and Narration: The Psychoanalytic Difference in Narrative Theory (Baltimore: Johns Hopkins UP, 1983), 860-70.

d183. Eagleton, Terry. Literary Theory: An Introduction (Minneapolis: U of Minnesota P, 1983) [chap. 5, "Psychoanalysis"].

d184. Edel, Leon. "Literature and Psychiatry," in S. Arieti, ed. American Handbook of Psychiatry, I: The Foundations of Psychiatry (NY: Basic Books, 1974), 1024-33.

d185. ----------. Stuff of Sleep and Dreams: Experiments in Literary Psychology (NY: Harper & Row, 1982).

d186. Edelson, Marshall. Language and Interpretation in Psychoanalysis (New Haven: Yale UP, 1975).

d187. ----------. "Two Questions About Psychoanalysis and Poetry." Psychiatry and the Humanities 4 (1980), 113-18.

d188. Efron, Arthur. "Reichian Criticism: The Human Body in *Wuthering Heights*," in J. Natoli, ed. Psychological Perspectives on Literature: Freudian Dissidents and Non-Freudians (Hamden CT: Archon, 1984), 53-78.

d189. "Ego Traps/Theory of Literature." Semiotext(e) 1.3 (1975) [special issue].

d190. Eifermann, Rivka R. "Interactions Between Textual Analysis and Related Self-Analysis,"in S. Rimmon-Kenan, ed. Discourse in Psychoanalysis and Literature (London and NY: Methuen, 1987), 38-56.

d191. Eissler, Kurt R. Discourse on Hamlet and *Hamlet* (NY: International Universities P, 1971).

d192. Ellis, David. Wordsworth, Freud, and the Spots of Time: Interpretation in the Prelude (Cambridge: Cambridge UP, 1985).

d193. Ellman, Neil. "Transactional Analysis for Literary Analysis and Self-Awareness." EngR 26.3 (1975), 42-44.

d194. Ende, Stuart A. "The Melancholy of the Descent of Poets: Harold Bloom's *The Anxiety of Influence: A Theory of Poetry* ." Boundary 2 (1974), 608-15.

d195. Enriquez, Eugene. "La Gardien des clés: Systeme et volupté chez Sade." Topique 19 (1977), 117-62.

d196. Eyssalet, C. "En guise de bonjour," in Littérature et psychanalyse: Une Clinique de l'écriture (Nantes: Dept. of Psych. U of Nantes, 1986), 135-40.

d197. "Esthétiques." Revue française de psychanalyse 38.1 (1974) [special issue].

d198. Faber, M. D., ed. Psychoanalytic Approaches to Shakespeare (NY: Science House, 1970).

d199. Fages, Jean-Baptiste. Comprendre Jacques Lacan (Toulouse: Privat, 1971).

d200. ----------. Histoire de la psychanalyse apres Freud (Toulouse: Privat, 1976).

d201. Felman, Shoshana. "Women and Madness: The Critical Phallacy." Diacritics 7 (1975), 2-10.

d202. ----------, ed. Literature and Psychoanalysis: The Question of Reading: Otherwise (Baltimore: Johns Hopkins UP, 1982; rpt. of YFS 55-56 (1977)].

d203. ----------. La folie et la chose littéraire (Paris: Seuil, 1978).

d204. ----------. "On Reading Poetry: Reflections on the Limits and Possibilities of Psychoanalytic Approaches." Psychiatry and the Humanities 4 (1980), 119-48.

d205. ----------. "The Originality of Jacques Lacan." PoT 2 (1980-81), 45-57.

d206. ----------. "Turning the Screw of Interpretation," in S. Felman, ed. Literature and Psychoanalysis: The Question of Reading: Otherwise (Baltimore: Johns Hopkins UP, 1982), 94-207.

d207. ----------. "Beyond Oedipus: The Specimen Story of Psychoanalysis," in R. C. Davis, ed. Lacan and Narration: The Psychoanalytic Difference in Narrative Theory (Baltimore: Johns Hopkins UP, 1983), 1021-53.

d208. ----------. Jacques Lacan and the Adventure of Insight: Psychoanalysis in Contemporary Culture (Cambridge: Harvard UP, 1987).

d209. Ferguson, Margaret W. "Border Territories of Defense: Freud and Defenses of Poetry." Psychiatry and the Humanities 4 (1980), 149-80.

d210. Fineman, Joel. "The Structure of Allegorical Desire," in S. Greenblatt, ed. Allegory and Representation (Baltimore: Johns Hopkins UP, 1981), 26-60.

d211. Fischer, Eileen. "The Discourse of the Other in Not I : A Confluence of Beckett and Lacan." Theatre 10.3 (1979), 101-03.

d212. Fischer, Jens Malte, ed. Psychoanalytische Literaturinterpretation (Tubingen: Max Niemeyer, 1980).

d213. Fisher, David James, ed. "Psychoanalysis and Interpretation." HIS 4.2-3 (1981) [special issue].

d214. Fizer, John. Psychologism and Psychoaesthetics: A Historical and Critical View of Their Relations (Amsterdam: Benjamins, 1981).

d215. Fleming, Keith. "Hamlet and Oedipus Today: Jones and Lacan." Hamlet Studies 4.1-2 (1982), 54-71.

d216. Flieger, Jerry Aline. "Trial and Error: The Case of the Textual Unconscious." Diacritics 11.1 (1981), 56-67 [on Jean Bellamin-Noel and Jacques Lacan].

d217. ----------. "The Prison-House of Ideology: Critic as Inmate."
Diacritics 12.3 (1982), 47-56.
d218. ----------. "The Purloined Punchline: Joke as Textual Paradigm," in R.
C. Davis, ed. Lacan and Narration: The Psychoanalytic Difference in
Narrative Theory (Baltimore: Johns Hopkins UP, 1983), 941-67.
d219. ----------. "Baudelaire and Freud: The Poet as Joker," in M. Charney
and J. Reppen, eds. Psychoanalytic Approaches to Literature and Film
(Rutherford NJ: Fairleigh Dickinson UP, 1987), 266-81.

d220. Forrester, John. "Michel Foucault and the History of Psychoanalysis."
History of Science 18 (1980), 286-302.
d221. ----------. "Philology and the Phallus," in C. MacCabe, ed. The
Talking Cure: Essays in Psychoanalysis and Language (NY: St. Martin's P,
1981), 45-69.
d222. ----------. "Psychoanalysis or Literature" French Studies 35 (1981),
170-79.
d223. ----------. "Who is in Analysis with Whom: Freud, Lacan, Derrida."
Economy and Society 13.2 (1984), 153-77.

d224. Frank, Lawrence. Charles Dickens and the Romantic Self (Lincoln: U
of Nebraska P, 1984).

d225. Franz, Marie-Louise von. "Analytical Psychology and Literary
Criticism." NLH 12 (1980), 119-26.

d226. Franzosa, John C., Jr. "Criticism and the Uses of Psychoanalysis." CE
34 (1973), 927-33.

d227. "French Freud: Structural Studies in Psychoanalysis." YFS 48 (1972)
[special issue].

d228. Friedman, Norman. "Psychology and Literary Form: Toward a
Unified Approach." PsyculR 2 (1978), 75-95 [Gestalt].

d229. Friedman, Susan Stanford. Psyche Reborn: The Emergence of H.D.
(Bloomington: Indiana UP, 1981).
d230. ----------. "Creativity and the Childbirth Metaphor: Gender
Differences in Literary Discourse." Feminist Studies 13.1 (1987), 49-82.
d231. ----------. "Against Discipleship: Collaboration and Intimacy in the
Relationship of H.D. and Freud." L&P 33.3-4 (1987), 89-108.

d232. Frosh, Steven. The Politics of Psychoanalysis: An Introduction to
Freudian and Post-Freudian Theory (New Haven: Yale UP, 1987).

d233. Frost, David. "Constructing Hamlet's Mind." Sydney Studies in English 12 (1986-87), 3-20.

d234. Fuller, Peter. Art and Psychoanalysis (London: Writers and Readers Publishing Cooperative, 1980).

d235. Gaillard, Françoise. "Literary Code(s) and Ideology: Towards a Contestation of Semiology." Sub-Stance 15 (1976), 68-81.
d236. ----------. "Au nom de la Loi: Lacan, Althusser et idéologie," in C. B. Duchet, et al , eds. Sociocritique (Paris: Nathan, 1979), 11-24.

d237. Gallagher, Catherine and Thomas Laqueur, eds. The Making of the Modern Body: Sexuality and Society in the Nineteenth Century (Berkeley: U of California P, 1987).

d238. Gallas, Helga. Das Textbegrehen des 'Michael Kohlhaas': Die Sprache des Unbewussten und der Sinn der Literatur (Reinbeck bei Hamburg: Rowohlt, 1981).

d239. Gallop, Jane. "The Ghost of Lacan, the Trace of Language." Diacritics 5.4 (1975), 18-24.
d240. ----------. "Psychoanalysis and France." W&L 7.1 (1979), 57-63.
d241. ----------. "Impertinent Questions: Irigaray, Sade, Lacan." Sub-Stance 26 (1980), 57-67.
d242. ---------- and Carolyn Burke. "Psychoanalysis and Feminism in France," in H. Eisenstein and A. Jardine, eds. The Future of Difference (Boston: G. K. Hall, 1980), 106-22.
d243. ----------. The Daughter's Seduction: Feminism and Psychoanalysis (Ithaca: Cornell UP, 1982).
d244. ----------. "Phallus/Penis: Same Difference." W&L 2 (1982), 243-51.
d245. ----------. "Lacan's 'Mirror Stage': Where to Begin." Sub-Stance 37-38 (1983), 118-28.
d246. ----------. "Lacan and Literature: A Case for Transference." Poetics 13.4-5 (1984), 301-08.
d247. ----------. Reading Lacan (Ithaca: Cornell UP, 1985).
d248. ----------. "Reading the Mother Tongue: Psychoanalytic Feminist Criticism." CritI 13 (1987), 314-29.

d249. Galperin, William H. "Marvell and the Death Instinct: 'The Iron Gates of Life,'" in M. Charney and J. Reppen, eds. Psychoanalytic Approaches to Literature and Film (Rutherford NJ: Fairleigh Dickinson UP, 1987), 249-65.

d250. Garber, Marjorie. Shakespeare's Ghost Writers: Literature as Uncanny Causality (NY: Methuen, 1987).

d251. ----------, ed. Cannibals, Witches, and Divorce: Estranging the Renaissance (Baltimore: Johns Hopkins UP, 1987).

d252. Gardiner, Judith Kegan. "Psychoanalytic Criticism and the Female Reader." L&P 26 (1976), 100-07.

d253. Garner, Shirley Nelson, Clair Kahane, and Madelon Sprengnether, eds. The (M)other Tongue: Essays in Feminist Psychoanalytic Interpretation (Ithaca: Cornell UP, 1985).

d254. Gasché, Rodolphe. "La Sorciere métapsychologique." Digraphe 3 (1974), 83-122 [on Lacan].

d255. Gault, J. L. "Notes sur la lettre et le signifiant," in Littérature et psychanalyse: Une Clinique de l'écriture (Nantes: Dept. of Psych. U of Nantes, 1986), 78-83 [Lacan].

d256. Gay, Peter. The Bourgeois Experience: Victoria to Freud. Vol. 2: The Tender Passions (Oxford: Oxford UP, 1987).
d257. ----------. Freud: A Life for Our Time (NY: Norton, 1988).

d258. Gear, Maria Carmen and Ernesto Cesar Liendo. Sémiologie psychanalytique (Paris: Minuit, 1975).

d259. George, Diane Hume. Blake and Freud (Ithaca: Cornell UP, 1980).
d260. ----------. Oedipus Anne: The Poetry of Anne Sexton (Urbana: U of Illinois P, 1987).

d261. Georgin, Robert. Lacan: Théorie et pratiques (Lausanne: L'Age d'homme, 1977).

d262. Ghiselin, Brewster. "Art and Psychiatry: Characterization as Therapy, Therapy as Characterization." MQR 16 (1977), 12-22.
d263. ----------. "Literature and Psychological Insight." WHR 31 (1977), 31-42.

d264. Gilman, Sander L., ed. Introducing Psychoanalytic Theory (NY: Brunner/Mazel, 1982) [includes Gilman's "Freud's Three Essays on the Theory of Sexuality : A Problem in Intellectual History," 181-204].
d265. ----------. Difference and Pathology: Stereotypes of Sexuality, Race, and Madness (Ithaca: Cornell UP, 1985).

d266. Girard, René. Deceit, Desire and the Novel: Self and Other in Literary Discourse (Baltimore: Johns Hopkins UP, 1965).

d267. ----------. Violence and the Sacred (Baltimore: Johns Hopkins UP, 1977).
d268. ----------. To Double Business Bound (Baltimore: Johns Hopkins UP, 1978).
d269. ----------. "Interdividual Psychology." UDQ 14.3 (1979), 3-19.
d270. ----------. "Narcissism: The Freudian Myth Demythified by Proust," in E. Kurzweil and W. Phillips, eds. Literature and Psychoanalysis (NY: Columbia UP, 1983), 363-77.
d271. ----------. Things Hidden Since the Foundation of the World (Stanford: Stanford UP, 1987).

d272. Girgus, Sam B. "R. D. Laing and Literature: Readings of Poe, Hawthorne, and Kate Chopin," in J. Natoli, ed. Psychological Perspectives on Literature: Freudian Dissidents and Non-Freudians (Hamden CT: Archon, 1984), 181-97.

d273. Goeppert, Sebastian, ed. Perspektiven psychoanalytischer Literaturkritik (Freiburg: Rombach, 1978).

d274. Gohin, Yves. "Progres et problemes de la psychanalyse littéraire." La Pensée 215 (1980), 58-81.

d275. Goldstein, Jan Ellen. "The Woolfs' Response to Freud: Water Spiders, Singing Canaries, and the Second Apple," in E. Kurzweil and W. Phillips, eds. Literature and Psychoanalysis (NY: Columbia UP, 1983), 232-55.

d276. Goldstein, Melvin. "Literature and Psychology, 1948-1968: A Commentary." L&P 17 (1967), 159-76.

d277. Gordon, David J. Literary Art and the Unconscious (Baton Rouge: Louisiana State UP, 1976).
d278. ----------. "Literature and Repression: The Case of Shavian Drama." Psychiatry and the Humanities 4 (1980), 181-204.

d279. Green, André. Un Oeil en trop: Le Complexe d'Oedipe dans la tragédie (Paris: Minuit, 1969).
d280. ----------. "Sur l'Anti-Oedipe ." Revue française de psychanalyse 36 (1972), 491-99 [on Deleuze and Guattari].
d281. ----------. Le discours vivant (Paris: PUF, 1973).
d282. ----------. "Idealization and Catharsis." Psychoanalytic Study of Society 6 (1975), 11-19.
d283. ----------. The Tragic Effect: The Oedipus Complex in Tragedy (NY: Cambridge UP, 1979).
d284. ----------. "The Unbinding Process." NLH 12 (1980), 11-19.

d285. ----------. "The Logic of Lacan's *objet a* and Freudian Theory:
Convergences and Questions." Psychiatry and the Humanities 6 (1983), 161-
92.
d286. ----------. On Private Madness (Madison CT: International
Universities P, 1986).
d287. ----------. "Oedipus, Freud, and Us," in M. Charney and J. Reppen,
eds. Psychoanalytic Approaches to Literature and Film (Rutherford NJ:
Fairleigh Dickinson UP, 1987), 215-37.

d288. Green, Geoffrey. Freud and Nabokov (Lincoln: U of Nebraska P,
1988).

d289. Greenblatt, Stephen. "Psychoanalysis and Renaissance Culture," in P.
Parker and D. Quint, eds. Literary Theory/Renaissance Texts (Baltimore:
Johns Hopkins UP, 1986), 210-24.

d290. Grimaud, Michel. "Petit psychanalyse du *Cid* ." Sub-Stance 3 (1972),
77-84.
d291. ----------. "Recent Trends in Psychoanalysis: A Survey, with Emphasis
on Psychological Criticism in English Literature and Related Areas." Sub-
Stance 13 (1976), 136-62.
d292. ----------. "Psychoanalysis, Contemporary Science, and the
Quandaries of Psychocriticism." L&P 27 (1977), 183-89.
d293. ----------. "Sur une métaphore métonymique hugolienne selon Jacques
Lacan." Littérature 29 (1978), 98-104.
d294. ----------. "La Rhétorique du reve: Swann et la psychanalyse."
Poétique 33 (1978), 90-106.
d295. ----------. "Les Mysteres du *Ptyx* : Hypotheses sur le remotivation
psychopoétique a partir de Mallarmé et Hugo." Michigan Romance Studies 1
(1980), 98-162.
d296. ----------. "Psychologie et littérature," in A. K. Varga, ed. Théorie de
la littérature (Paris: Picard, 1981), 256-81.
d297. ----------. "An Overview of Psychoanalytic Theory and the
Psychoanalytic Approach in Literary Theory and Practice, with Emphasis
on French Studies," in W. J. Berg, M. Grimaud, and G. Moskos.
Saint/Oedipus: Psychocritical Approaches to Flaubert's Art (Ithaca: Cornell
UP, 1982).
d298. ----------. "Poetics from Psychoanalysis to Cognitive Psychology."
Poetics 13.4-5 (1984), 325-46.

d299. Groeben, Norbert, Literaturpsychologie: Literaturwissenschaft
zwischen Hermeneutik und Empire (Stuttgart: Kohlhammer, 1972).
d300. ----------. "Metatheoretical Problems of the Psychoanalytical
Interpretation of Literature." Poetics 13.4-5 (1984), 407-20.

d301. Grosskurth, Phyllis. Melanie Klein: Her World and Her Work (NY: Knopf, 1986).

d302. Guattari, Félix. Psychanalyse et tranversalité (Paris: Maspéro, 1972).

d303. Gwin, Minrose. "Repetition and Recollection: The Unconscious Discourse of Mark Twain's Autobiography." L&P 33.3-4 (1987), 120-30.

d304. Haas, Norbert. "Unter dem Titel der Realitat," in J. Horisch and G. C. Tholen, eds. Eingebildete Texte: Affairen zwischen Psychoanalyse und Literaturwissenschaft (Munich: Fink, 1985), 49-63.

d305. Hahn, Claire. "Yeats Studies and the Parameters of Psychoanalytic Criticism." L&P 24 (1974), 171-76.

d306. Hamilton, James W. "Object Loss, Dreaming, and Creativity: The Poetry of John Keats." Psychoanalytic Study of the Child 24 (1969), 488-531.

d307. Handwerk, Gary. "Irony as Intersubjectivity: Lacan on Psychoanalysis and Literature." Comparative Criticism 7 (1985), 105-26.
d308. ----------. Irony and Ethics in Narrative: From Schlegel to Lacan (New Haven: Yale UP, 1986).

d309. Hansen, Hans-Sievert. "Neuere deutsche Beitrage zur psychanalytischen Literaturbetrachtung (1971-1976)." LWU 11 (1978), 97-114.

d310. Hanzo, Thomas A. "Paternity and Subject in Bleak House ," in R. C. Davis, ed. The Fictional Father: Lacanian Readings of the Text (Amherst: U of Massachusetts P, 1981), 27-47.

d311. Harris, Jean. "'But He was His Father': The Gothic and the Impostorious in Dickens' The Pickwick Papers ," in M. Charney and J. Reppen, eds. Psychoanalytic Approaches to Literature and Film (Rutherford NJ: Fairleigh Dickinson UP, 1987), 69-82.

d312. Hartman, Geoffrey. "A Touching Compulsion: Wordsworth and the Problem of Literary Representation." Georgia Rev 31 (1977), 345-61.
d313. ----------, ed. Psychoanalysis and the Question of the Text (Baltimore: Johns Hopkins UP, 1978) [includes Hartman's "Psychoanalysis: The French Connection," 86-113, later rptd. in Hartman's Saving the Text (Baltimore: Johns Hopkins UP, 1981)].
d314. ----------. "Centaur: Remarks on the Psychology of the Critic." Salmagundi 43 (1979), 130-39.

d315. ----------. "Diction and Defense in Wordsworth." Psychiatry and the Humanities 4 (1980), 205-15.

d316. Harvey, Irene. "Structures of Exemplarity in Poe, Freud, Lacan, and Derrida," in J. P. Muller and W. J. Richardson, eds. The Purloined Poe: Lacan, Derrida & Psychoanalytic Reading (Baltimore: Johns Hopkins UP, 1988), 252-67.

d317. Hayes, Francis. "The Great Dismal Swamp of Amateur Freudian Literary Criticism." MLJ 58 (1974), 339-42.

d318. Heller, Erich. "Observations on Psychoanalysis and Modern Literature." Psychiatry and the Humanities 1 (1976), 35-50.
d319. ----------. "The Dismantling of a Marionette Theatre; or, Psychology and the Misinterpretation of Literature." CritI 4 (1978), 417-32.

d320. Heller, Terry. The Delights of Terror: An Aesthetics of the Tale of Terror (Urbana: U of Illinois P, 1987).

d321. Hennighaus, Lothar. Tod und Verwandlung: Elias Canettis poetische Anthropologie aus der Kritik der Psychoanalyse (Frankfurt am Main: Lang, 1984).

d322. Herring, Henry D. "Constructivist Interpretation: The Value of Cognitive Psychology for Literary Understanding," in J. Natoli, ed. Psychological Perspectives on Literature: Freudian Dissidents and Non-Freudians (Hamden CT: Archon, 1984), 225-45.

d323. Hertz, Neil, ed. "A Fine Romance: Freud and Dora." Diacritics 13.1 (1983) [special issue].
d324. ----------. The End of the Line: Essays on Psychoanalysis and the Sublime (NY: Columbia UP, 1985).

d325. Hesnard, André. De Freud a Lacan (Paris: E.S.F., 1970).

d326. Hess-Luttich, Ernest W. B. "Notation des Psycholekts? Literaturkritik und Psycholinguistik," in his Literatur und Konversation: Sprachsoziologie und Pragmatik in der Literaturwissenschaft (WiebadenL Athenaion, 1980).

d327. Hiebel, Hans. "Witz und Metapher in der psychoanaltischen Wirkungsasthetik." GRM 28 (1978), 129-54.

d328. Hobson, Irmagard. "Goethe's Iphigenie : A Lacanian Reading." Goethe Yearbook 2 (1984), 51-67.

d329. Holland, Eugene W. "The Anti-Oedipus: Postmodernism in Theory, or the Post-Lacanian Historical Contextualization of Psychoanalysis." Boundary 2 14.1 (1985-86), 291-308.

d330. ----------. "Schizoanalysis: The Postmodern Contextualization of Psychoanalysis," in C. Nelson and L. Grossberg, eds. Marxism and the Interpretation of Culture (Urbana: U of Illinois P, 1987), 405-16.

d331. Holland, Norman N. "Toward a Psychoanalysis of Poetic Form: Some Mixed Metaphors Unmixed." L&P 15 (1965), 79-91.

d332. ----------. "Psychoanalytic Criticism and Perceptual Psychology: An Article-Review." L&P 14 (1966), 81-92.

d333. ----------. Psychoanalysis and Shakespeare (NY: McGraw-Hill, 1966).

d334. ----------. The Dynamics of Literary Response (NY: Oxford UP, 1968).

d335. ----------. "The 'Unconscious' of Literature: The Psychoanalytic Approach," in M. Bradbury and D. Palmer, eds. Contemporary Criticism (NY: St. Martin's P, 1970), 131-53.

d336. ----------. Poems in Persons: An Introduction to the Psychoanalysis of Literature NY: Norton, 1973).

d337. ----------. 5 Readers Reading (New Haven: Yale UP, 1975).

d338. ----------. The Psychoanalytic Study of Literature (Saratoga Springs NY: Empire State College of S.U.N.Y., 1975).

d339. ----------. "UNITY IDENTITY TEXT SELF." PMLA 90 (1975), 814-22.

d340. ----------. "Hamlet--My Greatest Creation." Journal of the American Academy of Psychoanalysis 3 (1975), 419-27.

d341. ---------- and Murray Schwartz. "The Delphi Seminar." CE 36 (1975), 789-800.

d342. ----------. "Literary Interpretation and Three Phases of Psychoanalysis." CritI 3 (1976), 221-33.

d343. ----------. "Transactive Criticism: Re-Creation through Identity." Criticism 18 (1976), 334-52.

d344. ----------. "Identity: An Interrogation at the Border of Psychology." Lang&S 10 (1977), 199-209.

d345. ----------. "Human Identity." CritI 4 (1977-78), 451-69.

d346. ----------. "What Can a Concept of Identity Add to Psycholinguistics?" Psychiatry and the Humanities 3 (1978), 171-234.

d347. ----------. "How do Dr. Johnson's Remarks on Cordelia's Death Add to My Own Response?" in G. Hartman, ed. Psychoanalysis and the Question of the Text (Baltimore: Johns Hopkins UP, 1978), 18-44.

d348. ----------. "Literature as Transaction," in P. Hernadi, ed. What Is Literature? (Bloomington: Indiana UP, 1978), 206-18.

d349. ----------. "Why This is Transference, Nor Am I Out of It." Psychoanalysis & Contemp. Thought 5.1 (1982), 27-34.

d350. ----------. "Freud, Physics, and Literature." Jour of the Amer. Acad. of Psychoanalysis 12.3 (1984), 301-20.

d351. ----------. The I (New Haven: Yale UP, 1985).

d352. ----------. "Re-covering 'The Purloined Letter': Reading as a Personal Transaction,"in J. P. Muller and W. J. Richardson, eds. The Purloined Poe: Lacan, Derrida & Psychoanalytic Reading (Baltimore: Johns Hopkins UP, 1988), 307-22.

d353. Holloway, Robin. "Jacques Lacan: Language is Foundational of the Unconscious," in M. Danesi, ed. Issues in Language (Lake Bluff IL: Jupiter P, 1981), 135-47.

d354. Hollwitz, John. "The Performance Psychology of Jacques Lacan." Literature in Performance 4.1 (1983), 27-30.

d355. Holzapfel, Heinrich. Subversion und Differenz: das Spiegelmotiv bei Freud, Thomas Mann, Rilke und Jacques Lacan (Essen: Blaue Eule, 1986).

d356. Homans, Peter. Jung in Context (Chicago: U of Chicago P, 1979).

d357. Horisch, Jochen and Georg-Christoph Tholen, eds. Eingebildete Texte: Affairen zwischen Psychoanalyse und Literaturwissenschaft (Munich: Fink, 1985).

d358. Hottois, Gilbert. "La hantise contemporaine du langage. Essai sur la situation philosophique du discours lacanien." Confrontations psychiatriques 19 (1981), 163-88.

d359. Huber, R. J. "Adlerian Theory and Its Application to *The Catcher in the Rye*-- Holden Caulfield," in J. Natoli, ed. Psychological Perspectives on Literature: Freudian Dissidents and Non-Freudians (Hamden CT: Archon, 1984), 43-52.

d360. Hutcheon, Linda. Formalism and the Freudian Aesthetic: The Example of Charles Mauron (Cambridge: Cambridge UP, 1984).

d361. Hyde, Michael J. "Jacques Lacan's Psychoanalytic Theory of Speech and Language." Quarterly of Speech 66.1 (1980), 96-108.

d362. Ionescu, Marina. "La Psychocritique: Delimitations et convergences." ASUI 24 (1978), 41-50.

d363. Irigaray, Luce. Speculum de l'autre femme (Paris: Minuit, 1974) [Speculum of the Other Woman (Ithaca: Cornell UP, 1985)].

d364. ----------. Ce Sexe qui n'en est pas un (Paris: Minuit, 1977).

d365. Irwin, John T. Doubling and Incest/Repetition and Revenge: A Speculative Reading of Faulkner (Baltimore: Johns Hopkins UP, 1975).
d366. ----------. "Figurations of the Writer's Death: Freud and Hart Crane." Psychiatry and the Humanities 4 (1980), 217-60.
d367. ----------. "Critical Introduction: The Family in Literature." Arizona Quarterly 36 (1980), 5-19 [Freudian].
d368. ----------. "The Dead Father in Faulkner," in R. C. Davis, ed. The Fictional Father: Lacanian Readings of the Text (Amherst: U of Massachusetts P, 1981),147-68.

d369. James, Sydney. "Transactional Analysis in Drama Criticism." DA 29 (1969), 3254A.

d370. Jameson, Fredric. The Political Unconscious: Narrative as a Socially Symbolic Act (Ithaca: Cornell UP, 1981).
d371. ----------. "Imaginary and Symbolic in Lacan: Marxism, Psychoanalytic Criticism, and the Problem of the Subject," in S. Felman, ed. Literature and Psychoanalysis: The Question of Reading: Otherwise (Baltimore: Johns Hopkins UP, 1982), 338-95.

d372. Jardine, Alice. Gynesis: Configurations of Women and Modernity (Ithaca: Cornell UP, 1985) ["Toward the Hysterical Body: Jacques Lacan and His Others," 159-77].

d373. Jenkins, Lee. Faulkner and Black-White Relations: A Psychoanalytic Approach (NY: Columbia UP, 1981).

d374. Jenny, Laurent. "Il n'y a pas de récit cathartique." Poétique 41 (1980), 1-21.

d375. Johnson, Barbara. The Critical Difference: Essays in the Contemporary Rhetoric of Reading (Baltimore: Johns Hopkins UP, 1980) [Lacan, Derrida].
d376. ---------- and Marjorie Johnson. "Secret Sharing: Reading Conrad Psychoanalytically." CE 49.6 (1987), 628-40.

d377. Johnson, Carroll B. Madness and Lust: A Psychoanalytical Approach to Don Quixote (Berkeley: U of California P, 1983).

d378. Joly, Raymond, ed. "Lectures psychanalytiques." ELit 11.3 (1978) [special issue].

d379. Jung, Carl. The Spirit in Man, Art, and Literature (NY: Pantheon, 1966) [vol. 15 of the Collected Works in the Bollingen Series].

d380. Juranville, Alain. Lacan et la philosophie (Paris: PUF, 1984).

d381. Kahane, Claire and Janice Doane. "Psychoanalysis and American Fiction: The Subversion of Q.E.D." SAF 9.2 (1981), 137-57 [Freud and Lacan].

d382. Kahn, Coppelia. Man's Estate: Masculine Identity in Shakespeare (Berkeley: U of California P, 1981).

d383. Kann, David J. "Reading One's Self and Others: Holland's Approach to Interpretive Behavior," in J. Natoli, ed. Psychological Perspectives on Literature: Freudian Dissidents and Non-Freudians (Hamden CT: Archon, 1984), 120-33.

d384. Kaplan, Linda J. "The Concept of the Family Romance." Psychoanalytic Rev 61 (1974), 169-202.

d385. Kaplan, Louise. The Family Romance of the Imposter-Poet Thomas Chatterton (NY: Atheneum, 1988).

d386. Kaplan, Morton and Robert Kloss. The Unspoken Motive: A Guide to Psychoanalytic Literary Criticism (NY: Free Press, 1973).

d387. Kearney, Richard. Modern Movements in European Philosophy (Manchester: Manchester UP, 1986) ["Jacques Lacan," 268-82].

d388. Kearns, Michael. Metaphors of Mind in Fiction and Psychology (Lexington: UP of Kentucky, 1987).

d389. Kennedy, J. Gerald. Poe, Death, and the Life of Writing (New Haven: Yale UP, 1987).

d390. Kerrigan, William. "The Articulation of the Ego in the English Renaissance." Psychiatry and the Humanities 4 (1980), 261-308.
d391. ----------. The Sacred Complex: On the Psychogenesis of Paradise Lost (Cambridge: Harvard UP, 1983).
d392. ----------. "Atoms Again: The Deaths of Individualism," in J. H. Smith and W. Kerrigan, eds. Taking Chances: Derrida, Psychoanalysis, and Literature (Baltimore: Johns Hopkins UP, 1984), 86-106.

d393. Khan, Asif Iqbal. "Psychological Criticism and the English Literary Tradition." Explorations 4.2 (1977), 26-32.

d394. Kiell, Norman. Psychiatry and Psychology in the Visual Arts and Aesthetics: A Bibliography (Madison: U of Wisconsin P, 1965).

d395. ----------. Varieties of Sexual Experience: Psychosexuality in Literature (NY: International Universities P, 1976).
d396. ----------. Psychoanalysis, Psychology, and Literature: A Bibliography, 2nd ed. (Metuchen NJ: Scarecrow P, 1982).

d397. Kimball, Jean. "From Eve to Helen: Stages of the Anima Figure in Joyce's Ulysses ." Mosaic 20.2 (1987), 29-40.

d398. Kimball, Samuel. "Uncanny Narration in Moby-Dick ." AL 59.4 (1987), 528-47.

d399. Kittler, Friederich and Horst Turk, eds. Urszenen: Literaturwissenschaft als Diskurskritik (Frankfurt am Main: Suhrkamp, 1977).

d400. Klein, Richard and Philip E. Lewis, eds. "The Tropology of Freud." Diacritics 9.1 (1979) [special issue].
d401. ----------. "In the Body of the Mother." Enclitic 7.1 (1983), 66-75 [Kristeva].

d402. Knapp, Bettina. Dream and Image (Troy NY: Whitston Pub., 1977).
d403. ----------. Theatre and Alchemy (Detroit: Wayne State UP, 1980).
d404. ----------. A Jungian Approach to Literature (Carbondale: Southern Illinois UP, 1984).
d405. ----------. Word/Image/Psyche (University AL: U of Alabama P, 1985).
d406. ----------. Archetype, Architecture, and the Writer (Bloomington: Indiana UP, 1986).
d407. ----------. Women in Twentieth-Century Literature: A Jungian View (University Park: Pennsylvania State UP, 1987).
d408. ----------. Music and the Writer: A Jungian Archetype (University Park: Pennsylvania State UP, 1988).

d409. Knapp, John V. "A Response to Mieke Bal's Psychopoetics ." Style 21.2 (1987), 259-80.

d410. Knutson, Harold C. Moliere: An Archetypal Approach (Toronto: U of Toronto P, 1976).

d411. Kofman, Sarah. Quatres romans analytiques (Paris: Galilée, 1974).
d412. ----------. The Childhood of Art: An Interpretation of Freud's Aesthetics (NY: Columbia UP, 1988).

d413. Kohut, Heinz. The Analysis of the Self (NY: International Universities P, 1971).

d414. ----------. "Psychoanalysis and the Interpretation of Literature: A Correspondence with Erich Heller." CritI 4 (1977-78), 433-50.

d415. ----------. The Restoration of the Self (NY: International Universities P, 1978).

d416. ----------. Self Psychology and the Humanities: Reflections on a New Psychoanalytic Approach (NY: W. W. Norton, 1985).

d417. Krauss, Henning and Reinhold Wolff, eds. Psychoanalytische Literaturwissenschaft und Literatursoziologie (Frankfurt: Lang, 1982).

d418. Kremer-Marietti, Angele. Lacan et la rhetorique de l'inconscient (Paris: Aubier-Montaigne, 1978).

d419. Kristeva, Julia. Desire in Language (NY: Columbia UP, 1980).

d420. ----------. Powers of Horror: An Essay on Abjection (NY: Columbia UP, 1982).

d421. ----------. "Psychoanalysis and the Polis." CritI 9.1 (1982), 77-92.

d422. ----------. "Within the Microcosm of 'The Talking Cure.'" Psychiatry and the Humanities 6 (1983), 33-48.

d423. ----------. Histoires d'amour (Paris: Denoel, 1983) [Tales of Love (NY: Columbia UP, 1987)].

d424. ----------. "The Pain of Sorrow in the Modern World: The Works of Marguerite Duras." PMLA 102.2 (1987), 138-52.

d425. ----------. "On the Melancholic Imaginary,"in S. Rimmon-Kenan, ed. Discourse in Psychoanalysis and Literature (London and NY: Methuen, 1987), 104-23.

d426. ----------. In the Beginning was Love: Psychoanalysis and Faith (NY: Columbia UP, 1987).

d427. Kucich, John. "Repression and Representation: Dickens' Generational Economy." NCF 38.1 (1983), 62-77.

d428. ----------. Repression in Victorian Fiction: Charlotte Bronte, George Eliot, and Charles Dickens (Berkeley: U of California P, 1987).

d429. Kudzus, U. G. "Reflections on the Double Bind of Literature and Psychopathology." Sub-Stance 20 (1978), 19-36.

d430. Kugler, Paul K. "Involuntary Poetics." NLH 15.3 (1984), 491-501 [Jung].

d431. Kuhns, Richard. Psychoanalytic Theory of Art: A Philosophy of Art on Developmental Principles (NY: Columbia UP, 1983).

d432. Kuriyama, Constance Brown. Hammer or Anvil: Psychological Patterns in Christopher Marlowe's Plays (New Brunswick NJ: Rutgers UP, 1980).

d433. Kurzweil, Edith. The Age of Structuralism: Lévi-Strauss to Foucault (NY: Columbia UP, 1980) [chap. 6: "Jacques Lacan: Structuralist Psychoanalysis"].
d434. ---------- and William Philips, eds. Literature and Psychoanalysis (NY: Columbia UP, 1983).

d435. Kytasty, Victor George. "Toward an Identity Theory of Literature." DAI 45 (1985), 3127A [Freudian].

d436. Lacan, Jacques. Ecrits (Paris: Seuil, 1966).
d437. ----------. "Of Structure as an Inmixing of an Otherness Prerequisite to Any Subject Whatever," in R. Macksey and E. Donato, eds. The Languages of Criticism and the Sciences of Man: The Structuralist Controversy (Baltimore: Johns Hopkins UP, 1970), 186-200.
d438. ----------. "Radiophonie." Scilicet 2-3 (1970), 55-99.
d439. ----------. Ecrits, 2 vols. (Paris: Seuil, 1970-71).
d440. ----------. "The Seminar on 'The Purloined Letter.'" YFS 48 (1972), 39-72 [also in J. P. Muller and W. J. Richardson, eds. The Purloined Poe: Lacan, Derrida & Psychoanalytic Reading (Baltimore: Johns Hopkins UP, 1988),28-99].
d441. ----------. Télévision (Paris: Seuil, 1974).
d442. ----------. Premiers Ecrits sur la paranoia (Paris: Seuil, 1975).
d443. ----------. Le Séminaire: Livre I. Les écrits techniques de Freud (Paris: Seuil, 1975).
d444. ----------. Le Séminaire: Livre XX. Encore (Paris: Seuil, 1975).
d445. ----------. Ecrits inspirés (Besançon: Arep, 1977).
d446. ----------. Ecrits: A Selection (NY: Norton, 1977).
d447. ----------. The Four Fundamental Concepts of Psycho-Analysis (NY: Norton, 1978).
d448. ----------. Le Séminaire: Livre II. Le moi dans la théorie et dans la technique de la psychanalyse (Paris: Seuil, 1978).
d449. ----------. Le Séminaire: Livre III: Les psychoses (Paris: Seuil, 1981).
d450. ----------. "Desire and the Interpretation of Desire in Hamlet ," in S. Felman, ed. Literature and Psychoanalysis: The Question of Reading: Otherwise (Baltimore: Johns Hopkins UP, 1982), 11-52.
d451. ----------. Speech and Language in Psychoanalysis (Baltimore: Johns Hopkins UP, 1982) [revision of The Language of the Self (1968)].
d452. ----------, et al . Feminine Sexuality (NY: Norton, 1982).
d453. ----------. Le Séminaire: Livre VII: L'éthique de la psychanalyse (Paris: Seuil, 1986).

d454. LaCapra, Dominick. "History and Psychoanalysis." CritI 13 (1987), 222-51.

d455. Lacoste, Patrick. Il écrit: une mise en scene de Freud (Paris: Galilée, 1981).

d456. Lacoue-Labarthe, P. and J.-L. Nancy. Le Titre de la lettre (Une Lecture de Lacan) (Paris: Galilée, 1973).

d457. Laplanche, Jean and Serge Leclaire. "The Unconscious: A Psychoanalytic Study." YFS 48 (1972), 118-75.
d458. ---------- and Jean-Baptiste Pontalis. The Language of Psychoanalysis (NY: Norton, 1973).
d459. ----------. Life and Death in Psychoanalysis (Baltimore: Johns Hopkins UP, 1976).

d460. Lavers, Annette. "Sartre and Freud." French Studies 41.3 (1987), 298-317.

d461. Layton, Lynne. "From Oedipus to Narcissus: Literature and the Psychology of Self." Mosaic 18.1 (1985), 97-105.
d462. ---------- and Barbara Ann Schapiro, eds. Narcissism and the Text: Studies in Literature and the Psychology of the Self (NY: New York UP, 1986).

d463. Leavey, Stanley A. "The Significance of Jacques Lacan." Psychiatry and the Humanities 3 (1978), 271-92.
d464. ----------. The Psychoanalytic Dialogue (New Haven: Yale UP, 1980).
d465. ----------. "John Keats' Psychology of Creative Imagination," in E. Kurzweil and W. Phillips, eds. Literature and Psychoanalysis (NY: Columbia UP, 1983), 201-16.
d466. ----------. "The Image and the Word: Further Reflections on Jacques Lacan." Psychiatry and the Humanities 6 (1983), 3-20.

d467. Lebovici, Serge and Daniel Widlocher, eds. Psychoanalysis in France (NY: International Universities P, 1980).

d468. Leclaire, Serge. Psychanalyser (Paris: Seuil, 1968).
d469. ----------. Démasquer le réel: un essai sur l'objet en psychanalyse (Paris: Seuil, 1971).

d470. Le Galliot, Jean. Psychanalyse et langages littéraires: Théories et pratique (Paris: Nathan, 1977).

d471. Leitch, Vincent. Deconstructive Criticism: An Advanced Introduction (NY: Columbia UP, 1983) [discusses Bloom, Lacan, Deleuze and Guattari].

d472. Lejeune, Philippe. "Ecriture et sexualité." Europe 502-03 (1971), 113-43.

d473. Lemaire, Anika. Jacques Lacan (London: Routledge, 1977).

d474. Lerner, Arthur. Psychoanalytically Oriented Criticism of Three American Poets: Poe, Whitman, and Aiken (Rutherford NJ: Fairleigh Dickinson UP, 1970).

d475. Lesser, Simon O. The Whispered Meanings: Selected Essays (Amherst: U of Massachusetts P, 1977) [Freudian].

d476. Lidz, Theodore. Hamlet's Enemy: Madness and Myth in Hamlet (NY: Basic Books, 1975).

d477. Lifton, Robert J. "From Analysis to Form: Towards a Shift in Psychological Paradigm." Salmagundi 28 (1975), 43-78.

d478. Lindauer, Martin S. The Psychological Study of Literature: Limitations, Possibilities, and Accomplishments (Chicago: Nelson-Hall, 1974).
d479. ----------. "An Empirical Approach to the Psychology of Literature," in J. Natoli, ed. Psychological Perspectives on Literature: Freudian Dissidents and Non-Freudians (Hamden CT: Archon, 1984), 246-66.

d480. Litowitz, Bonnie E. and Norman S. Litowitz. "The Influence of Linguistic Theory on Psychoanalysis: A Critical Historical Survey." International Review of Psychoanalysis 4 (1977), 419-48.

d481. Lockerd, Benjamin G., Jr. The Sacred Marriage: Psychic Integration in "The Faerie Queene" (Lewisburg: Bucknell UP, 1987).

d482. Lohmann, Hans-Martin, ed. Das Unbehagen in der Psychoanalyse: Eine Streitschrift (Frankfurt am Main and Paris: Qumran, 1983).

d483. Lukacher, Ned. "K(Ch)ronosology." Sub-Stance 25 (1980), 55-73 [Freud and Lacan].

d484. Lussier, André. "Des mythes et de l'inconscient." RUO 55.4 (1985), 45-58 [on Ricoeur].

d485. Lynch, David. Yeats, the Poetics of the Self (Chicago: U of Chicago P, 1979).

d486. Lyotard, Jean-François. Discours, Figure (Paris: Klincksieck, 1971).
d487. ----------. Dérive a partir de Marx et Freud (Paris: Union Générale d'Editions, 1973).
d488. ----------. Des dispositifs pulsionnels (Paris: Union Générale d'Editions, 1973).
d489. ----------. "Jewish Oedipus." Genre 10.3 (1977), 395-42.
d490. ----------. "The Dream-Work does Not Think." Oxford Literary Rev 6.1 (1983), 3-34.
d491. ----------. "Fiscourse, Digure: The Utopia Behind the Scenes of the Phantasy." TJ 35.3 (1983), 333-59.

d492. MacCabe, Colin, ed. The Talking Cure: Essays in Psychoanalysis and Language (NY: St. Martin's P, 1981) [Freud and Lacan].

d493. MacCannell, Juliet Flower. "Oedipus Wrecks: Lacan, Stendhal, and the Narrative Form of the Real," in R. C. Davis, ed. Lacan and Narration: The Psychoanalytic Difference in Narrative Theory (Baltimore: Johns Hopkins UP, 1983), 910-40.
d494. ----------. Figuring Lacan: Criticism and the Cultural Unconscious (Lincoln: U of Nebraska P, 1986).

d495. MacCary, W. Thomas. Friends and Lovers: The Phenomenology of Desire in Shakespearean Comedy (NY: Columbia UP, 1985).

d496. Macksey, Richard. "'Alas, Poor Yorick': Sterne Thoughts," in R. C. Davis, ed. Lacan and Narration: The Psychoanalytic Difference in Narrative Theory (Baltimore: Johns Hopkins UP, 1983), 1006-20.

d497. Mahony, Patrick. Psychoanalysis and Discourse (London and NY: Tavistock, 1987).
d498. ----------. Freud and the Rat Man (New Haven: Yale UP, 1987).
d499. ----------. Freud as a Writer (New Haven: Yale UP, 1987).

d500. Malin, Irving, ed. Psychoanalysis and American Fiction (NY: Dutton, 1965).

d501. Manheim, Leonard F. "Toward a Psychoanalytic Theory of Literature." L&P 16 (1966), 192-97.
d502. ---------- and Eleanor Manheim, eds. Hidden Patterns: Studies in Psychoanalytic Literary Criticism (NY: Macmillan, 1966).

d503. Mannoni, Octave. Clefs pour l'imaginaire ou l'Autre Scene (Paris: Seuil, 1970).

d504. ----------. "A Brief Introduction to Jacques Lacan." Contemporary Psychoanalysis 8 (1971), 97-106.

d505. ----------. Freud: The Theory of the Unconscious (London: New Left Books; NY: Random House, 1971).

d506. ----------. Fictions freudiennes (Paris: Seuil, 1973).

d507. ----------. Freud (NY: Vintage Books, 1974).

d508. Marcus, Steven. "Freud and Dora: Story, History, Case History," in E. Kurzweil and W. Phillips, eds. Literature and Psychoanalysis (NY: Columbia UP, 1983), 153-74.

d509. Margolin, Uri. "Harold Bloom. *The Anxiety of Influence: A Theory of Poetry* ." CRCL 4 (1977), 103-09.

d510. Marotti, Arthur F. "Countertransference, the Communication Process, and the Dimensions of Psychoanalytic Criticism." CritI 4 (1978), 471-89.

d511. Marta, Jan. "Lacan and Post-Structuralism." Amer. Jour. of Psychoanalysis 47.1 (1987), 51-57.

d512. Martens, Lorna. "The Theme of the Repressed Memory in Hofmannsthal's Elektra." German Quarterly 60.1 (1987), 38-51.

d513. ----------. "Musil und Freud: Die 'Foreign Body' in die Versuchung der stillen Veronika." Euphorion 81.2 (1987), 100-18.

d514. Martin, Jay. Who Am I This Time? Uncovering the Fictive Personality (NY: Norton, 1988).

d515. Martin, Philip. Mad Women in Romantic Writing (NY: St. Martin's P, 1987).

d516. Martindale, Colin. "The Grammar of Altered States of Consciousness: A Semiotic Reinterpretation of Aspects of Psychoanalytic Theory." Psychoanalysis and Contemporary Science 4 (1975), 331-54.

d517. ----------. Romantic Progression: The Psychology of Literary History (Washington, D.C.: Hemisphere Pub. Co., 1975).

d518. ----------, ed. "Poetics and Psychology." Poetics 7.2 (1978) [special issue].

d519. Mathieu, Michel. "L'art et la psychanalyse." Critique 26 (1971), 1044-54.

d520. Mauron, Charles. L'Inconscient dans l'oeuvre et la vie de Jean Racine (Paris: Corty, 1969).
d521. ----------. Psychocritique du genre comique: Aristophane, Plaute, Térence, Moliere, 3rd ed. (Paris: Corti, 1985).

d522. McGregor, Gaile. "The 'Primal Scene' as a Culture-Specific Phenomenon: A Speculative Rereading of Freudian--or Freud's-- Psychology." Journal of Mind and Behavior 8.1 (1987), 133-51.

d523. McNamara, Robert. "'Prufrock' and the Problem of Literary Narcissism." ContL 27.3 (1986), 356-77.

d524. McSweeney, Kerry. "Melville, Dickinson, Whitman and Psychoanalytic Criticism." CritQ 19.1 (1977), 71-82.

d525. Mehlman, Jeffrey. "Entre psychanalyse et psychocritique." Poétique 3 (1970), 365-85.
d526. ----------. "The 'Floating Signifier': From Lévi-Strauss to Lacan." YFS 48 (1972), 10-37.
d527. ----------. A Structural Study of Autobiography: Proust, Leiris, Sartre, Lévi-Strauss (Ithaca: Cornell UP, 1974).
d528. ----------. "How to Read Freud on Jokes: The Critic as Schadchen ." NLH 6 (1975), 439-61.
d529. ----------. "Poe pourri: Lacan's Purloined Letter." Semiotexte 1.3 (1975), 51-58.
d530. ----------. "The Suture of an Allusion: Lacan with Léon Bloy." Sub-Stance 33-34 (1981-82), 99-110.

d531. Meisel, Perry, ed. Freud: A Collection of Critical Essays (Englewood Cliffs NJ: Prentice-Hall, 1981).

d532. Mellard, J. "Lacan and Faulkner: A Post-Freudian Analysis of Humor in Fiction," in D. Fowler and A. Abadie, eds. Faulkner and Humor: Faulkner and Yoknapatawpha (University: UP of Mississippi, 1986), 195-215.

d533. Meltzer, Françoise. "The Uncanny Rendered Canny: Freud's Blind Spot in Reading Hoffmann's 'Sandman,'" in S. L. Gilman, ed. Introducing Psychoanalytic Theory (NY: Brunner/Mazel, 1982), 218-39.

d534. Melville, Stephen W. Philosophy Beside Itself: On Deconstruction and Modernism (Minneapolis: U of Minnesota P, 1986) [chap. 3, "Psychoanalysis and Deconstruction"; and chap. 5, "Psychoanalysis, Criticism, Self-Criticism"].
d535. ----------. "Psychoanalysis and the Place of Jouissance." CritI 13.2 (1987), 349-70.

d536. Merigot, Bernard. "Freud et la critique littéraire: le lien du texte." Europe 539 (1974), 139-99.

d537. Meyer, Bernard. Joseph Conrad: A Psychoanalytic Biography (Princeton: Princeton UP, 1967).

d538. Miel, Jan. "Jacques Lacan and the Structure of the Unconscious." YFS 36-37 (1966), 104-11.

d539. Miller, Jacques-Alain. "Jacques Lacan: 1901-1981." Psychoanalysis and Contemporary Thought 7 (1984), 615-28.

d540. Miller, J. Hillis. "Thomas Hardy, Jacques Derrida, and the 'Dislocation of Souls,'" in J. H. Smith and W. Kerrigan, eds. Taking Chances: Derrida, Psychoanalysis, and Literature (Baltimore: Johns Hopkins UP, 1984), 135-45.

d541. Miller, Joan M. French Structuralism: A Multidisciplinary Bibliography (NY: Garland, 1981) ["Jacques Lacan," 262-305].

d542. Milner, Max. Freud et l'interprétation de la littérature (Paris: C.D.U.-SEDES, 1980).

d543. Mitchell, Juliet and Jacqueline Rose, eds. Feminine Sexuality: Jacques Lacan and the école freudienne (NY: Pantheon Books, 1982).

d544. Mitscherlich, Alexander, ed. Psycho-Pathographien des Alltags: Schrfitsteller un Psychanalyse (Frankfurt: Suhrkamp, 1982).

d545. Mitscherlich-Nielsen, Margarete. "Psychoanalytic Notes on Franz Kafka," in E. Kurzweil and W. Phillips, eds. Literature and Psychoanalysis (NY: Columbia UP, 1983), 270-89.

d546. Mollinger, Shernaz. "Psychoanalytic Criticism and the Knowing Subject." DQ 15.3 (1980), 55-69 [on Crews, Holland, M. Schwartz].

d547. Monk, Patricia. The Smaller Infinity: The Jungian Self in the Novels of Robertson Davies (Toronto: U of Toronto P, 1982).

d548. Morris, Humphrey. "The Need to Connect: Representations of Freud's Psychical Apparatus." Psychiatry and the Humanities 4 (1980), 309-44.

d549. Morris, Wesley. "The Irrepressible Real: Jacques Lacan and Poststructuralism," in I. Konigsberg, ed. American Criticism in the Poststructuralist Age (Ann Arbor: U of Michigan P, 1981), 116-34.

d550. Morrison, Claudia C. Freud and the Critic: The Early Use of Depth Psychology in Literary Criticism (Chapel Hill: U of North Carolina P, 1968).

d551. Morson, Gary Saul. "Literary Theory, Psychoanalysis, and the Creative Process." PoT 3.2 (1982), 157-72.

d552. Moser, Tilmann. Romans als Krankengeschichten: uber Handke, Meckel und Martin Walser (Frankfurt am Main: Suhrkamp, 1985).

d553. Mounin, Georges. "Quelques traits du style de Jacques Lacan." NRF 17 (janv. 1969), 84-92.

d554. Muller, John P. "The Analogy of Gap in Lacan's Ecrits: A Selection ." Psychohistory Review 8.3 (1979), 38-45.
d555. ---------- and William J. Richardson. "Psychosis and Mourning in Lacan's Hamlet ." NLH 11.1 (1980), 147-65.
d556. ---------- and William J. Richardson. Lacan and Language: A Reader's Guide to Ecrits (NY: International Universities P, 1982).
d557. ----------. "Language, Psychosis, and the Subject in Lacan." Psychiatry and the Humanities 6 (1983), 21-32.
d558. ---------- and William J. Richardson, eds. The Purloined Poe: Lacan, Derrida, and Psychoanalytic Reading (Baltimore: Johns Hopkins UP, 1988) [includes Muller's "Negation in 'The Purloined Letter: Hegel, Poe, and Lacan," 343-68].

d559. Myktyta, Larsya. "Lacan, Literature and the Look: Woman in the Eye of Psychoanalysis." Sub-Stance 39 (1982), 49-57.

d560. Nagele, Rainer. "Freud, Habermas and the Dialectic of Enlightenment: On Real and Ideal Discourses." NGC 22 (1981), 41-62.
d561. ----------. Reading After Freud: Essays on Goethe, Holderlin, Habermas, Nietzsche, Brecht, Celan, and Freud (Baltimore: Johns Hopkins UP, 1987).

d562. Natoli, Joseph, ed. Psychological Perspectives on Literature: Freudian Dissidents and Non-Freudians (Hamden CT: Archon, 1984) [includes Natoli's "Phenomenological Psychology and Literary Interpretation," 198-224].
d563. ---------- and Frederik L. Rusch. Psychocriticism: An Annotated Bibliography (Westport CT: Greenwood P, 1984).

d564. Nead, Lynda. Representations of Women: Victorian Sexuality (Oxford: Basil Blackwell, 1987).

d565. Nebel, Cecile. The Dark Side of Creativity: Blocks, Unfinished Works, and the Urge to Destroy (Troy NY: Whitston, 1987).

d566. Newman, Karen. "Writing the 'Talking Cure': Psychoanalysis and Literature." PoT 3.2 (1982), 173-82.

d567. Newman, Robert D. "The Transformative Quality of the Feminine in the 'Penelope' Episode of Ulysses ." Journal of Analytical Psychology 31.1 (1986), 63-74.

d568. Noland, Richard W. "Contemporary Psychoanalytic Criticism." HSL 3 (1971), 132-43.
d569. ----------. "Psychoanalytic Criticism: Past and Present." HSL 7 (1975), 48-58.
d570. ----------. "Psychology and Fiction." HSL 7 (1975), 26-32.

d571. Nordquist, Joan. Jacques Lacan: A Bibliography (Santa Cruz CA: Reference and Research Services, 1987).

d572. Noy, Pinchas. "Symbolism and Mental Representation." Annual of Psychoanalysis 1 (1973), 125-58.

d573. Nyborg, Eigil. "Zur theorie einer tiefenpsychologischen Literaturanalyse." T&K 10 (supp.. 1981), 53-66 [Jungian].

d574. Ohlmeier, Dieter. "Das psychoanalytische Interesse an literarischen Texten," in J. Horisch and G. C. Tholen, eds. Eingebildete Texte: Affairen zwischen Psychoanalyse und Literaturwissenschaft (Munich: Fink, 1985), 15-25.

d575. Orlando, Francesco. Toward a Freudian Theory of Literature with an Analysis of Racine's Phedre (Baltimore: Johns Hopkins UP, 1978).
d576. ----------. "Rhétorique des Lumieres et dénégation freudienne." Poétique 41 (1980), 78-89.
d577. ----------. "Freud and Literature: Eleven Ways He Did It." Poetics 13.4-5 (1984), 361-80.

d578. Osakabe, Norimichi. "La Psychocritique de Ch. Mauron." JJK 8 (Jan., 1981), 71-83.

d579. Oxenhandler, Neal. "The Horizons of Psychocriticism." NLH 14.1 (1982), 89-103.

d580. Palmier, Jean-Michel. Lacan (Paris: Editions Universitaires, 1970).

d581. Panken, Shirley. Virginia Woolf and the 'Lust of Creation': A Psychoanalytic Exploration (Albany: S.U.N.Y. P, 1987).

d582. Paris, Bernard J. A Psychological Approach to Fiction: Studies in Thackeray, Stendhal, George Eliot, Dostoevsky, and Conrad (Bloomington: Indiana UP, 1974) [applies theories of Karen Horney].
d583. ----------. Character and Conflict in Jane Austen's Novels (Detroit: Wayne Stet UP, 1978).
d584. ----------, ed. "Third Force Psychology and Literary Criticism." LitR 24.2 (1981) [special issue; includes Paris' "Third Force Psychology and the Study of Literature, Biography, Criticism, and Culture," 181-221].
d585. ----------. "Third Force Psychology and the Study of Literature," in J. Natoli, ed. Psychological Perspectives on Literature: Freudian Dissidents and Non-Freudians (Hamden CT: Archon, 1984), 155-80 [based on 1981 essay above].
d586. ----------, ed. Third Force Psychology and the Study of Literature (Rutherford NJ: Fairleigh Dickinson UP, 1986).
d587. ----------. "Brutus, Cassius, and Caesar: An Inter-destructive Triangle," in M. Charney and J. Reppen, eds. Psychoanalytic Approaches to Literature and Film (Rutherford NJ: Fairleigh Dickinson UP, 1987), 139-55.

d588. Pasche, Francis. A partir de Freud (Paris: Payot, 1969).

d589. Paul, Robert A. "The Question of Applied Psychoanalysis and the Interpretation of Cultural Symbolism." Ethos 15.1 (1987), 82-103.

d590. Payne, Michael. "Do Psychologists and Critics Speak the Same Language?" JGE 24 (1972), 179-83.

d591. Peckham, Morse. Man's Rage for Chaos: Biology, Behavior, and the Arts (NY: Schocken, 1967).

d592. Pederson-Krag, Geraldine. "Detective Stories and the Primal Scene," in G. W. Most and W. W. Stowe, eds. The Poetics of Murder: Detective Fiction and Literary Theory (NY: Harcourt Brace Jovanovich, 1983), 13-20.

d593. Pelckmans, Paul. Le sacre du pere: fictions des lumieres et historicité d'Oedipe 1699-1775 (Amsterdam: Rodopi, 1983).

d594. Peraldi, François. "A Note on Time in 'The Purloined Letter,'"in J. P. Muller and W. J. Richardson, eds. The Purloined Poe: Lacan, Derrida & Psychoanalytic Reading (Baltimore: Johns Hopkins UP, 1988), 335-42.

d595. Pietzcker, Carl. Trauma, Wunsch und Abwehr: psychoanalytische Studien zu Goethe, Jean Paul, Brecht, zur Atomliteratur und zur literarischen Form (Wurzberg: Neumann, 1985).

d596. Pons, Xavier. "The Psychoanalytic Approach to Literature." LiNQ 14.1 (1986), 36-46.

d597. Pontalis, Jean-Baptiste. Apres Freud (Paris: Gallimard, 1968).
d598. ----------. Entre le reve et la douleur (Paris: Gallimard, 1977).

d599. Poole, Roger. "Psychoanalytic Theory: D. H. Lawrence, St Mawr ," in D. Tallack, ed. Literary Theory at Work: Three Texts (Totowa NJ: Barnes and Noble, 1987), 89-113.

d600. Pops, Martin. The Melville Archetype (Kent OH: Kent State UP, 1970).

d601. Porter, Laurence M. The Literary Dream in French Romanticism: A Psychoanalytic Interpretation (Detroit: Wayne State UP, 1979).
d602. ----------. "Huysman's 'A rebours': The Psychodynamics of Regression." AI 44.1 (1987), 51-65.

d603. Pratt, Annis, et al . Archetypal Patterns in Women's Fiction (Bloomington: Indiana UP, 1981).

d604. Przybylowicz, Donna. Desire and Repression: The Dialectic of Self and Other in the Late Works of Henry James (University AL: U of Alabama P, 1986).

d605. "Psychoanalysis and the Classics of Literature." PsyR 62.1 (1975) [special issue].

d606. "Psychology and Literature: Some Contemporary Directions." NLH 12.1 (1980) [special issue].

d607. Rabaté, Jean-Michel. "A Clown's Inquest into Paternity: Fathers, Dead or Alive, in Ulysses and Finnegans Wake ," in R. C. Davis, ed. The Fictional Father: Lacanian Readings of the Text (Amherst: U of Massachusetts P, 1981), 73-114.
d608. ----------. Language, Sexuality, and Ideology in Ezra Pound's Cantos (Albany: S.U.N.Y. P, 1986).

d609. Ragland-Sullivan, Ellie. "Explicating Jacques Lacan: An Overview." HSL 11 (1979), 140-56.

d610. ----------. "Julien's Quest for 'Self': *Qui Suis-je?* " Nineteenth-Century French Studies 8 (1979), 1-13.

d611. ----------. "The Psychology of Narcissism: Jean Genet's *The Maids* ." Gradiva 2 (1979), 19-40.

d612. ----------. "Lacan, Language, and Literary Criticism." LitR 24.4 (1981), 562-77.

d613. ----------. "Jacques Lacan: Feminism and the Problem of Gender Identity." Sub-Stance 36 (1982), 6-20.

d614. ----------. "Jacques Lacan, Literary Theory, and *The Maids* of Jean Genet," in J. Natoli, ed. Psychological Perspectives on Literature: Freudian Dissidents and Non-Freudians (Hamden CT: Archon, 1984), 100-19.

d615. ----------. "The Magnetisim Between Reader and Text: Prolegomena to a Lacanian Poetics." Poetics 13.4-5 (1984), 381-406.

d616. Ragussis, Michael. The Subterfuge of Art: Language and the Romantic Tradition (Baltimore: Johns Hopkins UP, 1978).

d617. Rajchman, John. "Lacan and the Ethics of Modernity." Representations 15 (1986), 42-56.

d618. Rancour-Laferriere, Daniel. Sign and Subject: Semiotic and Psychoanalytic Investigations Into Poetry (Lisse: Peter de Ridder, 1978).

d619. ----------. Out from Under Gogol's Overcoat: A Psychoanalytic Study (Ann Arbor: Ardis, 1982).

d620. Rand, Nicholas and Marie Torok. "The Secret of Psychoanalysis: History Reads Theory." CritI 13 (1987), 278-86.

d621. Rapaport, Herman. "Lacan Disbarred: Translation as Ellipsis." Diacritics 6.4 (1976), 57-60.

d622. ----------. "Living On: Lacan and Freud." NOR 9.1 (1982), 89-100.

d623. Reed, Gail S. "*Candide* : Radical Simplicity and the Impact of Evil," in E. Kurzweil and W. Phillips, eds. Literature and Psychoanalysis (NY: Columbia UP, 1983), 189-200.

d624. Rella, Franco. "Melancholy and the Labyrinthine World of Things." Sub-Stance 16.2 (1987), 29-36.

d625. Rendon, Mario, ed. "Horney Theory and Literature: A Symposium." Amer. Jour. of Psychoanalysis 42.1 (1982), 3-59.

d626. Reppen, Joseph and Maurice Charney, eds. The Psychoanalytic Study of Literature (Hillsale NJ: Analytic P, 1985).

d627. Rey, Jean-Michel. Parcours de Freud: Economie et discours (Paris: Galilée, 1974).
d628. ----------. "Freud's Writing on Writing." YFS 55-56 (1977), 301-28.

d629. Richards, David G. The Hero's Quest for the Self: An Archetypal Approach to Hesse's Demian and Other Novels (Lanham MD: UP of America, 1987).

d630. Richardson, William J. "Lacan's View of Language and Being." Psychoanalytic Rev 69.2 (1982), 229-33.
d631. ----------. "Lacan and the Subject of Psychoanalysis." Psychiatry and the Humanities 6 (1983), 51-74.
d632. ----------. "Lacanian Theory," in A. Rothstein, ed. Models of the Mind: Their Relationships to Clinical Work (NY: International Universities P, 1985), 101-17.
d633. ----------. "Lacan and Psychosis," in Psychosis and Sexual Identity: Towards a Post-Analytic View of the Screber Case (Stony Brook: S.U.N.Y. P, 1987).

d634. Richmond, Hugh M. "Personal Identity and Literary Personae: A Study in Historical Psychology." PMLA 90 (1975), 209-21.

d635. Ricoeur, Paul. Freud and Philosophy: An Essay in Interpretation (New Haven: Yale UP, 1970).
d636. ----------. "Psychoanalysis and the Work of Art." Psychiatry and the Humanities 1 (1976), 3-34.
d637. ----------. "Image and Language in Psychoanalysis." Psychiatry and the Humanities 3 (1978), 293-324.

d638. Riffaterre, Michael. "The Intertextual Unconscious." CritI 13 (1987), 371-85.

d639. Riley, William Patrick. "Encounter Criticism: Identity Development Through Prose Fiction." DAI 36 (1975), 2202A-03A.

d640. Rimmon-Kenan, Shlomith, ed. Discourse in Psychoanalysis and Literature (London and NY: Methuen, 1987) [includes Rimmon-Kenan's "Narration as Repetition: The Case of Gunter Grass's Cat and Mouse ," 176-87].

d641. Roberts, Jeanne A. "Literary Criticism as Dream Analysis." CEA 33.1 (1970), 14-16.

d642. Roberts, Patrick. The Psychology of the Tragic Drama (London and Boston: Routledge & Kegan Paul, 1975).

d643. Robinson, Paul. "Freud and the Feminists." Raritan 6.4 (1987), 43-61.

d644. Rogers, Robert. The Double in Literature (Detroit: Wayne State UP, 1970).
d645. ----------. Metaphor: A Psychoanalytic View (Berkeley: U of California P, 1978).

d646. Roland, Alan. "Psychoanalytic Literary Criticism--Promise and Problems." BForum 1 (1974), 275-84.
d647. ----------. "Toward a Reorientation of Psychaoanalytic Literary Criticism." PsyR 65 (1978), 391-414.
d648. ----------, ed. Psychoanalysis, Creativity, and Literature: A French-American Inquiry (NY: Columbia UP, 1978).

d649. Ronel, Avital. "Goethezeit," in J. H. Smith and W. Kerrigan, eds. Taking Chances: Derrida, Psychoanalysis, and Literature (Baltimore: Johns Hopkins UP, 1984), 146-82.
d650. ----------. "Doing Kafka in The Castle," in A. Udoff, ed. Kafka and the Contemporary Critical Performance: Centenary Readings (Bloomington: Indiana UP, 1987), 214-35 [Lacanian analysis].

d651. Rorty, Richard. "Freud, Morality, and Hermeneutics." NLH 12 (1980), 177-86.

d652. Rosenfield, Claire. Paradise of Snakes: An Archetypal Analysis of Conrad's Political Novels (Chicago: U of Chicago P, 1967).

d653. Ross, Andrew. "Viennese Waltzes." Enclitic 8.1-2 (1984), 71-82 [Lacan and feminism].

d654. Roudinesco, Elizabeth. La Bataille de cent ans: Histoire de la psychanalyse en France (Paris: Ramsay, 1982).

d655. Roussel, J. "Introduction to Jacques Lacan." New Left Rev 51 (1968), 63-77.

d656. Roustaing, François. Discipleship from Freud to Lacan (Baltimore: Johns Hopkins UP, 1982).
d657. ----------. Psychoanalysis Never Lets Go (Baltimore: Johns Hopkins UP, 1983).
d658. ----------. "L'Illusion lacanienne." Critique (May, 1985), 470-77.
d659. ----------. "How Do You Make a Paranoic Laugh?" MLN 102.4 (1987), 706-18.

d660. Rowe, John Carlos. The Theoretical Dimensions of Henry James (Madison: U of Wisconsin P, 1984).

d661. Rubin, Bernard. "Freud and Hoffmann: 'The Sandman,'" in S. L. Gilman, ed. Introducing Psychoanalytic Theory (NY: Brunner/Mazel, 1982), 205-17.

d662. Rubinstein, Benjamin B. "On Metaphor and Related Phenomena." Psychoanalysis and Contemporary Science 1 (1972), 70-108.

d663. Rudnytsky, Peter Lysiak. "Siege of Contraries: An Essay in Psychoanalytic Criticism." DAI 40 (1979), 3323A.
d664. ----------. "Oedipus and Anti-Oedipus." WLT 56.3 (1982), 462-70.
d665. ----------. "Medea's Revenge: Psychoanalysis, Feminism, and Tragedy." DQ 18.4 (1984), 35-42.
d666. ----------. Freud and Oedipus (NY: Columbia UP, 1987).

d667. Ruitenbeek, Hendrik M., ed. The Literary Imagination: Psychoanalysis and the Genius of the Writer (Chicago: Quadrangle, 1965).

d668. Rusch, Frederik L. "Approaching Literature through the Social Psychology of Erich Fromm," in J. Natoli, ed. Psychological Perspectives on Literature: Freudian Dissidents and Non-Freudians (Hamden CT: Archon, 1984), 79-99.

d669. Rycroft, Charles. "The Artist as Patient." TLS (Sept. 22, 1972), 1089-90.
d670. ----------. "Freud and the Imagination." NYRB (Apr. 3, 1975), 26-30.

d671. Sadoff, Dianne F. Monsters of Affection: Dickens, Eliot, and Bronte on Fatherhood (Baltimore: Johns Hopkins UP, 1982).

d672. Safouan, Moustapha. Etudes sur Oedipe: Introduction a une théorie du sujet (Paris: Seuil, 1974).
d673. ----------. La sexualité féminine dans la doctrine freudienne (Paris: Seuil, 1976).

d674. Salber, Willhelm. Literaturpsychologie: Gelebte und erlebte Literatur (Bonn: Bouvier, 1972).

d675. Schafer, Roy. A New Language for Psychoanalysis (New Haven: Yale UP, 1976).
d676. ----------. "Narration in Psychoanalytic Dialogue," in W. J. T. Mitchell, ed. On Narrative (Chicago: U of Chicago P, 1981), 25-49.

d677. Schapiro, Barbara. The Romantic Mother: Narcissistic Patterns in Romantic Poetry (Baltimore: Johns Hopkins UP, 1983).

d678. Schleifer, Ronald. "The Space and Dialogue of Desire: Lacan, Greimas, and Narrative Temporality," in R. C. Davis, ed. Lacan and Narration: The Psychoanalytic Difference in Narrative Theory (Baltimore: Johns Hopkins UP, 1983), 871-90.

d679. Schlossman, Beryl. "From La Boétie to Montaigne: The Place of the Text," in R. C. Davis, ed. Lacan and Narration: The Psychoanalytic Difference in Narrative Theory (Baltimore: Johns Hopkins UP, 1983), 891-909.

d680. Schmidt, A. V. C. "'Latent Content' and 'The Testimony of the Text': Symbolic Meaning in Sir Gawain and the Green Knight ." RES 38 (1987), 145-68.

d681. Schneiderman, Stuart. "Afloat with Jacques Lacan." Diacritics 1.2 (1971), 27-34.
d682. ----------. "Lacan et la littérature." TelQ 14 (1980), 39-47.
d683. ----------. Returning to Freud: Clinical Psychoanalysis in the School of Lacan (New Haven: Yale UP, 1980).
d684. ----------. Jacques Lacan: The Death of an Intellectual Hero (Cambridge: Harvard UP, 1983).

d685. Schonau, Walter, ed. Literaturpsychologische Studien und Analysen (Amsterdam: Rodopi, 1983).

d686. Schwab, Gabriele. "The Subject Genesis, the Imaginary, and the Poetic Language." Diogenes 115 (1981), 55-80 [Lacan].
d687. ----------. "Genesis of the Subject, Imaginary Functions, and Poetic Language." NLH 15.3 (1984), 453-74 [Lacan].

d688. Schwartz, Murray. "Critic, Define Thyself," in G. Hartman, ed. Psychoanalysis and the Question of the Text (Baltimore: Johns Hopkins, 1978), 1-17.
d689. ----------, ed. "Psychology and Literature: Some Contemporary Directions." NLH 12.1 (1980) [special issue].
d690. ---------- and Coppelia Kahn, eds. Representing Shakespeare: New Psychoanalytic Essays (Baltimore: Johns Hopkins UP, 1980).
d691. ---------- and David Willbern. "Literature and Psychology," in J.-P. Barricelli and J. Gibaldi, eds. Interrelations of Literature (NY: MLA, 1982), 205-24.

d692. Sédat, Jacques, ed. Retour a Lacan (Paris: Fayard, 1981).

d693. Seem, Mark. "To Oedipalize or Not to Oedipalize, that Is the Question . . . ." Sub-Stance 11-12 (1975), 166-69 [on Deleuze and Guattari].

d694. Sharpe, R. A. "Psychoanalysis and Narrative: A Structuralist Approach." International Review of Psycho-Analysis 14.3 (1987), 335-42.

d695. Shechner, Marc. Joyce in Nighttown: A Psychoanalytic Inquiry into Ulysses (Berkeley: U of California P, 1974).

d696. Shell, Marc. The End of Kinship: "Measure for Measure," Incest, and the Ideal of Universal Siblinghood (Stanford: Stanford UP, 1987).

d697. Shullenberger, William. "Lacan and the Play of Desire in Poetry." MSE 7.1 (1978), 33-40.

d698. Shupe, Donald R. "Representation versus Detection as a Model for Psychological Criticism." JAAC 34 (1976), 431-40.

d699. Sibony, Daniel. "Hamlet : A Writing-Effect," in S. Felman, ed. Literature and Psychoanalysis: The Question of Reading: Otherwise (Baltimore: Johns Hopkins UP, 1982), 53-93.

d700. Siegel, Carol. "'Venus Metempsychosis' and Venus in Furs : Masochism and Fertility in Ulysses ." TCL 33.2 (1987), 179-95.

d701. Simon, Bennett. "Tragic Drama and the Family: The Killing of Children and the Killing of Story-Telling,"in S. Rimmon-Kenan, ed. Discourse in Psychoanalysis and Literature (London and NY: Methuen, 1987), 152-75.

d702. Sitterson, Joseph C., Jr. "Psychoanalytical Models and Literary Theory." UTQ 51.1 (1981), 78-92 [on Lacan].

d703. Skulsky, Harold. "The Psychoanalytical 'Reading' of Literature." Neophil 67.3 (1983), 321-40.

d704. Skura, Meredith Anne. "Revisions and Rereadings in Dreams and Allegories." Psychiatry and the Humanities 4 (1980), 345-79.
d705. ----------. The Literary Use of the Psychoanalytic Process (New Haven: Yale UP, 1981).

d706. Slochower, Harry, et al . "Genius, Psychopathology, and Creativity." AI 24 (1967), 3-150.
d707. ----------. "The Psychoanalytic Approach to Literature: Some Pitfalls and Promises." L&P 21 (1971), 107-11.

d708. Smith, Joseph H. "Epilogue: Lacan and the Subject of American Psychoanalysis." Psychiatry and the Humanities 6 (1983), 259-76.

d709. Snider, Clifton. "Jungian Theory, Its Literary Application, and a Discussion of *The Member of the Wedding* ," in J. Natoli, ed. Psychological Perspectives on Literature: Freudian Dissidents and Non-Freudians (Hamden CT: Archon, 1984), 13-42.

d710. Sollers, Philippe. "Freud's Hand," in S. Felman, ed. Literature and Psychoanalysis: The Question of Reading: Otherwise (Baltimore: Johns Hopkins UP, 1982), 329-37.

d711. Spector, Jack J. The Aesthetics of Freud (NY: Praeger, 1973).
d712. ----------. "Freud and Nineteenth-Century Aesthetic Thought." BForum 1 (1974), 263-74.

d713. Spence, Donald P. "Narrative Recursion,"in S. Rimmon-Kenan, ed. Discourse in Psychoanalysis and Literature (London and NY: Methuen, 1987), 188-210.

d714. Spencer, Jenny S. "Norman's *'night Mother* ': Psycho-drama of Female Identity." Modern Drama 30.3 (1987), 364-75.

d715. Speziale-Bagliacca, Roberto. "Monsieur Bovary, c'est moi: Portrait psychoanalytique de Charles Bovary, masochiste moral." Revue française de psychanalyse 38 (1974), 669-705.
d716. ----------. "Lacan l'ineludible." NC 82-83 (1980), 97-129.

d717. Spilka, Mark. "Unleashing the Third Force." Novel 9 (1976), 165-70.

d718. Spivak, Gayatri Chakravorty. "The Letter as Cutting Edge," in S. Felman, ed. Literature and Psychoanalysis: The Question of Reading: Otherwise (Baltimore: Johns Hopkins UP, 1982), 208-26 [Lacan and deconstruction].

d719. Splitter, Randolph. Proust's Recherche: A Psychoanalytic Interpretation (Boston and London: Routledge & Kegan Paul, 1981).

d720. Sprague, Claire. Rereading Doris Lessing: Narrative Patterns of Doubling and Repetition (Chapel Hill: U of North Carolina P, 1987).

d721. Sprich, Robert. "Pressed Flowers/Fresh Flowers: New Directions in Psychoanalytic Criticism." CLQ 13 (1977), 67-72.

d722. Stanton, Martin. <u>Outside the Dream: Lacan and French Styles of Psychoanalysis</u> (Boston and London: Routledge & Kegan Paul, 1983).

d723. Starobinski, Jean. "Psychanalyse et critique littéraire." <u>Preuves</u> 181 (1966), 21-32.
d724. ----------. "La littérature et l'irrationnel." <u>CREL</u> 2 (1974), 4-15.
d725. ----------. "On the Fundamental Gestures of Criticism." <u>NLH</u> 5 (1974), 491-514.

d726. Stavola, Thomas J. <u>Scott Fitzgerald: Crisis in an American Identity</u> (London: Vision, 1979).

d727. Steig, Michael. "Motives for Interpretation: Intention, Response, and Psychoanalysis in Literary Criticism," in V. A. Kramer, ed. <u>American Critics at Work: Intention, Response, and Psychoanalysis in Literary Criticism</u> (Troy NY: Whitston, 1984), 251-64.

d728. Steiner, George. "The Historicity of Dreams." <u>Salmagundi</u> 61 (1983), 6-21.

d729. Steinmetz, Devora. "Oedipus Again! Kinship and Continuity in Ancient Literature." <u>AnSch</u> 3.3 (1985), 43-64.

d730. Stevenson, John Allen. "A Vampire in the Mirror: The Sexuality of *Dracula* ." <u>PMLA</u> 103 (1988), 139-49.

d731. Stierlin, Helm. "Liberation and Self-Destruction in the Creative Process." <u>Psychiatry and the Humanities</u> 1 (1976), 35-50.

d732. Stockholder, Kay. "Worlds in Dreams and Drama: A Psychoanalytic Theory of Literary Representation." <u>DR</u> 62.3 (1982), 374-96.
d733. ----------. <u>Dream Works: Lovers and Families in Shakespeare's Plays</u> (Toronto: U of Toronto P, 1987).

d734. Stora-Sandor, Judith. "Littérature et psychanalyse: Propositions pour une methodologie." <u>LanM</u> 71 (1977), 391-417.

d735. Stout, Janis P. "The Fallen Woman and the Conflicted Author: Hawthorne and Hardy." <u>American Transcendental Quarterly</u> n.s. 1.3 (1987), 233-46.

d736. Strauch, Edward H. "The Scope and Limits of the Freudian Approach to Literature." <u>AJES</u> 5 (1980), 125-43.

d737. Strout, Cushing. "Psyche, Clio, and the Artist," in M. Albin, ed. New Directions in Psychohistory (Lexington MA: Heath, 1980), 97-115.
d738. ----------. "Henry James' Dream of the Louvre, 'The Jolly Corner,' and Psychological Interpretation," in E. Kurzweil and W. Phillips, eds. Literature and Psychoanalysis (NY: Columbia UP, 1983), 217-31.

d739. Strozier, Robert M. "Dynamic Patterns: A Psycho-Analytic Theory of Plot." SoRA 7 (1974), 254-63.

d740. Suleiman, Susan Rubin. "Nadja, Dora, Lol V. Stein: Women, Madness, and Narrative,"in S. Rimmon-Kenan, ed. Discourse in Psychoanalysis and Literature (London and NY: Methuen, 1987), 124-51.

d741. Sundquist, Eric J. Home as Found: Authority and Genealogy in Nineteenth-Century American Literature (Baltimore: Johns Hopkins UP, 1979).

d742. Swan, Jim. "Giving New Depth to the Surface: Psychoanalysis, Literature, and Society." Psychoanalytic Rev 62 (1975), 5-28.

d743. Swanson, Don R. "Toward a Psychology of Metaphor." CritI 5 (1978), 163-66.

d744. Tanner, Tony. Adultery in the Novel: Contract and Transgression (Baltimore: Johns Hopkins UP, 1979) [Lacanian].

d745. Tennenhouse, Leonard, ed. The Practice of Psychoanalytic Criticism (Detroit: Wayne State UP, 1976).

d746. Thoma-Herterich, Christa. Zur Kritik der Psychokritik: Eine literaturwissenschaftliche Auseinandersetzung am Beispiel französischer Arbeiten (Bern: Lang, 1976).

d747. Tobin, Patricia. "From Plague to Porn: The Sexual Text in Freud and John Hawkes," in M. Charney and J. Reppen, eds. Psychoanalytic Approaches to Literature and Film (Rutherford NJ: Fairleigh Dickinson UP, 1987), 282-306.

d748. Todorov, Tzvetan. Théories du symbole (Paris: Seuil, 1977) ["La Rhétorique du Freud"].

d749. Trosman, Harry. Freud and the Imaginative World (Hillsdale NJ: Analytic P, 1985).

d750. Turkle, Sherry. Psychoanalytic Politics: Freud's French Revolution (NY: Basic Books, 1978) [on Lacan].
d751. ----------. "The New Philoosphy and the Agony of Structuralism: Enter the Trojan Horse." ChiR 32.3 (1981), 11-28 [on Lacan].
d752. ----------. "Lacan and America: The Problem of Discourse," in S. L. Gilman, ed. Introducing Psychoanalytic Theory (NY: Brunner/Mazel, 1982), 240-54.

d753. Twitchell, James B. Forbidden Partners: The Incest Taboo in Modern Culture (NY: Columbia UP, 1987).

d754. Urban, Bernd, ed. Psychoanalyse und Literaturwissenschaft: Texte zur Geschichte ihrer Beziehungen (Tubingen: Niemeyer, 1973).

d755. van den Berg, Sara. "Describing Sonnets by Milton and Keats: Roy Schafer's Action Language and the Interpretation of Texts," in J. Natoli, ed. Psychological Perspectives on Literature: Freudian Dissidents and Non-Freudians (Hamden CT: Archon, 1984), 134-54.

d756. Ver Eecke, Wilfried. "Hegel as Lacan's Source for Necessity in Psychoanalytic Theory." Psychiatry and the Humanities 6 (1983), 113-38.

d757. Vergote, Antoine. "From Freud's 'Other Scene' to Lacan's 'Other.'" Psychiatry and the Humanities 6 (1983), 193-222.

d758. Verhoeff, Hans. "Does Oedipus Have His Complex?" Style 18.3 (1984), 261-83.

d759. Waldeck, Peter B. "Anxiety and the Biopsychology of Literature." SUS 10 (1976), 69-84.

d760. Ward, Aileen. "The Psychoanalytic Theory of Poetic Form: A Comment." L&P 17 (1967), 30-37.

d761. Warner, William Beatty. Chance and the Text of Experience: Freud, Nietzsche, and Shakespeare's Hamlet (Ithaca: Cornell UP, 1986).

d762. Watson, George. The Study of Literature (NY: Scribner's, 1969) [chap. 9: "Psycho-analysis"].

d763. Weber, Samuel. "The Sideshow, or: Remarks on a Canny Moment." MLN 88 (1973), 1102-1133.
d764. ----------. "The Divaricator: Remarks on Freud's Witz ." Glyph 1 (1977), 1-27.

d765. ----------. Ruckkehr zu Freud: Jacques Lacans Ent-stellung der Psychoanalyse (Frankfurt am Main: Ullstein, 1978).
d766. ----------. The Legend of Freud (Minneapolis: U of Minnesota P, 1982).
d767. ----------. "The Debts of Deconstruction and Other, Related Assumptions," in J. H. Smith and W. Kerrigan, eds. Taking Chances: Derrida, Psychoanalysis, and Literature (Baltimore: Johns Hopkins UP, 1984), 33-65.

d768. Weiss, David. The Critic Agonistes: Psychology, Myth, and the Art of Fiction (Seattle: U of Washington P, 1985).

d769. Weissman, Stephen M. His Brother's Keeper: A Psychobiography of Samuel Taylor Coleridge (NY: International Universities P, 1987).

d770. Westlund, Joseph. Shakespeare's Restorative Comedies: A Psychoanalytic View of the Middle Plays (Chicago: U of Chicago P, 1984).

d771. Wijsen, Louise. "Psychoanalysis and the Literary Symbol: A Structural Approach to Imagery, Language, and Thought in Literature." DAI 38 (1978), 4860A.

d772. Wilden, Anthony G. "Freud, Signorelli, and Lacan: The Repression of the Signifier." AI 23 (1966), 332-66.
d773. ----------. "Jacques Lacan: A Partial Bibliography." YFS 36-37 (1966), 263-68.
d774. ----------. System and Structure: Essays on Communication and Exchange, 2nd ed. (NY: Methuen, 1980).

d775. Willbern, David. "Freud and the Inter-penetration of Dreams." Diacritics 9.1 (1979), 98-110.

d776. Willemart, Philippe. "La critique littéraire et l'inconscient défini comme ensemble de signifiants censurés." ASEL 3 (1979), 97-102 [psychoanalysis and semiotics].

d777. Wilt, Judith. "'He Would Come Back': The Fathers of Daughters in Daniel Deronda ." Nineteenth Century Literature 47.3 (1987), 313-38.
d778. ----------. "Desperately Seeking Verena: A Resistant Reading of The Bostonians ." Feminist Studies 13.2 (1987), 293-316.

d779. Wiltshire, John. "Freud and the Scientific Imagination." CR 23 (1981), 82-88.

d780. Withim, Philip. "From Symptom to Process: The Movement of Psychoanalytic Criticism." JGE 25 (1973), 173-83.

d781. Wolf, Ernest S. "Psychoanalytic Psychology of the Self and Literature." NLH 12 (1980), 41-60.

d782. Wolf, Mary Ellen. Eros Under Glass: Psychoanalysis and Mallarmé's "Herodiade" (Columbus: Ohio State UP, 1987).

d783. Wolff, Reinhold, ed. Psychoanalytischen Literaturkritik (Munich: Fink, 1975).
d784. ----------. "Castration Symbolism in Baudelaire's Fleurs du mal : An Essay in Psychoanalytic Content Analyses of Literary Texts." Poetics 10.4-5 (1981), 409-56.

d785. Wollheim, Richard. "The Cabinet of Dr. Lacan." NYRB 25 (Jan 1979), 36-45.

d786. Worbs, Michael. Nervenkunst: Literatur und Psychanalyse im Wien der Jahrhundertwende (Frankfurt am Main: Europaische Verlagsanstalt, 1983).

d787. Wordsworth, Ann. "An Art that Will Not Abandon the Self to Language: Bloom, Tennyson and the Blind World of the Wish," in R. Young, ed. Untying the Text: A Post-Structuralist Reader (London: Routledge & Kegan Paul, 1981), 207-22.

d788. Wright, Elizabeth. "Modern Psychoanalytic Criticism," in A. Jefferson and D. Robey, eds. Modern Literary Theory (Totowa NJ: Barnes & Noble, 1982).
d789. ----------. Psychoanalytic Criticism: Theory in Practice (London: Methuen, 1984).
d790. ----------. "Klassische und strukturalistische Ansatze der psychoanalytischen Literaturforschung," in J. Horisch and G. C. Tholen, eds. Eingebildete Texte: Affairen zwischen Psychoanalyse und Literaturwissenschaft (Munich: Fink, 1985), 26-48.
d791. ----------. "Transmission in Psychoanalysis and Literature: Whose Text Is It Anyway?"in S. Rimmon-Kenan, ed. Discourse in Psychoanalysis and Literature (London and NY: Methuen, 1987), 90-103.

d792. Wyatt, David. Prodigal Sons: A Study in Authorship and Authority (Baltimore: Johns Hopkins UP, 1980).

d793. Wygotski, L. S. "Das psychologische Problem der Kunst." KuL 14 (1966), 884-97.

d794. Young, Robert. "The Eye and Progress of His Song: A Lacanian Reading of *The Prelude* ." OLR 3.3 (1979), 78-98.
d795. ----------. "Psychoanalytic Criticism: Has It Got Beyond a Joke." Paragraph 4 (1984), 87-114.

d796. Zwinger, Lynda A. "The Sentimental Gilt of Heterosexuality: James' *The Golden Bowl* ." Raritan 7.2 (1987), 70-92.

E. Sociological Criticism, Literature and Society

e1. Ackerman, James S. "Towards a New Social Theory of Art." NLH 4 (1973), 315-30.

e2. Adriaens, Mark. "Ideology and Literary Production: Kristeva's Poetics," in P. V. Zima, ed. Semiotics and Dialectics: Ideology and the Text (Amsterdam: Benjamins, 1981), 179-220.

e3. Albanese, Ralph, ed. "Sociocriticism." ECr 21.3 (1981) [special issue].

e4. Albrecht, Milton C., James H. Barnett, and Mason Griff, eds. The Sociology of Art and Literature (NY: Praeger, 1970).

e5. Alter, Jean. "Structures narratives: Histoire et fiction: Pour une nouvelle sociologie de la littérature." CREL 3 (1977), 81-86.

e6. Althaus, Horst. Asthetik, Okonomie und Gesellschaft (Berne: Francke, 1971).

e7. Altick, Richard. The English Common Reader: A Social History of the Mass Reading Public, 1800-1900 (Chicago: U of Chicago P, 1975).

e8. Angenot, Marc and Darko Suvin. "Theses sur la 'sociologie' de la littérature." Lit 44 (1981), 117-27.

e9. Anz, Thomas. "Vorschlage zur Grundlegung einer Soziologie literarischer Normen." IASL 9 (1984), 128-44.

e10. Arato, Andrew and Eike Gebhardt, eds. The Essential Frankfurt School Reader (NY: Continuum, 1982).

e11. Bader, Wolfgang. Grundprobleme der Literaturtheorie Lucien Goldmanns: Ein Beitrag zur Analyse des Gesamtwerkes unter dem Blickpunkt: Literatur und ihr Subjekt (Frankfurt: Lang, 1979).

e12. Baldinger, Kurt. "Die Begrundung der Literatursoziologie: Das Lebenswerk Erich Kohlers." RC 34.67-68 (1982), 158-71.

e13. Bantock, G. H. "Literature and the Social Sciences." CritQ 17 (1975), 99-127.

e14. Bark, Joachim, ed. Literatursoziologie. I: Begriff und Methodik. II: Beitrage zur Praxis (Stuttgart: Kohlhammer, 1974).

e15. Barker, F., et al . Literature, Society and the Sociology of Literature (Colchester: U of Essex, 1977).
e16. ----------, et al . 1848: The Sociology of Literature (Colchester: U of Essex, 1978).

e17. Barth, Peter. Literaturtheorie als Gesellschaftstheorie: Zum gesellschaftstheoretischen Traditionzusammenhang burglicher Literaturwissenschaft (Berlin: Author, 1975).

e18. Belleau, André. "La Démarche sociocritique au Québec." V&I 8.2 (1983), 299-310.
e19. ----------, et al . "Sociologies de la littérature." EF 19.3 (1983-84) [special issue].

e20. Bennett, Bruce. "The Truth About Eagles: Lucien Goldmann's Sociology of Literature." NLRev 3 (1977), 39-48.

e21. Bisztray, George. "Literary Sociology and Marxist Theory: The Literary Work as a Social Document." Mosaic 5.2 (1971-72), 47-56.

e22. Boelhower, William Q. "Antonio Gramsci's Sociology of Literature." ConL 22.4 (1981), 574-99.

e23. Booth, Wayne C. "Criticulture: Or, Why we Need at Least Three Criticisms at the Present Time," in P. Hernadi, ed. What Is Criticism? (Bloomington: Indiana UP, 1981), 162-76.

e24. Bourdieu, Pierre. La distinction: Critique sociale du jugement (Paris: Minuit, 1979).

e25. ----------. "The Aristocracy of Culture." Media, Culture and Society 2.3 (1980), 225-54.

e26. ----------. "The Field of Cultural Production, or: The Economic World Reversed." Poetics 12.4-5 (1983), 311-56.

e27. Bradbrook, M. C. Literature in Action: Studies in Continental and Commonwealth Society (London: Chatto & Windus, 1972).

e28. Bradbury, Malcolm. "Literature and Sociology." E&S 23 (1970), 87-100.

e29. ----------. The Social Context of Modern English Literature (NY: Schocken Books, 1971).

e30. Brang, Peter. "Sociological Methods in Twentieth-Century Russian Criticism." YCC 5 (1973), 209-51.

e31. Bruford, Walter H. "Literary Criticism and Sociology." YCC 5 (1973), 3-20.

e32. Burger, Peter. "Zum Problem des Funktionswandels von Kunst und Literatur in der Epoche des Ubergangs von der feudalen zur burglichen Gesellschaft." LiLi 32 (1978), 11-27.

e33. ----------, ed. Seminar: Literatur- und Kunstsoziologie (Frankfurt: Suhrkamp, 1978).

e34. ----------. "Literary Institution and Modernization." Poetics 12.4-5 (1983), 419-33.

e35. Burns, Elizabeth and Tom Burns, eds. Sociology of Literature and Drama (Harmondsworth: Penguin, 1973).

e36. Charvat, William. The Profession of Authorship in America, 1800-1870 (Columbus: Ohio State UP, 1968).

e37. Clark, Priscilla B. The Battle of the Bourgeois: The Novel in France, 1789-1848 (Paris: Didier, 1973).

e38. ----------. "The Comparative Method: Sociology and the Study of Literature." YCGL 23 (1974), 5-13.

e39. ----------. "Literary Culture in France and the United States." American Journal of Sociology 84 (1979), 1057-77.

e40. ----------. "Literature and Sociology," in J.-P. Barricelli and J. Gibaldi, eds. Interrelations of Literature (NY: MLA, 1982), 107-22.

e41. Corner, John. "Criticism as Sociology: Reading the Media," in J. Hawthorn, ed. Criticism and Critical Theory (London: Arnold, 1984), 29-41.

e42. Corradi, Juan E. "Textures: Approaching Society, Ideology, Literature." I&L 1.2 (1977), 5-21.

e43. Corredor, Eva. "Sociocritical and Marxist Literary Theory," in J. Natoli, ed. Tracing Literary Theory (Urbana: U of Illinois P, 1987), 104-26.

e44. Craig, David. "Towards Laws of Literary Development." Mosaic 5.2 (1971-72), 11-30.
e45. ----------. The Real Foundation: Literature and Social Change (NY: Oxford UP, 1974).

e46. Creedy, Jean, ed. The Social Context of Art (London: Tavistock, 1970).

e47. Cros, Edmund. "Foundations of a Sociocriticism: Methodological Proposals and an Application to the case of the Buscon (Part II)." I&L 1.4 (1977), 63-80.
e48. ----------. "Eléments de sociocritiqe." Imprévue 1 (1982), 1-160.
e49. ----------. Théorie et pratiques sociocritiques (Montpellier: Centre d'Etudes et de Recherches Sociocrit., n.d.) [Theory and Practice of Sociocriticism (Minneapolis: U of Minnesota P, 1988)].
e50. ----------. "Sociocritique et génétique textuelle." Degrés 46-47 (1986), d1-d13.

e51. Darnton, Robert. "Reading, Writing, and Publishing in Eighteenth-Century France: A Case Study in the Sociology of Literature." Daedalus 100 (1971), 214-56.

e52. Dubois, Jacques. "Théories et positions actuelles, IV: Sociologie de la lecture et concept de lisibilité." RLV 41 (1975), 471-83.
e53. ----------. L'Institution de la littérature: Introduction a une sociologie (Brussels: Labor, 1970).

e54. Duchet, Claude. "Pour une socio-critique, ou variations sur un incipit." Littérature 1 (1971), 5-14.
e55. ----------, B. Merigot, and A. P. van Teslaar, eds. Sociocritique. Colloque organisé par l'Univ. de Paris-VIII et New York Univ. (Paris: Nathan, 1979).

e56. Duvignand, Jean. The Sociology of Art (NY: Harper & Row, 1972).
e57. ----------. "Esquisse d'une methode d'analyse sociologique d'un text littéraire." ECr 21.3 (1981), 5-14.

e58. Eibl, Karl. "Die aesthetische Rolle: Fragmente einer literatursoziologie in literaturgeschichtlicher Absicht." SG 24 (1971), 1091-1120.

e59. Escarpit, Robert. Sociology of Literature (Painesville OH: Lake Erie College Studies, 1965).
e60. ----------. The Book Revolution (London: Harrap; Paris: UNESCO, 1966).
e61. ----------. "The Sociology of Literature." International Encyclopedia of the Social Sciences, 9 (NY: Macmillan and Free Press, 1968), 417-25.
e62. ----------, ed. La Littéraire et le social (Paris: Flammarion, 1970).

e63. Evans, Mary. Lucien Goldmann: An Introduction (Sussex: Harvester P; Atlantic Highlands NJ: Humanities P, 1981).

e64. Feenberg, Andrew. "Aesthetics as Social Theory: Introduction to Feher's 'Is the Novel Problematic?'" Telos 15 (1973), 41-46.

e65. Feher, Ferenc. "Ideology as Demiurge in Modern Art." Praxis 3 (1976), 184-95.

e66. Fokkema, Douwe W. "The Social Significance of Literature as Art." YCGL 26 (1977), 5-9.

e67. Forster, Peter G. and Celia Kennford. "Sociological Theory and the Sociology of Literature." British Journal of Sociology 24.3 (1973), 355-64.

e68. Frye, Northrop. The Critical Path: An Essay on the Social Context of Literary Criticism (Bloomington: Indiana UP, 1971).

e69. Fugen, Hans N., ed. Wege der Literatursoziologie (Neuwied: Luchterhand, 1968).
e70. ----------. Die Hauptrichtungen der Literatursoziologie und ihre Methoden, 5th ed. (Bonn: Bouvier, 1971).
e71. ----------. Dichtung in der burgerlichen Gesellschaft (Bonn: Bouvier, 1972).
e72. ----------. "Literary Criticism and Sociology in Germany." YCC 5 (1973), 252-69.

e73. Garnham, Nicholas and Raymond Williams. "Pierre Bourdieu and the Sociology of Culture: An Introduction." Media, Culture and Society 2.3 (1980), 209-23.

e74. Giotta, Francesco. "La recherche sociologique du normatif littéraire." RITL 23 (1974), 217-26.

e75. Gohler, Helma. "Soziologische Aspekte der Bezeihung Personlichkeit und Literatur." WZUB 26 (1977), 131-39.

e76. Goldmann, Lucien. "The Sociology of Literature: Status and Problems of Method." ISSJ 19 (1967), 493-516.

e77. ----------. The Human Sciences and Philosophy (London: Jonathan Cape, 1969).

e78. ----------. Structures mentales et création culturelle (Paris: Anthropos, 1970).

e79. ----------. Marxisme et sciences humaines (Paris: Gallimard, 1970).

e80. ----------. Situation de la critique Racinienne (Paris: L'Arche, 1971).

e81. ----------. Racine (Cambridge: Rivers P, 1972).

e82. ----------. Towards the Sociology of the Novel (London: Methuen, 1975).

e83. ----------. Cultural Creation in Modern Society (St. Louis, Telos, 1976).

e84. ----------. "Genesis and Structure." Gradiva 1 (1978), 259-66 [followed by a discussion, 267-72].

e85. ----------. Methodology in the Sociology of Literature (St. Louis: Telos, 1980).

e86. [Goldmann and l'Institut de Sociologie]. Littérature et Société. Problemes de methodologie en sociologie de la littérature (Brussels: Free University of Brussels, 1967).

e87. ----------. Sociologie de la littérature: Recherches récentes et discussions (Brussels: Free University of Brussels, 1969).

e88. ----------. Critique sociologique et critique psychoanalytique (Brussels: Free University of Brussels, 1970).

e89. Gombrich, E. H. In Search of Cultural History (Oxford: Clarendon P, 1969).

e90. Goodlad, J. S. R. A Sociology of Popular Drama (Totowa NJ: Rowman and Littlefield, 1972).

e91. Graff, Gerald. "Literary Criticism as Social Diagnosis," in H. L. Sussman, ed. At the Boundaries (Boston: Northeastern UP, 1983), 1-21.

e92. Graña, César. Fact and Symbol: Essays in the Sociology of Art and Literature (NY: Oxford UP, 1971).

e93. Gunn, Daniel P. "Toward Social Criticism," in R. Sanderlin and C. Barrow, eds. Politics, Society, and the Humanities (Chattanooga TN: Southern Humanities, 1984), 75-81.

e94. Hall, John. The Sociology of Literature (London: Longman, 1979).

e95. Hamburger, Michael. Vernunft und Rebellion: Aufsatze zur Gesellschaftskritik in der deutschen Literatur (Munich: Hanser, 1969).

e96. Hansen, Olaf. "Hermeneutik und Literatursoziologie: Zwei Modelle. Marxistische Literaturtheorie in America. Zum Problem der *American Studies* ," in T. E. Metscher, *et al* . Literaturwissenschaft und Sozialwissenschaften: Grundlagen und Modellanalysen (Stuttgart: Metzler, 1971), 357-99.

e97. Hardt, Manfred. "Struktur und Vermittlung: Zu einem Hauptproblem der Literatursoziologie (Am Beispiel der *Madam Bovary*)." ZFSL 90 (1980), 47-65.

e98. Harold, Brent. "The Intrinsic Sociology in Fiction." MFS 23 (1977-78), 593-99.

e99. Harth, Dietrich. "Begriffsbildung in der Literaturwissenschaft. Beobachtungen zum Wandel der 'semantischen Orientierung.'" DVLG 45 (1971), 397-433.
e100. ----------. "Anmerkungen zur empirischen und ideologiekritischen Literatursoziologie." Archiv 222.2 (1985), 252-64.

e101. Hartwig, Helmut. "Literatursoziologie und das Problem der Klassenuberschreibung: Zur Soszologie asthetischer Fragestellungen," in T. E. Metscher, *et al* . Literaturwissenschaft und Sozialwissenschaften: Grundlagen und Modellanalysen (Stuttgart: Metzler, 1971), 315-40.

e102. Hegedus, Andras. "Literature and the Social Sciences as Specific Forms of Cognition: A Sociological Inquiry." HungS 3 (1968), 123-31.

e103. Heyndels, Ralph and Edmund Cros, eds. Operativité des méthodes sociocritiques (Montpellier: Centre d'Etudes et Recherches Sociocrits., 1984) [includes Heyndels' "Sociocritique du texte discontinu: Quelques réflexions premieres," 45-53].

e104. Hoggart, Richard. "Literature and Society," in N. MacKenzie, ed. A Guide to the Social Sciences (London: Weidenfeld and Nicolson, 1966), 225-48.

e105. Hohendahl, Peter Uwe. "Empfindsamkeit und gesellschaftliches Bewusstein. Zur Sociologie des empfindsamen Romans am Beispiel von *La Vie de Marianne, Clarissa, Fraulein von Sternheim,* und *Werther* ." Jahrbuch der deutschen Schillergesellschaft 16 (1972), 176-207.

e106. Jahn, Gary R. "The Aesthetic Theory of Leo Tolstoy's *What Is Art?* " JAAC 34 (1975), 59-65.

e107. Jameson, Fredric. The Political Unconscious: Narrative as a Socially Symbolic Act (Ithaca: Cornell UP, 1981).

e108. Jauss, Hans-R. and Claus Muller-Daehn, eds. Gerhard Hess. Gesellschaft, Literatur, Wissenschaft: Gesammelte Schriften, 1938-1966 (Munchen: Fink, 1967).

e109. Karbusicky, Vladimir. "The Interaction Between 'Reality--Work of Art--Society." International Social Science Journal 20 (1968), 644-55.

e110. Kavolis, Vytautas. Artistic Expression: A Sociological Analysis (Ithaca: Cornell UP, 1968).
e111. ----------. History on Art's Side: Social Dynamism in Artistic Efflorescences (Ithaca: Cornell UP, 1972).

e112. Khalizev, V. "Die Literatur undter historisch-funktionalem Aspekt." KuL 28.11 (1980), 1132-47.

e113. Kogan, L. and L. Iwanko. "Soziologische Methoden in der Literaturkritik? Steitgesprache zwischen Soziologen und Literaturkritikern--Rechnen, um zu streiten." KuL 23 (1975), 115-24.

e114. Kohler, Erich. "Einige Thesen zur Literatursoziologie." Germanisch-romanische Monatsschrift n.s. 24 (1974), 257-64.

e115. Kowski, Wadim. "Soziologische Methoden in der Literaturkritik? Streitgesprache zwischen Soziologen und Literaturkritikern--Soziologie der Literatur oder Soziologie gegen Literatur?" KuL 23 (1975), 131-40.

e116. Kreuzer, Helmut and Kate Hamburger. Gestaltungsgeschichte und Gesellschaftsgeschichte: Literatur-, Kunst-, und Musikwissenschaftliche Studien (Stuttgart: Metzler, 1969).

e117. Kristensen, Sven Moller. Literary Sociology: Four Lectures (Brugge: De Tempel, 1975).

e118. Kroeber, Karl. "Fictional Theory and Social History: The Need for a Synthetic Criticism." VS 19 (1975), 99-106.

e119. Laurenson, Diana. "A Sociological Study of Authorship." British Journal of Sociology 20 (1969), 311-25.
e120. ---------- and Alan Swingewood. The Sociology of Literature (London: MacGibbon and Kee; NY: Schocken, 1972).
e121. ----------, ed. The Sociology of Literature: Applied Studies (Keele: Sociological Review, 1977).

e122. Leenhardt, Jacques. "The Sociology of Literature: Some Stages in Its History." International Social Science Journal 19 (1967), 517-33.

e123. ----------. "Introduction a la sociologie de la littérature." Mosaic 5.2 (1971-72), 1-10.

e124. ----------. "Towards a Sociological Aesthetic: An Attempt at Constructing the Aesthetic of Lucien Goldmann." Sub-Stance 15 (1976), 94-104.

e125. ----------. "Lecture critique de la théorie goldmannienne du roman," in C. B. Duchet, et al . Sociocritique (Paris: Nathan, 1979), 172-82.

e126. ----------. "Introduction a la sociologie de la lecture." RSH 177 (1980), 39-55.

e127. ----------. "Toward a Sociology of Reading." in S. R. Suleiman and I. Crosman, eds. The Reader in the Text: Essays on Audience and Interpretation (Princeton: Princeton UP, 1980), 205-24.

e128. ----------. "Les Procédures critiques de la sociologie de la littérature." Degrés 12.39-40 (1984), k1-k13.

e129. ----------. "L'Opérationnalisation des procédures critiques de la sociologie de la littérature," in R. Heyndels and E. Cros, eds. Opérativité des méthodes sociocritiques (Montpellier: Centre d'Etudes et Recherches Sociocrit., 1984), 67-83.

e130. Lefebvre, Joel. "Bemerkungen zur literatursoziologischen Forschung in Frankreich." JIG 17.1 (1985), 8-24.

e131. Literaturwissenschaft und Sozialwissenschaften: Grundlagen und Modellanalysen (Stuttgart: Metzler, 1971).

e132. Lowenthal, Leo. "Literature and Sociology," in J. Thorpe, ed. Relations of Literary Study: Essays on Interdisciplinary Contributions (NY: MLA, 1967), 89-110.

e133. ----------. Erzahlkunst und Gesellschaft in der deutschen Literatur des 19. Jahrhunderts (Neuwied: Luchterhand, 1971).

e134. ----------. "Literatursoziologie im Ruckblick," in H. von Alemann and H. P. Thurn, eds. Soziologie in weltburgerlicher Absicht: Festschrift fur René Konig (Opladen: Westdeutscher, 1981), 101-13.

e135. Macherey, Pierre. Pour une théorie de la production littéraire (Paris: Maspero, 1966).

e136. Marcus, Steven. Representations: Essays on Literature and Society (NY: Random, 1976).

e137. Markiewicz, Henryk. "Gesellschaftliche Bedingtheit und soziologischer Schematismus in der Literaturtheorie." WB 18.8 (1972), 136-49.

e138. McGuire, Steven. "Interpretive Sociology and Paul Ricoeur." HumanS 4.2 (1981), 179-200.

e139. McHoul, Alexander. "Ethnomethodology and Literature: Preliminaries to a Sociology of Reading." Poetics 7 (1978), 113-20.

e140. Medvedev, P. N. and M. M. Bakhtin. The Formal Method in Literary Scholarship: A Critical Introduction to Sociological Poetics (Baltimore: Johns Hopkins UP/Goucher Coller, 1978).

e141. Metscher, Thomas W. "Hegel und die philosophische Grundlegung der Kunstsoziologie," in T. E. Metscher, et al . Literaturwissenschaft und Sozialwissenschaften: Grundlagen und Modellanalysen (Stuttgart: Metzler, 1971), 13-80.

e142. Meyersohn, Rolf. Sociology and Cultural Studies: Some Problems (Birmingham: Center for Contemporary Cultural Studies, 1969).

e143. Miles, David H. "Literary Sociology: Some Introductory Notes." GQ 48 (1975), 1-35.

e144. Mills, Gordon. Hamlet's Castle: The Study of Literature as a Social Experience (Austin: U of Texas P, 1976).

e145. Minder, Robert. Dichter in der Gesellschaft: Erfahrungen mit deutscher und franzosischer Literatur (Frankfurt am Main: Insel, 1966).

e146. Morrow, Raymond A. "La Théorie critique de l'Ecole de Francfort: Implications pour une sociologie de la littérature." EF 19.3 (1983-84), 35-49.

e147. Muhlmann, Wilhelm Emil. "Tradition and Revolution in Literature: Socioliterary Sketches in the Light of German Writing." YCC 5 (1973), 124-73.

e148. Muir, Edwin. Essays on Literature and Society, rev. and enl. ed. (Cambridge: Harvard UP, 1967).

e149. Muller-Seidel, Walter, et al . Historizitat in Sprach- und Literaturwissenshcaft (Munich: Fink, 1974).

e150. Nair, S. and M. Lowy. Lucien Goldmann, ou la dialectique de la totalité (Paris: Seghers, 1973).

e151. Naumann, Manfred. "Remaques sur le rapport du 'littéraire' et du 'social.'" PP 26.3-4 (1983), 131-36.

e152. Neumann, Thomas. Der Kunstler in der burgerlichen Gesellschaft: Entwurf einer Kunstsoziologie am Beispiel der Kunstlerasthetik Friedrich Schillers (Stuttgart: Enke, 1968).

e153. Nielsen, Greg Marc. "Esquisse d'une sociologie critique au dela de Lukacs et Goldmann." EF 19.3 (1983-84), 83-92.

e154. Ohmann, Richard. "Speech, Literature, and the Space Between." NLH 4 (1972-73), 47-63.
e155. ----------. "The Social Definition of Literature," in P. Hernadi, ed. What Is Literature? (Bloomington: Indiana UP, 1978), 89-101.
e156. ----------. "The Social Relations of Criticism," in P. Hernadi, ed. What Is Criticism? (Bloomington: Indiana UP, 1981), 189-98.

e157. Orr, John. Tragic Realism and Modern Society: Studies in the Sociology of the Modern Novel (Pittsburgh: U of Pittsburgh P, 1978).
e158. ----------. Tragic Drama and Modern Society (London: Macmillan, 1981).

e159. Philippi, Klaus-Peter. "Methodologische Probleme der Literatursoziologie. Kritische Bemerkungen zu einer fragwurdigen Situation." Wirkendes Wort 20 (1970), 217-30.
e160. ----------. "Uberlegungen zu den wissenschaftstheoretischen Voraussetzungen 'soziologischer' Interpretation." DVLG 49 (1975), 425-48.

e161. Pratt, Mary. "Art without Critics and Critics without Readers, or Pantagruel versus The Incredible Hulk," in P. Hernadi, ed. What Is Criticism? (Bloomington: Indiana UP, 1981), 177-88.

e162. Ramsey, Paul. "Society and Poetry," in A. Preminger, ed. Princeton Encyclopedia of Poetry and Poetics (Princeton: Princeton UP, 1965), 775-79.
e163. ----------. "Literary Criticism and Sociology." YCC 5 (1973), 21-29.

e164. Remak, Henry H. H. "The Comparative Method: Sociology and the Study of Literature." YCGL 23 (1975), 25-28.

e165. Ricken, Ulrich. "La description littéraire des structures sociales" Essai d'une approche sémantique." Lit 4 (1971), 53-62.

e166. Roberts, Thomas J. "The Network of Literary Identification: A Sociological Preface." NLH 5 (1973), 67-90.

e167. Robinson, David. "Manifestations of the Utopian Mentality: Literayr and Social Criticism." ELUD 1.1 (1973), 35-50.

e168. Rosengren, Karl Erik. Sociological Aspects of the Literary System (Stockholm: Natur och kultur, 1968).

e169. Rossbacher, Karlheinz. Heimatkunstbewegung und Heimatroman: Zu einer Literatursoziologie der Jahrhundertwende (Stuttgart: Klett, 1975).

e170. Rothe, Wolfgang. "Schriftsteller und Gesellschaft im 20. Jahrhundert," in O. Mann and W. Rothe, eds. Deutsche Literatur im 20. Jahrhundert: Strukturen und Gestalten, 5ht ed. (Berne: Francke, 1967), 1. 189-221.

e171. Routh, Janet. and J. Wolff, eds. The Sociology of Literature: Theoretical Approaches (Keele: Sociological Review, 1977).

e172. Rudnick, Hans H. "Recent British and American Studies Concerning Sociology of Literature." YCC 5 (1973), 270-81.

e173. Ruff, Ivan. "Can There Be a Sociology of Literature?" British Jour. of Sociology 25.3 (1974), 367-72.

e174. Sagarra, Eda. Tradition and Revolution: German Literature and Society 1830-1890 (London: Weidenfeld and Nicolson, 1971).

e175. Sammons, Jeffrey L. "The Threat of Literary Sociology and What to Do About It." YCC 5 (1973), 30-40.
e176. ----------. "Truth and Time: A Literary-Sociological Inquiry." CollG 8 (1974), 222-39.
e177. ----------. Literary Sociology and Practical Criticism: An Inquiry (Bloomington: Indiana UP, 1978).

e178. Sampson, David. "Literature versus Society: Recent Trends in Literary Criticism." SoRA 12.3 (1979), 264-84.

e179. Sarkany, Stephané. Le point du vue social dans les études littéraires: Panorama critique (Ottawa: Carleton U, Dept. of French, 1976).
e180. ----------. La Théorie de la littérature en tant que socience sociale (Bucharest: Kriterion, 1979).

e181. Scharfschwerdt, Jurgen. Grundprobleme der Literatursoziologie: Ein wissenschaftlicher Uberblick (Stuttgart: Kohlhammer, 1977).

e182. Schlaffer, Heinz. Der Burger als Held: Sozialgeschichtliche Auflosungen literarischer Widerspruche (Frankfurt am Main: Suhrkamp, 1973).

e183. Schmidt, Wolf-Heinrich. "Probleme der Soziologie literarischer Gattungen," in W.-H. Schmidt and K.-D. Seemann, eds. Gattungsprobleme der alteren slavischen Literaturen (Wiesbaden: Harrassowitz, 1984), 291-310.

e184. Schucking, Levin I. The Sociology of Literary Taste (Chicago: U of Chicago P; London: Routledge & Kegan Paul, 1966).

e185. Seaton, James. "Critical Theory and Popular Culture: The Example of Marcuse." MarkhamR 9 (1980), 56-60.

e186. Silbermann, Alphons. "Literaturphilosophie, soziologische Literaturasthetik oder Literatursoziologie." Kolner Zeitschrift fur Soziologie und Sozialpsychologie 18 (1966), 139-48.
e187. ----------. "Introduction: A Definition of the Sociology of Art." Int. Social Science Journal 20 (1968), 567-88.
e188. ----------. "On the Effects of Literature as a Means of Mass Communication." YCC 5 (1973), 174-94.
e189. ----------. "Erkenntnisinteressen der empirischen Literatursoziologie,"in H. von Alemann and H. P. Thurn, eds. Soziologie in weltburgerlicher Absicht: Festschrift fur René Konig (Opladen: Westdeutscher, 1981), 114-21.

e190. "Socio-Criticism." Sub-Stance 15 (1976) [special issue].

e191. "La Sociologie et les recherches littéraires." CREL 2 (1980) [special issue].

e192. Sommer, Dietrich and Dietrich Loffler. "Soziologische Probleme der literarischen Wirkungsforschung." WB 16, Heft 8 (1970), 51-77.
e193. ----------, et al , eds. Funktion und Wirkung: Soziologische Untersuchungen zur Literatur und Kunst (Berlin: Aufbau, 1978).

e194. Spearman, Diana. The Novel and Society (London & Routledge & Kegan Paul, 1966).

e195. Spivak, Gayatri Chakravorty. "Explanation and Culture: Marginalia." HIS 2 (1979), 201-21.

e196. Stock, Brian. "Literary Discourse and the Social Historian." NLH 8 (1977), 183-94.

e197. Stocklein, Paul. "Literatursoziologie. Gesichtspunkte zur augenblicken Diskussion," in R. Grimm and C. Wiedemann, eds. Literatur und Geistesgeschichte (Berlin: Erich Schmidt, 1968), 406-21.

e198. Strachan, Peter. "Literature as Manipulation: Towards a Social Application of Literary Studies." BJA 19 (1979), 342-51.

e199. Strelka, Joseph. Die gelenkten Musen: Dichtung und Gesellschaft (Vienna: Europa, 1971).

e200. Suvin, Darko. "Some Introductory Remarks on Sociological Approaches to Literature and Paraliterature." Culture & Context 1 (1980), 33-55.

e201. Swingewood, Alan. "Literature and *Praxis* : A Sociological Commentary." NLH 5 (1973), 169-76.
e202. ----------. The Novel and Revolution (London: Macmillan; NY: Barnes & Noble, 1975).
e203. ----------. The Myth of Mass Culture (London: Macmillan, 1977).
e204. ----------. Sociological Poetics and Aesthetic Theory (NY: St. Martin's P, 1987).

e205. Thomson, George. Aeschylus and Athens: A Study in the Social Origins of Drama, 3rd ed. (NY: Haskell House, 1967).

e206. Tober, Karl. "Poetry, History, and Society? Reflections on Method." YCC 5 (1973), 41-55.

e207. Todd, William Mills. "Between Marxism and Semiotics: Lidiia Ginzburg and Soviet Literary Sociology." CASS 19.2 (1985), 159-66.

e208. Ulmer, Gregory. "Sociocriticism." Novel 11 (1977), 70-76.

e209. Varga, Karoly. "The Sociological Approach to Literature," in Lajos Nyiro, ed. Literature and Its Interpretation (The Hague: Mouton, 1979), 231-302.

e210. Virden, Phil. "The Social Determinants of Aesthetic Styles." BJA 12 (1972), 175-85.

e211. Ward, Albert. Book Production, Fiction, and the German Reading Public 1740-1800 (Oxford: Clarendon, 1974).

e212. Warneken, Bernd J. "Zur Kritik positivistischer Literatusoziologie: Anhand von Fugens *Die Hauptrichtungen der Literatursoziologie* ," in T. W. Metscher, *et al* . Literaturwissenschaft und Sozialwissenschaften: Grunlagen und Modellanalysen (Stuttgart: Metzler, 1971), 81-150.

e213. Watson, George. The Study of Literature: A New Rationale of Literary History (NY: Scribner's, 1969) [chap. 10: "Sociology"].

e214. Wolff, Janet. The Social Production of Art (London: Macmillan, 1981).
e215. ----------. Aesthetics and the Sociology of Art (London: Allen & Unwin, 1983).

e216. Zéraffa, Michel. Roman et société (Paris: PUF, 1971).

e217. Zima, Peter V. Goldmann: Dialectique de l'Immanente (Paris: Universitaires, 1973).
e218. ----------. Textsoziologie (Stuttgart: Metzler, 1980).
e219. ----------. "Text and Context: The Socio-Linguistic Nexus," in Zima, ed. Semiotics and Dialectics: Ideology and the Text (Amsterdam: Benjamins, 1981), 103-35.
e220. ----------. "Literatursoziologie-Textsoziologie," in D. Harth and P. Gebhardt, eds. Erkenntnis der Literatur: Theorien, Konzepte, Methoden der Literaturwissenschaft (Stuttgart: Metzler, 1982), 161-94.
e221. ----------. "Die Komparatistik zwischen Asthetik und Textsoziologie." Sprachkunst 16.1 (1985), 113-40.

e222. Zolkiewski, Stefan. "Conceptions fof a Theory of Literary Production," in J. Odmark, ed. Language, Literature & Meaning II: Current Trends in Literary Research (Amsterdam: Benjamins, 1980), 141-99.

F. Marxist Criticism, Literature and Politics

f1. Aaron, Daniel. Writers on the Left (NY: Avon Books, 1965).

f2. Aarsleff, Hans. "Scholarship and Ideology: Joseph Bédier's Critique of Romantic Medievalism," in J. J. McGann, ed. Historical Studies and Literary Criticism (Madison: U of Wisconsin P, 1985), 93-113.

f3. Abicht, Ludo. "Marx, Freud, and the Writers: A New Attempt at Integration." Style 18.3 (1984), 377-86 [Jameson].

f4. Adereth, Maxwell. Commitment in Modern French Literature (London: Gollancz, 1967).

f5. Adorno, Theodor W. Noten zur Literatur, 4 vols. (Frankfurt: Suhrkamp, 1958-74).
f6. ----------. Kierkegaard. Konstruktion des Aesthetischen (Frankfurt am Main: Suhrkamp, 1966).
f7. ----------. Ohne Leitbild (Frankfurt am Main: Suhrkamp, 1967).
f8. ----------. Prisms: Cultural Criticism and Society (London: Spearman, 1967; Cambridge: MIT Press, 1981).
f9. ----------, ed. Uber Walter Benjamin (Frankfurt am Main: Suhrkamp, 1968).
f10.----------. Gesammelte Schriften, 23 vols. (Frankfurt: Suhrkamp, 1970--).
f11. ----------. Asthetische Theorie (Frankfurt am Main: Suhrkamp, 1970 [Aesthetic Theory (London & Boston: Routledge & Kegan Paul, 1984)].

f12. Alter, Jean. "Aux limites du marxisme: Fredric Jameson, l'inconscient politique, et au dela." ECr 21.3 (1981), 79-94.

f13. Anderson, Perry. "Modernity and Revolution," in C. Nelson and L. Grossberg, eds. Marxism and the Interpretation of Culture (Urbana: U of Illinois P, 1988), 317-38.

f14. Apostolides, Jean-Marie. Le prince sacrifié: théatre et politique au temps de Louis XIV (Paris: Minuit, 1985).

f15. Apple, Max. "Marxism and Comedy." RUS 61.1 (1975), 1-11.

f16. Arac, Jonathan, ed. "Engagements: Postmodernism, Marxism, Politics." Boundary 11.1-2 (1982-83) [special issue].
f17. ----------, ed. Postmodernism and Politics (Minneapolis" U of Minnesota P, 1986).
f18. ----------. Critical Genealogies: Historical Situations for Postmodern Literary Studies (NY: Columbia UP, 1987) [chap. 8 on Walter Benjamin; chap. 11 on Fredric Jameson].

f19. Arato, Andrew and Eike Gerhardt, eds. The Essential Frankfurt School Reader (NY: Urizen, 1978).
f20. ---------- and Paul Breines. The Young Lukacs and the Origins of Western Marxism (NY: Seabury P, 1979).

f21. Aronowitz, Stanley. "Culture and Politics." Politics and Society 6.3 (1976), 347-96.

f22. "Art and Ideology." Praxis 6 (1982) [special issue].

f23. Arvon, Henri. Marxist Esthetics (Ithaca: Cornell UP, 1973).

f24. Aubery, Pierre. "Culture proletarienne et littérature ouvriere." ELit 6 (1973), 353-61.

f25. Bahr, Ehrhard and Ruth G. Kunzer. George Lukacs (NY: Ungar, 1972).

f26. Bahti, Timothy. "History as Rhetorical Enactment: Walter Benjamin's Theses 'On the Concept of History.'" Diacritics 9 (1979), 2-17.

f27. Baldwin, Anna P. The Theme of Government in Piers Plowman (Cambridge: D. S. Brewer, 1981).

f28. Balibar, Etienne and Pierre Macherey. "Sur la littérature comme forme idéologique: Quelques hypothéses marxistes." Lit 13 (1974), 29-48.

f29. Bance, A. F., ed. Weimar Germany: Writers and Politics (Edinburgh: Scottish Academic Press, 1982).

f30. Barber, Benjamin R. and Michael J. Gargas McGrath, eds. The Artist and Political Vision (New Brunswick NJ: Transaction Books, 1982) [includes Barber's "Rousseau and Brecht: Political Virtue and the Tragic Imagination," 1-30].

f31. Barck, Karlheinz and Brigitte Burmeister, eds. Ideologie-Literatur-Kritik: Franzosische Beitrage zur marxistischen Literaturtheorie (Berlin: Akademie, 1977).

f32. Barker, Francis. "Ideology, Production, Text: Pierre Macherey's Materialist Criticism." Praxis 5 (1981), 99-108.
f33. ----------, et al. The Politics of Theory (Colchester: U of Essex, 1983).

f34. Barnett, Raymond. "Raymond Williams and Marxism: A Rejoinder to Terry Eagleton." New Left Review 99 (1976), 47-64.

f35. Barrett, Michele, et al. Ideology and Cultural Production (London: Croom Helm, 1979).
f36. ---------- and Jean Radford. "Modernism in the 1930s: Dorothy Richardson and Virginia Woolf," in 1936: The Sociology of Literature: Vol. 1, The Politics of Modernism (Colchester: U of Essez, 1979), 252-72.
f37. ----------. "The Place of Aesthetics in Marxist Criticism," in C. Nelson and L. Grossberg, eds. Marxism and the Interpretation of Culture (Urbana: U of Illinois P, 1988), 697-713.

f38. Barth, P. "Literaturtheorie als Gesellschaftstheorie: Zum gesellschaftstheoretischen Traditionszusammenhang burgerlicher Literaturwissenschaft." DAI 38 (1978), 4625C.

f39. Barthes, Roland. Writing Degree Zero (NY: Hill & Wang, 1968).
f40. ----------. Mythologies (NY: Hill & Wang, 1972).

f41. Bathrick, David. "Marxism and Modernism." NGC 33 (1984), 207-17.

f42. Baxandall, Lee. "Marxism and Aesthetics: A Critique of the Contribution of George Plekhanov." JAAC 25 (1967), 267-79.
f43. ----------. Marxism and Aesthetics: A Selective Annotated Bibliography. Books and Articles in the English Language (NY: Humanities, 1968).

f44. ----------, ed. <u>Radical Perspectives in the Arts</u> (Baltimore: Penguin, 1972).

f45. ---------- and Stefan Morawski, eds. <u>Marx and Engels on Literature and Art</u> (St. Louis: Telos, 1973).

f46. ----------. "The Marxist Orientation to Art and Literature." <u>NGC</u> 3 (1974), 163-80.

f47. Beker, Miroslav. "Marxism and the Determinants of Critical Judgment." <u>JAAC</u> 29 (1970), 33-41.

f48. Bell, Gene H. "Ideology and American Literary Criticism." <u>Science and Society</u> 37 (1973), 300-25.

f49. Belsey, Catherine. "Literature, History, Politics." <u>L&H</u> 9.1 (1983), 17-27.

f50. Benjamin, Walter. <u>Illuminations</u> (NY: Harcourt, 1969).

f51. ----------. <u>Charles Baudelaire: A Lyric Poet in the Era of High Capitalism</u> (London: New Left Books, 1972).

f52. ----------. <u>Gesammelte Schriften</u>, 6 vols. (Frankfurt am Main: Suhrkamp, 1972-85).

f53. ----------. <u>Understanding Brecht</u> (London: New Left Books, 1973).

f54. ----------. <u>Origin of German Tragic Drama</u> (London: New Left Books, 1977).

f55. ----------. <u>Reflections: Essays, Aphorisms, Autobiographical Writings</u> (NY: Harcourt, 1978).

f56. ----------. <u>One-Way Street and Other Writings</u> (London: New Left Books, 1979).

f57. ----------. <u>Benjamin uber Kafka: Texte, Briefzeugnisse, Aufzeichnungen</u> (Frankfurt am Main: Suhrkamp, 1981).

f58. Bennett, Tony. <u>Formalism and Marxism</u> (London: Methuen, 1979).

f59. ----------. "Marxism and Popular Fiction." <u>L&H</u> 7.2 (1981), 138-65.

f60. ----------. "*Formalism and Marxism* Revisited." <u>SoRA</u> 15.1 (1982), 3-21.

f61. ----------. "Marxism and Popular Fiction: Problems and Prospects." <u>SoRA</u> 15.2 (1982), 218-33.

f62. ----------. "Text and History," in P. Widdowson, ed. <u>Re-Reading English</u> (London: Methuen, 1982), 223-36.

f63. ----------. "Marxist Cultural Politics: In Search of 'The Popular.'" <u>AJCS</u> 1.2 (1983), 2-28.

f64. ----------. "Texts in History: The Determinations of Readings and Their Texts." <u>JMMLA</u> 18.1 (1985), 1-16.

f65. Bennington, Geoffrey. "Not Yet." Diacritics 12.3 (1982), 23-32 [on Jameson].

f66. Berg, Jan, *et al* . Sozialgeschichte der deutschen Literatur von 1918 bis Gegenwart (Frankfurt am Main: Fischer Taschenbuch, 1981).

f67. Berger, Christel, *et al* . Kunstlerisches Schaffen im Sozialismus (Berline: Dietz, 1975).

f68. Bergonzi, Bernard. "Further Thoughts About Marxism and Literature." CritQ 20.4 (1978), 49-54.

f69. Bernstein, J. M. The Philosophy of the Novel: Lukacs, Marxism and the Dialectics of Form (Minneapolis: U of Minnesota P, 1984).

f70. Bevington, David M. Tudor Drama and Politics: A Critical Approach to Topical Meaning (Cambridge: Harvard UP, 1968).

f71. Bhattacharya, Mihir. "Developing a Science of Literature: Marxism and Raymond Williams." JSL 7.1-2 (1980-81), 20-23.

f72. Birchall, Ian. "The Total Marx and the Marxist Theory of Literature," in P. Walton and S. Hall, eds. Situating Marx: Evaluations and Departures (London: Human Context Books, 1972), 118-45.

f73. Bird, Elizabeth. "Aesthetic Neutrality and the Sociology of Art," in M. Barrett, *et al* . Ideology and Cultural Production (London: Croom Helm, 1979).

f74. Bisztray, George. "Literary Sociology and Marxist Theory: The Literary Work as a Social Document." Mosaic 2 (1971-72), 47-56.
f75. ----------. "Marxism and the Pluralism of Critical Methods." YCGL 26 (1977), 10-16.
f76. ----------. Marxist Models of Literary Realism (NY: Columbia UP, 1978).

f77. Blanchard, Margaret. "Sozialization in *Mrs. Dalloway* ." CE 34.2 (1972), 287-305.

f78. Bloch, Ernst, *et al* . Aesthetics and Politics (London: NLB, 1977).

f79. Blotner, Joseph. The Modern American Political Novel, 1900-1960 (Austin: U of Texas P, 1966).

f80. Bodenheimer, Rosemarie. The Politics of Story in Victorian Social Fiction (Ithaca: Cornell UP, 1988).

f81. Bouche, Claude. "Materialist Literary Theory in France 1965-1975." Praxis 5 (1981), 3-20.

f82. Bourdieu, Pierre. La distinction: critique sociale du jugement (Paris: Minuit, 1979).
f83. ----------. "The Aristocracy of Culture." Media, Culture and Society 2.3 (1980), 225-54.

f84. Boutet, Dominique. Littérature, politique et société dans la France du Moyen Age (Paris: PUF, 1979).

f85. Bowra, C. M. Poetry and Politics, 1900-1960 (Cambridge: Cambridge UP, 1966).

f86. Brachet, Pierre. "Quelques rémarques sur les vues esthétiques de Marx et Engels," in Aspects de la civilisation germanique (St.-Etienne: Centre Interdisciplinaire d'Etude et de Recherche sur l'Expression Contemp., 1975), 123-48.

f87. Brantlinger, Patrick. The Spirit of Reform: British Literature and Politics, 1832-1867 (Cambridge: Harvard UP, 1977).

f88. Brecht, Bertolt. Gesammelte Werke, 8 vols. (Frankfurt: Suhrkamp, 1967).

f89. Breslin, Paul. The Psycho-political Muse: American Poetry Since the Fifties (Chicago: U of Chicago P, 1987).

f90. Brewster, Philip and Carl Howard Buchner. "Language and Critique: Jurgen Habermas on Walter Benjamin." New German Critique 17 (1979), 15-29.

f91. Bristol, Michael D. Carnival and Theater: Plebeian Culture and the Structure of Authority in Renaissance England (NY: Methuen, 1985).

f92. Bronner, Stephen Eric. "Expressionism and Marxism: Towards an Aesthetic of Emancipation," in S. E. Bronner and D. Kellner, eds. Passion and Rebellion: The Expressionist Heritage (South Hadley MA: Bergin, 1983), 411-53.
f93. ----------. "Marxism and Critical Aesthetics." Enclitic 8.1-2 (1984), 37-55.

f94. Brooks-Davies, Douglas. The Mercurian Monarch: Magical Politics from Spenser to Pope (Manchester: Manchester UP, 1983).

f95. Brown, Cynthia Jane. The Shaping of History and Poetry in Late Medieval France: Propaganda and Artistic Expression in the Works of the Rhétoriqueurs (Birmingham AL: Summa, 1985).

f96. Buch, Hans Manfred, ed. Parteilichkeit der Literatur oder Parteiliteratur? Materialien zu einer undogmatischen marxistischen Asthetik (Reinbeck bei Hamburg: Rowohlt, 1972).

f97. Buck-Morss, Susan. The Origin of Negative Dialectics: Theodor W. Adorno, Walter Benjamin and the Frankfurt Institute (NY: Free Press, 1977).
f98. ----------. "Walter Benjamin: Revolutionary Writer." New Left Review, 128 and 129 (1981), 50-75, 77-95.
f99. ----------. "Benjamin's Passagen-Werk: Redeeming Mass Culture for the Revolution." New German Critique 29 (1981), 211-40.

f100. Bullitt, Margaret M. "Toward a Marxist Theory of Aesthetics: The Development of Socialist Realism in the Soviet Union." RusR 35 (1976), 53-76.

f101. Bullock, Chris. "Teaching Mass Culture: An Introductory Reading List." RadT 15 (1979), 38-42.
f102. ---------- and David Peck. Guide to Marxist Literary Criticism (Bloomington: Indiana UP, 1980).

f103. Burns, Wayne. "Marxism, Criticism and the Disappearing Individual." RecL 12 (1984), 7-28.

f104. Buttigieg, Joseph A. "The Exemplary Worldliness of Antonio Gramsci's Literary Criticism." Boundary 11.1-2 (1982-83), 21-39.

f105. Cahn, Michael. "Subversive Mimesis: Theodor W. Adorno and the Modern Impasse of Critique," in M. Spariosu, ed. Mimesis in Contemporary Theory: An Interdisciplinary Approach: Volume I: The Literary and Philosophical Debate (Philadelphia: Benjamins, 1984), 27-64.

f106. Calinescu, Matei. "Marxism as a Work of Art: Post-Structuralist Readings of Marx." SFR 3 (1979), 123-35.
f107. ----------. "Literature and Politics," in J.-P. Barricelli and J. Gibaldi, eds. Interrelations of Literature (NY: MLA, 1982), 123-49.

f108. Cantarow, Ellen. "A Wilderness of Opinions Confounded: Allegory and Ideology." CE 34.2 (1972), 215-52.

f109. Cantor, Jay. The Space Between: Literature and Politics (Baltimore: Johns Hopkins UP, 1981).

f110. Carib, Ian. *Criticism and Ideology* : Theory and Experience." ConL 22.4 (1981), 489-501 [on Eagleton and Althusser].

f111. Carretta, Vincent. The Snarling Muse: Verbal and Visual Political Satire from Pope to Churchill (Philadelphia: U of Pennsylvania P, 1983).

f112. Caute, David. The Illusion: An Essay on Politics, Theatre, and the Novel (NY: Harper & Row, 1972).
f113. ----------. "Commitment without Empathy: A Writer's Notes on Politics, Theatre and the Novel." TriQ 30 (1974), 51-70.
f114. ----------. "A Portrait of the Artist as Midwife: Lucien Goldmann and the 'Transindividual Subject,'" in Collisions: Essays and Reviews (London: Quartet, 1974), 219-27.

f115. Chace, William M. The Political Idenitities of Ezra Pound and T. S. Eliot (Stanford: Stanford UP, 1973).

f116. Champigny, Robert. "Larvatus Prodeo." Diacritics 2.3 (1972), 25-29 [on Jameson].

f117. Chernaik, Warren L. The Poet's Time: Politics and Religion in the Work of Andrew Marvell (Cambridge: Cambridge UP, 1983).

f118. Clark, Michael. "Imagining the Real: Jameson's Use of Lacan." NOR 11.1 (1984), 67-72.

f119. Clarke, Simon, *et al* . One-Dimensional Marxism: Althusser and the Politics of Culture (London: Allison & Busby, 1980).

f120. Clecak, Pete Emmett. "Marxism and American Literary Criticism." DA 26 (1965), 366.
f121. ----------. "Marxism, Literary Criticism, and the American Academic Scene." Science and Society 31 (1967), 275-301.

f122. Cohen, Walter and Peter U. Hohendahl. "Marxist Literary Criticism: Problems and Proposals." Humanities in Soc 6.2-3 (1983), 161-77.

f123. Colls, Robert and Philip Dodd, eds. Englishness: Politics and Culture 1880-1920 (London: Croom Helm, 1986).

f124. Combes, Patrick. La littérature et le mouvement de mai 68: écriture, mythes, critique, écrivains, 1968-1981 (Paris: Seghers, 1984).

f125. Congdon, Lee. The Young Lukacs (Chapel Hill: U of North Carolina P, 1983).

f126. Cooper, Stephen. The Politics of Ernest Hemingway (Ann Arbor: UMI Research P, 1987).

f127. Corredor, Eva. "Lukacs and Bakhtin: A Dialogue on Fiction." RUO 53.1 (1983), 97-107.
f128. ----------. "Sociocritical and Marxist Literary Theory," in J. Natoli, ed. Tracing Literary Theory (Urbana: U of Illinois P, 1987), 105-26.

f129. Couto, Maria. Graham Greene: On the Frontier: Politics and Religion in the Novels (NY: St. Martin's P, 1988).

f130. Craig, Cairns. Yeats, Eliot, Pound, and the Politics of Poetry: Richest to the Richest (Pittsburgh: U of Pittsburgh P, 1982).

f131. Craig, David. "Lukacs' Views on How History Moulds Literature," in G. H. R. Parkinson, ed. Georg Lukacs: The Man, His Work and His Ideas (NY: Vintage, 1970), 191-218.
f132. ----------. The Real Foundations: Literature and Social Change (NY: Oxford UP, 1974).
f133. ----------, ed. Marxists on Literature: An Anthology (Baltimore: Penguin, 1975).

f134. Crews, Frederick. "Do Literary Studies Have an Ideology?" PMLA 85 (1970), 423-28.
f135. ----------. "Offing Culture: Literary Study and the Movement," in G. A. White and C. Newman, eds. Literature in Revolution (NY: Holt, Rinehart & Winston, 1972), 34-56.

f136. Dahl, Mary Karen. Political Violence in Drama: Classical Models, Contemporary Variations (Ann Arbor: UMI Research P, 1987).

f137. Das Gupta, Kalyan. "Principles of Literary Evaluation in English Marxist Criticism: Christopher Caudwell, Raymond Williams and Terry Eagleton." DAI 47 (1986), 1332A.

f138. David, R. G. "Benjamin, Storytelling and Brecht in the USA." NGC 17 (1979), 143-56.

f139. Davis, Lennard J. Resisting Novels: Ideology and Fiction (NY and London: Methuen, 1987).

f140. Dawson, P. M. S. The Unacknowledged Legislator: Shelley and Politics (Oxford: Clarendon; NY: Oxford UP, 1980).

f141. Deane, Seamus. Celtic Revivals (London and Boston: Faber & Faber, 1985).

f142. Delany, Paul. "Joyce: Political Development and the Aesthetic of Dubliners ," in B. R. Barber and M. J. G. McGrath, eds. The Artist and Political Vision (New Brunswick NJ: Transaction Books, 1982), 221-31.

f143. Della Volpe, Galvano. Critique of Taste (London: New Left Books, 1978).

f144. Demaitre, Ann. "The Great Debate on Socialist Realism." MLJ 50 (1966), 263-68.

f145. Demetz, Peter. Marx, Engels, and the Poets: Origins of Marxist Literary Criticism (Chicago: U of Chicago P, 1967).
f146. ----------. "Marxist Literary Criticism Today." Survey 82 (1972), 63-72.
f147. ----------. "Uber die Fiktionen des Realismus." NRs 88 (1977), 554-67.

f148. Denkler, Horst. Restauration und Revolution: polit. Tendenzen im dt. Drama zwischen Wiener Kongress u. Marzrevolution (Munchen: Fink, 1973).

f149. Dewhirst, Martin. "Soviet Literary Criticism: A Survey." Studies on the Soviet Union 8.3 (1969), 54-66.

f150. DiSalvo, Jackie. War of Titans: Blake's Critique of Milton and the Politics of Religion (Pittsburgh: U of Pittsburgh P, 1983).

f151. Dolan, Paul. Of War and War's Alarms: Fiction and Politics in the Modern World (NY: Free Press, 1976).

f152. Dowling, William C. Jameson, Althusser, Marx: An Introduction to The Political Unconscious (Ithaca: Cornell UP, 1984).

f153. Duke, David C. Distant Obligations: Modern American Writers and Foreign Causes (NY: Oxford UP, 1983).

f154. Dukore, Bernard F. Money and Politics in Ibsen, Shaw, and Brecht (Columbia: U of Missouri P, 1980).

f155. Dunham, Vera S. In Stalin's Time: Middleclass Values in Soviet Fiction (Cambridge: Cambridge UP, 1976).

f156. Durzak, Manfred. "Walter Benjamin und die Literaturwissenschaft." Montashefte 58 (1966), 217-31.

f157. Dymsic, A. L. "Sozialismus und Literaturwissenschaft." ZS 15 (1970), 471-76.

f158. Eagleton, Terry. Shakespeare and Society (London: Chatto & Windus, 1967).
f159. ----------. Exiles and Emigrés (London: Chatto & Windus, 1970).
f160. ----------. Myths of Power: A Marxist Study of the Brontes (NY: Barnes & Noble, 1975).
f161. ----------. Criticism and Ideology: A Study in Marxist Literary Theory (Atlantic Highlands NJ: Humanities, 1976).
f162. ----------. Marxism and Literary Criticism (Berkeley: U of California P, 1977).
f163. ----------. "Marxist Literary Criticism," in H. Schiff, ed. Contemporary Approaches to English Studies (London: Heinemann; NY: Barnes & Noble, 1977), 94-103.
f164. ----------. "Aesthetics and Politics." New Left Review 107 (1978), 21-34.
f165. ----------. "Liberality and Order: The Criticism of John Bayley." New Left Review 110 (1978), 29-40.
f166. ----------. "Tennyson: Politics and Sexuality in *The Princess* and *In Memoriam* ," in F. Barker, *et al* . 1848: The Sociology of Literature (Colchester: U of Essex, 1978), 97-106.
f167. ----------. "The End of Criticism." SoRA 14.2 (1981), 99-106.
f168. ----------. Walter Benjamin, or Towards a Revolutionary Criticism (London: New Left Books, 1981).
f169. ----------. "Marxism and Deconstruction." ConL 22.4 (1981), 477-88.
f170. ----------. The Rape of Clarissa: Writing, Sexuality and Class Struggle in Samuel Richardson (Minneapolis: U of Minnesota P, 1982).
f171. ----------. "Fredric Jameson: The Politics of Style." Diacritics 12.3 (1982), 14-22.
f172. ----------. Literary Theory: An Introduction (Minneapolis: U of Minnesota P, 1983).
f173. ----------. "The Rise of English Studies: An Interview with Terry Eagleton." SoRA 17.1 (1984), 18-32.
f174. ----------, *et al* . "The 'Text in Itself': A Symposium." SoRA 17.2 (1984), 115-46.

f175. ----------. The Function of Criticism: From *The Spectator* to Post-Structuralism (London: Verso, 1984).

f176. ----------. "Literature and History." CritQ 27.4 (1985), 23-26.

f177. ----------. "Ideology and Scholarship," in J. J. McGann, ed. Historical Studies and Literary Criticism (Madison: U of Wisconsin P, 1985), 114-25.

f178. ----------. "Marxism and the Past." Salmagundi 68-69 (1985-86), 271-90.

f179. ----------. Against the Grain: Essays 1975-1985 (London: Verso, 1986).

f180. ----------. William Shakespeare (Oxford & NY: Blackwell, 1986).

f181. ----------. "The Critic as Clown," in C. Nelson and L. Grossberg, eds. Marxism and the Interpretation of Culture (Urbana: U of Illinois P, 1988), 619-31.

f182. Easthope, Anthony. "Literature, History, and the Materiality of the Text." L&H 9.1 (1983), 28-37 [on Tony Bennett].

f183. Edwards, Thomas R. Imagination and Power: A Study of Poetyr on Public Themes (NY: Oxford UP, 1971).

f184. Egbert, Donald Drew. Social Radicalism and the Arts: Western Europe: A Cultural History from the French Revolution to 1968 (NY: Knopf, 1970).

f185. Ehrmann, Jacques, ed. Literature and Revolution (Boston: Beacon P, 1970).

f186. Eimermacher, Karl and Renate Eimermacher, eds. Dokumente zur sowjetischen Literaturpolitik 1917-1932 (Stuttgart: Kohlhammer, 1972).

f187. Elkins, Charles L. "The Development of British Marxist Literary Theory: Toward a Genetic Functional Approach to Literary Criticism." DAI 35 (1973), 5119A.

f188. Elliott, Gregory. Althusser: The Detour of Theory (London & NY: Verso, 1987).

f189. Empson, William. Some Versions of the Pastoral (NY: New Directions, 1968) ["Proletarian Literature," 3-23].

f190. Eorsi, Istvan. "Gyorgy Lukacs and the Theory of Lyric Poetry." New Hungarian Quarterly 6.18 (1965), 33-46.

f191. Erlich, Bruce. "Social Action and Literary Fable." MinnR 5 (1975), 40-52.

f192. Erlich, Victor, ed. Twentieth-Century Russian Literary Criticism
(New Haven: Yale UP, 1975).

f193. Evans, Richard Claypool. "Marxist Hermeneutics: Post-War Literary
Theory in Italy." DAI 40 (1979), 3282A.

f194. Fan, K. H, ed. The Chinese Cultural Revolution: Selected Documents
(NY: Grove Press, 1968).

f195. Farbstein, A. "Die marxistisch-leninistische Asthetik heute in den
sozialistischen Landern Europas." KuL 24 (1976), 115-37.

f196. Farrell, John P. Revolution as Tragedy: The Dilemma of the Moderate
from Scott to Arnold (Ithaca: Cornell UP, 1980).

f197. Federici, Silvia. "Notes on Lukacs' Aesthetics." Telos 11 (1972), 141-
51.

f198. Feenberg, Andrew. Lukacs, Marx, and the Sources of Critical Theory
(Totowa NJ: Rowman and Littlefield, 1981).

f199. Feher, Ferenc. "Is the Novel Problematic? A Contribution to the
Theory of the Novel." Telos 15 (1973), 47-74.

f200. Fekete, John. "Reflections on Literary Theory and Culture." Praxis
1.1 (1975), 25-36 [on Lukacs].
f201. ----------. The Critical Twilight: Explorations in the Ideology of
Anglo-American Literary Theory from Eliot to McLuhan (Boston:
Routledge & Kegan Paul, 1978).

f202. Field, Frank. Three French Writers and the Great War: Studies in the
Rise of Communism and Fascism (Cambridge: Cambridge UP, 1975).

f203. Fietkau, Wolfgang. Schwanengesang auf 1848: Studien zu Baudelaire,
Marx, und Benjamin (Munich: Rogner und Bernhard, 1972).

f204. Fischbach, Fred. Lukacs, Bloch, Eisler: Contribution a l'histoire d'une
controverse (Lille: PU de Lille, 1979).

f205. Fischer, David James. Romain Rolland and the Politics of Intellectual
Engagement (Berkeley: U of California P, 1988).

f206. Fischer, Ernst. "Chaos and Form." Mosaic 1.1 (1967), 132-40.
f207. ----------. Art against Ideology (NY: Braziller, 1969).

f208. ----------. "Reflections Upon the State of the Arts." Mosaic 4.1 (1970), 21-34.

f209. Fischer, Michael. "The Literary Importance of E. P. Thompson's Marxism." ELH 50.4 (1983), 811-29.

f210. Flieger, Jerry Aline. "The Prison-House of Ideology: Critic as Inmate." Diacritics 12.3 (1982), 47-56 [on Jameson].

f211. Flottes, Pierre. Histoire de la poésie politique et sociale en France de 1815 a 1939 (Paris: La Pensée Universelle, 1976).

f212. Flower, J. E., J. A. Morris, and E. E. Williams. Writers and Politics in Modern Britain, France, and Germany (NY: Holmes & Meier, 1977).
f213. ----------. Literature and the Left in France: Society, Politics, and the Novel Since the Late Nineteenth Century (Totowa NJ: Barnes & Noble, 1983).

f214. Fokkema, Douwe W. Literary Doctrine in China and Soviet Influence, 1956-1960 (The Hague: Mouton, 1965).
f215. ----------. Theories of Literature in the Twentieth Century: Structuralism, Marxism, Aesthetics of Receptions (NY: St. Martin's P, 1978) [chap. 4 on Marxist criticism].
f216. ----------. "Strength and Weakness of the Marxist Theory of Literature with Reference to Marxist Criticism in the People's Republic of China," in J. J. Deeney, ed. Chinese-Western Comparative Literature Theory and Strategy (Hong Kong: Chinese UP, 1980), 113-28.

f217. Folsom, Michael B., ed. Shakspeare: A Marxist Bibliography (NY: American Institute for Marxist Studies, 1965).

f218. Forgacs, David. "Beyond Lukacs." PNR 16 (1980), 34-37.
f219. ----------. "Marxist Literary Theories," in A. Jefferson and D. Robey, eds. Modern Literary Theory: A Comparative Introduction (Totowa NJ: Barnes & Noble, 1982), 134-69.

f220. Foulkes, A. P. Literature and Propaganda (London and NY: Methuen, 1983).

f221. "Fragen der Wertung von Literatur und Kunst in der entwickelten sozialistischen Gesellschaft: Eine Umfrage." WB 26.2 (1980), 97-137.

f222. Frankel, Edith Rogovin. Novy mir: A Case Study in the Politics of Literature, 1952-1958 (Cambridge & NY: Cambridge UP, 1981).

f223. Freyer, Grattan. W. B. Yeats and the Anti-Democratic Tradition (Dublin: Gill & Macmillan; Totowa NJ: Barnes & Noble, 1981).

f224. Fridlender, G. "Marx und Engels und Probleme des Realismus." KuL 18 (1970), 675-97, 801-22.

f225. Friedman, Jonathan. "Marxism, Structuralism and Vulgar Materialism." Man 9 (1974), 444-69.

f226. Frisby, David. Fragments of Modernity: Theories of Modernity in the Work of Simmel, Kracauer, and Benjamin (Cambridge MA: MIT Press, 1986).

f227. Frith, Simon. "Art Ideology and Pop Practice," in C. Nelson and L. Grossberg, eds. Marxism and the Interpretation of Culture (Urbana: U of Illinois P, 1988), 461-75.

f228. Frow, John Anthony. "Literature and the Language of Ideology: A Study in Marxist Literary Theory." DAI 41 (1980), 1575A.
f229. ----------. "System and Norm in Literary Evolution: For a Marxist Literary History." ClioI 10.2 (1981), 154-81.
f230. ----------. "Structuralist Marxism." SoRA 15.2 (1982), 208-17 [Macherey, Eagleton].
f231. ----------. "Marxism After Structuralism." SoRA 17.1 (1984), 33-50 [Benjamin, Eagleton, Jameson].
f232. ----------. "Textual Historicities." L&H 11.2 (1985), 264-80 also in JMMLA 18.1 (1985), 17-41).
f233. ----------. Marxism and Literary History (Cambridge: Harvard UP, 1986).

f234. Fruchtl, Josef. Mimesis: Konstellation eines Zentralbegriffs bei Adorno (Wurzburg: Konighausen und Neumann, 1986).

f235. Fry, Paul H. The Reach of Criticism: Method and Perception in Literary Theory (New Haven: Yale UP, 1983 ["The Instance of Walter Benjamin: Distraction and Perception in Criticism," 168-205].

f236. Fulberth, Georg. Proletarische Partei und bergerliche Literatur (Neuwied: Luchterhand, 1972).

f237. Fuld, Werner. "Die Aura. Zur Geschichte eines Begriffs bei Benjamin." Akzente 29 (1979), 274-86.
f238. ----------. Walter Benjamin: Zwischen den Stuhlen (Munich: Hanser, 1979).

f239. Gagnebin, Jeanne-Marie. Zur Geschichtsphilosophie Walter Benjamins: Die Unabgeschlossenheit des Sinns (Erlangen: Palm & Enke, 1978).

f240. Galik, Marian. "Studies in Modern Chinese Literary Criticism, iv: The Proletarian Criticism of Kuo Mo-jo." AAS 6 (1970), 145-60.

f241. Gallagher, Catherine. The Industrial Reformation of English Fiction: Social Discourse and Narrative Form, 1832-1867 (Chicago: U of Chicago P, 1985).

f242. Gallas, Helga. Marxistische Literaturtheorie (Neuwied: Luchterhand, 1971).

f243. Garnham, Nicholas and Raymond Williams. "Pierre Bourdieu and the Sociology of Culture: An Introduction." Media, Culture and Society 2.3 (1980), 209-23.

f244. Gatt-Rutter, John. Writers and Politics in Modern Italy (NY: Holmes & Meier, 1978).

f245. Gay, N. K. "Truth in Art and Truth in Life," in G. C. LeRoy and U. Beitz, eds. Preserve and Create: Essays in Marxist Literary Criticism (NY: Humanities, 1973), 76-92.

f246. Gebhardt, Peter, et al . Walter Benjamin: Zeitgenosse der Moderne (Kronberg: Scriptor, 1976).

f247. Geissler, Klaus. "Neue DDR-Beitrage zu Theorie und Geschichte des sozialistischen Realismus." ZS 20 (1975), 483-90.
f248. ---------- and Waltraud Geissler. "Forschungs- und darstellungsmethodische Probleme der Theorie und Geschichte des sozialistischen Realismus: Ein Literaturbericht." WB 22.12 (1976), 141-56.

f249. Gej, N. and W. Piskunow. "An den Quellen der marxistischen Literaturkritik." KuL 16 (1968), 181-98.

f250. Gibson, Donald B. The Politics of Literary Expression: A Study of Major Black Writers (Westport CT: Greenwood P, 1981).

f251. Giles, Steve. "Marxism and Form: D. H. Lawrence, St Mawr ," in D. Tallack, ed. Literary Theory at Work: Three Texts (Totowa NJ: Barnes & Noble, 1987), 49-66.

f252. Girnus, Wilhelm. Zur 'Asthetik' von Georg Lukacs: Zweitausend Jahre Verfalschung der aristotelischen 'Poetik' (Frankfurt: Marxistische Blatter, 1972).
f253. ----------. "On the Problem of Ideology and Literature." NLH 4 (1973), 483-500.

f254. Glicksberg, Charles I. The Literature of Commitment (Lewisburg: Bucknell UP, 1976).

f255. Gluck, Mary. Georg Lukacs and His Generation, 1900-1918 (Cambridge: Harvard UP, 1985).

f256. Goldberg, Jonathan. James I and the Politics of Literature: Jonson, Shakespeare, Donne, and their Contemporaries (Baltimore: Johns Hopkins UP, 1983).

f257. Goldgar, Bertrand A. Walpole and the Wits: The Relation of Politics to Literature, 1722-1742 (Lincoln: U of Nebraska P, 1976).

f258. Goldmann, Lucien. "Ideology and Writing." TLS (Sept. 28, 1967), 903-05.
f259. ----------. The Philosophy of the Enlightenment (Cambridge MA: MIT P, 1973) ["Marxist Criticism," 86-97].
f260. ----------. "Dialectical Materialism and Literary History." New Left Review 92 (1975), 39-51.
f261. ----------. Lukacs and Heidegger: Towards a New Philosophy (London & Boston: Routledge & Kegan Paul, 1977).

f262. Goldsmith, Arnold L. American Literary Criticism: 1905-1965 (Boston: Twayne, 1979) [chap. 3: "Marxist and Sociological Criticism: The Extrinsic Approach"].

f263. Good, Graham. "Lukacs' Theory of the Novel ." Novel 6 (1973), 175-85.

f264. Goodin, George. The Poetics of Protest: Literary Form and Political Implication in the Victim-of-Society Novel (Carbondale: Southern Illinois UP, 1985).

f265. Grauer, Michael. Die entzauberte Welt: Tragik und Dialektik der Moderne im fruhen Werk von Georg Lukacs (Konigstein/Ts.: A. Hain, 1985).

f266. Green, Leonard, ed. "Special Issue on Fredric Jameson: *The Political Unconscious* ." Diacritics 12.3 (1982) [includes interview with Jameson, 72-91].

f267. Green, Philip and Michael Walzer, eds. The Political Imagination in Literature: A Reader (NY: Free Press, 1969).

f268. Greffath, Krista. Metaphorischer Materialismus: Untersuchungen zum Geschichtsbegriff Walter Benjamins (Munich: Hanser, 1981).

f269. Grenz, Friedemann. "Adornos Vorschlag zu Theorie und Praxis der Literaturwissenschaften." ActaG 11 (1979), 191-214.

f270. Groman, George L., ed. Political Literature of the Progressive Era (East Lansing: Michigan State UP, 1967).

f271. Grossman, Marshall. "Formalism, Structuralism, Marxism: Fredric Jameson's Critical Narrative." Dispositio 4 (1979), 259-72.

f272. Gunther, Hans. "Michail Bachtins Konseption als Alternative zum sozialistischen Realismus," in P. V. Zima, ed. Semiotics and Dialectics: Ideology and the Text (Amsterdam: Benjamins, 1981), 137-77.

f273. Gunther, Henning. Walter Benjamin: Zwischen Marxismus und Theologie (Olten, Switzerland: Walter, 1974).

f274. Habermas, Jurgen. "Consciousness Raising or Redemptive Criticism." NGC 17 (1979), 30-59.

f275. Hall, John. "Totality and the Dialogic: Two Versions of the Novel?" TkR 16 (1984-85), 5-30 [on Lukacs and Bakhtin].

f276. Hamilton, Alastair. The Appeal of Fascism: A Study of Intellectuals and Fascism, 1919-1945 (London: Blond, 1971).

f277. Hardt, Hanno. "Critical Theory in Historical Perspective." JC 36.3 (1986), 144-54 [on Frankfurt School].

f278. Harlow, Barbara. Resistance Literature (NY & London: Methuen, 1987).

f279. Harrison, John R. The Reactionaries: A Study of the Anti-Democratic Intelligentsia (NY: Schocken, 1967).

f280. Hartinger, Walfried and Klaus Werner. "Zur Konfliktgestaltung in der sozialistisch-realistischen Literatur und Kunst." WB 18.9 (1973), 119-30.

f281. Hartung, Gunter. "Zu einer marxistischen Theorie der 'Autonomie der Kunst.'" WB 26.7 (1980), 44-58.

f282. Hartwick, Larry. "On *The Aesthetic Dimension* : A Conversation with Herbert Marcuse." ConL 22.4 (1981), 416-24.

f283. Harvey, J. R. "Criticism, Ideology, Raymond Williams and Terry Eagleton." CQ 8 (1978), 56-65.

f284. Hawthorn, Jeremy. Identity and Relationship: A Contribution to Marxist Theory of Literary Criticism (London: Lawrence & Wishart, 1973).
f285. ----------. "*Ulysses* , Modernism, and Marxist Criticism," in W. J. McCormack and A. Stead, eds. James Joyce and Modern Literature (London: Routledge, 1982), 112-25.

f286. Hayward, Max. "The Decline of Socialist Realism." Survey 8.1 (1972), 73-97.

f287. Heimonet, Jean-Michel. Politiques de l'écriture, Bataille/Derrida: le sens du sacré dans la pensée française du surréalisme a nos jours (Chapel Hill: U of North Carolina Dept. of Romance Languages, 1987).

f288. Heise, Wolfgang. "Zur Grundlegung der Realismustheorie durch Marx und Engels, I and II." WB 22.2 (1976), 99-120, 22.3 (1976), 123-44.

f289. Held, David. Introduction to Critical Theory: Horkheimer to Habermas (London: Hutchinson, 1980).

f290. Heller, Agnes and Ferenc Fehér, eds. Reconstructing Aesthetics: Writings the Budapest School (Oxford: Blackwell, 1986).

f291. Hering, Christoph. Die Intellektuelle als Revolutionar: Walter Benjamins Analyse intellektueller Praxis (Munchen: Fink, 1979).

f292. Hermassi, Karen. Polity and Theater in Historical Perspective (Berkeley: U of California P, 1977).

f293. Herr, Cheryl. Joyce's Anatomy of Culture (Urbana: U of Illinois P, 1986).

f294. Hess, James C. "Literary Production and Consumption." <u>DAI</u> 42 (1982), 4819A [on Raymond Williams, Terry Eagleton, Fredric Jameson].

f295. Higgins, John. "Raymond Williams and the Problem of Ideology." <u>Boundary</u> 11.1-2 (1982-83), 145-54.

f296. Higonnet, Anne, *et al* . "Façades: Walter Benjamin's Paris." <u>CritI</u> 10 (1984), 391-419.

f297. Hines, Samuel H., Jr. "Hermann Hesse: Passion and Politics," in B. R. Barber and M. J. G. McGrath, eds. <u>The Artist and Political Vision</u> (New Brunswick NJ: Transaction Books, 1982), 145-62.

f298. Hohendahl, Peter Uwe. "Asthetik und Sozialismus: Zur neuren Literaturtheorie der DDR." <u>JDSG</u> 18 (1974), 606-41.
f299. ----------. "George Lukacs in the GDR: On Recent Developments in Literary Theory." <u>NGC</u> 12 (1977), 169-74.

f300. Holland, Henry M. Jr., ed. <u>Politics through Literature</u> (Engelwood Cliffs NJ: Prentice-Hall, 1968).

f301. Holzman, Michael. "Georg Lukacs' Myth of the Golden Age." <u>ClioI</u> 10.3 (1981), 265-78.

f302. Homberger, Eric. <u>American Writers and Radical Politics, 1900-39: Equivocal Commitments</u> (NY: St. Martin's P, 1986).

f303. Horn, Andras. "The Concept of 'Mimesis' in Georg Lukacs." <u>BJA</u> 14 (1974), 26-40.

f304. Howard, June. "Toward a 'Marxist-Feminist Cultural Analysis.'" <u>MinnR</u> 20 (1983), 77-92.

f305. Howard, Roger. "Contradiction and the Poetic Image." <u>MinnR</u> 5 (1975), 89-97.

f306. Hoyles, John. "Radical Critical Theory and English," in P. Widdowson, ed. <u>Re-Reading English</u> (London: Methuen, 1982), 44-60.

f307. Hughes, Kenneth, ed. <u>Franz Kafka: An Anthology of Marxist Criticism</u> (Hanover: Clark University/UP of New England, 1981).

f308. Humm, Peter, *et al* , eds. <u>Popular Fictions: Essays in Literature and History</u> (London and NY: Methuen, 1986).

f309. Hurtgen, James R. "Meville: Billy Budd and the Context of Political Rule," in B. R. Barber and M. J. G. McGrath, eds. The Artist and Political Vision (New Brunswick NJ: Transaction Books, 1982), 245-65.

f310. Huttel, Martin. Marxistisch-Leninistische Literaturtheorie: Die theoretische Bedeutung der Literaturkritik von Marx, Engels und Lenin (Stuttgart: Heinz, 1977).

f311. Huyssen, Andreas, ed. "Critical Theory and Modernity." NGC 26 (1982) [special issue: Frankfurt School].

f312. Hynes, Samuel. The Auden Generation: Literature and Politics in England in the 1930s (NY: Viking Press, 1977).

f313. Illés, Laszlo. "Versuche einer theoretischen Grundlegung der proletarischen Literatur." ALitASH 27.1-2 (1985), 127-52.

f314. Jacobs, Carol. The Dissimulating Harmony: The Image of Interpretation in Nietzsche, Rilke, Artaud, and Benjamin (Baltimore: Johns Hopkins UP, 1978) ["Walter Benjamin: Image of Proust," 89-110].

f315. James, C. Vaughan. Soviet Socialist Realism: Origins and Theory (London: St. Martin's P, 1974).

f316. Jameson, Fredric. "T. W. Adorno, or, Historical Tropes." Salmagundi 2 (1967), 3-43.
f317. ----------. "The Case for George Lukacs." Salmagundi 13 (1970), 3-35.
f318. ----------. Marxism and Form: Twentieth Century Dialectical Theories of Literature (Princeton: Princeton UP, 1972).
f319. ----------. "The Great American Hunter, or, Ideological Content in the Novel." CE 34.2 (1972), 180-97.
f320. ----------. "The Ideology of the Text." Salmagundi 31-32 (1975), 204-46.
f321. ----------. "Notes Towards a Marxist Cultural Politics." MinnR 5 (1975), 35-39.
f322. ----------. "Ideology and Symbolic Action." CritI 5 (1978), 417-22.
f323. ----------. "Marxism and Historicism." NLH 11.1 (1979), 41-73.
f324. ----------. Fables of Aggression: Wyndham Lewis, the Modernist as Fascist (Berkeley: U of California P, 1979).
f325. ----------. The Political Unconscious: Narrative as a Socially Symbolic Act (Ithaca: Cornell UP, 1981).
f326. ----------. "Ulysses in History," in W. J. McCormack and A. Stead, eds. James Joyce and Modern Literature (London: Routledge, 1982), 126-41.

f327. ----------. "Beyond the Cave: Modernism and Modes of Production," in P. Hernadi, ed. The Horizon of Literature (Lincoln: U of Nebraska P, 1982), 157-82.

f328. ----------. "World Literature in an Age of Multinational Capitalism," inC. Koelb and V. Lokke, eds. The Current in Criticism: Essays on the Present and Future of Literary Theory (West Lafayette IN: Purdue UP, 1987), 139-58.

f329. ----------. "Cognitive Mapping," in C. Nelson and L. Grossberg, eds. Marxism and the Interpretation of Culture (Urbana: U of Illinois P, 1988), 347-57.

f330. Janz, Rolf-Peter. "Zur Historizitat und Aktualitat der *Theorie des Romans* von Georg Lukacs." JDSG 22 (1978), 674-99.

f331. Jauss, Hans-Robert. "The Idealist Embarrassment: Observations on Marxist Aesthetics." NLH 7 (1975), 191-208.

f332. Jay, Gregory S. "America the Scrivener: Economy and Literary History." Diacritics 14.1 (1984), 36-51.

f333. Jay, Martin. The Dialectic Imagination: A History of the Frankfurt School and the Institute of Social Research (Boston: Little, Brown, 1973) [chap. 6 on aesthetics].

f334. ----------. Adorno (Cambridge: Harvard UP, 1984).

f335. ----------. Marxism and Totality: The Adventures of a Concept from Lukacs to Habermas (Berkeley: U of California P, 1984).

f336. Jean, Raymond. "Marxisme et littérature: L'Exemple de Gramsci," in J. Onimus and A.-M. Rousseau, eds. Littérature et société (Paris: de Brouwer, 1973), 365-70.

f337. Jennings, Michael. "Benjamin as a Reader of Holderlin: The Origins of Benjamin's Theory of Literary Criticism." German Quarterly 56 (1983), 544-62.

f338. ----------. Dialectical Images: Walter Benjamin's Theory of Literary Criticism (Ithaca: Cornell UP, 1987).

f339. Jesuitow, A. "Der Kampf um das asthetische Erbe von Karl Marx." KuL 16 (1968), 1042-53.

f340. ----------. "Fragen der Asthetik im *Kapital* von Marx." KuL 18 (1970), 823-32.

f341. ----------. "Die Haupttypen der Darstellung in der Literatur des sozialistischen Realismus." KuL 24 (1976), 3-19.

f342. Jimenez, Marc. "Benjamin-Adorno: Vers une esthetique negative." RE 1 (1981), 79-100.

f343. John, E. "Das Kunstwerk als dialektische Einheit von Inhalt und Form." WZUL 15 (1966), 661-86.

f344. Johnson, Pauline. Marxist Aesthetics: The Foundations within Everyday Life for an Emancipated Consciousness (London & Boston: Routledge & Kegan Paul, 1984).

f345. Johnson, Priscilla, ed. Khrushchev and the Arts: The Politics of Soviet Culture, 1962-1964 (Cambridge MA: MIT P, 1965).

f346. Jones, Howard Mumford. Jeffersonianism and the American Novel (NY: Teachers College P, 1966).

f347. Jones, Richard, ed. Poetry and Politics: An Anthology of Essays (NY: Morrow, 1985).

f348. Jose, Nicholas. Ideas of the Restoration in English Literature, 1660-71 (Cambridge: Harvard UP, 1984).

f349. Jung, Werner. Wandlungen einer asthetischen Theorie: Georg Lukacs' Werke 1907 bis 1923: Beitrage zur deutschen Ideologiegeschichte (Koln: Pahl-Rugenstein, 1981).

f350. Jungheinrich, Hans-Klaus, ed. Nicht versohnt: Musikasthetik nach Adorno (Kassel: Barenreiter, 1987).

f351. Kagan, M. "Die Dialektik der Kunst: Methodologische Prinzipien der theoretischen Untersuchung der Kunst." KuL 13 (1965), 661-67.

f352. Kaiser, Gerhard. Benjamin, Adorno: Zwei Studien (Frankfurt: Athenaum, 1974).

f353. Kandler, Klaus. Drama und Klassenkampf (Berlin: Aufbau-Verlag, 1970).

f354. Karbusicky, Vladimir. Widerspiegelungstheorie und Strukturalismus: Zur Enstehungsgeschichte und Kritik der marxistisch-leninistischen Asthetik (Munchen: Fink, 1973).

f355. Kavanagh, James H. "Constucting a Critical Ideology." Praxis 5 (1981), 118-21.

f356. ----------. "'Marks of Weakness': Ideology, Science and Textual Criticism." Praxis 5 (1981), 23-28.
f357. ---------- and Thomas E. Lewis. "Etienne Balibar and Pierre Macherey." Diacritics 12.1 (1982), 46-51.
f358. ----------. "Terry Eagleton." Diacritics 12.1 (1982), 53-64.
f359. ----------. "Marxism's Althusser: Toward a Politics of Literary Theory." Diacritics 12.1 (1982), 25-45.
f360. ----------. "The Jameson Effect." NOR 11.1 (1984), 20-28 [Jameson, Althusser].

f361. Keller, Ernst. "Georg Lukacs' Concept of Literary Realism." AUMLA 47 (1977), 30-38.
f362. ----------. Der junge Lukacs: Antiburger und wesentliches Leben: Literatur und Kulturkritik, 1902-1915 (Frankfurt am Main: Sendler, 1984).

f363. Kempski, Jugen von. "Zur Asthetik von Georg Lukacs." NRs 79)1965), 109-20.

f364. Kennedy, Andrew K. "Lukacs and Modern Literature." CritQ 24.4 (1979), 53-60.

f365. Kennedy, James G. "The Content and Form of Native Son ." CE 34.2 (1972), 269-83.

f366. King, Noel. "Rewriting Richardson." JMMLA 18.1 (1985), 42-63 [on Eagleton].

f367. Kinney, John. "Metaphor and Method: Georg Lukacs' Debt to Organic Theory." JAAC 39 (1980), 175-84.

f368. Kiralyfalvi, Bela. The Aesthetics of Gyorgy Lukacs (Princeton: Princeton UP, 1975).

f369. Klatt, Gudrun. Vom Ungang mit der Moderne: asthetische Konzepte der dreissiger Jahre: Lifschitz, Lukacs, Lunatscharskii, Bloch, Benjamin (Berlin: Akademie, 1984).

f370. Koch, Hans. "Stichworte zum sozialistischen Realismus." WB 16, Heft 1 (1970), 10-38.

f371. Kopeczi, Bela. "Realisme socialiste: Legende et verité." ALitASH 13 (1971), 325-48.
f372. ----------. "A Marxist View of Form in Literature." NLH 3 (1972), 355-72.

f373. Krostof, Jane. "Critic and Commisar: A. V. Lunacharskii on Art." DAI 33 (1972), 2837A.

f374. Kruckeberg, Edzard. Der Begriff des Erzahlens im 20. Jahrhundert: zu den Theorien Benjamins, Adornos und Lukacs' (Bonn: Bouvier, 1981).

f375. Kuppers, Bernhard. Die Theorie vom Typischen in der Literatur: ihre Auspragung in der russischen Literaturkritik und in der sowjetischen Literaturwissenschaft (Munchen: Sagner, 1966).

f376. Kurrik, Marie. "The Novel's Subjectivity: Georg Lukacs' *Theory of the Novel* ." Salmagundi 28 (1975), 104-24.

f377. Kurz, Gerhard. "Benjamin kritischer gelesen." Philosophische Rundschau 23 (1976), 161-90.

f378. Kurzweil, Edith and William Phillips, eds. Writers & Politics: A Partisan Review Reader (Boston & London: Routledge & Kegan Paul, 1983).

f379. LaCapra, Dominick. Rethinking Intellectual History: Texts, Contexts, Language (Ithaca: Cornell UP, 1983).
f380. ----------. History and Criticism (Ithaca: Cornell UP, 1985).
f381. ----------. History, Politics, and the Novel (Ithaca: Cornell UP, 1987).

f382. Laing, David. The Marxist Theory of Art (Atlantic Highlands NJ: Humanities P, 1978).

f383. Lang, Berel and Forrest Williams, eds. Marxism and Art: Writings in Aesthetics and Criticism (NY: McKay, 1972).

f384. Lang, Peter Christian. Hermeneutik, Ideologiekritik, Asthetik: Uber Gadamer und Adorno sowie Fragen einer aktuellen Asthetik (Konigstein/Ts.: Forum Academicum, 1981).

f385. Langen, Bill. "Class Struggle in Literary Form and Deformation." Praxis 5 (1981), 122-26.

f386. Lapointe, François. Georg Lukacs and his Critics: An International Bibliography with Annotations (1910-1982) (Westport CT: Greenwood P, 1983).

f387. Laqueur, Walter and George L. Mosse, eds. Literature and Politics in the Twentieth Century (NY: Harper & Row, 1967).

f388. Lee, Leo Ou-Fan. "Problems of Marxist Literary Criticism on Mainland China." TkR 14 (1983-84), 381-93.

f389. Leenhardt, Jacques. Lecture politique du roman: "La Jalousie" d'Alain Robbe-Grillet (Paris: Minuit, 1973).

f390. Lehmann, A. G. "The Marxist as a Literary Critic," in G. H. R. Parkinson, ed. Georg Lukacs: The Man, His Work and His Ideas (NY: Vintage, 1970), 172-90.

f391. Lenin, Vladimir Il'ich. On Culture and Cultural Revolution (Moscow: Progress, 1966).
f392. -----------. On Literature and Art (Moscow: Progress, 1970).

f393. LeRoy, Gaylord and Ursula Beitz, eds. Preserve and Create: Essays in Marxist Literary Criticism (NY: Humanities, 1973).
f394. -----------. "The Marxist Approach to Modernism." JML 3 (1974), 1158-74.
f395. -----------. Marxism and Modern Literature (NY: American Institute for Marxist Studies, 1976).

f396. Lever, Julius Walter. The Tragedy of State (London: Methuen, 1971) [politics and Elizabethan drama].

f397. Levin, Harry. "Shakespeare and 'The Revolution of the Times,'" in G. A. White and C. Newman, eds. Literature in Revolution (NY: Holt, Rinehart & Winston, 1972), 228-47.

f398. Levine, Ira A. Left-wing Dramatic Theory in the American Theatre (Ann Arbor: UMI Research P, 1985).

f399. Lewis, Thomas. "Aesthetic Effect/Ideological Effect." Enclitic 7.2 (1983). 4-16 [Althusser, Bennett, Macherey, Balibar].

f400. Lichtheim, George. Georg Lukacs (NY: Viking, 1970).

f401. Liehm, Antonin. The Politics of Culture (NY: Grove, 1972).

f402. Lifshitz, Mikhail. The Philosophy of Art of Karl Marx (London: Pluto, 1973).

f403. Limon, Jerzy. Dangerous Matter: English Drama and Politics in 1623/24 (Cambridge and NY: Cambridge UP, 1986).

f404. Lindner, Burkhardt, ed. <u>Benjamin im Kontext</u> (Frankfurt am Main: Syndikat, 1978).
f405. ---------- and W. Martin Ludke, eds. <u>Materialien zur asthetischen Theorie Theodor W. Adornos: Konstruktion der Moderne</u> (Frankfurt am Main: Suhrkamp, 1980).

f406. Lindsay, Jack. "The Achievement of Georg Lukacs: The Problem of the Creative Norm." <u>Meanjin</u> 31 (1972), 117-29.
f407. ----------. "What Is Marxist Criticism?" <u>Meanjin</u> 35 (1976), 339-46.

f408. Loewy, Ernst, *et al* . <u>Exil: literarische und politische Texte aus dem deutschen Exil, 1933-1945</u> (Stuttgart: Metzler, 1979).

f409. Lomidse, G. I. "Sozialistischer Realismus und Romantismus." <u>WB</u> 17, Heft 6 (1971), 131-47.

f410. Loose, Gerhard. "Grundbegriffe des sozialistischen Realismus." <u>Monatshefte</u> 57 (1965), 162-70.

f411. Lovell, Terry. "Jane Austin and the Gentry: A Study in Literature and Ideology," in F. Barker, *et al* . <u>Literature, Society, and the Sociology of Literature</u> (Colchester: U of Essex, 1977), 118-32.
f412. ----------. <u>Pictures of Reality: Aesthetics, Politics and Pleasure</u> (London: British Film Institute, 1980).

f413. Lowenthal. David. "Orwell: Ethics and Politics in the Pre-*Nineteen Eighty-Four* Writings," in B. R. Barber and M. J. G. McGrath, eds. <u>The Artist and Political Vision</u> (New Brunswick NJ: Transaction Books, 1982), 335-61.

f414. Lowy, Michael. <u>Georg Lukacs--From Romanticism to Bolshevism</u> (London: NLB, 1979).

f415. Lucas, John, ed. <u>Literature and Politics in the Nineteenth Century</u> (London: Methuen, 1971).
f416. ----------, ed. <u>The 1930s: A Challenge to Orthodoxy</u> (Hassocks: Harvester: NY: Barnes & Noble, 1978).

f417. Lucid, Daniel P. "Preface to Revolution: Russian Marxist Literary Criticism, 1883-1917." <u>DAI</u> 33 (1972), 758A.

f418. Lukacher, Ned. "Walter Benjamin's Chthonian Revolution." <u>Boundary</u> 11.1-2 (1982-83), 41-57.

f419. Lukacs, Georg. Uber die Besonderheit als Kategorie der Asthetik (Neuwied u. Berlin: Luchterhand, 1967).

f420. ----------. Probleme der Asthetik (Neuwied: Luchterhand, 1969).

f421. ----------. Solzhenitsyn (London: Merlin, 1970).

f422. ----------. Realism in Our Time: Literature and the Class Struggle (NY: Harper & Row, 1971).

f423. ----------. Writer & Critic, and other Essays (NY: Grosset & Dunlap, 1971).

f424. ----------. The Theory of the Novel: A Historico-Philosophical Essay on the Forms of Great Epic Literature (Cambridge: MIT P, 1971).

f425. ----------. Asthetik (Neuwied: Luchterhand, 1972).

f426. ----------. "The Philosophy of Art ('The Heidelberg Aesthetics')." NHQ 47 (1972), 57-87.

f427. ----------. "Art and Society." NHQ 47 (1972), 44-56.

f428. ----------. "On the Phenomenology of the Creative Process." Philosophical Forum 3 (1972), 371-85.

f429. ----------. Soul and Form (Cambridge MA: MIT P,1974).

f430. ----------. "About the Principles of Dramatic Form." ETJ 26 (1974), 512-20.

f431. ----------. Fruhe Schriften zur Asthetik, 2 vols. (Darmstadt: Luchterhand, 1974-75).

f432. ----------. Essays on Realism (Cambridge MA: MIT P, 1981).

f433. Luking, Bernd. "Introducing Theodor W. Adorno: The Use of Aesthetic Theory for Literature and Criticism." UES 16.2 (1978), 59-63.

f434. Lunn, Eugene. Marxism and Modernism: An Historical Study of Lukacs, Brecht, Benjamin, and Adorno (Berkeley: U of California P, 1982).

f435. Lyotard, Jean-François. "The Unconscious, History, and Phrases: Notes on The Political Unconscious ." NOR 11.1 (1984), 73-79 [on Jameson].

f436. MacCabe, Colin. James Joyce and the Revolution of the Word (London: Macmillan, 1978).

f437. Macherey, Pierre and Etienne Balibar. "Literature as an Ideological Form: Some Marxist Propositions." OLR 3.1 (1978), 4-12.

f438. Malekin, Peter. Liberty and Love: English Literature and Society, 1640-88 (NY: St. Martin's P, 1981).

f439. Maniquis, Robert, ed. "Marxists and the University." Humanities in Soc 6.2-3 (1983) [special issue].

f440. Marcuse, Herbert. Negations: Essays in Critical Theory (London: Allen Lane, 1968).
f441. ----------. Eros and Civilization (London: Pluto, 1969).
f442. ----------. An Essay on Liberation (Boston: Beacon P, 1969).
f443. ----------. The Aesthetic Dimension: Toward a Critique of Marxist Aesthetics (Boston: Beacon P, 1978).

f444. Margolies, David N. The Function of Literature: A Study of Christopher Caudwell's Aesthetics (NY: International Pubs., 1969).

f445. Makler, Philip. "A Marxist Theory of Literary Tragedy: From Marx to Althusser." DAI40 (1979), 2652A-53A.

f446. Manganiello, Dominic. Joyce's Politics (London and Boston: Routledge & Kegan Paul, 1980).

f447. Mao Tse-Tung. On Literature and Art (Peking: Foreign Languages Press, 1967).

f448. Markow, Dmitri. "Uber die Beziehungen des socialistischen Realismus zu anderen literarischen Stromungen." WB 17, Heft 3 (1971), 80-97.
f449. ----------. "Der sozialistische Realismus--ein neues asthetisches System." KuL 23 (1975), 899-916.
f450. ----------. "On the Theoretical Foundations of the Poetics of Socialist Realism." SovL 7 (1976), 120-26.

f451. Markus, Gyorgy. "On George Lukacs' Unpublished Aesthetics." Philosophical Forum 3 (1972), 309-13.

f452. Martinson, Steven D. "'Wo die Wege sich scheiden': Georg Lukacs' Case Against Modernism." FMLS 17.1 (1981), 18-25.

f453. Marx, Karl and Friedrich Engels. Uber Kunst und Literatur, 2 vols. (Berlin: Dietz, 1967-68).
f454. ----------. Marx and Engels on Literature and Art (St. Louis: Telos, 1973).

f455. Maxwell-Mahon, W. D. "Marxist Dialecticism and Literary Criticism." UES 16.2 (1978), 51-57.

f456. McCanles, Michael. Dialectical Criticism and Renaissance Literature (Berkeley: U of California P, 1975).

f457. McCoy, Richard C. Sir Philip Sidney: Rebellion in Arcadia (New Brunswick NJ: Rutgers UP, 1979).

f458. McCrea, Brian. Henry Fielding and the Politics of Mid-Eighteenth-Century England (Athens: U of Goergia P, 1981).

f459. McDiarmid, Lucy. Saving Civilization: Yeats, Eliot, and Auden between the Wars (Cambridge and NY: Cambridge UP, 1984).

f460. McDonnell, Kevin and Kevin Robins. "Marxist Cultural Theory: The Althusserian Smokescreen," in S. Clarke, et al . One-Dimensional Marxism: Althusser and the Politics of Culture (London: Allison & Busby, 1980), 157-231.

f461. McGann, Jerome J. "Introduction: A Point of Reference," in J. J. McGann, ed. Historical Studies and Literary Criticism (Madison: U of Wisconsin P, 1985), 3-21.

f462. McLeod, Anne. "The Socialist Realist Perspective: A Theoretical Critique." ISlSt 6 (1985), 46-63.

f463. Meehan, Michael. Liberty and Politics in Eighteenth-Century England (London: Croom Helm, 1986).

f464. Mehlman, Jeffrey. Revolution and Repetition: Marx/Hugo/Balzac (Berkeley: U of California P, 1977).

f465. Meintema, Annie. "Friedrich Engels' Influence on the Rise and Development of Soviet Russian Literary Theories," in A. G. F. Holk, ed. Dutch Contributions to the Ninth International Congress of Slavists (Amsterdam: Rodopi, 1983), 110-24.

f466. Melada, Ivan. Guns for Sale: War and Capitalism in English Literature, 1851-1939 (Jefferson NC: McFarland, 1983).

f467. Menard, Jacques. "Lukacs et la théorie du roman historique." NRF (Oct. 1972), 229-38.

f468. Menninghaus, Winfried. Walter Benjamins Theorie der Sprachmagie (Frankfurt: Suhrkamp, 1980).
f469. ----------. "Walter Benjamins romantische Idee des Kunstwerks und seiner Kritik." Poetica 12 (1980), 421-42.

f470. Mercer, Colin. "After Gramsci." Screen Education 36 (1980), 5-15.
f471. ----------. "Paris Match: Marxism, Structuralism and the Problem of Literature," in J. Hawthorn, ed. Criticism and Critical Theory (London: Arnold, 1984), 43-57.

f472. Metschler, Thomas. "Literature and Art as an Ideological Form." NLH 11 (1979), 21-39.

f473. Miles, David H. "Portrait of the Artist as a Young Hegelian: Lukacs' *Theory of the Novel* ." PMLA 94 (1979), 22-35.

f474. Miller, Nikolaus. "Kritische Asthetik (Benjamin, Adorno, Szondi)," in F. Nemec and W. Solms, eds. Literaturwissenschaft Heute (Munich: Fink, 1979), 91-127.

f475. Milne, Gordon. The American Political Novel (Norman: U of Oklahoma P, 1966).

f476. Milner, Andrew. "Poor Protected Inwardness: Georg Lukacs and Social Realism." NLRev 5 (1978), 27-37.

f477. Mitchell, Stanley. "Lukacs' Concept of 'the Beautiful,'" in G. H. R. Parkinson, ed. Georg Lukacs: The Man, His Work and His Ideas (NY: Vintage, 1970), 219-35.

f478. Mittenzwei, Werner. "The Brecht-Lukacs Debate," in G. C. LeRoy and U. Beitz, eds. Preserve and Create: Essays in Marxist Literary Criticism (NY: Humanities, 1973).
f479. ----------, ed. Dialog und Kontroverse mit Georg Lukacs: Der Methodenstreit deutscher sozialistischer Schriftsteller (Leipzig: Reclam, 1975) [includes Mittenzwei's "Gesichtspunkte: Zur Entwicklung der literaturtheoretischen Position Georg Lukacs," 9-104].

f480. Mjasnikov, A. S. "Sozialistischer Realismus und Literaturtheorie." SuF 19 (1967), 669-716.
f481. ----------. "Aesthetics of Struggle and Truth (V.I. Lenin's Article 'Party Organization and Party Literature' and Problems of the Theory of Literature)." SovL 8 (1969), 146-67.
f482. ----------. "Die Vielfalt der Kunstlerischen Formen des sozialistischen Realismus." WB 17, Heft 3 (1971), 195-212.

f483. Mocnik, Rastko. "Toward a Materialist Concept of Literature." Cultural Critique 4 (1986), 171-89.

f484. Mohanty, S. P. "History at the Edge of Discourse: Marxism, Culture, Interpretation." Diacritics 12.3 (1982), 33-46 [on Jameson].

f485. Moore, Madeline. The Short Season Between Two Silences: The Mystical and the Political in the Novels of Virginia Woolf (Boston: Allen & Unwin, 1984).

f486. Morawski, Stefan. "Lenin as Literary Theorist." Science & Society 29 (1965), 3-25.

f487. ----------. "The Aesthetic Views of Marx and Engels." JAAC 28 (1970), 301-14.

f488. ----------. "Politicians versus Artists." Arts in Society 10 (1973), 8-18.

f489. ----------. Inquiries into the Fundamentals of Aesthetics (Cambridge: M.I.T. Press, 1974).

f490. ----------. "Art, Censorship and Socialism." Praxis 1 (1975), 38-47.

f491. ----------. "Contemporary Approaches to Aesthetic Inquiry: Absolute Demands and Limited Possibilities." CritI 4 (1977), 55-83.

f492. ----------. "Historicism and the Philosophy of Art." Praxis 4 (1978), 71-85.

f493. ----------. "The School of Althusser and Aesthetic Thought." Praxis 5 (1981), 73-76.

f494. Moretti, Franco. "The Spell of Indecision," in C. Nelson and L. Grossberg, eds. Marxism and the Interpretation of Culture (Urbana: U of Illinois P, 1988), 339-46.

f495. Morris, Tom. "On the Alienation of Marxist Literary Criticism." Sphinx 9 (1979), 59-64.

f496. Morson, Gary Saul. "The Heresiarch of *Meta* ." PTL 3 (1978), 407-27.

f497. ----------. "Socialist Realism and Literary Theory." JAAC 37 (1979), 121-33.

f498. Mozejko, Edward. Der Sozialistische Realismus: Theorie, Entwicklung und Versagen einer Literaturmethode (Bonn: Bouvier, 1977).

f499. Mueller, Marlies. Les idées politiques dans le roman héroique de 1630 a 1670 (Cambridge: Dept. of Romance Languages and Literatures, Harvard University, 1984).

f500. Mulhern, Francis. "The Marxist Aesthetics of Christopher Caudwell." New Left Review 85 (1974), 37-58.

f501. Mullenbrock, Heinz-Joachim. Whigs contra Tories: Studien zum Einfluss der Politik auf die englische Literatur des fruhen 18. Jahrhunderts (Heidelberg: C. Winter, 1974).

f502. Muller, Harro. "Materialismus und Hermeneutik: Zu Benjamins spaten theoretischen Schriften," in U. Nassen, ed. Studien zur Entwicklung einer Materialen Hermeneutik (Munich: Fink, 1979), 212-33.

f503. ----------. "Gesellschaftliche Funktion und asthetische Autonomie: Benjamin, Adorno, Habermas," in H. Brackert and J. Stuckrath, eds.

Literaturwissenschaft: Grundkurs 2 (Reinbeck bei Hamburg: Rowohlt, 1981), 329-40.

f504. Munton, Alan and Alan Young. Seven Writers of the English Left: A Bibliography of Literature and Politics, 1916-1980 (NY: Garland, 1981).

f505. Munz-Koenen, Ingeborg. "Auf dem Wege zu einer marxistischen Literaturtheorie: Die Debatte proletarisch-revolutionarer Schriftsteller mit Georg Lukacs," in W. Mittenswei, ed. Dialog und Kontroverse mit Georg Lukacs: Der Methodenstreit deutscher sozialistischer Schriftsteller (Leipzig: Reclam, 1975), 105-52.

f506. Musselwhite, David E. Partings Welded Together: Politics and Desire in the Nineteenth-Century English Novel (London and NY: Methuen, 1987).

f507. Mykyta, Larsya. "Jameson's Utopias." NOR 11.1 (1984), 46-51.

f508. Naeher, Jurgen. Walter Benjamins Allegorie-Begriff als Modell: Zur Konstitution philosophischer Literaturwissenschaft (Stuttgart: Klett, 1977).

f509. Nagele, Rainer. "The Scene of the Other: Theodor W. Adorno's Negative Dialectic in the Context of Poststructuralism." Boundary 11.1-2 (1982-83), 59-79.

f510. Naumann, M. "Literary Production and Reception." NLH 8 (1976), 107-26.

f511. Nelson, Brian. "Lukacs, Zola and the Aesthetics of Realism." NLRev 10 (1982), 39-44.

f512. Nelson, Cary. Our Last First Poets: Vision and History in Contemporary American Poetry (Urbana: U of Illinois P, 1981).
f513. ---------- and Lawrence Grossberg, eds. Marxism and the Interpretation of Culture (Urbana: U of Illinois P, 1988).

f514. Nicolas, Annne. "Pour la poétique d'Henri Meschonnic." Lit 12 (1973), 114-23.

f515. Nixon, Cornelia. Lawrence's Leadership Politics and the Turn Against Women (Berkeley: U of California P, 1986).

f516. Norbrook, David. Poetry and Politics in the English Renaissance (London and Boston: Routledge & Kegan Paul, 1984).

f517. Nordquist, Joan. Louis Althusser: A Bibliography (Santa Cruz CA: Reference and Research Services, 1986).

f518. Norris, Christopher. "Image and Parable: Readings of Walter Benjamin." P&L 7.1 (1982), 15-31.
f519. ----------. "On Marxist Deconstruction: Problems and Prospects." SoRA 17.2 (1984), 203-11.
f520. ----------. "Dialectics and Difference: On the Politics of Deconstruction." SHR 19.2 (1985), 159-69.

f521. Notter, Werner. Die Asthetik der kritischen Theorie (Frankfurt am Main and NY: Lang, 1986) [on Adorno].

f522. O'Brien, Conor Cruise. Writers and Politics (NY: Pantheon, 1965).
f523. ----------. "Passion and Cunning: The Politics of W. B. Yeats," in G. A. White and C. Newman, eds. Literature in Revolution (NY: Holt, Rinehart & Winston, 1972), 142-203.
f524. ----------. The Suspecting Glance (London: Faber & Faber, 1972).

f525. Oglesby, Carl. "Melville, or Water Consciousness and Its Madness," in G. A. White and C. Newman, eds. Literature in Revolution (NY: Holt, Rinehart & Winston, 1972), 123-41.

f526. O'Kane, John. "Althusser, Ideology, and Oppositional Politics." Enclitic 7.1 (1983), 104-16.

f527. Onderlinden, J. W. "Literatur und Engagement." LT 253 (1968), 738-50.

f528. Ovcharenko, Alexander. Socialist Realism and the Modern Literary Process (Moscow: Progress, 1978).

f529. Padgug, Richard. "Select Bibliography on Marxism and the Study of Antiquity." Arethusa 8 (1975), 201-25.

f530. Paetzold, Heinz. "Walter Benjamin's Theory of the End of Art." International Journal of Sociology 7 (1977), 25-75.

f531. Panichas, George, ed. The Politics of Twentieth-Century Novelists (NY: Crowell, 1974).

f532. Parkhomenko, M. and A. Miasnikov, eds. Socialist Realism in Literature and Art: A Collection of Articles (Moscow: Progress, 1971).

f533. Parkinson, G. H. R., ed. Georg Lukacs: The Man, His Work, and His Ideas (NY: Random House, 1970) [includes Parkinson's "Lukacs on the Central Category of Aesthetics," 109-46].
f534. ----------. Georg Lukacs (London: Routledge & Kegan Paul, 1977).

f535. Parrinder, Patrick. "The Accents of Raymond Williams." CritQ 26.1-2 (1984), 47-57.

f536. Pascal, Roy. "Georg Lukacs: the Concept of Totality," in G. H. R. Parkinson, ed. Georg Lukacs: The Man, His Work and His Ideas (NY: Vintage, 1970), 147-71.

f537. Pasternack, Gerhard. Georg Lukacs: spate Asthetik und Literaturtheorie (Konigstein/Ts.: A. Hain, 1985).

f538. Paulin, Tom. Ireland & the English Crisis (Newcastle upon Tyne: Bloodaxe, 1984).

f539. Pechey, Graham. "Formalism and Marxism." OLR 4.2 (1980), 72-81.
f540. ----------. "Scrutiny , English Marxism, and the Work of Raymond Williams." L&H 11.1 (1985), 65-76.

f541. Peck, David M. "The New Marxist Criticism: A Bibliography." MinnR 2-3 (1974), 127-32.
f542. ----------. "Salvaging the Marxist Criticism of the 30s." MinnR 4 (1975), 59-84.
f543. ----------. "The New Marxist Criticism: A Bibliography, II." MinnR 7 (1976), 100-05.

f544. Peper, Jurgen. "Im Namen der Wirklichkeit: Robert Weimanns marxistischer Beitrag zum Selbstverstandnis 'burgerlicher Literaturwissenschaft." DVLG 42 (1968), 573-89.

f545. Pérus, Jean. "Situation de la critique marxiste en France." PP 26.3-4 (1983), 125-31.

f546. Petrow, S. M. "Die Leninische Widerspiegelungstheorie und das Problem des Realismus." WB 17, Heft 3 (1971), 131-59.

f547. Pfaelzer, Jean. The Utopian Novel in America, 1886-1896: The Politics of Form (Pittsburgh: U of Pittsburgh P, 1984).

f548. Pfeil, Fred. "Towards a Portable Marxist Criticism: A Critique and a Suggestion." CE 41 (1980), 753-68.

f549. Pfotenhauer, Helmut. Asthetische Erfahrung und gesellschaftliches System: Untersuchungen zum Spatwerk Walter Benjamins (Stuttgart: J. B. Metzlersche, 1975).

f550. Piercy, Marge and Dick Lourie. "Tom Eliot Meets the Hulk at Little Big Horn: The Political Economy of Poetry," in G. A. White and C. Newman, eds. Literature in Revolution (NY: Holt, Rinehart & Winston, 1972), 57-91.

f551. Pike, David. Lukacs and Brecht (Chapel Hill: U of North Carolina P, 1985).

f552. Piskunov, Vladimir. "The Aesthetic Ideal of Soviet Literature." SovL 8 (1971), 131-38.

f553. Podhoretz, Norman. The Bloody Crossroads: Where Literature and Politics Meet (NY: Simon and Schuster, 1986).

f554. Poirier, Richard. "The Aesthetics of Radicalism." PR 41 (1974), 176-96.

f555. Poster, Mark. Existential Marxism in Post-war France: From Sartre to Althusser (Princeton: Princeton UP, 1975).

f556. Pracht, Erwin. "Socialist Realism," in G. C. LeRoy and U. Beitz, eds. Preserve and Create: Essays in Marxist Literary Criticism (NY: Humanities, 1973).

f557. Pradhan, S. V. "Caudwell's Theory of Poetry: Some Problems of a Marxist Synthesis." BJA 17 (1977), 266-74.

f558. Prawer, S. S. Marx and World Literature Oxford: Oxford UP, 1976).

f559. Quilligan, Maureen. Milton's Spenser: The Politics of Reading (Ithaca: Cornell UP, 1983).

f560. Rabey, David Ian. British and Irish Political Drama in the Twentieth Century: Implicating the Audience (NY: St. Martin's P, 1986).

f561. Rabine, Leslie W. "Searching for the Connections: Marxist-Feminists and Women's Studies." Humanities in Soc 6.2-3 (1983), 195-221.

f562. Raddatz, Fritz J., ed. Marxismus und Literatur, 3 vols. (Reinbeck bei Hamburg: Rowohlt, 1969).

f563. ----------. "Der holzerne Eisenring: Die moderne Literatur zwischen zweierlei Asthetik: Lukacs and Adorno." Merkur 31 (1977), 28-44.

f564. Rader, Melvin. "Marx's Interpretation of Art and Aesthetic Value." BJA 7 (1967), 237-49.

f565. Radnoti, Sandor. "The Early Aesthetics of Walter Benjamin." International Journal of Sociology 7 (1977), 76-123.

f566. Rahv, Philip. Essays on Literature and Politics, 1932-1972 (Boston: Houghton Mifflin, 1978).

f567. Raitiere, Martin N. Faire bitts: Sir Philip Sidney and Renaissance Political Theory (Pittsburgh: Duquesne UP, 1984).

f568. Rance, Nicholas. The Historical Novel and Popular Politics in Nineteenth-Century England (London: Vision, 1975).

f569. Reboussin, Marcel. Drieu La Rochelle et le mirage de la politique (Paris: Nizet, 1980).

f570. Rehar, Jack. "Radical Unworldliness." ELWIU 12.1 (1985), 125-37 [on Jameson].

f571. Reilly, Anne and Prospero Saiz. "Volosinov, Bennett, and the Politics of Writing." ConL 22.4 (1981), 510-43 [Voloshinov, Tony Bennett].

f572. Reis, Thomas. Das Bild des klassischen Schriftstellers bei Georg Lukacs: eine Untersuchung zur Wirkungsgeschichte literarischer Topoi in seiner Literaturtheorie und Asthetik (Frankfurt: R. G. Fischer, 1984).

f573. Reiss, Timothy J. "Social Context and the Failures of Theory." CRCL 13.1 (1986), 76-86.

f574. Reszler, André. L'Esthétique anarchitse (Paris: PUF, 1973).
f575. ---------- and T. G. Sauer, eds. "Politics and Literature." YCGL 22 (1973) [special issue].
f576. ----------. "Bakounine, Marx et l'heritage esthétique du socialisme." Esprit 438 (1974), 222-34.
f577. ----------. L'Intellectuel contre l'Europe (Paris: PUF, 1977).

f578. Reuben, Michael Barrett. "Praxis Made Perfect: The Interpretation of Ontological Marxism." DAI 41 (1980), 670A-71A.

f579. Richter, Dieter. "History and Dialectics in the Materialist Theory of Literature." NGC 6 (1975), 31-47.

f580. Roberts, Julian. Walter Benjamin (London: Macmillan, 1982).

f581. Rochlitz, Rainer. "De la philosophie comme critique littéraire: Walter Benjamin et le jeune Lukacs." RE 1 (1981), 41-59.
f582. ----------. Le jeune Lukacs: 1911-1916: théorie de la forme et philosophie de l'histoire (Paris: Payot, 1983).

f583. Rockmore, Tom, ed. Lukacs Today: Essays in Marxist Philosophy (Dordrecht & Boston: D. Reidel, 1988).

f584. Rodriguez, Iliana and Marc Zimmerman. "First Aesthetic Meditations on Capital." Sub-Stance 15 (1976), 160-86.

f585. Rogin, Michael Paul. Subversive Genealogy: The Politics and Art of Herman Melville (NY: Knopf, 1983).

f586. Roller, Judi M. The Politics of the Feminist Novel (Westport CT: Greenwood P, 1986).

f587. Rose, Gillian. The Melancholy Science: An Introduction to the Thought of Theodor W. Adorno (NY: Columbia UP, 1978).

f588. Rose, Margaret A. Reading the Young Marx and Engels: Poetry, Parody, and the Censor (Totowa NJ: Rowman and Littlefield, 1978).
f589. ----------. Marx's Lost Aesthetic: Karl Marx and the Visual Arts (Cambridge: Cambridge UP, 1984).

f590. Rosen, Robert C. John Dos Passos: Politics and the Writer (Lincoln: U of Nebraska P, 1981).

f591. Ross, Andrew. "The New Sentence and the Commodity Form: Recent American Writing," in C. Nelson and L. Grossberg, eds. Marxism and the Interpretation of Culture (Urbana: U of Illinois P, 1988), 361-80.

f592. Rowe, John Carlos. The Theoretical Dimensions of Henry James (Madison: U of Wisconsin P, 1984).

f593. Rudich, Norman, ed. Weapons of Criticism: Marxism in America and the Literary Tradition (Palo Alto CA: Ramparts P, 1976).

f594. Ruhle, Jurgen. Literature and Revolution: A Critical Study of the Writer and Communism in the Twentieth Century (London: Pall Mall P; NY: Praeger, 1969).

f595. Ryan, Michael. Marxism and Deconstruction: A Critical Introduction (Baltimore: Johns Hopkins UP, 1982).
f596. ----------. "Literary Criticism and Cultural Science: Transformation in the Dominant Paradigm of Literary Study." NDQ 51.1 (1983), 100-12.
f597. ----------. "The Marxism-Deconstruction Debate in Literary Theory." NOR 11.1 (1984), 29-35.

f598. Saalfeld, Lerke von. Die ideologische Funktion des Nibelungenliedes in der preussisch-deutschen Geschichte von seiner Wiederentdeckung bis zum Nationalsozializmus (n.p.: n.p., 1977).

f599. Said, Edward. Beginnings: Intention and Method (NY: Basic, 1975).
f600. ----------. Orientalism (NY: Random House, 1978).
f601. ----------. The World, the Text, and the Critic (Cambridge MA: Harvard UP, 1983).

f602. Saiz, Prospero and Anne Reilly, eds. "Marxism and the Crisis of the Word." ConL 22.4 (1981) [special issue].

f603. Sale, Roger. English Literature in History, 1780-1830: Pastoral and Politics (NY: St. Martin's P, 1983).

f604. Sander, Hans-Dietrich. Marxistische Ideologie und allgemeine Kunsttheorie (Tubingen: Mohr, 1970).

f605. Sanders, Scott. D. H. Lawrence: The World of Five Major Novels (NY: Viking, 1973).
f606. ----------. "Towards a Social Theory of Literature." Telos 18 (1973-74), 107-21.

f607. San Juan, Epifanio, Jr. "Marxism and the Poetics of Georg Lukacs." QQ 80 (1973), 547-55.

f608. Sargent, Lyman Tower. "Camus: The Absurdity of Politics," in B. R. Barber and M. J. G. McGrath, eds. The Artist and Political Vision (New Brunswick NJ: Transaction Books, 1982), 87-115.

f609. Sartre, Jean-Paul. Politics and Literature (London: Calder & Boyers, 1973).

f610. Sauerland, Karol. Einfuhrung in die Asthetik Adornos (Berlin & NY: de Gruyter, 1979).

f611. Scanlan, James P. "Can Realism be Socialist?" BJA 14 (1974), 41-55.
f612. ----------. "The Impossibility of a Uniquely Authentic Marxist Aesthetic." BJA 16 (1976), 128-36.

f613. Scattergood, V. J. Politics and Poetry in the Fifteenth Century (London: Blandford, 1971).

f614. Schamber, Ellie Nower. The Artist as Politician: The Relationship between the Art and the Politics of the French Romantics (Lanham MD: UP of America, 1984).

f615. Scheckner, Peter. Class, Politics, and the Individual: A Study of the Major Works of D. H. Lawrence (Rutherford NJ: Fairleigh Dickinson UP, 1985).

f616. Scheinman, Marc. "Trotsky and Malraux: The Political Imagination," in B. R. Barber and M. J. G. McGrath, eds. The Artist and Political Vision (New Brunswick NJ: Transaction Books, 1982), 117-44.

f617. Schoolman, Morton. "Marcuse's Aesthetics and the Displacement of Critical Theory." NGC 8 (1976), 54-79.

f618. Schrader, Gerd. Expressive Sachlichkeit: Anmerkungen zur Kunstphilosophie und Essayistik Theodor W. Adornos (Konigstein/Ts.: Hain, 1986).

f619. Schultz, Karl. "Vorlaufige Bibliographie der Schriften Theodor W. Adornos," in H. Schweppenhauser, ed. Theodor W. Adorno zum Gedachtnis (Frankfurt am Main: Suhrkamp, 1971), 177-239.

f620. Seaton, James. "Marxism Without Difficulty: Fredric Jameson's The Political Unconscious ." CentR 28-29 (1984-85), 122-42.

f621. Seehas, Ilse. "Der tschechische Beitrag zur Theorie des sozialistischen Realismus." WB 18.1 (1972), 46-72.

f622. Shanley, Mary Lyndon and Peter G. Stillman. "Mark Twain: Technology, Social Change, and Political Power," in B. R. Barber and M. J. G. McGrath, eds. The Artist and Political Vision (New Brunswick NJ: Transaction Books, 1982), 267-89.

f623. Sharpe, Kevin. Criticism and Compliment: The Politics of Literature in the England of Charles I (Cambridge and NY: Cambridge UP, 1987).
f624. ---------- and Steven N. Zwicker, eds. Politics of Discourse: The Literature and History of Seventeenth-Century England (Berkeley: U of California P, 1987).

f625. Shepherd, Simon. Marlowe and the Politics of Elizabethan Theater (NY: St. Martin's P, 1986).

f626. Shor, Ira. "Notes on Marxism and Method." CE 34 (1972), 173-77.
f627. ----------. "Questions Marxists Ask About Literature." CE 34 (1972), 178-79.

f628. Sibjoris, Rimvydas. "Tolstoy's Aesthetics in Soviet Perspective." Bucknell Rev (1970), 103-16.

f629. Siegel, Holger. Sowjetische Literaturtheorie (1917-1940): Von der historische-materialistischen zur marxistisch-leninistischen Literaturtheorie (Stuttgart: Metzler, 1981).

f630. Siegel, Paul N., ed. Leon Trotsky on Literature and Art (NY: Pathfinder, 1971).

f631. Siegmund-Schultze, Dorothea. "Raymond Williams' Concept of Culture." Zeitschrift fur Anglistik und Amerikanistik 22 (1974), 131-45.

f632. Simons, Elisabeth. "Socialist Realism--Development of the Theory in the German Democratic Republic since 1955," in G. C. LeRoy and U. Beitz, eds. Preserve and Create: Essays in Marxist Literary Criticism (NY: Humanities, 1973), 246-68.

f633. Slaughter, Cliff. Marxism, Ideology, and Literature (Atlantic Highlands NJ: Humanities P, 1980).

f634. Smith, Duncan. "Prose and Found Poetry and Anti-Modernist Aesthetics: A Modernist Response to Capitalist and Socialist Aesthetic Neutralization." MinnR 15 (1980), 98-111.

f635. Smith, John B. "Toward a Marxist Poetics." Style 16.1 (1982), 1-21.

f636. Smith, Steve. "Marxism and Ideology: Joseph Conrad, Heart of Darkness ," in D. Tallack, ed. Literary Theory at Work: Three Texts (Totowa NJ: Barnes & Noble, 1987), 181-200.

f637. Smith, Steven B. Reading Althusser: An Essay on Structural Marxism (Ithaca: Cornell UP, 1984).

f638. Socialist Realism in Literature and Art: A Collection of Articles (Moscow: Progress, 1971).

f639. Solomon, Maynard, ed. Marxism and Art (NY: Vintage, 1974).

f640. Sontag, Susan. Against Interpretation (NY: Farrar, Straus & Giroux, 1966).
f641. ----------. Styles of Radical Will (NY: Farrar, Straus & Giroux, 1969).

f642. Spender, Stephen. "Writers and Politics." Partisan Rev 34 (1967), 359-81.
f643. ----------. The Thirties and After: Poetry, Politics, People, 1933-1970 (NY: Random, 1978).

f644. Sperber, Murray. Literature and Politics (Rochelle NJ: Hayden, 1979).

f645. Spivak, Gayatri Chakravorty. "Marx after Derrida," in W. Cain, ed. Philosophical Approaches to Literature: New Essays on Nineteenth and Twentieth-Century Texts (Lewisburg: Bucknell UP, 1984), 227-46.
f646. ----------. "Can the Subaltern Speak?" in C. Nelson and L. Grossberg, eds. Marxism and the Interpretation of Culture (Urbana: U of Illinois P, 1988), 271-313.

f647. Sprinker, Michael. "The Part and the Whole." Diacritics 12.3 (1982), 57-71 [on Lukacs, Jameson].
f648. ----------. "Politics and Theory: Althusser and Sartre." MLN 100.5 (1985), 989-1011.

f649. Stacy, R. H. Russian Literary Criticism: A Short History (Syracuse NY: Syracuse UP, 1974) [chap. 9: "Marxist and Soviet Criticism"].

f650. Staden, Heinrich von. "Greek Art and Literature in Marx's Aesthetics." Arethusa 8 (1975), 119-44.
f651. ----------. "Nietzsche and Marx on Greek Art and Literature: Case Studies in Reception." Daedalus 105 (1976), 79-96.

f652. Stadtke, Klaus. "G. W. Plechanow zu Fragen der Asthetik und Literaturwissenschaft." WB 23.3 (1977), 44-77.

f653. Stallybrass, Peter and Allon White. The Politics and Poetics of Transgression (Ithaca: Cornell UP, 1986).

f654. Stanfield, Paul Scott. Yeats and Politics in the 1930s (NY: St. Martin's P, 1988).

f655. Staton, Shirley F., ed. Literary Theories in Praxis (Philadelphia: U of Pennsylvania P, 1987) [pt. 5: "Sociological Criticism: Historical, Marxist, Feminist"].

f656. Stein, Peter, ed. Theorie der politischen Dichtung (Munich: Nymphenburger, 1973).

f657. Steiner, George. Language and Silence: Essays on Language, Literature, and the Inhuman (NY: Atheneum, 1967) ["Marxism and Literature," 303-92].
f658. ----------. Extraterritorial: Papers on Literature and the Language Revolution (NY: Atheneum, 1971).

f659. Stephan, Alexander. "Georg Lukacs' erste Beitrage zur marxistischen Literaturtheorie." BrechtJ (1975), 79-111.

f660. Stierle, Karlheinz. "Walter Benjamin und die Erfahrung des Lesens." Poetica 12 (1980), 227-48.

f661. Stoekl, Allan. Politics, Writing, Mutilation: The Case of Bataille, Blanchot, Roussel, Leiris, and Ponge (Minneapolis: U of Minnesota P, 1985).

f662. Stoessel, Marleen. Aura: Das vergessene Menschliche: Zu Sprache und Erfahrung bei Walter Benjamin (Munich: Hanser, 1983).

f663. Stoljar, Margaret. "Cultural Politics and Literary Theory in the German Democratic Republic." JES 12.2 (1982), 130-49.

f664. Stone, Lawrence. "Modern Marxist Criticism and Lucien Goldmann." PRom 2, supp. 1 (1980), 31-39.

f665. Strong, Tracy B. "Shakespeare: Elizabethan Statecraft and Machiavellianism," in B. R. Barber and M. J. G. McGrath, eds. The Artist and Political Vision (New Brunswick NJ: Transaction Books, 1982), 193-220.

f666. Stuben, Jens. Parteilichkeit: Zur Kritik der marxistischen Literaturtheorie (Bonn: Bouvier, 1974).

f667. Suchkov, Boris. "Lenin and the Problems of Modern Art." SovL 4 (1980), 139-44.

f668. Sullivan, J. P. Literature and Politics in the Age of Nero (Ithaca: Cornell UP, 1985).

f669. Sutherland, John. "The Politics of English Studies in the British University, 1960-1984," in J. J. McGann, ed. Historical Studies and Literary Criticism (Madison: U of Wisconsin P, 1985), 126-40.

f670. Suvin, Darko. "The Cognitive Commodity: Fictional Discourse as Novelty and Circulation." Mosaic 19.2 (1986), 85-99.
f671. ----------. "Can People be (Re)Presented in Fiction?: Toward a Theory of Narrative Agents and a Materialist Critique beyond Technocracy or Reductionism," in C. Nelson and L. Grossberg, eds. Marxism and the Interpretation of Culture (Urbana: U of Illinois P, 1988), 663-96.

f672. Swingewood, Alan. The Novel and Revolution (London: Macmillan; NY: Barnes & Noble, 1975).

f673. "Symposium on Marxist Aesthetic Thought." ASoc 12 (1975), 216-41.

f674. Sypher, Eileen. "Towards a Theory of the Lyric: Georg Lukacs and Christopher Caudwell." Praxis 3 (1976), 173-83.

f675. Szanto, George. Narrative Taste and Social Perspectives: The Matter of Quality (NY: St. Martin's P, 1987).

f676. Szili, Joseph. "Recent Trends of Marxist Criticism in the Countries of Eastern Europe," in S. G. Nichols, Jr. and R. B. Vowles, eds. Comparatists at Work: Studies in Comparative Literature (Waltham MA: Blaisdell, 1968), 91-107.

f677. Szondi, Peter. "Hope in the Past: On Walter Benjamin." CritI 4 (1977-78), 491-506.

f678. Tar, Zoltan. The Frankfurt School: The Critical Theories of Max Horkheimer and Theodor W. Adorno (NY: Wiley, 1977).

f679. Tarrow, Susan. Exile from the Kingdom: A Political Rereading of Albert Camus (University AL: U of Alabama P, 1985).

f680. Tennenhouse, Leonard. Power on Display: The Politics of Shakespeare's Genres (NY: Methuen, 1986).

f681. Thibaudeau, Jean. "Preliminary Notes on the Prison Writings of Gramsci: The Place of Literature in Marxian Theory." Praxis 3 (1976), 3-29.

f682. Thomas, Andrew and Ian White. "A Bibliographical Note on Althusserian Approaches to Literature." Praxis 5 (1981), 89-93.

f683. Thornton, Ronald Wayne. "Marcel Proust and Marxist Literary Criticism from the Nineteen Twenties to the Nineteenth Seventies." DAI 40 (1979), 2050A.

f684. Tiedemann, Rolf. Studien zur Philosophie Walter Benjamins (Frankfurt am Main: Suhrkamp, 1965).
f685. ----------. "Bibliographie der Erstdrucke von Benjamins Schriften," in S. Unseld, ed. Zur Aktualitat Walter Benjamins (Frankfurt am Main: Suhrkamp, 1979), 225-79.
f686. ----------. Dialektik im Stillstand (Frankfurt am Main: Suhrkamp, 1983).

f687. Trager, Claus. "Materialistische Dialektik in den Literatur- und Kunstwissenschaften." WB 18.5 (1972), 10-28.
f688. ----------. Studien zur Realismustheorie und Methodologie der Literaturwissenschaft (Leipzig: Reclam, 1972).

f689. Transue, Pamela J. Virginia Woolf and the Politics of Style (Albany: SUNY P, 1986).

f690. Trueblood, Paul Graham, ed. Byron's Political and Cultural Influence in Nineteenth-Century Europe: A Symposium (Atlantic Highlands NJ: Humanities P, 1981).

f691. Truitt, Willis H. "Towards an Empirical Theory of Art: A Retrospective Comment on Max Raphael's Contribution to Marxian Aesthetics." BJA 2 (1971), 227-36.
f692. ---------- and Sheila M. Meeha. "A Note on Revolutionary Art and Ideology." Praxis 1.2 (1976), 81-90.

f693. Turner, James. The Politics of Landscape: Rural Scenery and Society in English Poetry, 1630-1660 (Cambridge: Harvard UP, 1979).

f694. Turner, John. Wordsworth: Play and Politics: A Study of Wordsworth's Poetry, 1787-1800 (NY: St. Martin's P, 1985).

f695. Ulle, Dieter. "Burgerliche Kulturkritik und Asthetik: Bemerkungen zu Theodor W. Adornos Schrift Asthetische Theorie ." WB 18.6 (1972), 133-54.
f696. ----------. "'Kulturrevolution' und Kunst: Bemerkungen zur Kunstauffassung Herbert Marcuses." WB 19.12 (1973), 93-104.

f697. Unger, Peter. Walter Benjamin als Rezensent: Die Reflexion eines Intellektuellen auf die zeitgeschichtliche Situation (Berlin: Peter Lang, 1974).

f698. Unseld, Siegfried, ed. Zur Aktualitat Walter Benjamins (Frankfurt am Main: Suhrkamp, 1972).

f699. Vassen, Florian. Methoden der Literaturwissenschaft. II: Marxistische Literaturtheorie und Literatursoziologie (Dusseldorf: Bertelsmann, 1972).

f700. Vazquez, Adolfo Sanchez. Art and Society: Essays in Marxist Aesthetics (NY: Monthly Review P, 1973).

f701. Vivas, Eliseo. "Marcuse on Art." ModA 14 (1970), 140-49.

f702. Waldman, Diane. "Critical Theory and Film: Adorno and 'The Cultural Industry' Revisited." NGC 12 (1977), 39-60.

f703. Waldvogel, Markus. Die Lyriktheorie Th. W. Adornos (Zurich: Juris, 1978).

f704. Wang, Fengzhen. "Marxist Literary Criticism in China," in C. Nelson and L. Grossberg, eds. Marxism and the Interpretation of Culture (Urbana: U of Illinois P, 1988), 715-22.

f705. Ward, Aileen. "The Forging of Orc: Blake and the Idea of Revolution," in G. A. White and C. Newman, eds. Literature in Revolution (NY: Holt, Rinehart & Winston, 1972), 204-27.

f706. Wartofsky, Marx W. "Art as Humanizing Praxis." Praxis 1 (1975), 56-65.

f707. Wasson, Richard. "New Marxist Criticism: Introduction." CE 34 (1972), 169-72.
f708. ----------. "'The True Possession of Time': Paul Nizan, Marxism, and Modernism." Boundary 5 (1977), 395-410.

f709. Watkins, Evan. "Raymond Williams and Marxist Criticism." Boundary 4 (1976), 933-46.

f710. Watson, George. Politics and Literature in Modern Britain (Totowa NJ: Rowman and Littlefield, 1977).

f711. Wawrzyn, Lienhard. Walter Benjamins Kunsttheorie: Kritik einer Rezeption (Darmstadt: Luchterhand, 1973).

f712. Weber, Samuel. "Capitalizing History: Notes on *The Political Unconscious*." Diacritics 13.2 (1983), 14-28 [on Jameson].

f713. Weber, Shierry. "Walter Benjamin: Commodity Fetishism, the Modern and the Experience of History," in The Unknown Dimensions: European Marxism Since Lenin (NY: Basic Books, 1972).

f714. Weigmann, Hermann. Ernst Blochs asthetische Kriterien und ihre interpretative Funktion in seinen literarischen Aufsatze (Bonn: Bouvier, 1975).

f715. Weimann, Robert. Structure and Society in Literary History (Charlottesville: U of Virginia P, 1976).

f716. Weimar, Klaus. Anatomie marxistischer Literaturtheorien (Bern: Francke, 1977).

f717. Wellek, René. "The Early Literary Criticism of Walter Benjamin." Rice University Studies 57 (1971), 123-34.
f718. ----------. "Walter Benjamin's Literary Criticism in His Marxist Phase," in J. P. Strelka, ed. The Personality of the Critic (University Park PA: Pennsylvania State UP, 1973).
f719. ----------. "Marxist Literary Criticism." YR 62 (1972), 119-26 [on Jameson].
f720. ----------. Four Critics: Croce, Valery, Lukacs, and Ingarden (Seattle: U of Washington P, 1981).
f721. ----------. A History of Modern Criticism: 1750-1950: Vol. 6: American Criticism, 1900-1950 (New Haven: Yale UP, 1986) ["Marxist Criticism," 89-98].

f722. Wellmer, Albrecht. Zur Dialektik von Moderne und Postmoderne: Vernunftkritik nach Adorno (Frankfurt am Main: Suhrkamp, 1985).

f723. Werckmeister, O. K. "Marx on Ideology and Art." NLH 4 (1973), 501-19.

f724. "Wertung von Kunst und Literatur in der entwickelten sozialistischen Gesellschaft." WB 26.10 (1980) [special issue].

f725. Wess, Robert. "Notes Toward a Marxist Rhetoric." BuR 28.2 (1983), 126-48.

f726. Wessell, Leonard P., Jr. "The Aesthetics of Living Form in Schiller and Marx." JAAC 37 (1978), 189-201.

f727. Wessely, Anna. "Antal and Lukacs: The Marxist Approach to the History of Art." NHQ 73 (1979), 114-25.

f728. West, Cornell. "Lukacs: A Reassessment." MinnR 19 (1982), 86-102.
f729. ----------. "Fredric Jameson's Marxist Hermeneutics." Boundary 11.1-2 (1982-83), 177-200.

f730. Whigham, Frank. Ambition and Privilege: The Social Tropes of Elizabethan Courtesy Theory (Berkeley: U of California P, 1984).

f731. White, George Abbott and Charles Newman, eds. Literature in Revolution (NY: Holt, Rinehart & Winston, 1972) [includes White's "Ideology and Literature: *American Renaissance* and F. O. Matthiessen," 430-500].

f732. White, Hayden. "Getting Out of History." Diacritics 12.3 (1982), 2-13 [on Jameson].

f733. Widdowson, Peter, ed. Re-reading English (London and NY: Methuen, 1982).

f734. Widmer, Kingsley. "The End of Criticism: Some Reflections on Radical Practice." Praxis 1.1 (1975), 88-97.

f735. Wiesenthal, Liselotte. Zur Wissenschaftstheorie Walter Benjamins (Frankfurt: Athenaum, 1973).

f736. Williams, Raymond. Communications, rev. ed. (NY: Barnes & Noble, 1967).
f737. ----------. "On Solzhenitsyn," in G. A. White and C. Newman, eds. Literature in Revolution (NY: Holt, Rinehart & Winston, 1972), 318-34.
f738. ----------. The Country and the City (NY: Oxford UP, 1973).
f739. ----------. Television: Technology and Cultural Form (NY: Schocken Books, 1975).
f740. ----------. "Post-war British Marxism." New Left Review 100 (1976-77), 81-94.
f741. ----------. Marxism and Literature (Oxford: Oxford UP, 1977).
f742. ----------. "Literature *in* Society," in H. Schiff, ed. Contemporary Approaches to English Studies (London: Heinemann; NY: Barnes & Noble, 1977), 24-37.
f743. ----------. Politics and Letters: Interviews with 'New Left Review' (London: New Left Books, 1979).
f744. ----------. Problems in Materialism and Culture (London: New Left Books, 1980).

f745. ----------. Culture (Glasgow: Fontana/Collins, 1981) [pubd. in USA as The Sociology of Culture (NY: Schocken Books, 1982)].

f746. ----------. Writing in Society (London: Verso, [1983?]).

f747. ----------. The Year 2000 (NY: Pantheon Books, 1983).

f748. ----------. Keywords: A Vocabulary of Culture and Society, rev. ed. (NY: Oxford UP, 1985).

f749. Willig, Herbert. "Die Aktualitat der kritischen Theorie von Adorno." FH 35.3 (1980), 55-69.

f750. Wilson, William Garrett, Jr. "V. N. Voloshinov: A Marriage of Formalism and Marxism," in P. V. Zima, ed. Semiotics and Dialectics: Ideology and the Text (Amsterdam: Benjamins, 1981), 39-102.

f751. Winegarten, Renée. Writers and Revolution: The Fatal Lure of Action (NY: Watts, 1974).

f752. Wirkus, Bernd. Zur Dialektik der Aufklarung in der Asthetik: Struktur- und Methodenprobleme der Asthetik Georg Lukacs (Cologne: author, 1975).

f753. Witte, Bernd. "Benjamin and Lukacs: Historical Notes on the Relationship between Their Political and Aesthetic Theories." New German Critique 5 (1975), 3-26.

f754. ----------. Walter Benjamin: Der Intellektuelle als Kritiker (Stuttgart: Metzlersche, 1976).

f755. ----------. "Negative Asthetik: Zu Benjamins Theorie und Praxis der literarischen Kritik." Colloquia Germanica 12 (1979), 193-200.

f756. ----------. Walter Benjamin (Reinbek bei Hamburg: Rowohlt, 1985).

f757. Wohlfart, Gunter. "Anmerkungen zur asthetischen Theorie Adornos." PJGG 83 (1976), 370-91.

f758. Wohlfarth, Irving. "On the Messianic Structure of Walter Benjamin's Last Reflections." Glyph 3 (1978), 148-212.

f759. ----------. "No Man's Land: On Walter Benjamin's 'Destructive Character.'" Diacritics 8 (1978), 47-65.

f760. ----------. "Hibernation: On the Tenth Anniversary of Adorno's Death." MLN 94 (1979), 956-87.

f761. ----------. "Walter Benjamin's Image of Interpretation." NGC 17 (1979), 70-98.

f762. ----------. "Die eigene, bis zum Verschwinden reife Einsamkeit." Merkur 35 (1981), 70-91.

f763. ----------. "History, Literature, and the Text: The Case of Walter Benjamin." MLN 96.5 (1981), 1002-14.

f764. Wolin, Richard. Walter Benjamin: An Aesthetic of Redemption (NY: Columbia UP, 1981).

f765. Woodring, Carl. Politics in English Romantic Poetry (Cambridge: Harvard UP, 1970).

f766. Yanarella, Ernest J. and Lee Sigelman, eds. Political Mythology and Popular Fiction (Westport CT: Greenwood P, 1988).

f767. Zaniello, Thomas A. "Ten Propositions of Contemporary Chinese Aesthetics." MinnR 5 (1975), 145-63.

f768. Zeiler, Eberhard. "Heritage and Tradition in Literature: Fundamental Positions of Marxism-Leninism and Some Practical Questions." JSL 8.1-2 (1981-82), 49-60.

f769. Zenck, Martin. Kunst als begriffslose Erkenntnis: zum Kunstbegriff der asthetischen Theorie Theodor W. Adornos (Munchen: W. Fink, 1977).

f770. Zima, P. V., ed. "Texte et idéologie." Degrés 24-25 (1980-81) [special issue].
f771. ----------. "L'Ambivalence dialectique: Entre Benjamin et Bakhtine." RE 1 (1981), 131-40.
f772. ----------, ed. Semiotics and Dialectics: Ideology and the Text (Amsterdam: Banjamins, 1981).
f773. ----------. "Adorno et la crise du langage: Pour une critique de la parataxis." RE 8 (1985), 105-25.

f774. Zimmerman, Marc. "Polarities and Contradictions: Theoretical Bases of the Marxist-Structuralist Encounter." NGC 7 (1976), 69-90.
f775. ----------. "Structural Historicism and Literature: A Brief Survey towards a Marxist Synthesis." ClioW 7 (1977), 53-73.
f776. ----------. "Marxism, Structuralism and Literature: Orientations and Schemata." I&L 2.6 (1978), 27-53.
f777. ----------. "Exchange and Production: Structuralist and Marxist Approaches to Literary Theory." Praxis 4 (1978), 151-68.

f778. Zmegac, Viktor. Kunst und Wirklichkeit: zur Literaturtheorie bei Brecht, Lukacs und Broch (Bad Homburg: Gehlen, 1969).
f779. ----------, ed. Marxistische Literaturkritik (Frankfurt: Athenaum Fischer, 1972).

f780. Zwicker, Steven N. Dryden's Political Poetry: The Typology of King and Nation (Providence: Brown UP, 1972).

f781. ----------. Politics and Language in Dryden's Poetry: The Arts of Disguise (Princeton: Princeton UP, 1984).

G. Feminist Criticism, Gender Criticism

g1. Abel, Elizabeth, ed. <u>Writing and Sexual Difference</u> (Chicago: U of Chicago P, 1982).

g2. ---------- and Emily Abel, eds. <u>The 'Signs' Reader: Women, Gender, and Scholarship</u> (Chicago: U of Chicago P, 1983).

g3. Adelman, Janet. "'This Is and Is Not Cressid': The Characterization of Cressida," in S. N. Garner, C. Kahane, and Madelon Sprengnether, eds. <u>The (M)other Tongue: Essays in Feminist Psychoanalytic Interpretation</u> (Ithaca: Cornell UP, 1985), 119-41.

g4. Allen, Carolyn. "Feminist Criticism and Postmodernism," in J. Natoli, ed. <u>Tracing Literary Theory</u> (Urbana: U of Illinois P, 1987), 278-305.

g5. Archer, Jan, *et al* . "Initiating a Context: A Collective Approach to Feminist Critical Theory." <u>RadT</u> 18 (1980), 33-39.

g6. Ascher, Carol, Louise DeSalvo, and Sara Ruddick, eds. <u>Between Women: Biographers, Novelists, Critics, Teachers, and Artists Write About Their Work on Women</u> (Boston: Beacon, 1984).

g7. Atack, Margaret. "The Other Feminist." <u>Paragraph</u> 8 (1986), 25-39 [discusses Kristeva].

g8. Auerbach, Nina. <u>Communities of Women: An Idea in Fiction</u> (Cambridge: Harvard UP, 1978).

g9. ----------. "Feminist Criticism Reviewed." <u>W&L</u> 1 (1980), 258-68.

g10. ----------. "Magi and Maidens: The Romance of the Victorian Freud," in E. Abel, ed. <u>Writing and Sexual Difference</u> (Chicago: U of Chicago P, 1982), 111-30.

g11. ----------. <u>Woman and the Demon: The Life of a Victorian Myth</u> (Cambridge: Harvard UP, 1982).

g12. ----------. "Why Communities of Women Aren't Enough." <u>TSWL</u> 3.1-2 (1984), 153-57.

g13. ----------. "Engorging the Patriarchy," in J. J. McGann, ed. <u>Historical Studies and Literary Criticism</u> (Madison: U of Wisconsin P, 1985), 229-39 [also in S. Benstock, ed. <u>Feminist Issues in Literary Scholarship</u> (Bloomington: Indiana UP, 1987), 150-60].

g14. Bal, Mieke. <u>Lethal Love: Feminist Literary Readings of Biblical Love Stories</u> (Bloomington: Indiana UP, 1987).

g15. Bamber, Linda. <u>Comic Women, Tragic Men</u> (Stanford: Stanford UP, 1982).

g16. Bammer, Angelika. "Women and Revolution: Their Theories, Our Experience." <u>BuR</u> 27.1 (1982), 143-56 [feminism and Marxism].

g17. Barickman, Richard, *et al* . <u>Corrupt Relations: Dickens, Thackeray, Trollope, Collins, and the Victorian Sexual System</u> (NY: Columbia UP, 1982).

g18. Barr, Marlene S., ed. <u>Future Females: A Critical Anthology</u> (Bowling Green OH: Bowling Green U Popular P, 1981).

g19. ----------. <u>Alien to Femininity: Speculative Fiction and Feminist Theory</u> (Westport CT: Greenwood P, 1987) [includes excellent bibliography].

g20. Barrett, Michele, ed. <u>Virginia Woolf: Women and Writing</u> (London: Women's Press, 1979).

g21. Bassnet, Susan. "Textuality/Sexuality." <u>EiP</u> 9.1 (1984), 1-15.

g22. Baym, Nina. <u>Woman's Fiction: A Guide to Novels by and About Women in America, 1820-1870</u> (Ithaca: Cornell UP, 1978).

g23. ----------. "The Madwoman and Her Languages: Why I Don't Do Feminist Theory." <u>TSWL</u> 3.1-2 (1984), 45-59 [also in S. Benstock, ed. <u>Feminist Issues in Literary Scholarship</u> (Bloomington: Indiana UP, 1987), 45-61].

g24. Bazin, Nancy Topping. <u>Virginia Woolf and the Androgynous Vision</u> (New Brunswick NJ: Rutgers UP, 1973).

g25. Beer, Gillian. "Beyond Determinism: George Eliot and Virginia Woolf," in M. Jacobus, ed. Women Writing and Writing About Women (London: Croom Helm, 1979), 80-99.

g26. Beer, Patricia. Reader, I Married Him: A Study of the Female Characters of Jane Austen, Charlotte Bronte, Elizabeth Gaskell and George Eliot (London: Macmillan, 1974).

g27. Bell, Roseann P., et al . Sturdy Black Bridges: Visions of Black Women in Literature (Garden City NY: Anchor P/Doubleday, 1979).

g28. Benstock, Shari. "The Feminist Critique: Mastering our Monstrosity." TSWL 2 (1983), 137-49.
g29. ----------. "Women's Literary History: To Be Continued." TSWL 5.2 (1986), 165-83.
g30. ----------. Women of the Left Bank: Paris, 1900-1940 (Austin: U of Texas P, 1986).
g31. ----------, ed. Feminist Issues in Literary Scholarship (Bloomington: Indiana UP, 1987) [includes Benstock's "Beyond the Reaches of Feminist Criticism: A Letter from Paris," 7-29].

g32. Berg, Christine and Philippa Berry. "'Spiritual Whoredom': An Essay on Female Prophets in the Seventeenth Century," in F. Barker, et al . 1642: Literature and Power in the Seventeenth Century (Colchester: U of Essex, 1981), 37-54.

g33. Berg, Elizabeth L. "The Third Woman." Diacritics 12.1 (1982), 11-21 [on S. Kofman, L. Irigaray, deconstruction].

g34. Blake, Kathleen. Love and the Woman Question in Victorian Literature: The Art of Self-Postponement (Totowa NJ: Barnes & Noble, 1983).

g35. Blanchard, Lydia. "Women and Fiction: The Limits of Criticism." SNNTS 9 (1977), 339-54.

g36. Booth, Wayne. "Freedom of Interpretation: Bakhtin and the Challenge of Feminist Criticism." CritI 9 (1982), 45-76.

g37. Boumelha, Penny. Thomas Hardy and Women: Sexual Ideology and Narrative Form (Brighton: Harvester P; Totowa NJ: Barnes & Noble, 1982).

g38. Bovenschen, Silvia. "Is There a Feminine Aesthetic?" NGC 10 (1977), 111-37.

g39. Bowlby, Rachel. "The Feminine Female." Social Text 7 (1983), 54-68.

g40. Bowles, Gloria and Renate Duelli Klein, eds. Theories of Women's Studies (London: Routledge, 1983) [includes bibliography, 229-68].

g41. Brooks, David. "'The Male Practice of Feminist Criticism': A Second Moment." LiNQ 13.1 (1985), 17-22.

g42. Brown, Cheryl L. and Karen Olson, eds. Feminist Criticism: Essays on Theory, Poetry and Prose (Metuchen NJ: Scarecrow P, 1978).

g43. Brown, Janet. Feminist Drama: Definition & Critical Analysis (Metuchen NJ: Scarecrow P, 1979).

g44. Brown, Lloyd Wellesley. Women Writers in Black Africa (Westport CT: Greenwood P, 1981).

g45. Brownstein, Rachel M. Becoming a Heroine (NY: Viking, 1982).

g46. Burke, Carolyn. "Introduction to Luce Irigaray's 'When Our Lips Speak Together.'" Signs 6.1 (1980), 66-68.
g47. ----------. "Irigaray through the Looking Glass." Feminist Studies 7.2 (1981), 288-306.
g48. ----------. "Gertrude Stein, the Cone Sisters, and the Puzzle of Female Friendship," in E. Abel, ed. Writing and Sexual Difference (Chicago: U of Chicago P, 1982), 221-42.

g49. Carter, Nancy Corson. "The Prodigal Daughter: A Parable Re-Visioned." Soundings 68.1 (1985), 88-105.

g50. Castle, Terry. Clarissa's Ciphers: Meaning and Disruption in Richardson's 'Clarissa' (Ithaca: Cornell UP, 1982).

g51. Castro, Ginette. "La Critique littéraire féministe: Une nouvelle lecture du roman féminin." RFEA (Nov., 1986), 399-413.

g52. Chase, Cynthia, Nelly Furman, and Mary Jacobus, eds. "Cherchez la femme : Feminist Critique/Feminist Text." Diacritics 12.2 (1982) [special issue].

g53. Chodorow, Nancy. The Reproduction of Mothering. Psychoanalysis and the Sociology of Gender (Berkeley: U of California P, 1978).

g54. Christ, Carol P. Diving Deep and Surfacing: Women Writers on Spiritual Quest (Boston: Beacon P, 1980).

g55. Christian, Barbara. Black Women Novelists: The Development of a Tradition, 1892-1976 (Westport CT: Greenwood P, 1980).
g56. ----------. Black Feminist Criticism: Perspectives on Black Women Writers (NY: Pergamon P, 1985).

g57. Cixous, Hélene. "The Laugh of the Medusa." Signs 1 (1976), 875-99.
g58. ----------. "La Missexualité, ou jouis je?" Poétique 26 (1976), 240-49.
g59. ----------. "Entretien avec Françoise van Rossum-Guyon." Revue des sciences humaines 168 (1977), 479-93.
g60. ----------, et al . La Venue a l'écriture (Paris: UGE, 1977).
g61. ----------. "L'Approche de Clarice Lispector." Poétique 40 (1979), 4018-19.
g62. ----------. "Castration or Decapitation?" Signs 7.1 (1981), 41-55.
g63. ----------. "Portrait of Dora." Diacritics 13.1 (1983), 2-32.

g64. Conley, Vera Andermatt. Hélene Cixous: Writing the Feminine (Lincoln: U of Nebraska P, 1984).

g65. Cornillon, Susan Koppelman, ed. Images of Women in Fiction: Feminist Perspectives (Bowling Green OH: Bowling Green U Popular P, 1972).
g66. ----------. "Development and Implementation of Feminist Literary Criticism." DAI 36 (1976), 5267A.

g67. Coste, Didier. "Rehearsal: An Alternative to Production/Reproduction in French Feminist Discourse," in I. Hassan and S. Hassan, eds. Innovation/Renovation: New Perspectives on the Humanities (Madison: U of Wisconsin P, 1983), 243-62.

g68. Coward, Rosalind and John Ellis. Language and Materialism (London: Routledge & Kegan Paul, 1977).
g69. ----------. Patriarchal Precedents: Sexuality and Social Relations (London: Routledge & Kegan Paul, 1983).
g70. ----------. Female Desire. Women's Sexuality Today (London: Paladin, 1984).
g71. ----------. "Female Desire and Sexual Identity," in M. Diaz-Diocretz and I. M. Zavala, eds. Women, Feminist Identity and Society in the 1980s: Selected Papers (Amsterdam: Benjamins, 1985), 25-36.

g72. Crawford, Mary and Roger Chaffin. "The Reader's Construction of Meaning: Cognitive Research on Gender and Comprehension," in E. A. Flynn and P. P. Schweickart, eds. Gender and Reading: Essays on Readers, Texts, and Contexts (Baltimore: Johns Hopkins UP, 1986), 3-30.

g73. Crosby, Christina. "Stranger than Truth: Feminist Literary Criticism and Speculations on Women." DR 64.2 (1984), 247-59.

g74. Crowder, Diane Griffith. "Amazons and Mothers? Monique Wittig, Hélène Cixous and Theories of Women's Writing." Contemporary Literature 24 (1983), 117-44.

g75. Cunningham, Stuart. "Some Problems of Feminist Literary Criticism." JWSL 1 (1978), 159-78.

g76. Dardigna, Anne-Marie. Les Chateaux d'Eros ou les infortunes du sexe des femmes (Paris: Maspero, 1981).

g77. Davidson, Cathy N. and E. M. Broner, eds. The Lost Tradition: Mothers and Daughters in Literature (NY: Ungar, 1980).

g78. Deutelbaum, Wendy and Cynthia Huff. "Class, Gender, and Family System: The Case of George Sand," in S. N. Garner, C. Kahane, and Madelon Sprengnether, eds. The (M)other Tongue: Essays in Feminist Psychoanalytic Interpretation (Ithaca: Cornell UP, 1985), 260-79.

g79. Diamond, Arlyn and Lee R. Edwards, eds. The Authority of Experience: Essays in Feminist Criticism (Amherst: U of Massachusetts P, 1977).

g80. Donovan, Josephine. "Feminist Style Criticism," in S. K. Cornillon, ed. Images of Women in Fiction: Feminist Perspectives (Bowling Green OH: Bowling Green U Popular P, 1972), 341-54.
g81. ----------, ed. Feminist Literary Criticism: Explorations in Theory (Lexington: UP of Kentucky, 1975).
g82. ----------. "Feminism and Aesthetics." CritI 3 (1977), 605-08.
g83. ----------. "Beyond the Net: Feminist Criticism as a Moral Criticism." DQ 17.4 (1983), 40-57.
g84. ----------. New England Local Color Literature: A Women's Tradition (NY: Ungar, 1983).
g85. ----------. Feminist Theory: The Intellectual Traditions of American Feminism (NY: Ungar, 1985).
g86. ----------. "Toward a Women's Poetics," in S. Benstock, ed. Feminist Issues in Literary Scholarship (Bloomington: Indiana UP, 1987), 98-109.

g87. Dronke, Peter. Women Writers of the Middle Ages (Cambridge: Cambridge UP, 1984).

g88. Dumais, Monique. "Voyage vers les sources: Quelques Discours féministes sur la nature." SRC 13.3 (1984), 345-52 [on Mary Daly].

g89. DuPlessis, Rachel Blau, *et al* . "For the Etruscans: Sexual Difference and Artistic Production--the Debate Over a Female Aesthetic," in H. Eisenstein and A. Jardine, eds. The Future of Difference (Boston: G. K. Hall, 1980), 128-56.
g90. ----------. Writing Beyond the Ending: Narrative Strategies of Twentieth-Century Women Writers (Bloomington: Indiana UP, 1985).

g91. Durham, Carolyn A. "Noman, Everywoman: Claudine Herrmann's *Les Voleuses de langue* ." BuR 27.1 (1982), 169-86.

g92. Durham, Margery. "The Mother Tongue: *Christabel* and the Language of Love," in S. N. Garner, C. Kahane, and Madelon Sprengnether, eds. The (M)other Tongue: Essays in Feminist Psychoanalytic Interpretation (Ithaca: Cornell UP, 1985), 169-93.

g93. Eagleton, Mary, ed. Feminist Literary Theory: A Reader (Oxford: Blackwell, 1986).

g94. Eagleton, Terry. The Rape of Clarissa: Writing, Sexuality, and Class Struggle in Samuel Richardson (Minneapolis: U of Minnesota P, 1982).

g95. Ecker, Gisela. "'A Map for Re-Reading': Intertextualitat aus der Perspektive einer feministischen Literaturwissenschaft," in U. Broich, M. Pfister, and B. Schulte-Middelich, eds. Intertextualitat: Formen, Funktionen, anglistische Fallstudien (Tubingen: Niemeyer, 1985), 297-310.

g96. Edwards, Lee R. Psyche as Hero (Middletown: Wesleyan UP, 1984).

g97. Eisenstein, Hester and Alice Jardine, eds. The Future of Difference (Boston: G. K. Hall, 1980).
g98. ----------. Contemporary Femninist Thought (London: Allen & Unwin, 1984).

g99. Ellmann, Mary. Thinking About Women (NY: Harcourt Brace, 1968).

g100. Elshtain, Jean Bethke. "Feminist Discourse and Its Discontents: Language, Power, and Meaning." Signs 7.3 (1982), 603-21.
g101. ----------. "The New Feminist Scholarship." Salmagundi 70-71 (1986), 3-26.

g102. Erickson, Joyce Quiring. "What Difference? The Theory and Practice of Feminist Criticism." C&L 33.1 (1983), 65-74.

g103. Evans, Mari. Black Women Writers (1950-1980): A Critical Evaluation (Garden City NY: Anchor P/Doubleday, 1984).

g104. Evans, Martha Noel. "Writing as Difference in Violette Leduc's Autobiography *La Batarde* ," in S. N. Garner, C. Kahane, and Madelon Sprengnether, eds. The (M)other Tongue: Essays in Feminist Psychoanalytic Interpretation (Ithaca: Cornell UP, 1985), 306-17.

g105. Farwell, Marilyn R. "Feminist Criticism and the Concept of the Poetic Persona." BuR 24.1 (1978), 139-56.

g106. Felman, Shoshana. "Women and Madness: The Critical Phallacy." Diacritics 5.4 (1975), 2-10.

g107. Féral, Josette. "Antigone or the Irony of the Tribe." Diacritics (Fall, 1978), 2-14.
g108. ----------. "The Powers of Difference," in H. Eisenstein and A. Jardine, eds. The Future of Difference (Boston: G. K. Hall, 1980), 88-94.

g109. Ferres, Kay, comp. "Since *Sexual Politics* : A Selected Bibliography of Feminist Literary Theory." LiNQ 8.3 (1980), 101-09.

g110. Finke, Laurie. "The Rhetoric of Marginality: Why I Do Feminist Theory." TSWL 5.2 (1986), 251-72.

g111. Fleischmann, Fritz, ed. American Novelists Revisited: Essays in Feminist Criticism (Boston: G. K. Hall, 1982).

g112. Flynn, Elizabeth Ann. "Feminist Critical Theory: Three Models." DAI 38 (1978), 4842A.
g113. ---------- and Patrocinio P. Schweickart, eds. Gender and Reading: Essays on Readers, Texts, and Contexts (Baltimore: Johns Hopkins UP, 1986).

g114. Fortunati, Vita and Giovanni Franci. "New Perspectives on Feminist Criticism." QFG 3 (1984), 111-21.

g115. Foster, Shirley. Victorian Women's Fiction: Marriage, Freedom, and the Individual (Totowa NJ: Barnes & Noble, 1985).

g116. Fox-Genovese, Elizabeth. "To Write My Self: The Autobiographies of Afro-American Women," in S. Benstock, ed. Feminist Issues in Literary Scholarship (Bloomington: Indiana UP, 1987), 161-80.

g117. Fox-Luckert, Lucia. Women Novelists in Spain and Spanish America (Metuchen NJ: Scarecrow P, 1979).

g118. Francis, Elizabeth. "Feminist Versions of the Pastoral." CLAQ 7.4 (1982), 7-9, 33.

g119. Freeman, Barbara. "Irigaray at *The Symposium* : Speaking Otherwise." OLR 8.1-2 (1986), 170-77.

g120. Friedman, Susan Stanford. "Modernism of the 'Scattered Remnant': Race and Politics in H. D.'s Development," in S. Benstock, ed. Feminist Issues in Literary Scholarship (Bloomington: Indiana UP, 1987), 208-31.

g121. Froula, Christine. "When Eve Reads Milton: Undoing the Canonical Economy." CritI 10 (1983), 321-47.

g122. Furman, Nelly. "Textual Feminism," in S. McConnell-Ginet, R. Borker, and N. Furman, eds. Women and Language in Literature and Society (NY: Praeger, 1980), 45-54.
g123. ----------. "The Politics of Language: Beyond the Gender Principle?" in G. Greene and C. Kahn, eds. Making a Difference: Feminist Literary Criticism (London: Methuen, 1985), 59-79.

g124. Gallop, Jane. "Psychoanalysis and Feminism in France," in H. Eisenstein and A. Jardine, eds. The Future of Difference (Boston: G. K. Hall, 1980), 106-22.
g125. ----------. Feminism and Psychoanalysis: The Daughter's Seduction (London: Macmillan, 1982).
g126. ----------. "*Writing and Sexual Difference* : The Difference Within." CritI 8.4 (1982), 797-804 [see E. Abel].
g127. ----------. "*Quand nos levres s'écrivent* : Irigaray's Body Politics." RR 74.1 (1983), 77-83.
g128. ----------. "The Mother Tongue," in F. Barker, *et al* . The Politics of Theory (Colchester: U of Essex, 1983), 49-56.
g129. ----------. "Beyond the *Jouissance* Principle." Representations 7 (1984), 110-15.
g130. ----------. "Feminist Criticism and the Pleasure of the Text." NDQ 54.2 (1986), 119-32.
g131. ----------. "French Theory and the Seduction of Feminism." Paragraph 8 (1986), 19-23.

g132. Gardiner, Judith Kegan. "On Female Identity and Writing by Women," in E. Abel, ed. Writing and Sexual Difference (Chicago: U of Chicago P, 1982), 177-92.
g133. ----------, *et al* . "An Interchange on Feminist Criticism in 'Dancing through the Minefield.'" FSt 8.3 (1982), 629-75 [see Kolodny].

g134. ----------. "Mind Mother: Psychoanalysis and Feminism," in G. Greene and C. Kahn, eds. Making a Difference: Feminist Literary Criticism (London: Methuen, 1985),113-45.

g135. ----------. "Gender, Values, and Lessing's Cats," in S. Benstock, ed. Feminist Issues in Literary Scholarship (Bloomington: Indiana UP, 1987), 110-23.

g136. Garner, Shirley Nelson, Claire Kahane, and Madelon Sprengnether, eds. The (M)other Tongue: Essays in Feminist Psychoanalytic Interpretation (Ithaca: Cornell UP, 1985) [includes Garner's "'Women Together' in Virginia Woolf's Night and Day ," 318-33].

g137. Gaudin, Colette, et al . "Feminist Readings: French Texts/American Contexts." YFS 62 (1981) [special issue].

g138. Gelfant, Blanche. Women Writing in America: Voices in Collage (UP of New England, 1984).

g139. Gilbert, Sandra and Susan Gubar. "A Revisionary Company." Novel 10 (1977), 158-66.

g140. ----------. "Life Studies, or, Speech After Long Silence: Feminist Critics Today." CE 40 (1979), 849-63.

g141. ---------- and Susan Gubar. The Madwoman in the Attic: The Woman Writer and the Nineteenth-Century Literary Imagination (New Haven: Yale UP, 1979).

g142. ---------- and Susan Gubar, eds. Shakespeare's Sisters: Feminist Essays on Women Poets (Bloomington: Indiana UP, 1979).

g143. ----------. "Costumes of the Mind: Transvestism as a Metaphor in Modern Literature," in E. Abel, ed. Writing and Sexual Difference (Chicago: U of Chicago P, 1982), 193-220.

g144. ----------. "The Education of Henrietta Adams." Profession 84 (1984), 5-9.

g145. ---------- and Susan Gubar. "'Forward into the Past': The Complex Female Affiliation Complex," in J. J. McGann, ed. Historical Studies and Literary Criticism (Madison: U of Wisconsin, 1985), 240-65.

g146. ----------. "Life's Empty Pack: Notes toward a Literary Daughteronomy." CritI 11.3 (1985), 355-84.

g147. ---------- and Susan Gubar. "Sexual Linguistics: Gender, Language, Sexuality." NLH 16.3 (1985), 515-43.

g148. Gilligan, Carol. In a Different Voice (Cambridge: Harvard UP, 1981).

g149. Ginsberg, Elaine. "Playwrights, Poets, and Novelists: Sisters Under the Skin," in B. Justice and R. Pore, eds. Toward the Second Decade: The

Impact of the Women's Movement on American Institutions (Westport CT: Greenwood P, 1981), 35-40.

g150. Goheen, Jutta. "From the Brothers Grimm to Alice Schwarzer: German Philology and the Feminist Critique." GerSR 5.3 (1982), 381-87.

g151. Goldberg, Rita. Sex and Enlightenment: Women in Richardson and Diderot (Cambridge: Cambridge UP, 1984).

g152. Greene, Gayle. "Feminist and Marxist Criticism: An Argument for Alliances." WS 9.1 (1981), 29-45.
g153. ----------. "Women and Men in Doris Lessing's Golden Notebook : Divided Selves," in S. N. Garner, C. Kahane, and Madelon Sprengnether, eds. The (M)other Tongue: Essays in Feminist Psychoanalytic Interpretation (Ithaca: Cornell UP, 1985), 280-305.
g154. ---------- and Coppélia Kahn, eds. Making a Difference: Feminist Literary Criticism (London: Methuen, 1985) [includes the editors' essay "Feminist Scholarship and the Social Contruction of Woman," 1-36].

g155. Greer, Germaine. "The Tulsa Center for the Study of Women's Literature: What We are Doing and Why We are Doing It." TSWL 1.1 (1982), 5-26.

g156. Gubar, Susan. "'The Blank Page' and the Issues of Female Creativity," in E. Abel, ed. Writing and Sexual Difference (Chicago: U of Chicago P, 1982), 73-94.

g157. Gunew, Sneja. "Feminist Criticism: Positions and Questions." SoRA 16.1 (1983), 151-60.

g158. Hartman, Joan E. and Ellen Messer-Davidow, eds. Women in Print, 2 vols. (NY: MLA, 1982).

g159. Hassauer, Frederike J. "Niemals nur 'eins' zu sein: Gibt es eine weibliche Asthetik?" Merkur 35.7 (1981), 710-16.

g160. Heath, Stephen. "Male Feminism." DR 64.2 (1984), 270-301.

g161. Heilbrun, Carolyn G. Towards Androgyny: Aspects of Male and Female in Literature (London: Victor Gollancz, 1973).
g162. ----------. "Women, Men, Theories, and Literature." ADEB 69 (1981), 13-17.
g163. ----------. "A Response to Writing and Sexual Difference ." CritI 8.4 (1982), 805-11 [see Abel].

g164. ---------- and Margaret Higonnet, eds. The Representation of Women in Fiction (Baltimore: Johns Hopkins UP, 1982).

g165. Henke, Suzette and Elaine Unkeless, eds. Women in Joyce (Urbana: U of Illinois P, 1982).

g166. Herrmann, Claudine. Les Voleuses de langue (Paris: des Femmes, 1976).

g167. Hickok, Kathleen. Representations of Women: Nineteenth-Century British Women's Poetry (Westport CT: Greenwood P, 1984).

g168. Holly, Marcia. "Consciousness and Authenticity: Towards a Feminist Aesthetic," in J. Donovan, ed. Feminist Literary Criticism: Explorations on Theory (Lexington: U of Kentucky P, 1975), 38-47.

g169. Homans, Margaret. Women Writers and Poetic Identity: Dorothy Wordsworth, Emily Bronte, and Emily Dickinson (Princeton: Princeton UP, 1980).
g170. ----------. "Eliot, Wordsworth, and the Scenes of the Sisters' Instruction," in E. Abel, ed. Writing and Sexual Difference (Chicago: U of Chicago P, 1982), 53-72.
g171. ----------. "'Her Very Own Howl': The Ambiguities of Representation in Recent Women's Fiction." Signs 9 (1983), 186-205.

g172. Hongo, Garrett and Catherine Parke. "A Conversation with Sandra M. Gilbert." MissR 9.1 (1985-86), 89-109.

g173. Howe, Florence. "Feminism and the Study of Literature." RadT 1.3 (1976), 3-11.

g174. Huf, Linda M. A Portrait of the Artist as a Young Woman (NY: Ungar, 1983).

g175. Humm, Maggie. Feminist Criticism: Women as Contemporary Critics (NY: St. Martin's P, 1986).

g176. Hutcheon, Linda. "Subject in/of/to History and His Story." Diacritics 16.1 (1986), 78-91.

g177. Iannone, Carol Ann. "Feminist Literary Criticism, 1968-1980: A Reappraisal." DAI 42 (1982), 4823A.
g178. ----------. "Feminist Literary Criticism: At War with Itself." CEA 45.2 (1983), 11-19.

g179. Irigaray, Luce. "Misere de la psychanalyse." Critique 30 (Oct. 1977), 879-903.

g180. ----------. Et l'une ne bouge pas sans l'autre (Paris: Minuit, 1979).

g181. ----------. Amante marine de Friedrich Nietzsche (Paris: Minuit, 1980).

g182. ----------. Le Corps-a-corps avec la mere (Montreal: de la Pleine Lune, 1981).

g183. ----------. Passions élémentaires (Paris: Minuit, 1982).

g184. ----------. Le Croyance meme (Paris: Galilée, 1983).

g185. ----------. L'Oubli de l'air chez Martin Heidegger (Paris: Minuit, 1983).

g186. ----------. "Femmes divines." Critique 41 (Mar. 1985), 294-308.

g187. ----------. The Sex Which Is Not One (Ithaca: Cornell UP, 1985).

g188. ----------. Speculum of the Other Woman (Ithaca: Cornell UP, 1985).

g189. Jacobus, Mary, ed. Women Writing and Writing About Women (London: Croom Helm, 1979) [includes Jacobus' "The Buried Letter: Feminism and Romanticism in Villette," 42-60].

g190. ----------. "The Question of Language: Men of Maxims and The Mill on the Floss," in E. Abel, ed. Writing and Sexual Difference (Chicago: U of Chicago P, 1982), 37-52 [applies Irigaray].

g191. ----------. "Is There a Woman in this Text?" NLH 14.1 (1982), 117-54 [feminism and psychoanalytic criticism].

g192. ----------. Reading Woman: Essays in Feminist Criticism (NY: Columbia UP, 1986).

g193. Jardine, Alice. "Introduction to Julia Kristeva's 'Women's Time.'" Signs 7.1 (1981), 5-12.

g194. ----------. "Pre-Texts for the Transatlantic Feminist." YFS 62 (1981), 220-36 [discusses Kristeva].

g195. ----------. "Gynesis." Diacritics 12.2 (1982), 54-65.

g196. ----------. Gynesis: Configurations of Woman and Modernity (Ithaca: Cornell UP, 1985) [rel. to post-structuralist criticism].

g197. Jardine, Lisa. Still Harping on Daughters: Women and Drama in the Age of Shakespeare (Sussex: Harvester P; Totowa NJ: Barnes & Noble, 1983).

g198. ----------. "'Girl Talk' (for Boys on the Left); Or, Marginalising Feminist Critical Praxis." OLR 8.1-2 (1986), 208-17.

g199. Jehlen, Myra. "Archimedes and the Paradox of Feminist Criticism." Signs 6.4 (1981), 575-601.

g200. Jelinek, Estelle C., ed. Women's Autobiography: Essays in Criticism (Bloomington: Indiana UP, 1980).

g201. Johnson, Julie Greer. Women in Colonial Spanish American Literature (Westport CT; Greenwood P, 1983).

g202. Jones, Ann Rosalind. "Writing the Body: Toward an Understanding of *l'écriture féminine* ." Feminist Studies 7.2 (1981), 247-63.
g203. ----------. "Inscribing Femininity: French Theories of the Feminine," in G. Greene and C. Kahn, eds. Making a Difference: Feminist Literary Criticism (London: Methuen, 1985), 80-112 [on Cixous, Irigaray, Kristeva].

g204. Jones, Anne Goodwyn. Tomorrow is Another Day: The Woman Writer in the South, 1859-1936 (Baton Rouge: Louisiana State UP, 1981).

g205. Juhasz, Suzanne. "The Feminist Mode in Literature and Criticism." Frontiers 2.3 (1977), 96-103.
g206. ----------. "The Critic as Feminist: Reflections on Women's Poetry, Feminism, and the Art of Criticism." WS 5 (1977), 113-27.

g207. Justice, Betty and Renate Pore, eds. Toward the Second Decade: The Impact of the Women's Movement on American Institutions (Westport CT: Greenwood P, 1981).

g208. Kahn, Coppélia. Man's Estate (Berkeley: U of California P, 1981).
g209. ----------. "Excavating 'Those Dim Minoan Regions': Maternal Subtexts in Patriarchal Literature." Diacritics 12.2 (1982), 32-41.
g210. ----------. "The Gothic Mirror," in S. N. Garner, C. Kahane, and Madelon Sprengnether, eds. The (M)other Tongue: Essays in Feminist Psychoanalytic Interpretation (Ithaca: Cornell UP, 1985), 334-51.

g211. Kamuf, Peggy. "Writing Like a Woman," in S. McConnell-Ginet, R. Borker, and N. Furman, eds. Women and Language in Literature and Society (NY: Praeger, 1980), 284-99.
g212. ----------. "Replacing Feminist Criticism." Diacritics 12.2 (1982), 42-47.
g213. ----------. "Penelope at Work: Interruptions in *A Room of One's Own* ." Novel 16 (1982), 5-18.
g214. ----------. Fictions of Feminine Desire: Disclosures of Heloise (Lincoln: U of Nebraska P, 1982).

g215. Kaplan, Cora. "Pandora's Box: Subjectivity, Class, and Sexuality in Socialist Feminist Criticism," in G. Greene and C. Kahn, eds. Making a Difference: Feminist Literary Criticism (London: Methuen, 1985), 146-76.

g216. Kaplan, Sydney Janet. "Literary Criticism." Signs 4 (1979), 514-27.

g217. ----------. "Varieties of Feminist Criticism," in G. Greene and C. Kahn, eds. Making a Difference: Feminist Literary Criticism (London: Methuen, 1985), 37-58.

g218. Katz-Stoker, Fraya. "The Other Criticism: Feminism vs. Formalism," in S. K. Cornillon, ed. Images of Women in Fiction: Feminist Perspectives (Bowling Green OH: Bowling Green U Popular P, 1972), 315-27.

g219. Kawin, Bruce F. The Mind of the Novel: Reflexive Fiction and the Ineffable (Princeton: Princeton UP, 1982) ["Feminism and the Dis-covery of Self," 298-323].

g220. Kelley, Mary. Private Woman, Public Stage: Literary Domesticity in Nineteenth-Century America (NY: Oxford UP, 1984).

g221. Kennard, Jean E. "Ourself behind Ourself: A Theory for Lesbian Readers," in E. A. Flynn and P. P. Schweickart, eds. Gender and Reading: Essays on Readers, Texts, and Contexts (Baltimore: Johns Hopkins UP, 1986), 63-80.

g222. Keohane, Nannerl O., et al , eds. Feminist Theory: A Critique of Ideology (Chicago: U of Chicago P, 1982).

g223. Keyssar, Helene. Feminist Theatre: An Introduction to Plays of Contemporary British and American Women (NY: Grove P, 1985).

g224. Knight, Diana, ed. "Feminism." Paragraph 8 (1986) [special issue].

g225. Kofman, Sarah. L'Enigme de la femme: la femme dans les textes de Freud (Paris: Galilée, 1980).

g226. Kolodny, Annette. "Some Notes on Defining a 'Feminist Literary Criticism.'" CritI 2 (1975), 75-92.
g227. ----------. "A Map of Misreading: Or, Gender and the Interpretation of Literary Texts." NLH 11 (1980), 451-67 [also in S. N. Garner, C. Kahane, and Madelon Sprengnether, eds. The (M)other Tongue: Essays in Feminist Psychoanalytic Interpretation (Ithaca: Cornell UP, 1985), 241-59].
g228. ----------. "Dancing through the Minefield: Some Observations of the Theory, Practice and Politics of a Feminist Literary Criticism." FSt 6 (1980), 1-25.
g229. ----------. "Turning the Lens on 'The Panther Captivity': A Feminist Exercise in Practical Criticism," in E. Abel, ed. Writing and Sexual Difference (Chicago: U of Chicago P, 1982), 159-76.
g230. ----------. The Land Before Her: Fantasy and Experience of the American Frontiers, 1630-1860 (Chapel Hill: U of North Carolina P, 1984).

g231. Kristeva, Julia. Des Chinoises (Paris: des Femmes, 1974) [About Chinese Women (London: Boyars, 1977)].

g232. ----------. La Révolution du langage poétique (Paris: Seuil, 1974) [Revolution in Poetic Language (NY: Columbia UP, 1984)].

g233. ----------. "La femme, ce n'est jamais ça." Tel Quel 59 (1974), 19-24.

g234. ----------. "The System and the Speaking Subject," in T. Sebeok, ed. The Tell-Tale Sign: A Survey of Semiotics (Lisse: Peter de Ridder, 1975), 47-55.

g235. ----------. Polylogue (Paris: Seuil, 1977).

g236. ----------. Desire in Language: A Semiotic Approach to Literature and Art (NY: Columbia UP, 1980).

g237. ----------. Pouvoirs de l'horreur (Paris: Seuil, 1980) [Powers of Horror (NY: Columbia UP, 1982)].

g238. ----------. "Women's Time." Signs 7.1 (1981), 13-35.

g239. ----------. Histoires d'amour (Paris: Denoel, 1983).

g240. Lanser, Susan S. "Toward a Feminist Narratology." Style 20.3 (1986), 341-63.

g241. Lasch, Christopher. "A Typology of Intellectuals: The Feminist Subject." Salmagundi 70-71 (1986), 27-32.

g242. ----------, Renata Adler, and Jean Bethke Elshtain. "The New Feminist Intellectual: A Discussion." Salmagundi 70-71 (1986), 33-43.

g243. Lauter, Estella and Carol Schreier Rupprecht, eds. Feminist Archetypal Theory: Interdisciplinary Re-Visions of Jungian Thought (Knoxville: U of Tennessee P, 1985).

g244. Lauter, Paul. "Race and Gender in the Shaping of the American Literary Canon: A Case Study from the Twenties." Feminist Studies 9 (1983), 435-63.

g245. ----------, ed. Reconstructing American Literature: Courses, Syllabi, Issues (Old Westbury NY: Feminist P, 1983).

g246. Lebowitz, Andrea. "Is Feminist Literary Criticism Becoming Anti-Feminist?" ROO 8.4 (1984), 97-108.

g247. Léger, Susan H. "The Lure of Symmetry: Or the Strange Impossibility of Feminist Criticism." MR 24.2 (1983), 330-36.

g248. Lenz, Carolyn, Gayle Greene, and Carol Thomas Neely, eds. The Woman's Part: Feminist Criticism of Shakespeare (Urbana: U of Illinois P, 1980).

g249. Leverenz, David. "Mrs. Hawthorne's Headache: Reading *The Scarlet Letter*," in S. N. Garner, C. Kahane, and Madelon Sprengnether, eds. The (M)other Tongue: Essays in Feminist Psychoanalytic Interpretation (Ithaca: Cornell UP, 1985), 194-216.

g250. Lipking, Lawrence. "Aristotle's Sister: A Poetics of Abandonment." CritI 10.1 (1983), 61-81.

g251. Loeb, Catherine R., Susan E. Searing, and Esther F. Stineman. Women's Studies: A Recommended Core Bibliography 1980-1985 (Littleton CO: Libraries Unlimited, 1987).

g252. Lovell, Terry. "Writing Like a Woman: A Question of Politics," in F. Barker, *et al* . The Politics of Theory (Colchester: U of Essex, 1983), 15-26.

g253. Lussier, Mark and Peggy McCormack, eds. "Feminist Literary Criticism." NOR 13.4 (1986) [special issue; includes interviews conducted by the editors with Annette Kolodny, Catherine R. Stimpson, Jane Gallop, and Carolyn Heilbrun].

g254. Lydon, Mary, ed. "Versions/Feminism's: A Stance of One's Own." Sub-Stance 32 (1981) [special issue].
g255. ----------. "Foucault and Feminism: A Romance of Many Dimensions." HIS 5.3-4 (1982), 245-56.

g256. Lyotard, Jean-François. "One of the Things as Stake in Women's Struggles." Sub-Stance 20 (1978), 9-16.

g257. Makward, Christiane. "Structures du silence/ du délire: Marguerite Duras, Hélene Cixous." Poétique 35 (1978), 314-24.
g258. ----------. "To Be or Not to Be. . . a Feminist Speaker," in H. Eisenstein and A. Jardine, eds. The Future of Difference (Boston: G. K. Hall, 1980), 95-105.

g259. Marcus, Jane, ed. New Feminist Essays on Virginia Woolf (Lincoln: U of Nebraska P, 1981).
g260. ----------. "Liberty, Sorority, and Misogyny," in C. Heilbrun and M. Higonnet, eds. The Representation of Women in Fiction (Baltimore: Johns Hopkins UP, 1982), 60-97.
g261. ----------, ed. Virginia Woolf: A Feminist Slant (Lincoln: U of Nebraska P, 1983).
g262. ----------. "Invisible Mending," in C. Ascher, L. DeSalvo, and S. Ruddick, eds. Between Women (Boston: Beacon, 1984), 381-95.

g263. ----------. "Still Practice, A/Wrested Alphabet: Toward a Feminist Aesthetic." TSWL 3.1-2 (1984), 79-97 [also in S. Benstock, ed. Feminist Issues in Literary Scholarship (Bloomington: Indiana UP, 1987), 79-97].
g264. ----------. Virginia Woolf and the Languages of Patriarchy (Bloomington: Indiana UP, 1987).

g265. Marcuse, Herbert. "Marxism and Feminism." WS 2 (1974), 279-88.

g266. Marder, Herbert. Feminism and Art: A Study of Virginia Woolf (Chicago: U of Chicago P, 1968).

g267. Marini, Marcelle. Territoires du féminin avec Marguerite Duras (Paris: Minuit, 1977).

g268. Marks, Elaine and Isabelle de Courtivron, eds. New French Feminisms (Brighton: Harvester; Amherst: U of Massachusetts P, 1980).

g269. Martin, Biddy. "Feminism, Criticism, and Foucault." NGC 27 (1982), 3-30.

g270. McConnell-Ginet, Sally, Ruth Borker, and Nelly Furman, eds. Women and Language in Literature and Society (NY: Praeger, 1980).

g271. McDowell, Deborah E. "New Directions for Black Feminist Criticism." BALF 14 (1980), 153-59.

g272. McLeod, Anne. "Gender Difference Relativity in GDR-Writing or; How to Oppose Without Really Trying." OLR 7.1-2 (1985), 41-61.

g273. Meese, Elizabeth. "The Whole Truth: Frameworks for the Study of Women's Noncanonical Literature," in L. Hoffmann and D. Rosenfelt, eds. Teaching Women's Literature from a Regional Perspective (NY: MLA, 1982), 15-22.
g274. ----------. Crossing the Double-Cross: The Practice of Feminist Criticism (Chapel Hill: U of North Carolina P, 1986).

g275. Michie, Helena. "Mother, Sister, Other: The 'Other Woman' in Feminist Theory." L&P 32.4 (1986), 1-10.

g276. Miller, Beth, ed. Women in Hispanic Literature: Icons and Fallen Idols (Berkeley: U of California P, 1983).

g277. Miller, Nancy K. The Heroine's Text: Readings in the French and English Novel 1722-1782 (NY: Columbia UP, 1980).

g278. ----------. "Emphasis Added: Plots and Plausibilities in Women's Fiction." PMLA 96 (1981), 36-48.

g279. ----------. "The Text's Heroine: A Feminist Critic and Her Fictions." Diacritics 12.2 (1982), 48-53 [on Peggy Kamuf].

g280. ----------. "Rereading as a Woman: The Body in Practice." PoT 6.1-2 (1985), 291-99.

g281. ----------. "Parables and Politics: Feminist Criticism in 1986." Paragraph 8 (1986), 40-54.

g282. ----------. "Changing the Subject: Authorship, Writing, and the Reader," in T. de Lauretis, ed. Feminist Studies: Critical Studies (Bloomington: Indiana UP, 1986), 102-20.

g283. Mitchell, Juliet. Psychoanalysis and Feminism (Harmondsworth: Penguin, 1974).

g284. ----------. Women: The Longest Revolution. Essays in Feminism, Literature and Psychoanalysis (London: Virago, 1984).

g285. Modleski, Tania. Loving with a Vengeance: Mass-Produced Fantasies for Women (Archon, 1982).

g286. ----------. "Feminism and the Power of Interpretation: Some Critical Readings," in T. de Lauretis, ed. Feminist Studies: Critical Studies (Bloomington: Indiana UP, 1986), 121-38.

g287. Moi, Toril. "Sexual/Textual Politics," in F. Barker, et al . The Politics of Theory (Colchester: U of Essex, 1983), 1-14 [on Kristeva].

g288. ----------. Sexual/Textual Politics: Feminist Literary Theory (London and NY: Methuen, 1985) [on Kristeva, Irigaray, Cixous].

g289. ----------, ed. The Kristeva Reader (Oxford: Basil Blackwell, 1986).

g290. Monteith, Moira, ed. Women's Writing: A Challenge to Theory (Sussex: Harvester; NY: St. Martin's P, 1986).

g291. Mora, Gabriela and Karen S. Van Hooft, eds. Theory and Practice of Feminist Literary Criticism (Ypsilanti MI: Bilingual, 1982).

g292. Morris, Meaghan. "Forum: Feminism and Interpretation Theory." SoRA 16.1 (1983), 149-73.

g293. Moss, Anita, ed. "Feminist Criticism and the Study of Children's Literature." CLAQ 7.4 (1982), 3-22 [special section].

g294. Mulford, Wendy. "Socialist-Feminist Criticism: A Case Study, Women's Suffrage and Literature, 1906-14," in P. Widdowson, ed. Re-reading English (NY: Methuen, 1982), 179-92.

g295. Munich, Adrienne. "Notorious Signs, Feminist Criticism and Literary Tradition," in G. Greene and C. Kahn, eds. Making a Difference: Feminist Literary Criticism (London: Methuen, 1985), 238-59.

g296. Mussell, Kay. Fantasy and Reconciliation: Contemporary Formulas of Women's Romance Fiction (Westport CT: Greenwood P, 1984).

g297. Natalle, Elizabeth J. Feminist Theatre (Metuchen NJ: Scarecrow P, 1985).

g298. Neely, Carol Thomas. "Feminist Criticism in Motion," in P. A. Treichler, C. Kramarae, and B. Stafford, eds. For Alma Mater: Theory and Practice in Feminist Scholarship (Urbana: U of Illinois P, 1985), 69-90.

g299. Nelson, Cary. "Envoys of Otherness: Difference and Continuity in Feminist Criticism," in P. A. Treichler, C. Kramarae, and B. Stafford, eds. For Alma Mater: Theory and Practice in Feminist Scholarship (Urbana: U of Illinois P, 1985), 91-118.

g300. Newton, Judith Lowder. Women, Power, and Subversion: Social Strategies in British Fiction 1778-1860 (Athens: U of Georgia P, 1981).
g301. ----------. "Making--and Remaking--History: Another Look at 'Patriarchy,'" in S. Benstock, ed. Feminist Issues in Literary Scholarship (Bloomington: Indiana UP, 1987), 124-40.

g302. Nussbaum, Felicity A. The Brink of All We Hate: English Satires on Women, 1660-1750 (Lexington: UP of Kentucky, 1984).

g303. Ostriker, Alicia. Writing Like a Woman (Ann Arbor: U of Michigan P, 1983).

g304. Patai, Daphne. "Beyond Defensiveness: Feminist Research Strategies," in M. Barr and N. D. Smith, eds. Women and Utopia (Lanham MD: UP of America, 1983), 148-69.

g305. Pearson, Carol and Katherine Pope. The Female Hero in American and British Literature (NY: Bowker, 1981).

g306. Perry, Ruth. Women, Letters, and the Novel (NY: AMS P, 1980).

g307. Pollak, Ellen. The Poetics of Sexual Myth (Chicago: U of Chicago P, 1985).

g308. Pratt, Annis. "The New Feminist Criticism." CE 32 (1971), 872-78.

g309. ----------. "Archetypal Approaches to the New Feminist Criticism."
BuR 21.1 (1973), 3-14.
g310. ----------. "Spinning Among Fields: Jung, Frye, Lévi-Strauss and
Feminist Archetypal Theory," in E. Lauter and C. S. Rupprecht, eds.
Feminist Archetypal Theory: Interdisciplinary Re-Visions of Jungian
Thought (Knoxville: U of Tennessee P, 1985), 93-136.

g311. Prenshaw, Peggy Whitman, ed. Women Writers of the Contemporary
South (Jackson: UP of Mississippi, 1984).

g312. Pryse, Marjorie and Hortense J. Spillers, eds. Conjuring: Black
Women, Fiction, and Literary Tradition (Bloomington: Indiana UP, 1985).

g313. Radway, Janice A. Reading the Romance: Women, Patriarchy, and
Popular Literature (Chapel Hill: U of North Carolina P, 1984).

g314. Register, Cheri. "American Feminist Literary Criticism: A
Bibliographical Introduction," in J. Donovan, ed. Feminist Literary
Criticism: Explorations in Theory (Lexington: UP of Kentucky, 1975), 1-
28.
g315. ----------. "Review Essay: Literary Criticism." Signs 6 (1980), 268-
82.

g316. Reinhardt, Nancy. "New Directions for Feminist Criticism in Theatre
and the Related Arts." Soundings 64.4 (1981), 361-87.

g317. Richardson, Betty. "Women and Writing: A Decade of Scholarship
and Criticism." PLL 18.1 (1982), 91-111.

g318. Richmond, Velma Bourgeois. "Women as Critics: A Look to the
Future." CEA 37.4 (1975), 20-22.

g319. Rigney, Barbara Hill. Madness and Sexual Politics in the Feminist
Novel: Studies in Bronte, Woolf, Lessing and Atwood (Madison: U of
Wisconsin P, 1978).
g320. ----------. Lilith's Daughters: Women and Religion in Contemporary
Fiction (Madison: U of Wisconsin P, 1982).
g321. ----------. "'A Wreath Upon the Grave': The Influence of Virginia
Woolf on Feminist Critical Theory," in J. Hawthorn, ed. Criticism and
Critical Theory (London: Arnold, 1984).

g322. Robinson, Lillian S. "Dwelling in Decencies: Radical Criticism and the
Feminist Perspective." CE 32 (1971), 879-89.
g323. ----------. Sex, Class and Culture (Bloomington: Indiana UP, 1978).

g324. ----------. "Treason Our Text: Feminist Challenges to the Literary Canon." TSWL 2 (1983), 83-98.
g325. ----------. "Feminist Criticism: How Do We Know When We've Won?" TSWL 3.1-2 (1984), 143-51 [also in S. Benstock, ed. Feminist Issues in Literary Scholarship (Bloomington: Indiana UP, 1987), 141-49].

g326. Rogers, Katharine M. The Troublesome Helpmate: A History of Misogyny in Literature (Seattle: U of Washington P, 1966).

g327. Rooney, Ellen. "Criticism and the Subject of Sexual Violence." MLN 98.5 (1983), 1269-78.

g328. Rosinsky, Natalie M. Feminist Futures--Contemporary Women's Speculative Fiction (Ann Arbor: UMI Research P, 1984).

g329. Rowe, John Carlos. The Theoretical Dimensions of Henry James (Madison: U of Wisconsin P, 1984) [chap. 3: "Feminist Issues: Women, Power, and Rebellion in *The Bostonians, The Spoils of Poynton*, and *The Aspern Papers* "].

g330. Ruderman, Judith. D. H. Lawrence and the Devouring Mother (Durham NC: Duke UP, 1984).

g331. Rule, Jane. Lesbian Images (Garden City NY: Doubleday, 1975).

g332. Russ, Joanna. How to Suppress Women's Writing (Austin: U of Texas P, 1983).

g333. Russo, Mary. "Notes on 'Post-Feminism,'" in F. Barker, *et al* . The Politics of Theory (Colchester: U of Essex, 1983), 27-37 [on Kristeva].
g334. ----------. "Female Grotesques: Carnival and Theory," in T. de Lauretis, ed. Feminist Studies: Critical Studies (Bloomington: Indiana UP, 1986), 213-29.

g335. Ruthven, K. K. "Male Critics and Feminist Criticism." EIC 33.4 (1983), 263-72.
g336. ----------. Feminist Literary Studies: An Introduction (Cambridge: Cambridge UP, 1984).

g337. Sage, Lorna. "The Available Space," in M. Monteith, ed. Women's Writing: A Challenge to Theory (Sussex: Harvester; NY: St. Martin's P, 1986), 15-33.

g338. Savona, Jeannette Laillou. "French Feminism and Theatre: An Introduction." MD 27.4 (1984), 540-45.

g339. Schor, Naomi. Breaking the Chain: Women, Theory, and French Realist Fiction (NY: Columbia UP, 1985).
g340. ----------. "*Eugénie Grandet* : Mirrors and Melancholia," in S. N. Garner, C. Kahane, and Madelon Sprengnether, eds. The (M)other Tongue: Essays in Feminist Psychoanalytic Interpretation (Ithaca: Cornell UP, 1985), 217-37.
g341. ----------. "Introducing Feminism." Paragraph 8 (1986), 94-101.

g342. Schweickart, Patrocinio Pagaduan. "A Theory of Feminist Criticism." DAI 41 (1981), 3093A.
g343. ----------. "Add Gender and Stir." Reader 13 (1985), 1-9.
g344. ----------. "Reading Ourselves: Toward a Feminist Theory of Reading," in E. A. Flynn and P. P. Schweickart, eds. Gender and Reading: Essays on Readers, Texts, and Contexts (Baltimore: Johns Hopkins UP, 1986), 31-62.

g345. Schwenger, Peter. Phallic Critiques: Masculinity and Twentieth-Century Literature Boston: Routledge & Kegan Paul, 1984).

g346. Scott, Bonnie Kime. Joyce and Feminism (Bloomington: Indiana UP, 1984).

g347. Segel, Elizabeth. "Cultural Fictions." CLAQ 7.4 (1982), 11-12.

g348. Sharistanian, Janet. "A Note on Using Feminist Literary Criticism in the Classroom." Frontiers 4.1 (1979), 31-34.

g349. Showalter, Elaine. "Women and the Literary Curriculum." CE 32 (1971).
g350. ----------. "Literary Criticism." Signs 1 (1975), 435-60.
g351. ----------. A Literature of Their Own: British Women Novelists from Bronte to Lessing (Princeton: Princeton UP, 1977).
g352. ----------. "Towards a Feminist Poetics," in M. Jacobus, ed. Women Writing and Writing About Women (London: Croom Helm, 1979), 22-41.
g353. ----------. "Feminist Criticism in the Wilderness," in E. Abel, ed. Writing and Sexual Difference (Chicago: U of Chicago P, 1982), 9-36.
g354. ----------. "Critical Cross-Dressing: Male Feminists and the Woman of the Year." Raritan 2 (1983), 130-49.
g355. ----------. "Women's Time, Women's Space: Writing the History of Feminist Criticism." TSWL 3.1-2 (1984), 29-43 [also in S. Benstock, ed. Feminist Issues in Literary Scholarship (Bloomington: Indiana UP, 1987), 30-44].
g356. ----------. "Women Writers and American Processions: Feminist Criticism 1984." OntarioR 21 (1984-85), 92-98.

g357. ----------, ed. The New Feminist Criticism: Essays on Women, Literature, and Theory (NY: Pantheon, 1985).

g358. ----------. "Shooting the Rapids: Feminist Criticism in the Mainstream." OLR 8.1-2 (1986), 218-24.

g359. Simpson, Hilary. D. H. Lawrence and Feminism (DeKalb: Northern Illinois UP, 1982).

g360. Simpson-Zinn, Joy. "The Différance of l'écriture féminine ." Chimeres 18.1 (1985), 77-93.

g361. Smith, Barbara. "Toward a Black Feminist Criticism," in J. Bowles, ed. In the Memory and Spirit of Frances, Zora, and Lorraine: Essays and Interviews on Black Women and Writing (Washington, DC: Howard U, 1979), 32-40.

g362. Smith, Paul. "A Question of Feminine Identity." NCA 1 (1984), 81-102.

g363. Spacks, Patricia Meyer. The Female Imagination: A Literary and Psychological Investigation of Women's Writing (London: Allen & Unwin, 1976).

g364. ----------. "The Difference It Makes." Soundings 64.4 (1981), 343-60.

g365. Spencer, Sharon. "Feminist Criticism and Literature," in R. Kostelanetz, ed. American Writing Today, 2 vols. (Washington DC: International Communication Agency, 1982), 2: 157-70.

g366. Spector, Judith A. "Gender Studies: New Directions for Feminist Criticism." CE 43.4 (1981), 374-78.

g367. Spillers, Hortense J. "A Hateful Passion, a Lost Love," in S. Benstock, ed. Feminist Issues in Literary Scholarship (Bloomington: Indiana UP, 1987), 181-207.

g368. Spivak, Gayatri Chakravorty. "Three Feminist Readings." Union Seminary Quarterly Rev 35.1-2 (1978-79), 15-38.

g369. ----------. "Making and Unmaking in To the Lighthouse," in S. McConnell-Ginet, R. Borker, and N. Furman, eds. Women and Language in Literature and Society (NY: Praeger, 1980), 310-27.

g370. ----------. "French Feminism in an International Frame." YFS 62 (1981), 154-84.

g371. ----------. "Feminism and Critical Theory," in P. A. Treichler, C. Kramarae, and B. Stafford, eds. For Alma Mater: Theory and Practice in Feminist Scholarship (Urbana: U of Illinois P, 1985), 119-42.

g372. ----------. "Three Women's Texts and a Critique of Imperialism."
CritI 12.1 (1985), 243-61.
g373. ----------. "Imperialism and Sexual Difference." OLR 8.1-2 (1986),
225-40.

g374. Squier, Susan Merrill, ed. Women Writers and the City: Essays in
Feminist Literary Criticism (Knoxville: U of Tennessee P, 1984).

g375. Staicar, Tom, ed. The Feminine Eye: Science Fiction and the Women
Who Write It (NY: Ungar, 1982).

g376. Staley, Thomas F., ed. Twentieth-Century Women Novelists (Totowa
NJ: Barnes & Noble, 1982).

g377. Stanton, Domna C. "Language and Revolution: The Franco-American
Dis-Connection," in H. Eisenstein and A. Jardine, eds. The Future of
Difference (Boston: G. K. Hall, 1980), 73-87 [on Kristeva and Cixous].

g378. Steinem, Gloria and Charlotte Bunch, eds. Building Feminist Theory:
Essays from Quest: A Feminist Quarterly (NY: Longman, 1981).

g379. Sternburg, Janet, ed. The Writer on Her Work (NY: Norton, 1980).

g380. Stimpson, Catherine R. "On Feminist Criticism," in P. Hernadi, ed.
What Is Criticism? (Bloomington: Indiana UP, 1981), 230-41.
g381. ----------. "Zero Degree Deviancy: The Lesbian Novel in English," in
E. Abel, ed. Writing and Sexual Difference (Chicago: U of Chicago P,
1982), 243-60.
g382. ----------. "Feminism and Feminist Criticism." MR 24.2 (1983), 271-
88.

g383. Stitzel, Judith. "Changing Curricular Assumptions: Teaching and
Studying Women's Literature from a Regional Perspective," in B. Justice
and R. Pore, eds. Toward the Second Decade: The Impact of the Women's
Movement on American Institutions (Westport CT: Greenwood P, 1981),
141-48.

g384. Stockinger, Jacob. "Toward a Gay Criticism." CE 36 (1974), 303-10.

g385. Stone, Jennifer. "The Horrors of Power: A Critique of 'Kristeva,'" in
F. Barker, et al . The Politics of Theory (Colchester: U of Essex, 1983), 38-
48.

g386. Stubbs, Patricia. Women and Fiction: Feminism and the Novel 1880-
1920 (Brighton: Harvester; London: Methuen, 1981).

g387. Suleiman, Susan Rubin. "Writing and Motherhood," in S. N. Garner, C. Kahane, and Madelon Sprengnether, eds. The (M)other Tongue: Essays in Feminist Psychoanalytic Interpretation (Ithaca: Cornell UP, 1985), 352-77.

g388. Swan, Jim. "Difference and Silence: John Milton and the Question of Gender," in S. N. Garner, C. Kahane, and Madelon Sprengnether, eds. The (M)other Tongue: Essays in Feminist Psychoanalytic Interpretation (Ithaca: Cornell UP, 1985), 142-68.

g389. Taylor, Barbara. Eve and the New Jerusalem: Socialism and Feminism in the Ninteenth Century (London: Virago, 1983).

g390. Terzian, Debra. "Luce Irigaray: Discours de l'homme ou de la femme?" Constructions (1985), 119-25.

g391. "Textual Politics: Feminist Criticism." Diacritics 5.4 (1975) [special issue].

g392. Todd, Jane Marie. Women's Friendship in Literature (NY: Columbia UP, 1980).
g393. ----------. "A Philosophy of Questions: Feminist Theory and the Politics of Enunciation." TSWL 5.2 (1986), 303-12.

g394. Toth, Emily, ed. Regionalism and the Female Imagination: A Collection of Essays (NY: Human Sciences P, 1985).

g395. Treichler, Paula A., Cheris Kramarae, and Betty Stafford, eds. For Alma Mater: Theory and Practice in Feminist Scholarship (Urbana: U of Illinois P, 1985).
g396. ----------. "Teaching Feminist Theory," in C. Nelson, ed. Theory in the Classroom (Urbana: U of Illinois P, 1986), 57-128.
g397. ----------. "Escaping the Sentence: Diagnosis and Discourse in 'The Yellow Paper,'" in S. Benstock, ed. Feminist Issues in Literary Scholarship (Bloomington: Indiana UP, 1987), 62-78.

g398. Trible, Phyllis. "A Daughter's Death: Feminism, Literary Criticism and the Bible." MQR 22.3 (1983), 177-89.

g399. Vickers, Nancy J. "Diana Described: Scattered Woman and Scattered Rhyme," in E. Abel, ed. Writing and Sexual Difference (Chicago: U of Chicago P, 1982), 95-110.

g400. Walker, Cheryl. The Nightingale's Burden: Women Poets and American Culture Before 1900 (Bloomington: Indiana UP, 1982).

g401. Warren, Joyce W. The American Narcissus: Individualism and Women in Nineteenth-Century American Fiction (New Brunswick NJ: Rutgers UP, 1984).

g402. Watson, Barbara Bellow. "On Power and the Literary Text." Signs 1 (1975), 111-18.

g403. Weedon, Chris. Feminist Practice and Poststructuralist Theory (Oxford: Basil Blackwell, 1987).

g404. Weir, Lorraine. "'Wholeness, Harmony, Radiance' and Women's Writing." ROO 8.4 (1984), 19-24.

g405. Westkott, Marcia. "Women's Studies as a Strategy for Change: Between Criticism and Vision," in G. Bowles and R. D. Klein, eds. Theories of Women's Studies (London: Routledge, 1983), 210-18.

g406. White, Allon. 'L'éclatement du sujet': The Theoretical Work of Julia Kristeva (Birmingham: U of Birmingham Centre for Contemporary Studies, 1977).

g407. Whitford, Margaret. "Luce Irigaray: The Problem of Feminist Theory." Paragraph 8 (1986), 102-05.

g408. Williamson, Marilyn L. "Toward a Feminist Literary History." Signs 10.1 (1984), 136-47.

g409. Wilson, Diana, ed. "The Rhetoric of Feminist Writing." DQ 18.4 (1984) [special issue].

g410. Wilson, Katharina M., ed. Medieval Women Writers (Athens: U of Georgia P, 1984).

g411. "Women in Literature and Criticism." CEA 37.4 (1975) [special issue].

g412. Woodbridge, Linda. Women and the English Renaissance: Literature and the Nature of Womankind, 1540-1620 (Urbana: U of Illinois P, 1983).

g413. Young, Robert, ed. "Sexual Difference." OLR 8.1-2 (1986) [special issue].

g414. Zeitlin, Froma I. "Travesties of Gender and Genre in Aristophanes' Thesmophoriazousae ," in E. Abel, ed. Writing and Sexual Difference (Chicago: U of Chicago P, 1982), 131-58.

g415. Zimmerman, Bonnie. "What Has Never Been: An Overview of Lesbian Feminist Literary Criticism." FSt 7.3 (1981), 451-76.

H. Reader-Response Criticism

h1. Alcorn, Marshall W., Jr. and Mark Bracher. "Literature, Psychoanalysis, and the Re-Formation of the Self: A New Direction in Reader-Response Criticism." <u>PMLA</u> 100.3 (1985), 342-54.

h2. Amigone, Grace Ritz. "Apprehending a Literary Work of Art: A Comparative Study of Interventions into a Poem by Experienced and Inexperienced Readers." <u>DAI</u> 44 (1983), 486A.

h3. Amossy, Ruth. "(Re)Lecture(s)." <u>RR</u> 72.2 (1981), 226-42.

h4. Anderson, Howard. "*Tristram Shandy* and the Reader's Imagination." <u>PMLA</u> 86 (1971), 966-73.

h5. Applebee, Arthur N. "Studies in the Spectator Role: An Approach to Response to Literature," in C. R. Cooper, ed. <u>Researching Response to Literature and the Teaching of Literature: Points of Departure</u> (Norwood NJ: Ablex, 1985), 87-102.

h6. Armstrong, Paul B. <u>The Challenge of Bewilderment: Understanding and Representation in James, Conrad, and Ford</u> (Ithaca: Cornell UP, 1987).

h7. Bagwell, J. Timothy. "Who's Afraid of Stanley Fish?" <u>PoT</u> 4.1 (1983), 189-201.

h8. Bales, Kent. "Intention and the Readers' Responses." <u>Neohelicon</u> 13.1 (1986), 177-94 [discusses Iser].

h9. Barnouw, Dagmar. "Critics in the Act of Reading." PoT 1.4 (1980), 213-22.

h10. Barthes, Roland. S/Z (Paris: Seuil, 1970) [S/Z (NY: Hill & Wang, 1977)].
h11. ----------. Le Plaisir du texte (Paris: Seuil, 1973) [The Pleasure of the Text (NY: Hill & Wang, 1975)].

h12. Bashford, Bruce. "The Rhetorical Method in Literary Criticism." P&R 9 (1976), 133-46 [discusses Bloom].

h13. Bauschatz, Cathleen M. "Montaigne's Conception of Reading in the Context of Renaissance Poetics and Modern Criticism," in S. R. Suleiman and I. Crosman, eds. The Reader in the Text: Essays on Audience and Interpretation (Princeton: Princeton UP, 1980), 264-91.

h14. Baym, Nina. Novels, Readers, and Reviewers: Responses to Fiction in Antebellum America (Ithaca: Cornell UP, 1984).

h15. Beach, Richard. "Discourse Conventions and Researching Response to Literary Dialogue," in C. R. Cooper, ed. Researching Response to Literature and the Teaching of Literature: Points of Departure (Norwood NJ: Ablex, 1985), 103-27.

h16. Beall, Chandler B. "Dante and His Reader." Forum Italicum 13.3 (1979), 299-343.

h17. Beaugrande, Robert-Alain de. "A Rhetorical Theory of Audience Response," in R. L. Brown, Jr. and M. Steinmann, Jr., eds. Rhetoric 78: Proceedings of Theory of Rhetoric: An Interdisciplinary Conference (Minneapolis: U of Minnesota Center for Advanced Studies in Lang., Style, and Lit. Theory, 1979), 9-20.

h18. Beaujour, Michel. "Exemplary Pornography: Barres, Loyola, and the Novel," in S. R. Suleiman and I. Crosman, eds. The Reader in the Text: Essays on Audience and Interpretation (Princeton: Princeton UP, 1980), 325-49.

h19. Beers, Terry Lynn. "Interpretive Schemata and Literary Response." DAI 47 (1986), 2155A-56A.

h20. Bennett, Tony. "Texts, Readers, Reading Formations." BMMLA 16.1 (1983), 3-17.

h21. Berg, Temma Fay. "Strategies of Reading: The Reader-Response Movement in America." DAI 41 (1980), 249A.
h22. ----------. "Psychologies of Reading," in J. Natoli, ed. Tracing Literary Theory (Urbana: U of Illinois P, 1987), 248-77.

h23. Berger, Carole. "The Rake and the Reader in Jane Austen's Novels." SEL 15 (1975), 531-44.
h24. ----------. "Viewing as Action: Film and Reader Response Criticism." LFQ 6 (1978), 144-51.

h25. Bilan, R. P. "'We Interpreters.'" UTQ 51.1 (1981), 102-12 [discusses S. Fish and P. D. Juhl].

h26. Bjorklund, Beth. "Cognitive Strategies in a Text." JLS 8 (1979), 84-99.

h27. Black, Stephen A. "On Reading Psychoanalytically." CE 39 (1977), 267-74.

h28. Bleich, David. "The Determination of Literary Value." Literature & Psychology 17 (1967), 19-30.
h29. ----------. "Emotional Origins of Literary Meaning." CE 31 (1969), 30-40.
h30. ----------. "Psychological Bases of Learning from Literature." CE 33 (1971), 32-45.
h31. ----------. "The Subjective Character of Critical Interpretation." CE 36 (1975), 739-55.
h32. ----------. Readings and Feelings: An Introduction to Subjective Criticism (Urbana IL: NCTE, 1975).
h33. ----------. "Pedagogical Directions in Subjective Criticism." CE 37 (1976), 454-67.
h34. ----------. "The Subjective Paradigm in Science, Psychology, and Criticism." NLH 7 (1976), 313-34.
h35. ----------. Literature and Self-Awareness: Critical Questions and Emotional Responses (NY: Harper & Row, 1977).
h36. ----------. "The Logic of Interpretation." Genre 10.3 (1977), 363-94.
h37. ----------. Subjective Criticism (Baltimore: Johns Hopkins UP, 1978).
h38. ----------. "Negotiated Knowldge of Language and Literature." Studies in the Literary Imagination 12.1 (1979), 73-92.
h39. ----------. "The Identity of Pedagogy and Research in the Study of Response to Literature." CE 42 (1980), 350-66.
h40. ----------. "Teleology and Taxonomy in Critical Explanation." BuR 26.1 (1981), 102-27 [discusses Culler, Ingarden, Iser].
h41. ----------. "The Identity of Pedagogy and Research in the Study of Response to Literature," in C. R. Cooper, ed. Researching Response to

Literature and the Teaching of Literature: Points of Departure (Norwood NJ: Ablex, 1985), 253-72.

h42. ----------. "Gender Interests in Reading and Language," in E. A. Flynn and P. P. Schweickart, eds. Gender and Reading: Essays on Readers, Texts, and Contexts (Baltimore: Johns Hopkins UP, 1986), 234-66.

h43. Blessin, Stefan. Erzahlstruktur und Leserhandlung: Zur Theorie der literarischen Kommunikation am Beispiel von Goethes Wahlverwandtschaften (Heidelberg: Winter, 1974).

h44. Block, Ed. "Bleich and Iser on the Reader's Role." Reader 9 (1983), 1-9.

h45. Block, Elizabeth. "Narrative Judgment and Audience Response in Homer and Vergil." Arethusa 19.2 (1986), 155-69.

h46. Bloom, Edward, ed. "In Defense of Authors and Readers." Novel 11.1 (1977) [special section].

h47. Bloom, Harold. "The Necessity of Misreading." GaR 29 (1975), 267-88.

h48. Booth, Stephen. "On the Value of Hamlet," in N. Rabkin, ed. Reinterpretations of Elizabethan Drama (NY: Columbia UP, 1969), 77-99.

h49. ----------. An Essay on Shakespeare's Sonnets (New Haven: Yale UP, 1969).

h50. Bové, Paul. "The Poetics of Coercion: An Interpretation of Literary Competence." Boundary 5 (1976), 263-84.

h51. Brinker, Menachem. "Two Phenomenologies of Reading: Ingarden and Iser on Textual Indeterminacy." PoT 1.4 (1980), 203-12.

h52. Brinkley, Robert A. "The Unfaithful Text." MSE 5.2 (1975), 31-39 [on H. Bloom].

h53. Brooke-Rose, Christine. "The Readerhood of Man," in S. R. Suleiman and I. Crosman, eds. The Reader in the Text: Essays on Audience and Interpretation (Princeton: Princeton UP, 1980), 120-48.

h54. Brooks, Cleanth. "The Primacy of the Reader." MissR 6.2 (1983), 189-201 [on Bloom and Fish].

h55. Brooks, Peter. "Competent Readers." Diacritics 6.1 (1976), 23-26 [on Culler].

h56. Brown, Homer Obed. "Ordinary Readers, Extraordinary Texts, and Ludmilla: Part One." Criticism 23.4 (1981), 335-48 [on Fish, Holland, Iser].

h57. Brown, Steven R. "Political Literature and the Response of the Reader: Experimental Studies of Interpretation, Imagery, and Criticism." American Political Science Review 71 (1977), 567-84.

h58. Brownlee, Marina Scordilis. The Status of the Reading Subject in the Libro de buen Amor (Chapel Hill: U of North Carolina Dept. of Romance Languages, 1985).

h59. Brownstein, Rachel M. Becoming a Heroine: Reading About Women in Novels (NY: Viking, 1982).

h60. Bruss, Elizabeth. "The Game of Literature and Some Literary Games." NLH 9 (1977), 153-72.

h61. Burger, Peter. Vermitterung, Rezeption, Funktion: Asthetische Theorie und Methodologie der Literaturwissenschaft (Frankfurt: Suhrkamp, 1979).

h62. Busch, Ulrich. "Zur literarischen Kompetenz des Literaturwissenschaftlichers und des Laienlesers am Beispiel von Anton Cechovs Drei Schwestern ." Poetica 16.3-4 (1984), 237-45.

h63. Buzzard, Sharon Kay. "Reader Response Criticism and the Reflexive Narrative: The Reader/Viewer Role in Creating a Narrative." DAI 46 (1986), 3348A.

h64. Cain, William. "'Lycidas' and the Reader's Response." Dalhousie Rev 58 (1978), 272-84.
h65. ----------. "Constraints and Politics in the Literary Theory of Stanley Fish." BuR 26.1 (1981), 75-88.

h66. Caraher, Brian Gregory. "Experience, Authority and Theoretical Ideals: A Methodological Critique of Some Recent Reader-Response Criticism and Theory." Reader 9 (1983), 10-31 [discusses Bleich and Holland].

h67. Castle, Terry. Clarissa's Ciphers: Meaning and Disruption in Richardson's 'Clarissa' (Ithaca: Cornell UP, 1982).

h68. Caws, Mary Ann. Reading Frames in Modern Fiction (Princeton: Princeton UP, 1985).

h69. Chabot, C. Barry. ". . . Reading Readers Reading Readers Reading. . . "
Diacritics 5.3 (1975), 24-38.
h70. ----------. "Understanding Interpretive Situations," in C. R. Cooper, ed.
Researching Response to Literature and the Teaching of Literature: Points of
Departure (Norwood NJ: Ablex, 1985), 22-32.

h71. Champagne, Roland A. Literary History in the Wake of Roland
Barthes: Re-Defining the Myths of Reading (Birmingham AL: Summa,
1984).

h72. Charles, Michel. Rhétorique de la lecture (Paris: Seuil, 1977).
h73. ----------. "La lecture critique." Poétique 34 (1978), 129-51.

h74. Charvat, William. "Melville and the Common Reader," in M. J.
Bruccoli, ed. The Profession of Authorship in America, 1800-1870
(Columbus: Ohio State UP, 1968), 262-82.

h75. Chase, Cynthia. "The Decomposition of the Elephants: Double-Reading
Daniel Deronda." PMLA 93 (1978), 215-25.

h76. Cohan, Steven. "Figures Beyond the Text: A Theory of Readable
Character in the Novel." Novel 17.1 (1983), 5-27.

h77. Cohen, Gillian. "The Psychology of Reading." NLH 4 (1972), 75-90.

h78. Cooper, Charles R., ed. Researching Response to Literature and the
Teaching of Literature: Points of Departure (Norwood NJ: Ablex, 1985).

h79. Coste, Didier. "Three Concepts of the Reader and Their Contribution to
a Theory of the Literary Text." OL 34 (1979), 271-86.

h80. Coward, David. "The Sociology of Literary Response," in J. Routh and
J. Wolff, eds. The Sociology of Literature: Theoretical Approaches (Keele:
U of Keele, 1977), 8-17.

h81. Craig, George. "Reading: Who Is Doing What to Whom?" in G.
Josipovici, ed. The Modern English Novel (NY: Barnes & Noble, 1976), 15-
36.

h82. Craig, Randall. "Reader-Response Criticism and Literary Realism."
ELWIU 11.1 (1984), 113-26.

h83. Crawford, Mary and Roger Chaffin. "The Reader's Construction of
Meaning: Cognitive Research on Gender and Comprehension," in E. Flynn

and P. P. Schweickart, eds. Gender and Reading: Essays on Readers, Texts, and Contexts (Baltimore: Johns Hopkins UP, 1986), 3-30.

h84. Creighton, Joanne V. "The Reader and Modern and Post-Modern Fiction." CollL 9.3 (1982), 216-30.

h85. Crosman, Robert. "Some Doubts About 'The Reader of *Paradise Lost*,'" CE 37 (1975), 372-82.
h86. ----------. Reading "Paradise Lost" (Bloomington: Indiana UP, 1980).
h87. ----------. "Do Readers Make Meaning?" in S. R. Suleiman and I. Crosman, eds. The Reader in the Text: Essays on Audience and Interpretation (Princeton: Princeton UP, 1980), 149-64.
h88. ----------. "How Readers Make Meaning." CollL 9.3 (1982), 207-15.

h89. Culler, Jonathan. "Reading and Misreading." YR 65 (1975), 88-95.
h90. ----------. "Stanley Fish and the Righting of the Reader." Diacritics 5.1 (1975), 26-31.
h91. ----------. "Prolegomena to a Theory of Reading," in S. R. Suleiman and I. Crosman, eds. The Reader in the Text: Essays on Audience and Interpretation (Princeton: Princeton UP, 1980), 46-66.

h92. Dallenbach, Lucien. "Reflexivity and Reading." NLH 11 (1980), 435-49.

h93. Daumer, Elisabeth. "Gender Bias in the Concept of Audience." Reader 13 (1985), 32-41.

h94. Davis, Frederick, ed. The Literature of Research in Reading with Emphasis on Models (New Brunswick NJ: Rutgers UP, 1971).

h95. DeMaria, Robert, Jr. "The Ideal Reader: A Critical Fiction." PMLA 93 (1978), 463-74.
h96. ----------. "'The Thinker as Reader': The Figure of the Reader in the Writing of Wallace Stevens." Genre 12 (1979), 243-68.

h97. Dentan, Michel. Le texte et son lecteur: études sur Benjamin Constant, Villiers de l'Isle-Adam, Ramuz, Cendrars, Bernanos, Gracq (Lausanne: l'Aire, 1983).

h98. Dilligan, Robert J. "Effective Stylistics: A Response to Affective Stylistics." Cahiers de lexicologie 30 (1977), 24-37.

h99. Dillon, George L. Language Processing and the Reading of Literature: Toward a Model of Comprehension (Bloomington: Indiana UP, 1978).
h100. ----------. "Styles of Reading." PoT 3.2 (1982), 77-88.

h101. Dolezel, Lubomir. "Eco and His Model Reader." PoT 1.4 (1980), 181-88.

h102. Drotner, Kristen. "Schoolgirls, Madcaps, and Air Aces: English Girls and Their Magazine Reading between the Wars." Feminist Studies 9 (1983), 33-52.

h103. Dryden, Edgar A. "Writer as Reader: An American Story." Boundary 8.1 (1979), 189-95.

h104. Dubois, Jacques. "Sociologie de la lecture et concept de lisibilité." Revue des Langues Vivantes 41 (1975), 471-83.

h105. Ducharme, Edward W. "The Reader in the Text: Implications of Objective and Subjective Theories of Interpretation for the Teaching of Literature." DAI 41 (1980), 2093A.

h106. Durgnat, Raymond. "Art and Audience." BJA 10 (1970), 11-24.

h107. Eagleton, Terry. "The Revolt of the Reader." NLH 13.3 (1982), 449-52.

h108. Easson, Roger R. "William Blake and His Reader in *Jerusalem,*" in S. Curran and J. A. Wittreich, Jr., eds. Blake's Sublime Allegory (Madison: U of Wisconsin P, 1973), 309-27.

h109. Eaton, Marcia M. "A Strange Kind of Sadness." JAAC 40 (1985), 51-63.

h110. Eco, Umberto. A Theory of Semiotics (Bloomington: Indiana UP, 1976).
h111. ----------. The Role of the Reader: Explorations in the Semiotics of Texts (Bloomington: Indiana UP, 1979).
h112. ----------, *et al* . "The Theory of Signs and the Role of the Reader." BMMLA 14.1 (1981), 33-55 [article and responses].

h113. Elliott, Susan M. "A New Critical Epistemology." HSL 7 (1975), 170-89.

h114. Erlich, Victor. "Reading Conscious and Unconscious." CE 36 (1975), 766-75 [on Fish and Holland].

h115. Felman, Shoshana. "Rereading Femininity." YFS 62 (1981), 19-44.

h116. Fetterley, Judith. The Resisting Reader: A Feminist Approach to American Fiction (Bloomington: Indiana UP, 1979).

h117. ----------. "Reading About Reading: 'A Jury of Her Peers,' 'The Murders in the Rue Morgue,' and 'The Yellow Wallpaper,'" in E. Flynn and P. P. Schweickart, eds. Gender and Reading: Essays on Readers, Texts, and Contexts (Baltimore: Johns Hopkins UP, 1986), 147-64.

h118. Fish, Stanley. Surprised by Sin: The Reader in "Paradise Lost" (NY: St. Martin's Press, 1967).

h119. ----------. "Letting Go: The Reader in Herbert's Poetry." ELH 37 (1970), 475-94.

h120. ----------. "Inaction and Silence: The Reader in Paradise Regained," in J. A. Wittreich, Jr., ed. Calm of Mind: Tercentenary Essays on "Paradise Regained" and "Samson Agonistes" (Cleveland: Case Western Reserve UP, 1971), 25-47.

h121. ----------. Self-Consuming Artifacts: The Experience of Seventeenth-Century Literature (Berkeley: U of California P, 1972).

h122. ----------. Is There a Text in this Class? The Authority of Interpretive Communities (Cambridge: Harvard UP, 1980).

h123. ----------. "Why No One's Afraid of Wolfgang Iser." Diacritics 11.1 (1981), 2-13.

h124. ----------. "Change." TkR 14.1-4 (1983-84), 277-96 [on interpretive communities].

h125. ----------. "La Théorie est sans conséquences." Critique 41 (1985), 445-69.

h126. Fitzgerald, Jill. "The Relationship Between Reading Ability and Expectations for Story Structures." DPr 7.1 (1984), 21-41.

h127. Flynn, Elizabeth. "Women Reading: A Phenomenological Approach." Reader 8 (1980), 16-22.

h128. ----------. "Women as Reader-Response Critics." NOR 10.2-3 (1983), 20-25 [on Rosenblatt, Suleiman, Tompkins].

h129. ---------- and Patrocinio P. Schweickart, eds. Gender and Reading: Essays on Readers, Texts, and Contexts (Baltimore: Johns Hopkins UP, 1986) [includes annotated bibliography, 289-303].

h130. ----------. "Gender and Reading," in E. Flynn and P. P. Schweickart, eds. Gender and Reading: Essays on Readers, Texts, and Contexts (Baltimore: Johns Hopkins UP, 1976), 267-88.

h131. Forunatow, N. "Kunstlerischer Schaffensprozess und Leser-Rezeption." KuL 19 (1971), 26-44.

h132. Foster, Dennis A. Confession and Complicity in Narrative (Cambridge & NY: Cambridge UP, 1987).

h133. Fowler, Roger. "Language and the Reader: Shakespeare's Sonnet 73," in Style and Structure in Literature: Essays in the New Stylistics (Ithaca: Cornell UP, 1975), 79-122.
h134. ----------. "'The Reader': A Linguistic View." CREL 4 (1977), 47-60.
h135. ----------. Linguistics and the Novel (London: Methuen, 1977) [chap. 5].

h136. French, Patricia Ross. "Reader-Response Theory: A Practical Application." JMMLA 20.2 (1987), 28-40.

h137. Freund, Elizabeth. The Return of the Reader: Reader-Response Criticism (London & NY: Methuen, 1987).

h138. Frey, Eberhard. "What Is Good Style? Reader Reactions to German Text Samples." MLJ 56 (1972), 310-23.

h139. Gagnier, Regenia A. Idylls of the Marketplace: Oscar Wilde and the Victorian Public (Stanford CA: Stanford UP, 1986).

h140. Galenbeck, Susan. "Higher Innocence: David Bleich, the Geneva School, and Reader Criticism." CE 40 (1979), 788-801.

h141. Gardiner, Judith Kegan. "Psychoanalytic Criticism and the Female Reader." Lit and Psychology 26 (1976), 100-07 [discusses Holland].

h142. Gasparov, Boris. "The Narrative Text as an Act of Communication." NLH 9 (1978), 245-61.

h143. Gelernt, Jules. "The Dynamics of Literary Response ." L&P 20 (1970), 129-34 [on Holland].

h144. Gibson, Eleanor J. and Harry Levin. The Psychology of Reading (Cambridge MA: MIT Press, 1975).

h145. Gill, Tejwant S. "Gramscian Hegemony: A Paradigm of Reader-Response Aesthetics." LCrit 21.4 (1986), 38-48.

h146. Glidden, Hope H. "Recouping the Text: The Theory and Practice of Reading." ECr 21.2 (1981), 25-36.

h147. Gloversmith, Frank, ed. The Theory of Reading (Sussex: Harvester; Totowa NJ: Barnes and Noble, 1984).

h148. Glowinski, Michal. "Der potentielle Leser in der Struktur eines poetischen Werkes." WB 21.6 (1975), 118-43.

h149. ----------. "Reading, Interpretation, Reception." NLH 11 (1979), 75-82.

h150. Goodman, Kenneth S., ed. The Psycholinguistic Nature of the Reading Process (Detroit: Wayne State UP, 1968).

h151. Graham, Joseph F. "Critical Persuasion: In Response to Stanley Fish." Boundary 8.1 (1979), 147-57.

h152. Greenfield, Catherine. "On Readers, Readerships, and Reading Practices." SoRA 16.1 (1983), 121-42.

h153. Greenstein, Susan. "Dear Reader, Dear Friend: Richardson's Readers and the Social Response to Character." CE 41.5 (1980), 524-34.

h154. Grivel Charles and Françoise Gaillard, eds. "L'Effet de lecture." RSH 177 (1980) [special issue].

h155. Guthrie, Jerry L. "Self-Deception and Emotional Response to Fiction." BJA 21.1 (1981), 65-75.

h156. Hagopian, John V. "In Defense of the Affective Fallacy." SoRA 1.3 (1965), 72-77.

h157. Hamann, Elsbeth. Theodor Fontanes "Effi Briest" aus erzahlteoretischer Sicht: unter besonderer Berucksichtigung der Interdependenzen zwischen Autor, Erzahlwerk und Leser (Bonn: Bouvier Verlag Herbert Grundmann, 1984).

h158. Harker, W. John. "Comprehending the Discourse of Poetry," in A. Flammer and W. Kintsch, eds. Discourse Processing (Amsterdam: North-Holland, 1982), 570-81.

h159. Harris, Victoria Frankel. "Criticism and the Incoporative Consciousness, I: The Garden of Meanings and Symbolicity." CentR 25.4 (1981), 417-34.

h160. Harris, Wendell. "On Choosing One's Allies: The Interimplication of Act and Response." Reader 12 (1984), 21-38.

h161. Harth, Dietrich. "Romane und ihre Leser." GRM 20 (1979), 159-79.

h162. Harvey, Robert Charles. "One Reader Reading: An Exploration of the Relationship between Conscious and Unconscious Response in Reading Five Prose Fictions." DAI 39 (1978), 296A.

h163. Hellenga, Robert R. "What Is a Literary Experience *Like* ?" NLH 14.1 (1982), 105-15.

h164. Hill, Leslie. "The Wandering Viewpoint." OLR 4.2 (1980), 94-101 [on Iser].

h165. Hirsch, Marianne. "Gender, Reading, and Desire in *Moderato Cantabile*." Twentieth Century Literature 28 (1982), 69-85.

h166. Holland, Norman N. The Dynamics of Literary Response (NY: Oxford UP, 1968).
h167. ----------. 5 Readers Reading (New Haven: Yale UP, 1975).
h168. ----------. "The New Paradigm: Subjective or Transactive?" NLH 7 (1976), 335-46 [on Bleich].
h169. ----------. "Stanley Fish, Stanley Fish." Genre 10 (1977), 433-41.
h170. ----------. "Literature as Transaction," in P. Hernadi, ed. What Is Literature? (Bloomington: Indiana UP, 1978), 206-18.
h171. ----------. "A Transactive Account of Transactive Criticism." Poetics 7 (1978), 177-89.
h172. ----------. "Transacting My 'Good-Morrow' or, Bring Back the Vanished Critic." Studies in the Literary Imagination 12.1 (1979), 61-72.
h173. ----------. "Re-Covering 'The Purloined Letter': Reading as a Personal Transaction," in S. R. Suleiman and I. Crosman, eds. The Reader in the Text: Essays on Audience and Interpretation (Princeton: Princeton UP, 1980), 350-70.
h174. ----------. "Criticism as Transaction," in P. Hernadi, ed. What Is Criticism? (Bloomington: Indiana UP, 1981), 242-52.
h175. ----------. "Driving in Gainesville, Florida: The Shared and the Individual in Literary Response." HSL 16.2-3 (1984), 1-15.
h176. ----------. "Reading Readers Reading," in C. R. Cooper, ed. Researching Response to Literature and the Teaching of Literature: Points of Departure (Norwood NJ: Ablex, 1985), 3-21.
h177. ----------. "The Miller's Wife and the Professors: Questions About the Transactive Theory of Reading." NLH 17.3 (1986), 423-47.
h178. ---------- and Leona F. Sherman. "Gothic Possibilities," in E. Flynn and P. P. Schweickart, eds. Gender and Reading: Essays on Readers, Texts, and Contexts (Baltimore: Johns Hopkins UP, 1986), 215-33.

h179. Horton, Susan R. "The Experience of Stanley Fish's Prose or the Critic as Self-Creating, Self-Consuming Artificer." Genre 10.3 (1977).
h180. ----------. The Reader in the Dickens World: Style and Response (Pittsburgh: U of Pittsburgh P, 1981).

h181. Hoyt, Reed J. "Reader-Response and Implication-Realization." JAAC 43.3 (1985), 281-90.

h182. Hughes, Daniel. "Reading in Critical Theory." <u>MLN</u> 96.5 (1981), 1149-59.

h183. Hunt, Russell A. and Douglas Vipond. "Crash-Testing a Transactional Model of Literary Reading." <u>Reader</u> 14 (1985), 23-39.

h184. Hunter, J. Paul. "The Loneliness of the Long-Distance Reader." <u>Genre</u> 10 (1977), 455-84.

h185. Iser, Wolfgang. "Indeterminacy and the Reader's Response in Prose Fiction," in J. Hillis Miller, ed. <u>Aspects of Narrative</u> (NY: Columbia UP, 1971), 1-45.
h186. ----------. "The Reading Process: A Phenomenological Approach." <u>NLH</u> 3 (1972), 279-99.
h187. ----------. <u>The Implied Reader: Patterns of Communication in Prose Fiction from Bunyan to Beckett</u> (Baltimore: Johns Hopkins UP, 1974).
h188. ----------. "The Reality of Fiction: A Functionalist Approach to Literature." <u>NLH</u> 7 (1975), 7-38.
h189. ----------. <u>The Act of Reading: A Theory of Aesthetic Response</u> (Baltimore: Johns Hopkins UP, 1978).
h190. ----------. "Narrative Strategies as a Means of Communication," in M. J. Valdes and O. J. Miller, eds. <u>Interpretation of Narrative</u> (Toronto: U of Toronto P, 1978), 100-17.
h191. ----------. "The Current Situation of Literary Theory: Key Concepts and the Imaginary." <u>NLH</u> 11 (1979), 1-20.
h192. ----------. "The Indeterminacy of the Text: A Critical Reply." <u>CCrit</u> 2 (1980), 27-47.
h193. ----------. "Interaction between Text and Reader," in S. R. Suleiman and I. Crosman, eds. <u>The Reader in the Text: Essays on Audience and Interpretation</u> (Princeton: Princeton UP, 1980), 106-19.
h194. ----------. "Interview." <u>Diacritics</u> 10.2 (1980), 57-74.
h195. ----------. "Talk Like Whales: A Reply to Stanley Fish." <u>Diacritics</u> 11.3 (1981), 82-87.

h196. Jack, Ian. <u>The Poet and His Audience</u> (Cambridge & NY: Cambridge UP, 1984).

h197. Jauss, Hans Robert. "Levels of Identification of Hero and Audience." <u>NLH</u> 5 (1974), 283-317.

h198. Jayne, Edward S. "Affective Criticism: Theories of Emotion and Synaesthesis in the Experience of Literature." <u>DAI</u> 31 (1971), 6612A-13A.

h199. Johnson, Nancy Jean. "Reader-Response Criticism and the Rhetorical Tradition." <u>DAI</u> 42 (1982), 4458A.

h200. Jordan, Robert M. Chaucer's Poetics and the Modern Reader (Berkeley: U of California P, 1987).

h201. Juhl, P. D. "Stanley Fish's Interpretive Communities and the Status of Critical Interpretation." CCrit 5 (1983), 47-58.

h202. Kaiser, Michael. "Zur begrifflichen und terminologischen Klarung einiger Vorgange beim literarischen Lesen." GRM 28 (1978), 87-94 [on Iser].

h203. Kamerbeek, J., Jr. "Le Concept du 'Lecteur ideal.'" Neophil 61 (1977), 2-7.

h204. Kennard, Jean E. "Ourself behind Ourself: A Theory for Lesbian Readers," in E. Flynn and P. P. Schweickart, eds. Gender and Reading: Essays on Readers, Texts, and Contexts (Baltimore: Johns Hopkins UP, 1986), 63-80.

h205. Kincaid, James R. "Coherent Readers, Incoherent Texts." CritI 3 (1977), 781-802.

h206. Kintgen, Eugene R. "Reader Response and Stylistics." Style 11.1 (1977), 1-18.
h207. ----------. The Perception of Poetry (Bloomington: Indiana UP, 1983).

h208. Koelb, Clayton. The Incredulous Reader: Literature and the Function of Disbelief (Ithaca: Cornell UP, 1984).

h209. Kotin, Armine. "On the Subject of Reading." Journal of Applied Structuralism 1 (1979), 11-34.

h210. Kritzman, Lawrence D. "Learning to Read: Literary Competence and Structuralist Poetics." Dispositio 2 (1977), 113-17.

h211. Kuenzli, Rudolf E. "The Intersubjective Structure of the Reading Process: A Communication-Oriented Theory of Literature." Diacritics 10.2 (1980), 47-56.

h212. Lamarque, Peter. "How Can We Fear and Pity Fictions?" BJA 21.4 (1981), 291-304.

h213. Lange, Victor. "The Reader in the Strategy of Fiction," in R. G. Popperwell, ed. Expression, Communication and Experience in Literature and Language (London: MHRA, 1973), 86-102.

h214. Langman, F. H. "The Idea of the Reader in Literary Criticism." BJA 7 (1967), 84-94.

h215. Latané, David E., Jr. Browning's *Sordello* and the Aesthetics of Difficulty (Victoria, B.C., Canada: ELS, U of Victoria, 1987).

h216. "Lecture et lectures." Cahiers 4 (1977) [special issue].

h217. Leenhardt, Jacques. "Toward a Sociology of Reading," in S. R. Suleiman and I. Crosman, eds. The Reader in the Text: Essays on Audience and Interpretation (Princeton: Princeton UP, 1980), 205-24.

h218. Leistner, Detlef B. Autor, Erzahltext, Leser: Sprachhandlungstheoretische Uberlegungen zur Sprachverwendung in Erzahltexten (Erlangen: Palm & Enke, 1975).

h219. Lewandowski, Theodor. "Uberlegungen zur Theorie und Praxis des Lesens." WW 30 (1980), 54-65.

h220. Link, Hannelore. "'Die Appellstruktur der Texte' und 'ein Paradigmawechsel in der Literaturwissenschaft." Jahrbuch der deutschen Schillergesellschaft 17 (1973), 532-83 [on Iser].

h221. Loesberg, Jonathan. "Intentionalism, Reader-Response and the Place of Deconstruction." Reader 12 (1984), 21-38 [on Derrida, Fish, E. D. Hirsch].

h222. Lotman, Iurii M. "The Text and the Structure of Its Audience." NLH 14.1 (1982), 81-87.

h223. Mace, C. A. "On the Directedness of Aesthetic Response." BJA 8 (1968), 155-60.

h224. Mailloux, Steven. "Evaluation and Reader Response Criticism: Values Implicit in Affective Stylistics." Style 10 (1976), 329-43.
h225. ----------. "Stanley Fish's 'Interpreting the *Variorum* ': Advance or Retreat?" CritI 3 (1976), 183-90.
h226. ----------. "Reader-Response Criticism?" Genre 10 (1977), 413-31.
h227. ----------. "Learning to Read: Interpretation and Reader-Response Criticism." Studies in the Literary Imagination 12 (1979), 93-108.
h228. ----------, ed. "Theories of Reading, Looking, and Listening." BuR 26.1 (1981) [special issue].
h229. ----------. "How to Be Persuasive in Literary Theory: The Case of Wolfgang Iser." Centrum 1.1 (1981), 65-73.
h230. ----------. "Reading in Critical Theory." MLN 96 (1981), 1149-59.

h231. ----------. Interpretive Conventions: The Reader in the Study of American Fiction (Ithaca: Cornell UP, 1982).

h232. ----------. "Learning to Read: Interpretation and Reader-Response Criticism," in V. Kramer, ed. American Critics at Work: Examinations of Contemporary Literary Theory (Troy NY: Whitston, 1984), 296-315.

h233. Mann, Peter H. "The Romantic Novel and Its Readers." Jour of Popular Culture 15 (1981), 9-18.

h234. Maranda, Pierre. "The Dialectic of Metaphor: An Anthropological Essay on Hermeneutics," in S. R. Suleiman and I. Crosman, eds. The Reader in the Text: Essays on Audience and Interpretation (Princeton: Princeton UP, 1980), 183-204.

h235. Marin, Louis. "Toward a Theory of Reading in the Visual Arts: Poussin's The Arcadian Shepherds," in S. R. Suleiman and I. Crosman, eds. The Reader in the Text: Essays on Audience and Interpretation (Princeton: Princeton UP, 1980), 293-324.

h236. Marlow, James. "Fish Doing Things with Austin and Searle." MLN 91 (1976), 1602-12.

h237. Marshall, Donald G. "Reading as Understanding: Hermeneutics and Reader-Response Criticism." C&L 33.1 (1983), 37-48.

h238. Maurer, Karl. "Formen des Lesens." Poetica 9 (1977), 472-98.

h239. McCormick, Kathleen. "Psychological Realism and Literary Interpretation: A Cognitive Approach to Studying the Interactions of Texts and Readers." DAI 45 (1985), 2523A-24A.

h240. ----------. "Psychological Realism: A New Epistemology for Reader-Response Criticism." Reader 14 (1985), 40-53.

h241. ----------. "Swimming Upstream with Stanley Fish." JAAC 44.1 (1985), 67-76.

h242. ----------. "Theory in the Reader: Bleich, Holland, and Beyond." CE 47.8 (1985), 836-51.

h243. McGann, Jerome J. "Formalism, Savagery, and Care; Or, the Function of Criticism Once Again." CritI 2 (1976), 605-30.

h244. McGillis, Rod. "Literary Incompetence." CLAQ 10.3 (1985), 144-45 [on Culler].

h245. Melnick, Daniel. "Fullness and Dissonance: Music and the Reader's Experience of Modern Fiction." MFS 25 (1979), 209-22.

h246. Mermin, Dorothy. The Audience in the Poem: Five Victorian Poets (New Brunswick NJ: Rutgers UP, 1983).

h247. Merrell, Floyd. "How We Perceive Texts." Dispositio 3 (1978), 167-73.

h248. Michaels, Walter Benn. "Writers Reading: James & Eliot." MLN 91 (1976), 827-49.
h249. ----------. "Saving the Text: Reference and Belief." MLN 93 (1978), 771-93.

h250. Miller, Bruce E. "Does Critical Consensus Exist? The Case of Keats's Nightingale Ode." RS 50.3-4 (1982), 133-45.

h251. Miller, Owen J. "Reading as a Process of Reconstruction: A Critique of Recent Structuralist Formulations," in M. J. Valdes and O. J. Miller, eds. Interpretation of Narrative (Toronto: U of Toronto P, 1978), 19-27.

h252. Miller, Robin Feuer. Dostoevsky and The Idiot : Author, Narrator, and Reader (Cambridge: Harvard UP, 1981).

h253. Miner, Madonne M. "Gender, Reading and Misreading." Reader 13 (1985), 10-18.
h254. ----------. "Guaranteed to Please: Twentieth-Century American Women's Bestsellers," in E. Flynn and P. P. Schweickart, eds. Gender and Reading: Essays on Readers, Texts, and Contexts (Baltimore: Johns Hopkins UP, 1986), 187-211.

h255. Mistacco, Vicki. "The Theory and Practice of Reading Nouveaux Romans: Robbe-Grillet's Topologie d'une cité fantome," in S. R. Suleiman and I. Crosman, eds. The Reader in the Text: Essays on Audience and Interpretation (Princeton: Princeton UP, 1980), 371-400.

h256. Mitchell, Ruth. "The Critical Relationship: A Theory of Reader Response." DAI 37 (1977), 5854A-55A.

h257. Montgomery, Robert L. The Reader's Eye: Studies in Didactic Literary Theory from Dante to Tasso (Berkeley: U of California P, 1979).

h258. Morse, David. "Author-Reader-Language: Reflections on a Critical Closed Circuit," in F. Gloversmith, ed. The Theory of Reading (Sussex: Harvester; Totowa NJ: Barnes and Noble, 1984), 52-92.

h259. Mullen, Judith. "Some Readings on Reading with a Brief Introductory Initiation into Structuralism." Rackham Literary Studies 9 (1979), 77-87.

h260. Mundhenk, Rosemary. "The Education of the Reader in *Our Mutual Friend*." NCF 34 (1979), 41-58.

h261. Mykyta, Larysa. "Literature Lost or the Politics of Justification." Reader 9 (1983), 32-37 [discusses Bleich].
h262. ----------. "The Politics of Subjective Criticism." PCL 11 (1985), 54-61 [on Bleich].

h263. Nabholtz, John R. "My Reader My Fellow-Labourer" A Study of English Romantic Prose (Columbia: U of Missouri P, 1986).

h264. Nardo, Anna K. "Fantasy Literature and Play: An Approach to Reader Response." CentR 22 (1978), 201-13.

h265. Naumann, Manfred. "Literatur und Leser." WB 16.5 (1970), 92-116.
h266. ----------. "Autor--Adressat--Leser." WB 17.11 (1971), 163-69.
h267. ----------. "Autor und Leser." WB 19.11 (1973), 5-9.

h268. Nelson, Cary. "Reading Criticism." PMLA 91 (1976), 801-15.

h269. Nelson, Lowry, Jr. "The Fictive Reader and Literary Self-Reflexiveness," in P. Demetz, T. Green, and L. Nelson, Jr., eds. The Disciplines of Criticism (New Haven: Yale UP, 1968), 173-91.

h270. Nojgaard, Morten. "The Function of a Narratee or How We Are Manipulated by Texts." OL supp. 4 (1979), 57-64.
h271. ----------. "La Lecteur dans le texte." OL 39.3 (1984), 189-212.

h272. Norman, Liane. "Bartleby and the Reader." NEQ 44 (1971), 22-39.
h273. ----------. "Risk and Redundancy." PMLA 90 (1975), 285-91.

h274. O'Brien, Barbara J. "Imaginative Reading: The Process of Responding to Literature." DAI 42 (1984), 202A.

h275. Odell, L. and Charles R. Cooper. "Describing Responses to Works of Fiction." Research in the Teaching of English 10 (1976), 203-25.

h276. Olsen, Michel. "'Lecteur modele,' codes et structures." OL 37.1 (1982), 83-94 [on Eco, Groeben, Iser].

h277. Ong, Walter J. "The Writer's Audience is Always a Fiction." PMLA 90 (1975), 9-21.
h278. ----------. "Beyond Objectivity: The Reader-Writer Transaction as an Altered State of Consciousness." CEA 40.1 (1977), 6-13.

h279. ----------. "Reading, Technology, and the Nature of Man: An Interpretation." YES 10 (1980), 132-49.

h280. Pagliaro, Harold E. "The Affective Question." BuR 20.1 (1972), 3-20.

h281. Pearson, Roger. Stendhal's Violin: A Novelist and His Reader (Oxford: Clarendon, 1988).

h282. Pedrick, Victoria and Nancy S. Rabinowitz, eds. "Audience-Oriented Criticism and the Classics." Arethusa 19.2 (1986) [special issue].

h283. Perez-Firmat, Gustavo. "Interpretive Assumptions and Interpreted Texts: On a Poem by Stanley Fish." ELWIU 11.1 (1984), 145-52.

h284. Perry, Menakhem. "Literary Dynamics: How the Order of a Text Creates Its Meanings, with an Analysis of Faulkner's 'A Rose for Emily.'" PoT 1 (1979), 35-64, 311-61.

h285. Persin, Margaret H. Recent Spanish Poetry and the Role of the Reader (Lewisburg PA: Bucknell UP, 1987).

h286. Pestino, Joseph Francis. "The Reader/Writer Affair: Instigating Repertoire in the Experimental Fiction of Susan Sontag, Walter Abish, Réjean Ducharme, Paul West, and Christine Brooke-Rose." DAI 47 (1986), 1314A-15A.

h287. Petersen, Bruce. "Writing About Responses: A Unified Model of Reading, Interpretation, and Composition." CE 44 (1982), 459-68.

h288. Peterson, Carla L. The Determined Reader: Gender and Culture in the Novel from Napoleon to Victoria (New Brunswick NJ: Rutgers UP, 1986).

h289. Petrosky, Anthony R. "Response: A Way of Knowing," in C. R. Cooper, ed. Researching Response to Literature and the Teaching of Literature: Points of Departure (Norwood NJ: Ablex, 1985), 70-83.

h290. Picard, Michel. "Pour la lecture littéraire." Littérature 26 (1977), 26-42.

h291. Piwowarczyk, Mary Ann. "The Narratee and the Situation of Enunciation: A Reconsideration of Prince's Theory." Genre 9 (1976), 161-77.

h292. Potter, Rosanne G. "Reader Responses and Character Syntax," in R. W. Bailey, ed. Computing in the Humanities (Amsterdam: North-Holland, 1982).

h293. Poulet, Georges. "Phenomenology of Reading." NLH 1 (1969), 53-68.
h294. ----------. "Criticism and the Experience of Interiority," in R. A. Macksey and E. Donato, eds. The Structuralist Controversy: The Languages of Criticism and the Sciences of Man (Baltimore: Johns Hopkins UP, 1972), 56-72.

h295. Pratt, Mary Louise. Toward a Speech Act Theory of Literary Discourse (Bloomington: Indiana UP, 1977).
h296. ----------. "Interpretive Strategies/Strategic Interpretations: On Anglo-American Reader Response Criticism." Boundary 11.1-2 (1982-83), 201-31 [discusses Culler, Prince].

h297. Preston, John. The Created Self: The Reader's Role in Eighteenth-Century Fiction (NY: Barnes & Noble, 1970).

h298. Prince, Gerald. "On Readers and Listeners in Narrative." Neophil 55 (1971), 117-22.
h299. ----------. "Introduction a l'étude du narrataire." Poétique 14 (1973), 178-96.
h300. ----------. "Notes on the Text as Reader," in S. R. Suleiman and I. Crosman, eds. The Reader in the Text: Essays on Audience and Interpretation (Princeton: Princeton UP, 1980), 225-40.
h301. ----------. "Reading and Narrative Competence." ECr 22.2 (1981), 81-88.

h302. Purves, Alan C. and Victoria Rippere. Elements of Writing About a Literary Work: A Study of Responses to Literature (Urbana IL: NCTE, 1968).
h303. ----------, ed. How Porcupines Make Love: Notes on a Response-Centered Curriculum (Lexington MA: Xerox, 1972).
h304. ---------- and Richard Beach. Literature and the Reader: Research in Response to Literature, Reading Interests, and the Teaching of Literature (Urbana IL: NCTE, 1972).
h305. ----------. "That Sunny Dome: Those Caves of Ice: A Model for Research in Reader Response." CE 40 (1979), 801-12 [another version in C. R. Cooper, ed. Researching Response to Literature and the Teaching of Literature: Points of Departure (Norwood NJ: Ablex, 1985), 54-69].
h306. ----------. "Putting Readers in Their Places: Some Alternatives to Cloning Stanley Fish." CE 42 (1980), 228-36.

h307. Quignard, Pascal. Le Lecteur (Paris: Gallimard, 1976).

h308. Rabinowitz, Nancy and Peter Rabinowitz. "The Critical Balance: Reader, Text, and Meaning." CE 41 (1980), 924-32.
h309. ----------. "Aphrodite and the Audience: Engendering the Reader." Arethusa 19.2 (1986), 171-85.

h310. Rabinowitz, Peter J. "Truth in Fiction: A Reexamination of Audiences." CritI 4 (1977-78), 121-41.
h311. ----------. "'What's Hecuba to Us?' The Audience's Experience of Literary Borrowing," in S. R. Suleiman and I. Crosman, eds. The Reader in the Text: Essays on Audience and Interpretation (Princeton: Princeton UP, 1980), 241-63.
h312. ----------. "Circumstantial Evidence: Musical Analysis and Theories of Reading." Mosaic 18.4 (1985), 159-73.
h313. ----------. "Shifting Stands, Shifting Standards: Reading, Interpretation, and Literary Judgment." Arethusa 19.2 (1986), 115-34.
h314. ----------. Before Reading: Narrative Conventions and the Politics of Interpretation (Ithaca: Cornell UP, 1987).

h315. Rader, Ralph. "Fact, Theory, and Literary Explanation." CritI 1 (1974), 245-72.

h316. Radway, Janice. "Women Read the Romance: The Interaction of Text and Context." Feminist Studies 9 (1983), 53-78.
h317. ----------. "Interpretive Communities and Variable Literacies: The Functions of Romance Reading." Daedalus 113.3 (1984), 49-73.
h318. ----------. Reading the Romance: Women, Patriarchy, and Popular Literature (Chapel Hill: U of North Carolina P, 1984).
h319. ----------. "American Studies, Reader Theory, and the Literary Text: From the Study of Material Objects to the Study of Social Processes," in D. E. Nye and C. K. Thomsen, eds. American Studies in Transition (Odense: Odense UP, 1985), 29-51.

h320. Raible, Wolfgang. "Vom Autor als Kopist zum Leser als Autor: Literaturtheorie in der literarischen Praxis." Poetica 5 (1972), 133-51.

h321. Ravaux, Françoise. "The Return of the Reader." FR 52 (1979), 708-13.

h322. Ray, William. "Recognizing Recognition: The Intra-Textual and Extra-Textual Critical Persona." Diacritics 7.4 (1977), 20-33 [on Iser, Piwowarczyk, Prince].
h323. ----------."Supersession and the Subject: A Reconsideration of Stanley Fish's 'Affective Stylistics.'" Diacritics 8.3 (1978), 60-71.
h324. ----------. "Reading Theory: The Role of the Semiotician." Diacritics 10.1 (1980), 50-59 [on Eco].

h325. ----------. Literary Meaning: From Phenomenology to Deconstruction
(Oxford: Basil Blackwell, 1984).

h326. "Readers and Spectators: Some Views and Reviews." NLH 8 (1976)
[special issue].

h327. "Reading, Interpretation, Response." Genre 10.3 (1977), 363-453
[special section].

h328. "The Reader and the Text." ECr 21.2 (1971) [special issue].

h329. Reeves, Charles Eric. "Literary Conventions and the Noumenal Text:
Stanley Fish's Egalitarian Poetics." Neophil 70.3 (1986), 334-40.

h330. Regis, Edward, Jr. "Literature *by* the Reader: The 'Affective' Theory
of Stanley Fish." CE 38 (1976), 263-80.

h331. Reichert, John. Making Sense of Literature (Chicago: U of Chicago P,
1977) [chap. 3: "Writer and Reader"].
h332. ----------. "But That Was in Another Ballpark: A Reply to Stanley
Fish." CritI 6 (1979), 164-72.

h333. Rendall, Steven. "The Critical *We*." OL 35 (1980), 32-49.
h334. ----------. "Fish vs. Fish." Diacritics 12 (1982), 49-56.
h335. ----------. "Reading Montaigne." Diacritics 15.2 (1985), 44-53.

h336. Richowsky, John Christopher. "Toward a Subjective Study of
Literature." DAI 36 (1976), 4464A-65A.

h337. Riffaterre, Michael. "The Self-Sufficient Text." Diacritics 3.3 (1973),
39-45.
h338. ----------. "Intertextual Scrambling." Romanic Review 68 (1977),
197-206.
h339. ----------. Semiotics of Poetry (Bloomington: Indiana UP, 1978).
h340. ----------. "The Reader's Perception of Narrative: Balzac's *Paix de
ménage*," in M. J. Valdes and O. J. Miller, eds. Interpretation of Narrative
(Toronto: U of Toronto P, 1978), 28-37.
h341. ----------. Production du texte (Paris: Seuil, 1979).
h342. ----------. "Interpretation and Undecidability." NLH 12.2 (1981), 227-
42.

h343. Riquelme, John Paul. "The Ambivalence of Reading." Diacritics 10.2
(1980), 75-86 [on Iser].

h344. Rogers, Robert. "Amazing Reader in the Labyrinth of Literature." PoT 3.2 (1982), 31-46.

h345. Roloff, Volker. "Der Begriff der Lekture in kommunikations-theoretischer und literaturwissenschaftlicher Sicht." RJ 29 (1978), 33-57.

h346. Rosenblatt, Louise M. "Towards a Transactional Theory of Reading." Journal of Reading Behavior 1 (1969), 31-47.
h347. ----------. The Reader, the Text, and Poem: The Transactional Theory of the Literary Work (Carbondale: Southern Illinois UP, 1978).
h348. ----------. "Act I, Scene I: Enter the Reader." LPer 1.2 (1981), 13-23.
h349. ----------. "On the Aesthetic as the Basic Model of the Reading Process." BuR 26.1 (1981), 17-32.
h350. ----------. "The Transactional Theory of the Literary Work: Implications for Research," in C. R. Cooper, ed. Researching Response to Literature and the Teaching of Literature: Points of Departure (Norwood NJ: Ablex, 1985), 33-53.
h351. ----------. "The Literary Transaction," in P. Demers, ed. The Creating Word (Edmonton: U of Alberta P, 1986), 66-85.

h352. Rosmarin, Adena. "Reading the Readers." DQ 19.4 (1985), 111-17 [on Mailloux].

h353. Ross, James F. "On the Concepts of Reading." Philosophical Forum 6 (1972), 93-141.

h354. Roudiez, Leon. "Notes on the Reader as Subject." Semiotext(e) 1.3 (1975), 69-80.

h355. Rowe, John Carlos. The Theoretical Dimensions of Henry James (Madison: U of Wisconsin P, 1984) [chap. 7: "Forms of the Reader's Act: Author and Reader in the Prefaces to the New York Edition"].

h356. Said, Edward. "Opponents, Audiences, Constituencies, and Communities." CritI 9 (1982), 1-26.

h357. Saldivar, Ramon. "Reading and Systems of Reading." SNNTS 11 (1979), 472-81.

h358. Sarkany, Stéphane. "Intentions créatrices et intentionnalité de fait: Ecriture, lecture et lecteurs." CJRS 4.3 (1977), 23-34.

h359. Schibanoff, Susan. "Taking the Gold Out of Egypt: The Art of Reading as a Woman," in E. Flynn and P. P. Schweickart, eds. Gender and

Reading: Essays on Readers, Texts, and Contexts (Baltimore: Johns Hopkins UP, 1986), 83-106.

h360. Schloss, Carol and Khachig Tololyan. "The Siren in the Funhouse: Barth's Courting of the Reader." Journal of Narrative Technique 11 (1981), 64-74.

h361. Schmidt, Siegfried J. "Receptional Problems with Contemporary Narrative Texts and Some of their Reasons." Poetics 9 (1980), 119-46.

h362. Scholes, Robert. "Cognition and the Implied Reader." Diacritics 5.3 (1975), 13-15 [on Iser].
h363. ----------. "Who Cares About the Text?" Novel 17.2 (1984), 171-80 [on Fish].

h364. Schor, Naomi. "Fiction as Interpretation/ Interpretation as Fiction," in S. R. Suleiman and I. Crosman, eds. The Reader in the Text: Essays on Audience and Interpretation (Princeton: Princeton UP, 1980), 165-82.

h365. Schwartz, Murray. "Where Is Literature?" CE 36 (1975), 756-65.

h366. Schweickart, Patrocinio P. "Reading Ourselves: Toward a Feminist Theory of Reading," in E. Flynn and P. P. Schweickart, eds. Gender and Reading: Essays on Readers, Texts, and Contexts (Baltimore: Johns Hopkins UP, 1986), 31-62.

h367. Segel, Elizabeth. "'As the Twig Is Bent. . .': Gender and Childhood Reading," in E. Flynn and P. P. Schweickart, eds. Gender and Reading: Essays on Readers, Texts, and Contexts (Baltimore: Johns Hopkins UP, 1986), 165-86.

h368. Selden, Raman. "The Reader and the Text." DUJ 74.2 (1982), 269-74.

h369. Seung, T. K. "Pragmatic Context and Textual Interpretation." JLS 9 (1980), 82-93.

h370. Sharratt, Bernard. Reading Relations: Structures of Literary Production: A Dialectical Text/Book (Atlantic Highlands NJ: Humanities P, 1982).

h371. Shepherd, David. "The Authority of Meanings and the Meanings of Authorities: Some Problems in the Theory of Reading." PoT 7.1 (1986), 129-45.

h372. Sherman, Carol. "Response Criticism: 'Do Readers Make Meaning?'" RomN 18 (1977), 288-92.

h373. Shevelow, Kathryn. "Fathers and Daughters: Women as Readers of the *Tatler*," in E. Flynn and P. P. Schweickart, eds. Gender and Reading: Essays on Readers, Texts, and Contexts (Baltimore: Johns Hopkins UP, 1986), 107-23.

h374. Singer, Harry and Robert B. Ruddell, eds. Theoretical Models and Processes of Reading (Newark DE: International Reading Association, 1976).

h375. Skulsky, Harold. "On Being Moved by Fiction." JAAC 39 (1980), 5-14.

h376. Slatoff, Walter. With Respect to Readers: Dimensions of Literary Response (Ithaca: Cornell UP, 1970).
h377. ----------. "Some of My Best Friends are Interpreters." NLH 4 (1973), 375-80.

h378. Smith, Allan Gardner. "The Occultism of the Text." PoT 3.4 (1982), 5-20 [discusses Iser].

h379. Smith, Frank. Understanding Reading: A Psycholinguistic Analysis of Reading and Learning How to Read (NY: Holt, Rinehart & Winston, 1971).

h380. Sosnoski, James. "Reading Acts and Reading Warrants: Some Implications for Readers Responding to Joyce's Portrait of Stephen." JJQ 16 (1978-79), 43-63.

h381. Spilka, Mark. "The Affective Fallacy Revisited." SoRA 1.3 (1965), 57-72, 77-79.

h382. Steig, Michael. "The Challenge of Subjectivism: A Personal Response." WRC 10.2 (1975), 15-23 [on Bleich and Holland].

h383. Steinberg, Gunter. Erlebte Rede: Ihre Eigenart und ihre Formen in neurer deutscher, franzosischer und englischer Erzahlliteratur (Goppingen: Kummerle, 1971).

h384. Steiner, George. "'Critic'/ 'Reader.'" NLH 10 (1979), 423-52.

h385. Stiebel, Arlene. "But Is It Life? Some Thoughts on Modern Critical Theory." MLS 14.3 (1984), 3-12 [discusses Fish and Iser].

h386. Stierle, Karlheinz. "The Reading of Fictional Texts," in S. R. Suleiman and I. Crosman, eds. The Reader in the Text: Essays on Audience and Interpretation (Princeton: Princeton UP, 1980), 83-105.

h387. Stonum, Gary Lee. "For a Cybernetics of Reading." MLN 92 (1977), 945-68.

h388. Stowe, William W. "Satisfying Readers: A Review-Essay." TSLL 24.1 (1982), 102-19.

h389. Suleiman, Susan R. "Ideological Dissent from Works of Fiction: Toward a Rhetoric of the roman a these." Neophilologus 60 (1976), 162-77.
h390. ----------. "Interpreting Ironies." Diacritics 6.2 (1976), 15-21.
h391. ----------. "Reading Robbe-Grillet: Sadism and Text in Projet pour une révolution a New York." Romanic Review 68 (1977), 43-62.
h392. ---------- and Inge Crosman, eds. The Reader in the Text: Essays on Audience and Interpretation (Princeton NJ: Princeton UP, 1980).
h393. ----------. "Introduction: Varieties of Audience-Oriented Criticism," in S. R. Suleiman and I. Crosman, eds. The Reader in the Text: Essays on Audience and Interpretation (Princeton: Princeton UP, 1980), 3-45.
h394. ----------. "The Question of Readability in Avant-Garde Fiction." STCL 6.1-2 (1980-81), 17-36.
h395. ----------. Authoritarian Fictions: The Ideological Novel as a Literary Genre (NY: Columbia UP, 1983) [esp. chap. 4: "Redundancy and the 'Readable' Text"].
h396. ----------. "Malraux's Women: A Re-Vision," in E. Flynn and P. P. Schweickart, eds. Gender and Reading: Essays on Readers, Texts, and Contexts (Baltimore: Johns Hopkins UP, 1986), 124-46.

h397. Thomas, Brook. "Not a Reading of, but the Act of Reading Ulysses." JJQ 16 (1978-79), 81-93.

h398. Todorov, Tzvetan. "Reading as Construction," in S. R. Suleiman and I. Crosman, eds. The Reader in the Text: Essays on Audience and Interpretation (Princeton: Princeton UP, 1980), 67-82.

h399. Tompkins, Jane P. "Criticism and Feeling." CE 39 (1977), 169-78.
h400. ----------, ed. Reader-Response Criticism: From Formalism to Post-Structuralism (Baltimore: Johns Hopkins UP, 1980) [includes Tompkins' "An Introduction to Reader-Response Criticism," ix-xxvi; and "The Reader in History: The Changing Shape of Literary Response," 201-32].

h401. Toolan, Michael. "Stanley Fish and the Interpretive Communities of Responding Readers." DQR 14.1 (1984), 62-73.

h402. Trotter, David. The Making of the Reader: Language and Subjectivity in Modern American, English, and Irish Poetry (NY: St. Martin's P, 1984).

h403. Valdes, Mario J. "A Functional View of Criticism," in P. Hernadi, ed. What Is Criticism? (Bloomington: Indiana UP, 1981), 126-33.

h404. Veley, Charles R. "Literature and the Emotions: A Psychology of Literary Response." DAI 32 (1971), 935A-36A.

h405. Verdaasdonk, H. and C. J. Van Rees. "Reading a Text vs. Analyzing a Text." Poetics 6 (1977), 55-76.

h406. Waldoff, Leon. "Perceiving and Creating in Interpretation." HSL 7 (1975), 154-69 [on Holland].

h407. Weinrich, Harald. Literatur fur Leser: Essays und Aufsatze zur Literaturwissenschaft (Stuttgart: Kohlhammer, 1971).

h408. Wells, Larry D. "Indeterminacy as Provocation: The Reader's Role in Annette von Droste-Hulshoff's 'Die Judenbuche.'" MLN 94 (1979), 475-92.

h409. Wijsen, Louk M. P. T. "From Text to Symbol: The Cognitive and Effective Response to Literature." PsyculR 2 (1978), 147-63.

h410. Williams, David A. "Audience Response and the Interpreter," in E. M. Doyle and V. H. Floyd, eds. Studies in Interpretation, vol. 2 (Amsterdam: Rodopi, 1977), 199-206.

h411. Wilson, W. Daniel. "Readers in Texts." PMLA 96.5 (1981), 848-63 [discusses W. Iser, H. Link, W. Ong. G. Prince, E. Wolff].

h412. Winterowd, R. Ross. "The Rhetorical Transaction of Reading." CCC 27 (1976), 185-91.

h413. Wiseman, Mary B. "Identifying with Characters in Literature." JCLA 4. 12 (1981), 47-57.

h414. Wood, Allen and Susan Cerasano. "A Conversation with Stanley Fish." RLSt 9 (1978), 51-61.

h415. Wyatt, David M. "Spelling Time: The Reader in Emerson's 'Circles.'" AL 48 (1976), 140-51.

I. Reception Aesthetics

i1. Adler, Gunter. "Identifikation und Distanzierung bei der Literaturrezeption." <u>WB</u> 26.2 (1980), 43-72.

i2. Amacher, Richard and Victor Lange, eds. <u>New Perspectives in German Literary Criticism</u> (Princeton: Princeton UP, 1979).

i3. Arnold, Armin and C. Stephen Jaeger, eds. <u>Der Gesunde Gelehrte: Literatur-, Sprach- und Rezeptionsanalysen</u> (Herisau: Schlapher, 1987).

i4. Bailey, Marianne. "Articles et livres récents consacrés a l'étude de la réception critique." <u>O&C</u> 2.2 (1978), 145-46.

i5. Barck, Karlheinz. "Rezeptionsasthetik und soziale Funktion der Literatur." <u>WB</u> 31.7 (1985), 1131-49.

i6. Bark, Joachim. "Mass Literature, Belles Lettres and Functional Texts: A Discussion of Current Positions and Classroom Praxis." <u>NGC</u> 5 (1975), 129-48.

i7. Barner, Wilfried. "Rezeptions- und Wirkungsgeschichte," in H. Brackert and J. Stuckrath, eds. <u>Literaturwissenschaft: Grundkurs 2</u> (Reinbeck bei Hamburg: Rowohlt, 1981).

i8. Bauer, Werner, <i>et al</i>. <u>Text und Rezeption: Wirkungsanalyse zeitgenossischer Lyrik am Beispiel des Gedichts "Fadensonnen" von Paul Celan</u> (Frankfurt: Athenaum, 1972).

i9. Baurmann, Jurgen. "Textrezeption empirisch: Wege zu einim Ziel, Behelfbrucken oder Holzwege?" in G. Kopf, ed. Rezeptionspragmatik: Beitrage zur Praxis des Lesens (Munich: Fink, 1981), 201-18.

i10. Berger, Albert. "Moderne Lyrik als Rezeptionsproblem: Theoretische Gesichtspunkte zum Umgang mit modernen Gedichten im Unterricht," in W. Schmidt=Dengler, ed. Formen der Lyrik in der osterreichischen Gegenwartsliteratur (Vienna: Osterreichischer Bundesverlag, 1981), 5-13.

i11. Billaz, André. "La Problématique de la 'réception' dans les deux Allemagnes." RHL 81.1 (1981), 21-36.
i12. ----------. "Le Point de vue de la réception: Prestiges et problemes d'une perspective." RSH 1 (1983), 21-36 [on Jauss].

i13. Bluher, Karl Alfred. "La fonction du 'public' dans la pensée esthétique de Valery: Ebauches d'une théorie de la réception littéraire." CaVS 11 (1979), 105-28.

i14. Boerner, Peter. "National Images and Their Place in Literary Research: Germany as Seen by 18th Century French and English Reading Audiences." Monatshefte 67 (1975), 358-70.

i15. Bollenbeck, Georg. Till Eulenspiegel, der dauerhafte Schwankheld: zum Verhaltnis von Productions- und Rezeptionsgeschichte (Stuttgart: J. B. Metzlersche, 1985).

i16. Brang, Peter. "A. I. Beleckijs 'Theorie der Leserrezeption.'" IASL 2 (1977), 40-55.

i17. Brunet, Manon. "Pour une esthétique de la production de la réception." EF 19.3 (1983-84), 65-82 [on Jauss].

i18. Burger, Christa. Textanalyse als Ideologiekritik: Zur Rezeption zeitgenossischer Unterhaltungsliteratur (Frankfurt: Athenaum, 1973).

i19. Burger, Peter. Theorie der Avantgarde (Frankfurt: Suhrkamp, 1974).
i20. ----------. "Rezeptionsasthetik-Zwischenbilanz (III): Probleme der Rezeptionsforschung." Poetica 9 (1977), 446-71.
i21. ----------. "La reception: Problemes de recherche." O&C 2.2 (1978), 5-18.
i22. ----------. Vermittlung, Rezeption, Funktion: Asthetische Theorie und Methodologie der Literaturwissenschaft (Frankfurt: Suhrkamp, 1979).

i23. Chevrel, Yves. "Théories de la réception: Perspectives comparatistes." Degrés 12 (1984), j1-j15.

i24. ----------. "Méthodologie de la réception: De la recherche a l'enseignement." Neohelicon 12.1 (1985), 47-57.

i25. Cogez, Gérard. "Premier bilan d'une théorie de la réception." Degrés 12 (1984), d1-d16.

i26. Conger, Syndy McMillen. "Hans Robert Jauss's *Rezeptionsasthetik* and England's Reception of Eighteenth-Century German Literature." Eighteenth Century 22.1 (1981), 74-93.

i27. Eco, Umberto. "The Problem of Reception." Gradiva 1 (1977), 115-19.

i28. Engelsing, Rolf. Analphabetentum und Lekture: Zur Sozialgeschichte des Lesers in Deutschland zwischen feudaler und industrieller Gesellschaft (Stuttgart: Metzler, 1973).

i29. Fargues, Alfred M. "Wirkungsgeschichte oder Ubereinkunft: Am Nullpunkt der Literatur?" GRM 22 (1972), 23-38.

i30. Faulstich, Werner. Domanen der Rezeptionsanalyse: Probleme, Losungsstrategien, Ergebnisse (Kronberg: Athenaum, 1977).

i31. Forster, Jurgen. "Rezeptionsasthetik und Literaturdidaktik: Zur Problematik der Aneirgnung rezeptionsasthetischer Theoreme in der Literaturdidaktik." WW 5 (1983), 295-309.

i32. Freese, Wolfgang and Karl Menges. Broch-Forschung: Uberlegungen zur Methode u. Problematik e. literarische Rezeptionsvorgangs (Munchen and Salzburg, 1977).

i33. Fuhrmann, Manfred, ed. Terror und Spiel (Munich: Fink, 1971) [Poetik und Hermeneutik: Arbeitsergebnisse einer Forschungsgruppe, IV].
i34. ----------, Hans Robert Jauss, and Wolfgang Pannenberg, eds. Text und Applikation (Munich: Fink, 1981) [Poetik und Hermeneutik: Arbeitsergebnisse einer Forschungsgruppe, IX].

i35. Fullner, Bernd. Heinrich Heine in deutschen Literaturgeschichten: eine Rezeptionsanalyse (Frankfurt am Main: Peter Lang, 1982).

i36. Galan, F. W. "Is Reception History a Literary Theory?" in P. Steiner, M. Cervenka, and R. Vroon, eds. The Structure of the Literary Process (Amsterdam and Philadelphia: John Benjamins, 1982), 161-86.
i37. ----------. Historic Structures: The Prague School Project, 1928-1946 (Austin: U of Texas P, 1985) [chap. 5: "Readers' Reception History and the Individual Poetic Talent"].

i38. Gilli, Yves. "Texte littéraire: Réalité sociale et histoire: Une Analyse de la critique de la RDA a l'encontre de l'esthétique de la réception," in D. Minary, ed. Texte littéraire et histoire: Approche théorique et pratique a la lumiere des récentes recherches européenes (Paris: Belles-Letts., 1985), 33-41.

i39. Goldschnigg, Dietmar. Rezeptions- und Wirkungsgeschichte Georg Buchners (Kronberg/Ts.: Scriptor, 1975).

i40. Grimm, Gunter, ed. Literatur und Leser: Theorien und Modelle zur Rezeption literarischer Werke (Stuttgart: Reclam, 1975).
i41. ----------. "Rezeptionsgeschichte: Pramissen und Moglichkeiten historischer Darstellungen." IASL 2 (1977), 144-86.
i42. ----------. Rezeptionsgeschichte: Grundlegung einer Theorie; mit Analysen und Bibliographie (Munich: Fink, 1977) [extensive bibliography].

i43. Grimminger, Rolf. "Abriss einer Theorie der literarischen Kommunikation." Linguistik und Didiaktik 3.4 (1972), 277-93; 4.1 (1973), 1-15.

i44. Grivel, Charles. "Au sujet d'une nouvelle défense et distraction de l'experience esthétique." RSH 177 (1980), 7-21 [interview with Jauss].

i45. Groeben, Norbert. "Wissenpsychologische Dimensionen der Rezeptionsforschung: Zur Prazisierung der kommunikationswissenschaftlichen Funktion einer empirischen Literaturwissenschaft." LiLi 15 (1974), 61-79.
i46. ----------. Rezeptionsforschung als empirische Literaturwissenschaft: Paradigma- durch Methodendiskussion an Untersuchungsbeispielen (Kronberg/Ts.: Athenaum, 1977).

i47. Gumbrecht, Hans Ulrich. "Konsequenzen der Rezeptionsasthetik oder Literaturwissenschaft als Kommunikationssoziologie." Poetica 7.3-4 (1975), 388-413.

i48. Heinekamp, Albert, ed. Beitrage zur Wirkungs- und Rezeptionsgeschichte von Gottfried Wilhelm Leibniz (Stuttgart: S. Steiner Wiesbaden, 1986).

i49. Heuermann, Hartmut, et al, eds. Literarische Rezeption: Beitrage zur Theorie des Text-Leser-Verhaltnisses und seiner Erforschung (Paderborn: Schoningh, 1975).
i50. ----------. "Kognitive Dissonanz als Phanomen der literarischen Rezeption: Zur Ubertragung und Anwendung einer sozialpsychologischen Theorie auf die Literaturwissenschaft." Archiv 217 (1980), 134-50.

i51. Hohendahl, Peter Uwe, ed. Sozialgeschichte und Wirkungsasthetik: Dokumente zur empirischen und marxistischen Rezeptionsforschung (Frankfurt: Athenaum, 1974).

i52. ----------. "Introduction to Reception Aesthetics." NGC 10 (1977), 29-63.

i53. ----------. The Institutions of Criticism (Ithaca: Cornell UP, 1982).

i54. ----------. "Beyond Reception Aesthetics." NGC 28 (1983), 108-46.

i55. Holub, Robert C. "Trends in Literary Theory: The American Reception of Reception Theory." GQ 55.1 (1982), 80-96.

i56. ----------. Reception Theory: A Critical Introduction (NY: Methuen, 1984).

i57. Hoogeveen, Jos. Funktionalistische Rezeptionstheorie: eine Ausseinandersetzung mit rezeptionsasthetischen Positionen in der Literaturwissenschaft (Leiden: Universiatire Pers, 1978).

i58. Huhn, Peter. "Zu den Grunden for die Popularitat des Detektivromans: Eine Untersuchung von Thesen uber die Motive seiner Rezeption." Arcadia 12 (1977), 273-96.

Ibsch, Elrud [see Kunne-Ibsch].

i59. Ingen, Ferdinand van. "Die Revolte des Lesers oder Rezeption versus Interpretation. Zu Fragen der Interpretation und der Rezeptionsasthetik." Amsterdamer Beitrage zur neuren Germanistik 3 (1974), 83-148.

i60. Iser, Wolfgang, ed. Immanente Asthetik--Asthetische Reflexion (Munich: Fink, 1966) [Poetik und Hermeneutik: Arbeitsergebnisse einer Forschungsgruppe, II].

i61. ----------. "Das Literaturverstandnis zwischen Geschichte und Zukunfte." DU 34.6 (1982), 8-25.

i62. Jauss, Hans Robert, ed. Die nicht mehr schonen Kunste (Munich: Fink, 1968) [Poetik und Hermeneutik: Arbeitsergebnisse einer Forschungsgruppe, III].

i63. ----------. "Paradigmawechsel in der Literaturwissenschaft." Linguistische Berichte 3 (1969), 44-56.

i64. ----------. Kleine Apologie der asthetischen Erfahrung (Konstanz: Konstanzer Universitatserden, 1972).

i65. ----------. Literaturgeschichte als Provokation, 4th ed. (Frankfurt: Suhrkamp, 1974).

i66. ----------. "Der Leser als Instanz einer neuen Geschichte der Literatur." Poetica 7.3-4 (1975), 325-44.

i67. ----------. "History of Art and Pragmatic History," in R. E. Amacher and V. Lange, eds. New Perspectives in German Literary Criticism (Princeton: Princeton UP, 1979), 432-64.
i68. ----------. Aesthetic Experience and Literary Hermeneutics (Minneapolis: U of Minnesota P, 1982).
i69. ----------. Toward an Aesthetics of Reception (Minneapolis: U of Minnesota P, 1982) [includes trans of the key 1967 essay "Literary History as a Challenge to Literary Theory"].

i70. Jimenez, Marc. "Reception et interprétation actuelles de l'Ecole de Francfort." RE 32.3-4 (1979), 367-89.

i71. Jost, Erhard. "Der Heldentod des Dichters Theodor Korner: Der Einfluss eines Mythos auf die Rezeption einer Lyrik und ihre literarische Kritik." OL 32 (1977), 310-40.

i72. Jurt, Joseph. "La Réception du roman par la critique de l'entre-deux-guerres." O&C 2.2 (1978), 87-98.
i73. ----------. "'L'Esthétique de la réception': Une Nouvelle approche de la littérature?" LR 37.3 (1983), 199-220.

i74. Juttner, Siegfried. "Im Namen des Lesers: Zur Rezeptionsdebatte in der deutschen Romanistik (1965-1975)." GRM 29 (1979), 1-26.

i75. Kaiser, Herbert. "Sachlichkeit, Verantwortung, KreativitatL Unpragmatische Uberlegungen zur Rezeptionspragmatik und Literaturdidaktik," in G. Kopf, ed. Rezeptionspragmatik: Beitrage zur Praxis des Lesens (Munich: Fink, 1981), 58-78.

i76. Kanzog, Klaus, ed. Text und Kontext: Quellen und Aufsatze zur Rezeptionsgeschichte der Werke Heinrich von Kleists (Berlin: Schmidt, 1979).

i77. Kempf, Franz R. Albrecht von Hallers Ruhm als Dichter: eine Rezeptionsgeschichte (NY: Peter Lang, 1986).

i78. Kern, Peter Christoph. "Wie baut sich im Leser eine fiktive Wirklichkeit auf? Sieben Thesen und eine Anwendung zur asthetischer Rezeption." LWU 18.2 (1985), 137-62.

i79. Kliche, Dieter. "Literaturrezeption und Literaturtheorie." WB 20.8 (1974), 155-62.

i80. Kolter, Gerhard. "Typen der Lyrikrezeption am Karl Krolows." TuK 77 (1983), 37-45.

i81. Kopf, Gerhard. "Asthetische Erfahrung und literarischen Verstehen: Voruberlegungen zu einer Rezeptionspragmatik," in G. Kopf, ed. Rezeptionspragmatik: Beitrage zur Praxis des Lesens (Munich: Fink, 1981), 79-104.

i82. Koselleck, Reinhart and Wolf-Dieter Stempel, eds. Geschichte-- Ereignis und Erzahlung (Munich: Fink, 1973) [Poetik und Hermeneutik: Arbeitsergebnisse einer Forschungsgruppe, V].

i83. Kruezer, Helmut. "Trivalliteratur als Forschungsproblem: Zur Kritk des deutschen Trivialromans seit der Aufklarrung." Deutsche Vierteljahrsschrift 41 (1967), 173-91.

i84. Kunne-Ibsch, Elrud. "Rezeptionsforschung: Konstanten und Variaten eines literaturwissenschaftlichen Konzepts in Theorie und Praxis." ABnG 3 (1974), 1-36.
i85. ----------. "Lesenrollen, Bedeutungstypen und literarische Kommunikation." ABnG 15 (1982), 335-49.

i86. Lehmann, Gunther K. "Die Theorie der literarischen Rezeption aus soziologischer und psychologischer Sicht." WB 20.8 (1974), 49-70.

i87. "Lesenprozesse im Unterricht," Der Deutschunterricht 33.2 (1981) [special issue].

i88. Leuschner, Brigette. "Erfinden und Erzahlen: Funktion und Kommunikation in autothematischer Dichtung." MLN 100.3 (1985), 498- 513.

i89. Link, Hannelore. Rezeptionsforschung: Eine Einfuhrung in Methoden und Probleme (Stuttgart: Kohlhammer, 1976).

i90. Mandelkow, Karl Robert. "Probleme der Wirkungsasthetik." Jahrbuch fur Internationale Germanistik 2 (1970), 71-84.
i91. ----------. Orpheus und Maschine (Heidelberg: Stiehm, 1976) [essays on receptions-aesthetics and Marxist criticism].
i92. ----------. Goethe in Deutschland: Rezeptionsgeschichte eines Klassikers (Munchen: Beck, 1980).

i93. Marino, Adrian. "Succes littéraire et réception sociale." CREL 1 (1973), 17-28.

i94. Marquand, Odo and Karlheinz Stierle, eds. Identitat (Munich: Fink, 1979) [Poetik und Hermeneutik: Arbeitsergebnisse einer Forschungsgruppe, VIII].

i95. Meregalli, Franco. "Sur la réception littéraire." RLC 54 (1980), 134-49.

i95. Minary, Daniel. "Une Méthode pour conjuguer la littérature du passé au présent: Problemes du texte et de l'histoire selon R. Weimann (R.D.A.)," in D. Minary, ed. Texte littéraire et histoire: Approche théorique et pratique a la lumiere des récentes recherches européenes (Paris: Belles-Letts., 1985), 43-70.

i96. Mobius, Friedrich. "Das 'Denkmal' als Produkt der Rezeption: Beobachtungen und Hypothesen zur Wirkungsgeschichte." WB 22.9 (1976), 43-66.

i97. Moog-Grunewald, Maria. "Einfluss- und Rezeptionsforschung," in M. Schmeling, ed. Vergleichende Literaturwissenschaft: Theorie und Praxis (Wiesbaden: Athenaion, 1981), 49-72.

i98. Muller-Seidel, Walter. "Rezeptionsforschung: Zu einem Buch von Hannelore Link und zu ihrem Andenken." JDSG 22 (1978), 722-27.

i99. Muller-Solger, Hermann. "Die Rezeptionsauffassung in der Dramaturgie des Sturm und Drang." LY 6 (1974), 179-98.

i100. Munzberg, Olav. Rezeptivitat und Spontaneitat: Die Frage nach dem asthetischen Subjekt oder Soziologische und politische implikationen des Verhaltnisses Kunstwerk-Rezipient in den asthetischen Theorien Kants, Schillers, Hegels, Benjamins, Brechts, Heideggers, Sartres und Adornos (Frankfurt: Akademische, 1974).

i101. Naumann, Manfred, et al . Gesellschaft, Literatur, Lesen: Literaturrezeption in theoretischer Sicht (Berlin: Aufabu, 1973).
i102. ----------. "Literary Production and Reception." NLH 8.1 (1976), 107-26.
i103. ----------. "Das Dilemma der 'Rezeptionsasthetik.'" WB 23.1 (1977), 5-21.

i104. Neubauer, John. "Trends in Literary Reception: Die Neuen Leiden der Wertherwirkung." German Quarterly 52 (1979), 69-79.

i105. Nies, Fritz. "A la recherche de la 'majorité silencieuse': Iconographie et réception littéraire." O&C 2.2 (1978), 65-74.

i106. Nojgaard, Morten. "La Lecteur et la critique: Quelques contributions récentes a l'étude de l'instance de la réception littéraire." Degrés 21 (1980), a1-a22.

i107. Noltenius, Rainer. Dichterfeiern in Deutschland: Rezeptionsgeschichte also Sozialgeschichte am Beispiel der Schiller- und Freiligrath-Feiern (Munchen: Fink, 1984).

i108. Pfeifer, Martin, ed. Hermann Hesses weltweite Wirkung: internationale Rezeptionsgeschichte (Frankfurt a.M.L Suhrkamp, 1977).

i109. Preisendanz, Wolfgang and Rainer Warning, eds. Das Komische (Munich: Fink, 1976) [Poetik und Hermeneutik: Arbeitsergebnisse einer Forschungsgruppe, VII].

i110. Probst, Gerhard F. "Gattungsbegriff und Rezeptionsasthetik." CollG 10 (1976-77), 1-14.

i111. Raynaud, Jean-Michel. "De l'irrecevabilité de l'esthétique de la réception mais encore." RSH 1 (1983), 159-80 [discusses Jauss].

i112. "'Reception asthetik': Contributions allemandes récentes a une nouvelle approche critique: L'Esthétique de la réception." O&C 2.2 (1978) [special issue].

i113. Reese, Walter. Literarische Rezeption (Stuttgart: Metzler, 1980).

i114. "Rezeption--Interpretation." Amsterdamer Beitrage zur neuren Germanistik 3 (1974) [special issue].

i115. "Rezeptionsasthetik." Der Deutschunterricht 29.2 (1977) [special issue].

i116. Riedel, Nicolai. Untersuchungen zur Geschichte der internationalen Rezeption Uwe Johnsons: ein Beitrag zur empirischen Rezeptionsforschung (Hildesheim and NY: Olms, 1985).

i117. Ruhe, Ernstpeter. "Rezeptionsgeschichte und Trivialliteratur: Ein Leser der Nouvelle Héloise im Jahre 1838." NM 78 (1977), 1-17.

i118. Rutten, Frans. "Sur les notions de texte et de lecture dans une théorie de la réception." RSH 177 (1980), 67-83.

i119. Scarf, Karla. "Zu einigen Fragen der Rezeption in theoretischer Sicht." WB 25.8 (1979), 104-14.

i120. Schaefer, Klaus. "Wesen und Funktion der 'Perspektive' im literarischen Produktions- und Rezeptionsprozess: Thesen." WB 26.12 (1980), 167-73.

i121. Scheiffele, Eberhard. "Wege und Aporien der 'Rezeptionsasthetik.'" NRs 90 (1979), 520-41.

i122. Schlaeger, Jurgen. "Recent German Contributions to Literary Theory," in G. Laprevotte, ed. Echanges: Actes du Congres de Strasbourg (Paris: Didier, 1982), 59-71 [discusses Iser, Jauss].

i123. Schlenstedt, Dieter. Wirkungsasthetische Analysen: Poetologie und Prosa in der neuren DDR-Literatur (Berlin: Akademie, 1979).
i124. ----------, et al, eds. Literarische Widerspiegelung: Geschichtliche und theoretische Dimensionen eines Problems (Berlin & Weimar: Aufbau, 1981).

i125. Schmidt, Henry J. "'Text-Adequate Concretizations' and Real Readers: Reception Theory and Its Applications." NGC 17 (1979), 157-69.

i126. Schmidt, Peter Lebrecht. "Reception Theory and Classical Scholarship: A Plea for Convergence," in W. M. Calder, et al , eds. Hypatia: Essays in Classics, Comparative Literature, and Philosophy Presented to Hazel E. Barnes on Her Seventieth Birthday (Boulder: Colorado Associated UP, 1985), 67-77.

i127. Schmidt, Siegfried J. Grundriss der empirischen Literaturwissenschaft, 2 vols. (Braunschweig: Viewig & Sohn, 1980-82).

i128. Schober, Otto. "Zur Orientierung heutiger Literaturdidaktik an der Rezeptionstheorie," in G. Kopf, ed. Rezeptionspragmatik: Beitrage zur Praxis des Lesens (Munich: Fink, 1981), 9-26.

i129. Schonert, Jorg, ed. Carl Sternheims Dramen: zur Textanalyse, Ideologiekritik und Rezeptionsgeschichte (Heidelberg: Quelle & Meyer, 1975).

i130. Schumacher, Alois. "De l'esthétique de la réception a l'expérience esthétique: Eléments de réflexion sur les théories de Hans Robert Jauss," in D. Minary, ed. Texte littéraire et histoire: Approche théorique et pratique a la lumiere des récentes recherches européenes (Paris: Belles-Letts., 1985), 11-32.

i131. Segers, Rien T. "Readers, Text and Author: Some Implications of Rezeptionsasthetik ." YCGL 24 (1975), 15-23.
i132. ----------. The Evaluation of Literary Texts: An Experimental Investigation into the Rationalization of Value Judgments with Reference to Semiotics and Esthetics of Reception (Lisse: Ridder, 1978).

i133. ----------. "An Interview with Hans Robert Jauss." NLH 11 (1979), 83-95.
i134. ----------. "La Détermination idéologique de lecteur: A propos de la necessité de la collaboration entre la sémiotique et l'esthétique de la réception." Degrés 24-25 (1980-81), h1-h14.

i135. Simon-Schaefer, Roland. "Die Rezeptionsasthetik und das Wertungsproblem in der Kunst." Archiv 214 (1977), 1-17.

i136. Sommer, Dietrich and Dietrich Loffler. "Soziologische Probleme der literarischen Wirkungsforschung." WB 16.8 (1970), 51-76.
i137. ----------, et al, eds. Funktion und Wirkung: Soziologische Untersuchungen zur Literatur und Kunst (Berlin & Weimar: Aufbau, 1978).

i138. Steinmetz, Horst. "Rezeption und Interpretation: Versuch einer Abgrenzung." ABnG 3 (1974), 37-81.
i139. ----------. "Rezeptionsasthetik und Interpretation," in H. Brackert and J. Stuckrath, eds. Literaturwissenschaft: Grundkurs 2 (Reinbeck bei Hamburg: Rowohlt, 1981), 421-35.

i140. Stierle, Karlheinz. "Was heisst Rezeption bei fiktionalen Texten?" Poetica 7 (1975), 345-87.
i141. ----------. Text als Handlung: Perspektiven einer systematischen Literaturwissenschaft (Munich: Fink, 1975).
i142. ----------. "The Reading of Fictional Texts," in S. R. Suleiman and I. Crosman, eds. The Reader in the Text (Princeton: Princeton UP, 1980).

i143. Stuckrath, Jorn. Historische Rezeptionsforschung: Ein kritischer Versuch zu ihrer Geschichte und Theorie (Stuttgart: Metzler, 1979).

i144. Tarot, Rolf. "Structure and Reception." YCC 8 (1978), 166-90.

i145. "Théorie de la réception en Allemagne." Poétique 39 (1979) [special issue].

i146. Turk, Horst. Wirkungsasthetik: Theorie und Interpretation der literarischen Wirkung (Munich: Text + Kritik, 1976).

i147. Vaget, Hans Rudolf. "Rezeptionsasthetik: Schwierigkeiten mit dem Erwartungshorizont am Beispiel der Buddenbrooks." Monatshefte 71 (1979), 399-409.

i148. Vajda, Gyorgy M. "Points de vue pour la théorie esthétique de la réception." Neohelicon 8 (1981), 291-97.

i149. Viehoff, Reinhold. "Uber einen Versuch, den Erwartungshorizont zeitgenossischer Literaturkritik empirisch zu objektivieren." Zeitschrift fur Literaturwissenschaft und Linguistik 6.21 (1976), 96-124.

i150. Vodicka, Felix. "The Concretization of the Literary Work: Problems of the Reception of Neruda's Work," in P. Steiner, ed. The Prague School: Selected Writings, 1929-1946 (Austin: U of Texas P, 1982), 103-34.

i151. Wagner, Irmgard. "Hans Robert Jauss and Classicity." MLN 99.5 (1984), 1173-84.

i152. Waldmann, Gunter. Kommunikationsasthetik I: Die Ideologie der Erzahlform (Munich: Fink, 1976).

i153. Warning, Rainer, ed. Rezeptionsasthetik: Theorie und Praxis (Munich: Fink, 1975).

i154. Weber, Heinz-Dieter, ed. Rezeptionsgeschichte oder Wirkungsasthetik (Stuttgart: Klett-Cotta, 1978).

i155. Weimann, Robert. Literaturgeschichte und Mythologie: Methodologische und historische Studien (Berlin & Weimar: Aufbau, 1974).
i156. ----------. "'Reception Aesthetics' and the Crisis of Literary History." ClioW 5 (1975), 3-33.

i157. Weinrich. Harald. "Fur eine Literaturgeschichte des Lesers." Merkur 21 (1967), 1026-38.
i158. ----------, ed. Positionen der Negativitat (Munich: Fink, 1975) [Poetik und Hermeneutik: Arbeitsergebnisse einer Forschungsgruppe, VI].

i159. Wienold, Gotz. "Textverarbeitung: Uberlegungen zur Kategorienbildung in einer strukturellen Literaturgeschichte." Zeitschrift fur Literaturwissenschaft und Linguistik 1.1-2 (1971), 59-89.

i160. Wittkowski, Wolfgang. "Unbehagen eines Praktikers an der Theorie: Zur Rezeptionsasthetik von Hans Robert Jauss." CollG 12 (1979), 1-17.

i161. Wolff, Erwin. "Der intendierte Leser: Uberlegungen und Beispiele zur Einfuhrung eines literaturwissenschaftlichen Begriffs." Poetica 4.2 (1971), 141-66.

i162. Wunsch, Marianne. "Wirkung und Rezeption," in K. Kanzog, D. Kanzog, and A. Masser, eds. Reallexikon der deutschen Literatur, IV: 9, 10 (Berlin: de Gruyter, 1984), 894-919.

i163. Zimmermann, Bernhard. "Der Leser als Produzent: Zur Problematik der rezeptionsasthetischen Methode." LiLi 15 (1974), 12-27.
i164. ----------. Literaturrezeption im historischen Prozess: Zur Theorie einer Rezeptionsgeschichte der Literatur (Munich: Beck, 1977).

J. Phenomenological Criticism

j1. Adamowski, T. H. "The Condemned of Rouen: Sartre's Flauberts." <u>Novel</u> 6 (1972), 79-83.

j2. Alexander, Ian W. <u>French Literature and the Philosophy of Consciousness: Phenomenological Essays</u> (NY: St. Martin's P, 1985).

j3. Alexander, Meena. "Embodied Space: Outline of a Concept Paradigmatic to a Post-Phenomenological Theory of Art." <u>JSL</u> 3.2 (1975-76), 53-62.

j4. Allen, Douglas. "Phenomenological Method and the Dialectic of the Sacred," in N. J. Girardot and M. L. Linscott, eds. <u>Imagination and Meaning: The Scholarly and Literary Worlds of Mircea Eliade</u> (NY: Seabury, 1982), 70-81.

j5. Armstrong, Paul B. <u>The Phenomenology of Henry James</u> (Chapel Hill: U of North Carolina P, 1983).

j6. Bachelard, Gaston. <u>The Poetics of Space</u> (Boston: Beacon, 1969).

j7. Barnes, Hazel. <u>Sartre and Flaubert</u> (Chicago: U of Chicago P, 1981).

j8. Bensman, Joseph and Robert Lilienfeld. "A Phenomenological Model of the Artistic and Critical Attitudes." <u>PPR</u> 28 (1968), 353-67.

j9. Berg, Richard Allan. "Towards a Phenomenological Aesthetic: A Critical Exposition of Mikel Dufrenne's Aesthetic Philosophy with Special Reference to Theory of Literature." <u>DAI</u> 39 (1979), 5550A.

j10. Berleant, Arnold. The Aesthetic Field: A Phenomenology of Aesthetic Experience (Springfield IL: Charles C. Thomas, 1970).

j11. Bersani, Leo. "From Bachelard to Barthes." PR 34 (1967), 215-32.

j12. Blanchot, Maurice. De Kafka a Kafka (Paris: Gallimard, 1981).
j13. ----------. The Gaze of Orpheus and Other Literary Essays (NY: Station Hill, 1981).
j14. ----------. The Space of Literature (Lincoln: U of Nebraska P, 1982).
j15. ----------. The Sirens' Song: Selected Essays (Bloomington: Indiana UP, 1982).
j16. ----------. The Writing of the Disaster (Lincoln: U of Nebraska P, 1986).

j17. Bochan, Bohdan. The Phenomenology of Freedom in Kleist's Die Familie Schroffstein and Penthesilea (Frankfurt a.M.: Lang, 1982).

j18. Brady, Patrick. "Phenomenology, Structuralism, Semiology." BuR 22.1 (1976), 13-25.

j19. Bratu, Horia and Ileana Marculescu. "Aesthetics and Phenomenology." JAAC 37 (1979), 335-49.

j20. Brodtkorb, Paul, Jr. Ishmael's White World: A Phenomenological Reading of Moby Dick (New Haven: Yale UP, 1965).

j21. Bruzina, Ronald. "Eidos: Universality in the Image or in the Concept?" in R. Bruzina and B. Wilshire, eds. Crosscurrents in Phenomenology (The Hague: Mouton, 1978), 144-65.
j22. ---------- and Bruce Wilshire, eds. Phenomenology: Dialogues and Bridges (Albany: SUNY P, 1982).

j23. Brunius, Teddy. "The Aesthetics of Roman Ingarden." PPR 30 (1970), 590-95.

j24. Carrard, Philippe. "Starobinski, Rousset et la question du récit." SFSt 1.2 (1980), 24-61 [Geneva school].

j25. Carvalho, Maria da Penha Petit Villela de. "Man and Nature: Does the Husserlian Analysis of Pre-Predicative Experience Shed Light on the Emergence of Nature in the Work of Art?" in A.-T. Tymieniecka, ed. The Philosophical Reflection of Man in Literature (Dordrecht: Reidel, 1982), 301-11 [discusses Husserl].

j26. Casey, Edward S. Imagining: A Phenomenological Study (Bloomington: Indiana UP, 1976).
j27. ----------. "Literary Description and Phenomenological Method." YFS 61 (1981), 176-201.

j28. Casteñada, Hector-Neri. "Fiction and Reality: Their Fundamental Connections: An Essay on the Ontology of Total Experience." Poetics 8 (1979), 31-62.

j29. Castro, Donald Frank. "A Phenomenological Approach to the Concept of Genre." DAI 39 (1978), 859A.

j30. Certeau, Michel de. "The Madness of Vision." Enclitic 7.1 (1983), 24-31 [on Merleau-Ponty].

j31. Champigny, Robert. "Trying to Understand L'Idiot." Diacritics 1 (1971), 2-6 [on Sartre].
j32. ----------. "Gaston Bachelard," in J. Simon, ed. Modern French Criticism: From Proust to Valéry to Structuralism (Chicago: U of Chicago P, 1972), 175-91.

j33. Cohen, Sibyl S. "Roman Ingarden's Aesthetics of Literature." DAI 37 (1976), 2232A.

j34. Collins, Douglas. Sartre as Biographer (Cambridge: Harvard UP, 1980).

j35. Columb, Gregory G. "Roman Ingarden and the Language of Art and Science." JAAC 35 (1976), 7-13.

j36. Contat, Michel and Michel Rybalka. Les Ecrits de Sartre: Chronologie, Bibliographie commenté (Paris: Gallimard, 1970).

j37. Corrigan, Matthew A. "Phenomenology and Literary Criticism: A Definition and an Application." DAI 31 (1971), 4761A.

j38. Creed, Walter G. "René Wellek and Karl Popper on the Mode of Existence of Ideas in Literature and Science." JHI 44.4 (1983), 639-56.

j39. Crowley, Ruth. "Roman Ingarden and Literary Truth Value," in M. Woodmansee and W. F. W. Lohnes, eds. Erkennen und Deuten: Essays zur Literatur und Literaturtheorie (Berlin: Schmidt, 1983), 42-53.

j40. Daemmrich, Horst S. Literaturkritik in Theorie und Praxis (Munich: Francke, 1974).

j41. Danto, Arthur C. "Narration and Knowledge." P&L 6.1-2 (1982), 17-32.

j42. Detweiler, Robert. Story, Sign, and Self: Phenomenology and Structuralism as Literary Critical Methods (Philadelphia: Fortress P, 1978).

j43. Dobrez, L. A. C. The Existential and Its Limits: Literary and Philosophical Perspectives on the Works of Beckett, Ionesco, Genet & Pinter (London: Athlone; NY: St. Martin's, 1986).

j44. Donato, Eugenio. "Language, Vision, and Phenomenology: Merleau-Ponty as a Test Case," in R. Macksey, ed. Velocities of Change (Baltimore: Johns Hopkins UP, 1974), 292-303.

j45. Dufrenne, Mikel. "L'Art est-il langage?" RdE 13 (1968), 161-77.
j46. ----------. Esthétique et philosophie, 2 vols. (Paris: Klincksieck, 1967-76).
j47. ----------. Phénomenologie de l'experience esthétique, 2 vols. (Paris: PUF, 1967)[The Phenomenology of Aesthetic Experience (Evanston: Northwestern UP, 1973)].
j48. ----------. In the Presence of the Sensuous: Essays in Aesthetics (Atlantic Highlands NJ: Humanities P, 1987).

j49. Ehrmann, Jacques. "Introduction to Gaston Bachelard." MLN 81 (1966), 572-78.

j50. Eykman, Christoph. "Eidetic Conception and the Analysis of Meaning in Literature," in A.-T. Tymieniecka, ed. The Philosophical Reflection of Man in Literature (Dordrecht: Reidel, 1982), 443-53 [discusses Husserl, Ingarden].

j51. Falk, Eugene H. The Poetics of Roman Ingarden (Chapel Hill: U of North Carolina P, 1981).

j52. Fellmann, Ferdinand. Phanomenologie und Expressionismus (Freiburg: Alber, 1982).

j53. Floyd, Sheryl Lynn. "A Phenomenological Account of Aesthetic Perception and Its Implications for Aesthetic Theory." DAI 40 (1979), 3355A.

j54. Foust, Ronald. "The Aporia of Recent Criticism and the Contemporary Significance of Spatial Form," in J. R. Smitten and A. Daghistany, eds. Spatial Form in Narrative (Ithaca: Cornell UP, 1981), 179-201.

j55. Fritz, Donald Eric. "Phenomenological Criticism: An Analysis and an Application to the Fiction of John Updike." DAI 36 (1976), 6655A-56A.

j56. Gardiner, Patrick. "Sartre on Character and Knowledge." NLH 9 (1977), 65-82.

j57. Gore, K. "Sartre and Flaubert: From Antipathy to Empathy." Journal of the British Society for Phenomenology 4.2 (1973), 104-12.

j58. Gras, Vernon, ed. European Literary Theory and Practice: From Existential Phenomenology to Structuralism (NY: Delta/Dell, 1973).

j59. Grossvogel, David I. "Perception as a Form of Phenomenological Criticism." HSL 1 (1969), 83-88.

j60. Guarino, Raimondo. "Le Théâtre du sens: Quelques remarques sur 'fiction' et perception." Degrés 31 (1982), g1-g10.

j61. Hahn, Otto. "Sartre's Criticism," in R. Macksey, ed. Velocities of Change (Baltimore: Johns Hopkins UP, 1974), 260-76.

j62. Halliburton, David. Edgar Allan Poe: A Phenomenological View (Princeton: Princeton UP, 1973) [esp. chap. 2: "A Methodological Introduction"].
j63. ----------. Poetic Thinking: An Approach to Heidegger (Chicago: U of Chicago P, 1981).

j64. Halpern, Joseph. Critical Fictions: The Literary Criticism of Jean-Paul Sartre (New Haven: Yale UP, 1976).

j65. Hanneborg, Knut. The Study of Literature: A Contribution to the Phenomenology of the Human Sciences (Oslo: Universitetsforlaget, 1967).

j66. Hans, James S. "Gaston Bachelard and the Phenomenology of the Reading Consciousness." JAAC 35 (1977), 315-27.
j67. ----------. The Play of the World (Amherst: U of Massachusetts P, 1981).

j68. Harrell, Jean G. and Alina Wierzbianska, eds. Aesthetics in Twentieth-Century Poland: Selected Essays (Lewisburg PA: Bucknell UP, 1973) [esp. Husserl and Ingarden].

j69. Herzberger, David K. "Ortega y Gasset and the 'Critics of Consciousness.'" JAAC 34 (1976), 455-60.

j70. Hess, Rainer. "Erkenntnis und Methode in der Literaturwissenschaft." GRM 22 (1972), 419-32.

j71. Holdheim, W. Wolfgang. "The Lessons of Phenomenology." Diacritics 9.2 (1979), 30-41.

j72. Holenstein, Elmar. "Jakobson phénomenologue?" L'Arc 60 (1974), 29-37.

j73. Hottois, Gilbert. "L'Insistance du langage dans la phénomenologie post-husserlienne." RPL 77 (1979), 51-70.

j74. Ingarden, Roman. Erlebnis, Kunstwerk und Wert: Vortrage zur Asthetik (Tubingen: Niemeyer, 1969).
j75. ----------. Gegenstand und Aufgaben der Literaturwissenschaft: Aufsatze und Diskussionsbeitrage (1937-1964) (Tubingen: Niemeyer, 1969).
j76. ----------. The Cognition of the Literary Work of Art (Evanston: Northwestern UP, 1973).
j77. ----------. The Literary Work of Art (Evanston: Northwestern UP, 1973).
j78. ----------. "Psychologism and Psychology in Literary Scholarship." NLH 5 (1974), 213-23.
j79. ----------. "Phenomenological Aesthetics: An Attempt at Defining Its Range." JAAC 33 (1975), 258-69.
j80. ----------. Man and Value (Washington DC: Catholic U of America P, 1983).
j81. ----------. Selected Papers in Aesthetics (Washington DC: Catholic U of America P, 1985).

j82. Jameson, Fredric. "Three Methods in Sartre's Literary Criticism," in J. Simon, ed. Modern French Criticism: From Proust to Valéry to Structuralism (Chicago: U of Chicago P, 1972), 193-227.

j83. Johnson, Bruce. True Correspondence: A Phenomenology of Thomas Hardy's Novels (Tallahassee: UP of Florida, 1983).

j84. Jones, Robert Emmet. Panorama de la nouvelle critique en France de Gaston Bachelard a Jean-Paul Weber (Paris: d'Enseignement Superieur, 1968).

j85. Kaelin, Eugene. An Existentialist Aesthetic: The Theories of Sartre and Merleau-Ponty (Madison: U of Wisconsin P, 1966).
j86. ----------. Art and Existence (Lewisburg PA: Bucknell UP, 1970).

j87. ----------. The Unhappy Consciousness: The Poetic Plight of Samuel Beckett: An Inquiry at the Intersection of Phenomenology and Literature (Dordrecht & Boston: D. Reidel, 1981).

j88. Kaplan, Edward K. "Gaston Bachelard's Philosophy of Imagination: An Introduction." PPR 33 (1972), 1-24.

j89. Keel, Erich Leon. "Beyond Structuralism and Phenomenology: The Critical Theory of Maurice Merleau-Ponty." DAI 40 (1979), 238A-39A.

j90. Kern, Edith. Existential Thought and Fictional Technique: Kierkegaard, Sartre, Beckett (New Haven: Yale UP, 1970).

j91. Kostantinovic, Zoran. Phanomenologie und Literaturwissenschaft: Skizzen zu einer wissenschaftstheoretischen Begrundung (Munchen: List, 1973).
j92. ----------. "Uber Ingarden hinaus: Forschungsgeschichtliche Hinweise zur Entwicklung des phanomenologischen Ansatzes in der Literaturwissenschaft." LiLi 17 (1975), 25-34.

j93. Krenzlin, Norbert. "Untersuchungen zur phanomenologischen Asthetik." WB (1968), 1236-84.
j94. ----------. Das Werk "rein tur sich": Zur Geschichte der Verhaltnisses von Phanomenologie, Asthetik und Literaturwissenschaft (Berline: Akademie, 1979).

j95. Kreuzer, Helmut, ed. Phanomenologie und Hermeneutik (Gottingen: Vandenhoek & Ruprecht, 1975).

j96. Langellier, Kristin. "A Phenomenology of Narrative in Performance," in S. Deetz, ed. Phenomenology in Rhetoric and Communication (Washington DC: UP of America, 1981), 83-90.

j97. Lapointe, François H. and Claire Lapointe. Maurice Merleau-Ponty and his Critics: An International Bibliography, 1942-1976 (NY: Garland, 1976).
j98. ----------. Jean-Paul Sartre and his Critics: An International Bibliography (1938-80), rev., 2nd ed. (Bowling Green OH: Philosophy Documentation Center, 1981).

j99. Lawall, Sarah N. Critics of Consciousness: The Existential Structures of Literature (Cambridge: Harvard UP, 1968).

j100. Ledebur, Ruth Freifrau von. "Uberlegungen zur Asthetik Roman Ingardens: An Beispielen neurer deutscher Shakespeare-Rezeption." Poetics 8 (1976), 134-44.

j101. Lesage, Laurent. The French New Criticism: An Introduction and a Sampler (University Park: Penn State UP, 1967).

j102. Lewis, Philip E. "Merleau-Ponty and the Phenomenology of Language." YFS 36-37 (1966), 19-40.

j103. Librach, Ronald S. "Narration and the Life-World." JAAC 41.1 (1982), 77-86.

j104. Lyster, Robert W. Hamlet and Man's Being: The Phenomenology of Nausea (Lanham MD: UP of America, 1984).

j105. MacCary, W. Thomas. Friends and Lovers: The Phenomenology of Desire in Shakespearean Comedy (NY: Columbia UP, 1985).

j106. Macksey, Richard. "The Consciousness of the Critic: Georges Poulet and the Reader's Share," in R. Macksey, ed. Velocities of Change (Baltimore: Johns Hopkins UP, 1971), 304-40.

j107. Magliola, Robert R. "The Phenomenological Approach to Literature: Its Theory and Methodology." Lang&S 5 (1972), 79-99.
j108. ----------. Phenomenology and Literature: An Introduction (West Lafayette IN: Purdue UP, 1977).
j109. ----------. "Permutation and Meaning: A Heideggerian troisieme voie," in A.-T. Tymieniecka, ed. The Philosophical Reflection of Man in Literature (Dordrecht: Reidel, 1982), 353-83.

j110. Man, Paul de. Blindness and Insight: Essays in the Rheotric of Contemporary Criticism, 2nd ed., rev. (Minneapolis: U of Minnesota P, 1983)["Impersonality in the Criticism of Maurice Blanchot," 60-78; and "The Literary Self as Origin: The Work of Georges Poulet," 79-101].

j111. Mandelkow, Karl R. "Probleme der Wirkungsgeschichte." JIG 2.1 (1970), 71-84.

j112. Mansuy, M. "L'Imagination de Bachelard, théoricien de l'imagination." IL 17 (1965), 54-63.

j113. Martineau, Emmanuel. "Mimesis dans la Poétique: Pour une solution phénomenologique." RMM 81 (1976), 438-66.

j114. Martinez Bonati, Félix. Fictive Discourse and the Structures of Literature: A Phenomenological Approach (Ithaca: Cornell UP, 1981).

j115. McEwen, Fred B. "Phenomenology in Literary Criticism." LHR 10 (1968), 47-55.

j116. Medina, Angel. Reflection, Time, and the Novel: Toward a Communicative Theory of Literature (Boston: Routledge & Kegan Paul, 1979).

j117. Miller, J. Hillis. "La critique de Georges Poulet." MdF 152 (1965), 652-74.
j118. ----------. Poets of Reality: Six Twentieth-Century Writers (Cambridge: Harvard UP, 1965).
j119. ----------. "Geneva or Paris? The Recent Work of Georges Poulet." UTQ 39 (1970), 212-28.
j120. ----------. Thomas Hardy: Distance and Desire (Cambridge: Harvard UP, 1970).
j121. ----------. "The Geneva School: The Criticism of Marcel Raymond, Albert Béguin, Georges Poulet, Jean Rousset, Jean-Pierre Richard, and Jean Starobinski," in J. Simon, ed. Modern French Criticism: From Proust to Valéry to Structuralism (Chicago: U of Chicago P, 1972), 277-310.
j122. ----------. The Linguistic Moment: From Wordsworth to Stevens (Princeton: Princeton UP, 1985).

j123. Mueller-Vollmer, Kurt. "Rezeption und Neuansatz: Phanomenologische Literaturwissenschaft in den Vereinigten Staaten." LiLi 17 (1975), 10-24.
j124. ----------. "Interpretation: Discourse or Discipline? A Phenomenological View." Monatshefte 71 (1979), 379-86.

j125. Murray, Michael. Modern Critical Theory: A Phenomenological Introduction (The Hague: Martinus Nijhoff, 1975).

j126. Nakjavani, Erik. "Phenomenology and Theory of Literature: An Interview with Paul Ricoeur." MLN 96.5 (1981), 1084-90.

j127. Natoli, Joseph. "Phenomenological Psychology and Literary Interpretation," in J. Natoli, ed. Psychological Perspectives on Fiction: Freudian Dissidents and Non-Freudians (Hamden CT: Archon, 1984), 198-224.

j128. Oppenheim, Lois. "Ontological Reference and the Horizon of Meaning." Criticism 24.3 (1982), 261-72.

j129. Orr, Leonard. Existentialism and Phenomenology: A Guide to Research (Troy NY: Whitston, 1978).

j130. ----------, ed. De-Structing the Novel: Essays in Applied Postmodern Hermeneutics (Troy NY: Whitston, 1982).

j131. Ortega y Gasset, José. Phenomenology and Art (NY: Norton, 1975).

j132. Oxenhandler, Neal. "Literature as Perception in the Work of Merleau-Ponty," in J. Simon, ed. Modern French Criticism: From Proust to Valéry to Structuralism (Chicago: U of Chicago P, 1972), 229-53.

j133. Pearce, Howard D. "A Phenomenological Approach to the *Theatrum Mundi*." PMLA 95 (1980), 42-57.

j134. Pfaff, Frank M. "First Questions." DAI 35 (1974), 2236A-37A.

j135. Pison, Thomas. "A Phenomenological Approach to Keats's 'To Autumn,'" in H. R. Garvin, ed. Phenomenology, Structuralism, Semiology (Lewisburg PA: Bucknell UP, 1976).

j136. Poulet, Georges. "La pensée critique de Charles Du Bos." Critique 21 (1965), 491-516.
j137. ----------. Bachelard et la connaissance de soi." RMM 70 (1965), 1-26.
j138. ----------. "Maurice Blanchot, critique et romancier." Critique 22 (1966), 485-97.
j139. ---------- and Jean Ricardou, eds. Les Chemins actuels de a critique (Paris: Plon, 1967).
j140. ----------. The Metamorphoses of the Circle (Baltimore: Johns Hopkins UP, 1967).
j141. ----------. "Phénomenologie de la conscience critique." SFr 12, supp. 34 (1968), 17-32.
j142. ----------. "Phenomenology of Reading." NLH 1 (1969), 53-68.
j143. ----------. La Conscience critique (Paris: José Corti, 1971).
j144. ----------. "Poulet on Poulet: The Self and the Other in Critical Consciousness." Diacritics 2.1 (1972), 46-50.
j145. ----------. Proustian Space (Baltimore: Johns Hopkins UP, 1977).
j146. ----------. Exploding Poetry: Baudelaire/ Rimbaud (Chicago: U of Chicago P, 1984).

j147. Radway, Janice A. "A Phenomenological Theory of Popular and Elite Literature." DAI 39 (1978), 288A-89A.
j148. ----------. "Phenomenology, Linguistics, and Popular Literature." JPC 12 (1978), 88-98.

j149. Rapaport, Herman. "Phenomenology and Contemporary Theory," in J. Natoli, ed. Tracing Literary Theory (Urbana: U of Illinois P, 1987), 148-76.

j150. Richard, Jean-Pierre. Paysage de Chateaubriand (Paris: Seuil, 1967).
j151. ----------. Microlectures, 2 vols. (Paris: Seuil, 1979).

j152. Rousset, Jean. Le mythe de Don Juan (Paris: Colin, 1978).
j153. ----------. Narcisse romancier: essai sur le premiere personne dans le roman, 2nd ed. (Paris: Corti, 1986).

j154. Rowe, John Carlos. The Theoretical Dimensions of Henry James (Madison: U of Wisconsin P, 1984) [chap. 6: "Phenomenological Hermeneutics: Henry James and Literary Impressionism"].

j155. Rudnick, Hans F. "Roman Ingarden's Aesthetics of Literature." CollG 8 (1974), 1-14.

j156. Ruthrof, Horst F. "A Phenomeno-Sociological Approach to Fiction." Philosophy and Phenomenological Research 33 (1972), 399-407.
j157. ----------."Aspects of a Phenomenological View of Narrative." JNT 4 (1974), 87-99.
j158. ----------. "Text and the Construction of Meaning: A Phenomenological Approach." SoRA 16.1 (1983), 110-20.

j159. Said, Edward. Joseph Conrad and the Fiction of Autobiography (Cambridge: Harvard UP, 1966).
j160. ----------. "Roads Taken and Not Taken in Contemporary Criticism." ConL 17.3 (1976), 327-48.

j161. Sallis, John C. "Phenomenology and Language." Personalist 48 (1967), 490-508.
j162. ----------, ed. Husserl and Contemporary Thought (Atlantic Highlands NJ: Humanities P, 1983).

j163. Sartre, Jean-Paul. L'Idiot de la famille, 3 vols. (Paris: Gallimard, 1971-72) [vol. 1: The Family Idiot (U of Chicago P, 1982)].
j164. ----------. Mallarmé, or the Poet of Nothingness (University Park: Pennsylvania State UP, 1988).

j165. Scholz, Bernhard F. "A Phenomenological Interpretation of the Organic Metaphor in Literary Theory and Criticism." DAI 32 (1972), 6392A.
j166. ----------. "Literatur als Bewusstsinsphanomen: Zum Ansatzpunkt phanomenologischer Literaturwissenschaft." LiLi 17 (1975), 35-53.

j167. Scriven, Michael. Sartre's Existential Biographies (NY: St. Martin's P, 1984).

j168. Silver, Philip. Ortega as Phenomenologist: The Genesis of *Meditations on Quixote* (NY: Columbia UP, 1978).

j169. Silverman, Hugh J., *et al*. The Horizons of Continental Philosophy: Essays on Husserl, Heidegger, and Merleau-Ponty (Dordrecht & Boston: Kluwer Academic, 1988).

j170. Starobinski, Jean, *et al*. Jean-Jacques Rousseau: quatre études (Neuchatel: A. la Baconniere, 1978).
j171. ----------. Words upon Words: The Anagrams of Ferdinand de Saussure (New Haven: Yale UP, 1979).
j172. ----------. 1789, the Emblems of Reason (Charlottesville: U of Virginia P, 1982).
j173. ----------. Montaigne in Motion (Chicago: U of Chicago P, 1985).
j174. ----------. The Invention of Liberty, 1700-1789 (NY: Rizzoli, 1987).
j175. ----------. Jean-Jacques Rousseau: Transparency and Obstruction (Chicago: U of Chicago P, 1988).

j176. Stewart, David and Algis Mickunas. Exploring Phenomenology: A Guide to the Field and Its Literature (Chicago: American Library Assoc., 1974).

j177. Stewart, Philip. "The Critical Tautology." Diacritics 5.1 (1975), 2-7.

j178. Straus, Erwin W. and Richard M. Griffith, eds. Aisthesis and Aesthetics (Pittsburgh: Duquesne UP, 1970).

j179. Strube, Werner. "Was heisst 'Wahrheit' auf Kunstwerke bezogen? Uberlegungen im Anschluss an Roman Ingarden." LJGG 22 (1981), 325-35.

j180. Suhl, Benjamin. Jean-Paul Sartre: The Philosopher as a Literary Critic (NY: Columbia UP, 1970).

j181. Survant, Joe. "Narrative Time and the Spatial Metaphor: Phenomenology as Problem and Cure." JEP 5.1-2 (1984), 36-42.

j182. Swearingen, James E. Reflexivity in *Tristram Shandy:* An Essay in Phenomenological Criticism (New Haven: Yale UP, 1977).

j183.Thomas, Johannes. "G. Poulet und der Wahrheitsanspruch der Literaturkritik." RLV 39 (1973), 520-25.

j184. Townsend, Dabney W., Jr. "Phenomenology and the Form of the Novel: Toward an Expanded Critical Method." PPR 34 (1974), 331-38.

j185. Tripet, Arnaud. "L'Ecole de Geneve: L'Oeuvre critique de Marcel Raymond." SFSt 1.2 (1980), 5-23.

j186. Tymieniecka, Anna-Teresa, ed. The Philosophical Reflection of Man in Literature (Dordrecht: Reidel, 1982).
j187. ----------, ed. The Existential Coordinates of the Human Condition: Poetic--Epic--Tragic: The Literary Genre (Dordrecht: Reidel, 1984).
j188. ----------, ed. Poetics of the Elements in the Human Condition: The Sea: From Elemental Stirrings to Symbolic Inspiration, Language, and Life-Significance in Literary Interpretation and Theory (Dordrecht: Reidel, 1985).

j189. Ungar, Steven R. "Sartre as Critic." Diacritics 1 (1971), 32-37.

j190. Vajda, Gyorgy. "Phénomenologie et sciences littéraires." ALitASH 11 (1969), 89-126.
j191. ----------. "Phenomenology and Literary Criticism," in L. Nyiro, ed. Literature and Its Interpretation (The Hague: Mouton, 1979), 163-230.
j192. ----------. "Phenomenology and Comparative Literature (A Kind of Fictitious Letter to Students)." Neohelicon 10.2 (1983), 133-46.

j193. Valdes, Mario J. Shadows in the Cave: A Phenomenological Approach to Literary Criticism Based on Hispanic Texts (Toronto: U of Toronto P, 1982).
j194. ----------. Phenomenological Hermeneutics and the Study of Literature (Toronto: U of Toronto P, 1987).

j195. Weinsheimer, Joel. Imitation (London & Boston: Routledge & Kegan Paul, 1984).

j196. Wellek, René. Four Critics: Croce, Valéry, Lukacs, and Ingarden (Seattle: U of Washington P. 1981).

j197. Wilcocks, R. Jean-Paul Sartre: A Bibliography of International Criticism (Edmonton: U of Alberta P, 1975).

j198. Wohrer, Franz K. Thomas Traherne: The Growth of a Mystic's Mind: A Study of the Evolution and the Phenomenology of Traherne's Mystical Consciousness (Salzburg: Insitut fur Anglistik und Amerikanistik, Universitat Salzburg, 1982).

j199. Yoos, George E. "A Phenomenological Look at Metaphor." PPR 32 (1971), 78-88.

K. Hermeneutics

k1. Aler, Jean. "Heidegger's Conception of Language in *Being and Time*," in J. J. Kockelmans, ed. On Heidegger and Language (Evanston: Northwestern UP, 1972), 33-62.

k2. Altenhofer, Norbert. "Geselliges Betragen--Kunst--Auslegung: Anmerkungen zu Peter Szondis Schleiermacher-Interpretation und zur Frage einer materialen Hermeneutik," in U. Nassen, ed. Studien zur Entwicklung einer materialen Hermeneutik (Munich: Fink, 1979), 165-211.

k3. Altieri, Charles. Act and Quality: A Theory of Meaning and Humanistic Understanding (Amherst: U of Massachusetts P, 1981).

k4. Apel, Karl-Otto. Analytic Philosophy of Language and the Geisteswissenschaften (Dordrecht: Reidel, 1967).
k5. ----------, *et al* , eds. Hermeneutik und Ideologiekritik (Frankfurt: Suhrkamp, 1973).
k6. ----------. "The A Priori of Communication and the Foundation of the Humanities," in F. Dallmayr and T. McCarthy, eds. Understanding and Social Inquiry (Notre Dame IN: U of Notre Dame P, 1977), 292-315.
k7. ----------. Towards a Transformation of Philosophy (London: Routledge & Kegan Paul, 1980).

k8. Armstrong, Paul B. "The Conflict of Interpretations and the Limits of Pluralism." PMLA 98.3 (1983), 341-52.

k9. Arthur, Christopher E. "Gadamer and Hirsch: The Canonical Work and the Interpreter's Intention." Cultural Hermeneutics 4 (1977), 183-97.

k10. Assmann, A. "Die Legitimitat der Fiktion: Ein Beitrag zur Geschichte der literarischen Kommunikation." DAI 42 (1981), 1541C.

k11. Beardsley, Monroe C. "Modes of Interpretation." JHI 32 (1971), 143-48.

k12. Behler, Ernst. "The New Hermeneutics and Comparative Literature." Neohelicon 10.2 (1983), 25-45 [discusses Gadamer].

k13. Berg, Richard. "Heidegger on Language and Poetry." Kinesis 7 (1977), 75-89.

k14. Bernstein, Richard J. Beyond Objectivism and Relativism: Science, Hermeneutics, and Praxis (Philadelphia: U of Pennsylvania P, 1983).
k15. ----------. "Philosophy in the Conversation of Mankind" and "From Hermeneutics to Praxis," in R. Hollinger, ed. Hermeneutics and Praxis (Notre Dame IN: U of Notre Dame P, 1985), 54-86, 272-96.

k16. Betti, Emilio. "Hermeneutics as the General Science of the Geisteswissenschaften ," in J. Bleicher, ed. Contemporary Hermeneutics: Hermeneutics as Method, Philosophy, and Critique (London: Routledge & Kegan Paul, 1980), 51-94.
k17. ----------. "The Epistemological Problem of Understanding as an Aspect of the General Problem of Knowing," in G. Shapiro and A. Sica, eds. Hermeneutics: Questions & Prospects (Amherst: U of Massachusetts P, 1984), 25-53.

k18. Biemel, Walter. "Poetry and Language in Heidegger," in J. J. Kockelmans, ed. On Heidegger and Language (Evanston: Northwestern UP, 1972), 65-105.

k19. Birault, Henri. "Thinking and Poetizing in Heidegger," in J. J. Kockelmans, ed. On Heidegger and Language (Evanston: Northwestern UP, 1972), 147-68.

k20. Bleicher, Josef, ed. Contemporary Hermeneutics: Hermeneutics as Method, Philiosophy, and Critique (London: Routledge & Kegan Paul, 1980).

k21. Bloom, Harold. A Map of Misreading (NY: Oxford UP, 1975).
k22. ----------. Agon: Towards a Theory of Revisionism (NY: Oxford UP, 1982).

k23. Boeckh, August. On Interpretation & Criticism (Norman: U of Oklahoma P, 1968).

k24. Bohler, Dietrich. "Philosophische Hermeneutik und Hermeneutische Methode," in M. Fuhrmann, et al, eds. Text und Applikation: Theologie, Jurisprudenz und Literaturwissenschaft im Hermeneutischen Gesprach (Munich: Fink, 1981), 483-512.

k25. Bolz, Norbert W. Geschichtsphilosophie des Asthetischen: Hermeneutische Rekunstruktion der Noten zur Literatur Theodor W. Adornos (Hildesheim: Gerstenberg, 1979).

k26. Borgmann, Albert. "Language in Heidegger's Philosophy." Journal of Existentialism (1966), 161-80.

k27. Boschenstein, Bernhard. "Peter Szondi: 'Studies on Holderlin': Exemplarity of a Path." Boundary 11.3 (1983), 93-110.

k28. Bourgeois, Patrick L. Extension of Ricoeur's Hermeneutic (The Hague: Martinus Nijhoff, 1973).
k29. ----------. "From Hermeneutics of Symbols to the Interpretation of Texts," in C. E. Reagan, ed. Studies in the Philosophy of Paul Ricoeur (Athens: Ohio UP, 1979), 83-95.

k30. Bové, Paul. "The Penitentiary of Reflection: Soren Kierkegaard and Critical Activity." Boundary 9.1 (1980), 233-58.
k31. ----------. Destructive Poetics: Heidegger and Modern American Poetry (NY: Columbia UP, 1980).

k32. Brandom, Robert. "Freedom and Constraint by Norms," in R. Hollinger, ed. Hermeneutics and Praxis (Notre Dame IN: U of Notre Dame P, 1985), 173-91.

k33. Bredella, Lothar. "Die Tatigkeit des Lesers beim sinnhaften Aufbau der fiktiven Welt literarischer Text: Zur Kritik von Ingardens Begriff der 'Unbestimmheitstelle,'" in J. Hasler, ed. Anglistentag 1981: Vortrage (Frankfurt am Main: Lang, 1983), 170-89.

k34. Bruns, Gerlad L. Inventions: Writing, Textuality, and Understanding in Literature and History (New Haven: Yale UP, 1982).

k35. Bubner, Rudiger, Konrad Cramer, and Reiner Wiehl, eds. Hermeneutik und Dialektik, 2 vols. (Tubingen: Mohr, 1970).
k36. ----------. "Theory and Practice in Light of the Hermeneutic-Criticist Controversy." Cultural Hermeneutics 2 (1975), 337-52.

k37. Buck, Gunther. "The Structure of Hermeneutic Experience and the Problem of Tradition." NLH 10 (1978), 31-47.

k38. ----------. "Hermeneutics of Texts and Hermeneutics of Action." NLH 12 (1980), 87-96.

k39. ----------. "Von Texthermeneutik zur Handlungshermeneutik," in M. Fuhrmann, H. R. Jauss, and W. Pannenberg, eds. Text und Applikation: Theologie, Jurisprudenz und Literaturwissenschaft im hermeneutischen Gesprach (Munich: Fink, 1981), 525-36.

k40. Burgos, Jean. "Thématique et herméneutiques ou le thématicien contre les interprétés." RLV 43 (1977), 522-34.

k41. Byrum, Charles Stephen. "Philosophy as Play." Man and World 8 (1975), 315-26.

k42. Cain, William E. "Authors and Authority in Interpretation." GaR 34 (1980), 617-34.

k43. Caputo, John D. "The Thought of Being and the Conversation of Mankind: The Case of Heidegger and Rorty," in R. Hollinger, ed. Hermeneutics and Praxis (Notre Dame IN: U of Notre Dame P, 1985), 248-71.

k44. ----------. Radical Hermeneutics: Repetition, Deconstruction, and the Hermeneutic Project (Bloomington: Indiana UP, 1987).

k45. Carravetta, Peter. "The Problem of Method and the Quest for Hermeneutics: A Study in the Foundations of Interpretive Thought in Twentieth Century Italian Literary Criticism." DAI 44 (1983), 481A.

k46. Carrithers, Gale H., Jr. "How Literary Things Go: Contra Hirsch." Genre 1 (1968), 195-208.

k47. Cavell, Stanley. Must We Mean What We Say? (NY: Scribners, 1969).

k48. Chabot, C. Barry. "The Fates of Interpretation." GaR 34 (1980), 639-57.

k49. Child, Arthur. "Hermeneutics Again." Genre 3 (1970), 97-110.

k50. Connerton, Paul. "Gadamer's Hermeneutics." CCrit 5 (1983), 107-28.

k51. Connolly, John M. "Gadamer and the Author's Authority: A Language-Game Approach." JAAC 44.3 (1986), 272-77.

k52. Corley, Paul. "Bedeutung und Geschichte: Vorstudien zu einer phanomenologischen Grundlegung der Texthermeneutik." DAI 35 (1974), 1617A.

k53. Corngold, Stanley. "*Sein und Zeit* : Implications for Poetics." Boundary 4 (1976), 439-54 [on Heidegger].

k54. Czaplejewicz, Eugeniusz. "Dialogue Theory of a Literary Work." ZRL 20.1 (1977), 49-66.

k55. Dallmayr, Fred R. and Thomas A. McCarthy, eds. Understanding and Social Inquiry (Notre Dame IN: U of Notre Dame P, 1977).

k56. Danneberg, Lutz and Hans-Harald Muller. "Wissenschaftstheorie, Hermeneutik, Literaturwissenschaft: Anmerkungen zu einem unterbliebenen und Beitrage zu einem kunftigen Dialog uber die Methodology des Verstehens." DVLG 58.2 (1984), 177-261.

k57. DeLoach, Bill. "On First Looking int Ricoeur's *Interpretation Theory* : A Beginner's Guide." Pre/Text 4.3-4 (1983), 225-36.

k58. Dilthey, Wilhelm. "The Rise of Hermeneutics." NLH 3 (1972), 229-44.

k59. Dockhorn, Klaus. "Hans-Georg Gadamer's *Truth and Method* ." Philosophy and Rhetoric 13 (1980), 160-80.

k60. Dostal, Robert J. "Kantian Aesthetics and the Literary Criticism of E. D. Hirsch." JAAC 38 (1980), 299-305.

k61. Dreyfus, Hubert L. "Holism and Hermeneutics," in R. Hollinger, ed. Hermeneutics and Praxis (Notre Dame IN: U of Notre Dame P, 1985), 227-47.

k62. Ducker, Danny. "Hermeneutics and Literary Criticism: A Phenomenological Mode of Interpretation with Particular Application to *Who's Afraid of Virginia Woolf* ." DAI 36 (1976), 8045A.

k63. Erickson, Stephen A. Language and Being: An Analytic Phenomenology (New Haven: Yale UP, 1970).

k64. Ermath, Michael. Wilhelm Dilthey: The Critique of Historical Reason (Chicago: U of Chicago P, 1978).
k65. ----------. "The Transformation of Hermeneutics: 19th-Century Ancients and 20th-Century Moderns." Monist 64 (1981), 175-94.

k66. Frank, Manfred. Das Individuelle Allgemeine: Textstrukturisierung und -interpretation nach Schleiermacher (Frankfurt: Suhrkamp, 1977).

k67. Freundlieb, Dieter. Zur Wissenschaftstheorie der Literaturwissenschaft: Eine Kritik der transzendentalen Hermeneutik (Munich: Fink, 1978).

k68. Fries, Thomas. "Critical Relation: Peter Szondi's Studies on Celan." Boundary 11.3 (1983), 139-67.

k69. Frow, John. "Reading as System and as Practice." CCrit 5 (1983), 87-105.

k70. Fuhrmann, Manfred, Hans Robert Jauss, and Wolfhart Pannenberg, eds. Text und Applikation: Theologie, Jurisprudenz und Literaturwissenschaft im hermeneutischen Gesprach (Munich: Fink, 1981).

k71. Gadamer, Hans-Georg, ed. Truth and Historicity (The Hague: Nijhoff, 1972).
k72. ----------. Wahrheit und Methode: Grundzuge einer Philosophischen Hermeneutik, 4th ed. (Tubingen: Mohr, 1975) [Truth and Method (NY: Seabury P, 1975), based on 3rd ed.].
k73. ----------. "The Problem of Historical Consciousness." Graduate Faculty Philosophy Journal 5 (1975), 8-52.
k74. ----------. Hegel's Dialectic: Five Hermeneutical Studies (New Haven: Yale UP, 1976).
k75. ----------. Kleine Schriften 1: Philosophie--Hermeneutik, 2nd ed. (Tubingen: Mohr, 1976).
k76. ----------. Kleine Schriften 2: Interpretationen, 2nd ed. (Tubingen: Mohr, 1979).
k77. ----------. Kleine Schriften 3: Idee und Sprache: Plato, Husserl, Heidegger (Tubingen: Mohr, 1972).
k78. ----------. Kleine Schriften 4: Variationen (Tubingen: Mohr, 1977).
k79. ----------. Philosophical Hermeneutics (Berkeley: U of California P, 1976).
k80. ----------. Rhetorik und Hermeneutik (Gottingen: Vandenhoeck and Ruprecht, 1976).
k81. ----------. Philosophische Lehrjahre: Eine Ruckschau (Frankfurt am Main: Klostermann, 1977).
k82. ----------. Die Akualitat des Schonen: Kunst als Spiel, Symbol, und Fest (Stuttgart: Reclam, 1977).
k83. ----------. Dialogue and Dialectic: Eight Hermeneutical Studies on Plato (New Haven: Yale UP, 1980).
k84. ----------. "Philosophie und Literatur," in E. W. Orth, ed. Was ist Literatur? (Freiburg: Abber, 1981), 18-45.

k85. ----------. Reason in the Age of Science (Cambridge: MIT P, 1981).
k86. ----------. "The Eminent Text and its Truth," in P. Hernadi, ed. The Horizon of Literature (Lincoln: U of Nebraska P, 1982), 337-67 [responses by G. Graff, G. L. Bruns, T. Conley, D. Marshall, 347-67].
k87. ----------. "The Hermeneutics of Suspicion," in G. Shapiro and A. Sica, eds. Hermeneutics: Questions & Prospects (Amherst: U of Massachusetts P, 1984), 54-65.

k88. Garrett, Jan Edward. "Hans-Georg Gadamer on 'Fusion of Horizons.'" Man and World 11 (1978), 392-400.

k89. Gebhard, Walter. "Hermeneutik als Rezeptionsanweisung," in G. Kopf, ed. Rezeptionspragmatik: Beitrage zur Praxis des Lesens (Munich: Fink, 1981), 27-57.

k90. Gerhart, Mary. The Question of Belief in Literary Criticism: An Introduction to the Hermeneutical Theory of Paul Ricoeur (Stuttgart: Heinz, 1979).

k91. Goebel, Rolf J. "Curtius, Gadamer, Adorno: Probleme literarischer Tradition." Monatshefte 78.2 (1986), 151-66.

k92. Gras, Vernon, ed. "A Symposium: Hermeneutics, Post-Structuralism, and 'Objective Interpretation.'" PLL 17.1 (1981), 48-87.

k93. Greene, Maxine. "Language, Literature, and the Release of Meaning." CE 41 (1979), 123-35.

k94. Grimm, Reinhold B. "Von der explikativen zur poetischen Allegorese," in M. Fuhrmann, H. R. Jauss, and W. Pannenberg, eds. Text und Applikation: Theologie, Jurisprudenz und Literaturwissenschaft im hermeneutischen Gesprach (Munich: Fink, 1981), 567-76.

k95. Grob, Karl. "Theory and Practice of Philology: Reflections on the Public Statements of Peter Szondi." Boundary 11.3 (1983), 169-90.

k96. Grondin, Jean. Hermeneutische Wahrheit? Zum Wahrheitsbegriff Hans-Georg Gadamers (Konigstein/Ts.: Forum Academicum, 1982).

k97. Gunther, Horst. "Philological Understanding: A Note on the Writings of Peter Szondi." CCrit 5 (1983), 245-50.

k98. Habermas. Jurgen. Knowledge and Human Interests (Boston: Beacon P, 1971).

k99. ----------. "A Postscript to *Knowledge and Human Interests.*" Philosophy of the Social Sciences 3 (1973), 157-89.

k100. ----------. Communication and the Evolution of Society (Boston: Beacon P, 1976).

k101. ----------. "A Review of Gadamer's *Truth and Method,*" in F. Dallmayr and T. McCarthy, eds. Understanding and Social Inquiry (Notre Dame IN: U of Notre Dame P, 1977), 335-63.

k102. ----------. "The Hermeneutic Claim to Universality," in J. Bleicher, ed. Contemporary Hermeneutics: Hermeneutics as Method, Philosophy, and Critique (London: Routledge & Kegan Paul, 1980), 181-212.

k103. Halliburton, David. "The Hermeneutics of Belief and the Hermeneutics of Suspicion." Diacritics 6.4 (1976), 2-9.

k104. ----------. Poetic Thinking: An Approach to Heidegger (Chicago: U of Chicago P, 1981).

k105. Hamburger, Kate. Wahrheit und Aesthetische Wahrheit (Stuttgart: Klett-Cotta, 1979).

k106. Hamlin, Cyrus. "The Limits of Understanding: Hermeneutics and the Study of Literature." Arion 3 (1976), 385-419.

k107. ----------. "The Conscience of Narrative: Towards a Hermeneutics of Transcendence." NLH 13.2 (1982), 205-30.

k108. Hans, James S. "Hans-Georg Gadamer and Hermeneutic Phenomenology." Philosophy Today 22 (1978), 3-19.

k109. ----------. "Hermeneutics, Play, Deconstruction." Philosophy Today 24 (1980), 299-317.

k110. Harries, Karsten. "Language and Silence: Heidegger's Dialogue with Georg Trakl." Boundary 4 (1976), 495-511.

k111. Harth, Dietrich. "Bemerkungen zur 'Objektivierung des Verstehens' als Aufgabe literarischer Hermeneutik." JIG 2.1 (1970), 155-60.

k112. Haverkamp, Anselm. "Allegorie, Ironie und Wiederholung: Zur zeiten Lektüre," in M. Fuhrmann, H. R. Jauss, and W. Pannenberg, eds. Text und Applikation: Theologie, Jurisprudenz und Literaturwissenschaft im hermeneutischen Gesprach (Munich: Fink, 1981), 561-66.

k113. Hays, Michael, ed. "The Criticism of Peter Szondi." Boundary 11.3 (1983) [special issue].

k114. Heidegger, Martin. Discourse on Thinking (NY: Harper & Row, 1966).

k115. ----------. What Is Called Thinking? (NY: Harper & Row, 1968).
k116. ----------. Poetry, Language, Thought (NY: Harper & Row, 1971).
k117. ----------. On the Way to Language (San Francisco: Harper & Row, 1971).
k118. ----------. On Time and Being (NY: Harper & Row, 1972).
k119. ----------. Early Greek Thinking (NY: Harper & Row, 1975).
k120. ----------. Heidegger: Basic Writings (NY: Harper & Row, 1977).

k121. Hinman, Lawrence M. "Quid Facti or Quid Juris: The Fundamental Ambiguity of Gadamer's Understanding of Hermeneutics." Philosophy and Phenomenological Research 40 (1980), 512-35.

k122. Hirsch, E. D., Jr. Validity in Interpretation (New Haven: Yale UP, 1967).
k123. ----------. "Literary Evaluation as Knowledge." ConL 9 (1968), 319-31.
k124. ----------. "The Norms of Interpretation--A Brief Response." Genre 2 (1969), 57-62.
k125. ----------. "Three Dimensions of Hermeneutics." NLH 3 (1972), 245-61.
k126. ----------. "'Intrinsic' Criticism." CE 36 (1974), 446-57.
k127. ----------. The Aims of Interpretation (Chicago: U of Chicago P, 1976).

k128. Hogan, John. "Gadamer and the Hermeneutical Experience." Philosophy Today 20 (1976), 3-12.

k129. Holdheim, W. Wolfgang. "The Hermeneutical Significance of Auerbach's Ansatz ." NLH 16.3 (1985), 627-31.

k130. Holenstein, Elmar. "The Structure of Understanding: Structuralism versus Hermeneutics." PTL 1 (1976), 223-38.

k131. Hollinger, Robert, ed. Hermeneutics and Praxis (Notre Dame IN: U of Notre Dame P, 1985).

k132. Howard, Roy J. Three Faces of Hermeneutics: An Introduction to Current Theories of Understanding (Berkeley: U of California P, 1982).

k133. Hoy, David Couzens. "Hermeneutic Circularity, Indeterminacy and Incommensurability." NLH 10 (1978), 161-73.
k134. ----------. The Critical Circle: Literature, History, and Philosophical Hermeneutics (Berkeley: U of California P, 1978).
k135. ----------. "Forgetting the Text: Derrida's Critique of Heidegger." Boundary 8.1 (1979), 223-35.

k136. Hufnagel, Erwin. Einfuhrung in die Hermeneutik (Stuttgart: Kohlhammer, 1976).

k137. Huntley, John. "A Practical Look at E. D. Hirsch's *Validity in Interpretation.*" Genre 1 (1968), 242-55.

k138. Hyde, Michael J. "Philosophical Hermeneutics and the Communicative Experience." Man and World 13 (1980), 81-98.
k139. ----------. "The Hermeneutic Phenomenon and the Authenticity of Discourse." VLang 17.2 (1983), 146-62 [discusses Heidegger].

k140. Ihde, Don. Hermeneutic Phenomenology: The Philosophy of Paul Ricoeur (Evanston: Northwestern UP, 1971).

k141. Ingram, David. "Hermeneutics and Truth," in R. Hollinger, ed. Hermeneutics and Praxis (Notre Dame IN: U of Notre Dame P, 1985), 32-53 [discusses Gadamer, Heidegger].

k142. Japp, Uwe. Hermeneutik (Munich: Fink, 1977).
k143. ----------. "Hermeneutik," in H. Brackert and J. Stuckrath, eds. Literaturwissenschaft: Grundkurs 2 (Reinbeck bei Hamburg: Rowohlt, 1981), 451-63.
k144. ----------. "Uber Kontext und Kritik," in M. Fuhrmann, H. R. Jauss, and W. Pannenberg, eds. Text und Applikation: Theologie, Jurisprudenz und Literaturwissenschaft im hermeneutischen Gesprach (Munich: Fink, 1981), 547-50.

k145. Jauss, Hans Robert. "Limits and Tasks of Literary Hermeneutics." Diogenes 109 (1980), 92-119.
k146. ----------. "Literature and Hermeneutics," in P. Hernadi, ed. What Is Criticism? (Bloomington: Indiana UP, 1981).
k147. ----------. "Zur Abgrenzung ind Bestimmung einer literarischer Hermeneutik," in M. Fuhrmann, H. R. Jauss, and W. Pannenberg, eds. Text und Applikation: Theologie, Jurisprudenz und Literaturwissenschaft im hermeneutischen Gesprach (Munich: Fink, 1981), 459-82.
k148. ----------. "Der fragende Adam: Zur Funktion von Frage und Antwort in literarischer Tradition," in M. Fuhrmann, H. R. Jauss, and W. Pannenberg, eds. Text und Applikation: Theologie, Jurisprudenz und Literaturwissenschaft im hermeneutischen Gesprach (Munich: Fink, 1981), 551-60.
k149. ----------. "Poiesis." CritI 8.3 (1982), 591-608.
k150. ----------. "The Identity of the Poetic Text in the Changing Horizon of Understanding," in M. J. Valdes and O. Miller, eds. Identity of the Literary Text (Toronto: U of Toronto P, 1985), 146-74.

k151. Jay, Martin. "Should Intellectual History Take a Linguistic Turn? Reflections on the Habermas-Gadamer Debate," in D. LaCapra and S. Kaplan, eds. Modern European Intellectual History: Reappraisals and New Perspectives (Ithaca: Cornell UP, 1982), 86-110.

k152. Juhl, P. D. "The Doctrine of 'Verstehen' and the Objectivity of Literary Interpretations." DVLG 49 (1975), 381-424.
k153. ----------. Interpretation: An Essay in the Philosophy of Literary Criticism (Princeton: Princeton UP, 1980).

k154. Kermode, Frank. The Classic (London: Faber and Faber, 1975).
k155. ----------. The Genesis of Secrecy: On the Interpretation of Narrative (Cambridge: Harvard UP, 1979).

k156. Kinneavy, James L. "The Relation of the Whole to the Part in Interpretation Theory and in the Composing Process." VLang 17.2 (1983), 120-45.

k157. Kirkland, Frank M. "Gadamer and Ricoeur: The Pardigm of the Text." Graduate Faculty Philosophy Journal 6 (1977), 131-44.

k158. Kisiel, Theodore. "Repetition in Gadamer's Hermeneutics." Analecta Husserliana 2 (1972), 196-203.
k159. ----------. "The Happening of Tradition: The Hermeneutics of Gadamer and Heidegger," in R. Hollinger, ed. Hermeneutics and Praxis (Notre Dame IN: U of Notre Dame P, 1985), 3-31.

k160. Klein, Jurgen. Beyond Hermeneutics: Zur Philosophie der Literatur-- und Geisteswissenschaften (Essen: Blaue Eule, 1985).

k161. Kline, Charles Robert, Jr., ed. "The Renascence of die Hermeneute." VLang 17.2 (1983) [special issue].

k162. Kloepfer, Rolf. "Escape into Reception: The Scientistic and Hermeneutic Schools of German Literary Theory." PoT 3.2 (1982), 47-75.

k163. Kockelmans, Joseph J. "Language, Meaning, and Ek-sistence," and "Ontological Difference, Hermeneutics, and Language," both in J. J. Kockelmans, ed. On Heidegger and Language (Evanston: Northwestern UP, 1972), 3-32, 195-234.

k164. Kresic, Stephen, ed. Contemporary Literary Hermeneutics and the Interpretation of Classical Texts (Ottawa: Ottawa UP, 1981).

k165. Lapointe, François H. "Ricoeur and His Critics: A Bibliographical Essay," in C. E. Reagan, ed. Studies in the Philosophy of Paul Ricoeur (Athens: Ohio UP, 1979), 163-77.

k166. Lawlor, Leonard. "Event and Repeatability: Ricoeur and Derrida in Debate." Pre/Text 4.3-4 (1983), 317-34.

k167. Lawry, Edward. "The Work-Being of the Work of Art in Heidegger." Man and World 11 (1978), 186-98.

k168. Lefevre, André. "Western Hermeneutics and Concepts of Chinese Literature Theory." TkR 6-7 (1975-76), 159-68.

k169. Leitch, Vincent B. Deconstructive Criticism: An Advanced Introduction (NY: Columbia UP, 1983), chap. 4.

k170. Leventhal, Robert Scott. "From Semiotic Interpretation to Critical Hermeneutics: The Emergence of Hermeneutic Critique in the Early Writings of Friedrich Schlegel." DAI 43 (1983), 3002A.

k171. Ley, Klaus. "Kunst und Kairos: Zur Konstitutionen der wirkungsasthetischen Kategorie von Gegenwartigkeit in der Literatur." Poetica 17.1-2 (1985), 46-82.

k172. Linge, David E. "Dilthey and Gadamer: Two Theories of Historical Understanding." Journal of the American Academy of Religion 41 (1973), 536-53.

k173. Lundin, Roger. "Hermeneutics and the Romantic Tradition." CSR 13.1 (1983), 3-18.
k174. ----------, et al. The Responsibility of Hermeneutics (Grand Rapids MI: Eerdmans, 1985).

k175. MacIntyre, Alasdair. "Contexts of Interpretation: Reflections on Hans-Georg Gadamer's Truth and Method." Boston University Journal 24 (1976), 41-46.

k176. Mailloux, Steven. "Rhetorical Hermeneutics." CritI 11.4 (1985), 620-42.

k177. Margot, Jean-Paul. "Herméneutique et fiction chez M. Foucault." Dialogue 23.4 (1984), 635-48.

k178. Marino, Adrian. "Mircea Eliade's Hermeneutics," in N. J. Girardot and M. L. Ricketts, eds. Imagination and Meaning: The Scholarly and Literary Worlds of Mircea Eliade (NY: Seabury P, 1982), 19-69.
k179. ----------. "Hermeneutics as Criticism." VLang 17.2 (1983), 206-15.

k180. Marquard, Odo. "Frage nach der Frage, auf die Hermeneutik die Antwort ist," in M. Fuhrmann, H. R. Jauss, and W. Pannenberg, eds. Text und Applikation: Theologie, Jurisprudenz und Literaturwissenschaft im hermeneutischen Gesprach (Munich: Fink, 1981), 581-89.

k181. Marshall, Donald. "The Aims of Interpretation, by E. D. Hirsch, Jr." PQ 56 (1977), 418-25.
k182. ----------. "Plot as Trap, Plot as Mediation," in P. Hernadi, ed. The Horizon of Literature (Lincoln: U of Nebraska P, 1982), 71-96.

k183. Martin, Wallace. "The Hermeneutic Circle and the Art of Interpretation." CL 24 (1972), 97-117.
k184. ----------. "Critical Truth as Necessary Error," in P. Hernadi, ed. What Is Criticism? (Bloomington: Indiana UP, 1981), 83-95.

k185. Martinez Bonati, Félix. "Hermeneutical Criticism and the Description of Form," in M. J. Valdes and O. J. Miller, eds. Interpretation of Narrative (Toronto: U of Toronto P, 1978), 78-99.
k186. ----------. Fictive Discourse and the Structures of Literature (Ithaca: Cornell UP, 1981).

k187. Maurer, Karl. "Textkritik und Interpretation." Poetica 16.3-4 (1984), 324-55.

k188. McCarthy, Thomas. "On Misunderstanding 'Understanding.'" Theory and Decision 3 (1973), 351-69.

k189. McGuire, Steven. "Interpretive Sociology and Paul Ricoeur." HumanS 4.2 (1981), 179-200.

k190. Mendelson, Jack. "The Habermas-Gadamer Debate." NGC 18 (1979), 44-73.

k191. Misgeld, Dieter. "Discourse and Conversation: The Theory of Communicative Competence and Hermeneutics in Light of the Debate Between Habermas and Gadamer." Cultural Hermeneutics 4 (1977), 321-44.
k192. ----------. "On Gadamer's Hermeneutics," in R. Hollinger, ed. Hermeneutics and Praxis (Notre Dame IN: U of Notre Dame P, 1985), 143-70.

k193. Mohanty, J. N. "Transcendental Philosophy and the Hermeneutic Critique of Consciousness," in G. Shapiro and A. Sica, eds. Hermeneutics: Questions & Prospects (Amherst: U of Massachusetts P, 1984), 96-120.

k194. Mueller-Vollmer, Kurt. "To Understand an Author Better than the Author Himself: On the Hermeneutics of the Unspoken." Lang&S 5 (1972), 43-52.

k195. Murray, Michael. Modern Critical Theory: An Introduction (The Hague: Nijhoff, 1975).
k196. ----------, ed. Heidegger and Modern Philosophy: Critical Essays (New Haven: Yale UP, 1978).
k197. ----------. "Heidegger's Hermeneutic Reading of Holderlin: The Signs of Time." Eighteenth Century 21 (1980), 41-66.
k198. ----------. "Poetic Sense and Poetic Reference." PLL 17.1 (1981), 53-61.

k199. Muto, Susan. "Reading the Symbolic Text: Some Reflections on Interpretation," in A. Van Kaam and S. Muto, eds. Creative Formation of Life and World (Washington DC: UP of America, 1982), 113-35 [on Ricoeur].

k200. Nagle, Rainer. "Text, History and the Critical Subject: Notes on Peter Szondi's Theory and Praxis of Hermeneutics." Boundary 11.3 (1983), 29-51.

k201. Nassen, Ulrich, ed. Studien zur Entwicklung einer materialen Hermeneutik (Munich: Fink, 1979).
k202. ----------, ed. Klassiker der Hermeneutik (Paderborn: Schoningh, 1982).

k203. Orr, Leonard. "From Procrustean Criticism to Process Hermeneutics." SubStance 25 (1980), 74-86.
k204. ----------. "The Hermeneutic Interplay." Journal of Thought 16.4 (1981), 85-97.
k205. ----------, ed. De-Structing the Novel: Essays in Applied Postmodern Hermeneutics (Troy NY: Whitston, 1982).
k206. ----------. "The Post-Turn Turn: Derrida, Gadamer, and the Re-Mystification of Language." Journal of Literary Criticism 1.2 (1984), 23-35.
k207. ----------. "Thinking and Poetry: Heidegger and Literary Criticism." Studia Neophilologica, forthcoming.

k208. Ott, Heinrich. "Hermeneutics and the Personal Structure of Language," in J. J. Kockelmans, ed. On Heidegger and Language (Evanston: Northwestern UP, 1972), 169-93.

k209. Palmer, Richard E. Hermeneutics: Interpretation Theory in Schleiermacher, Dilthey, Heidegger, and Gadamer (Evanston: Northwestern UP, 1969).
k210. ----------. "Postmodernity and Hermeneutics." Boundary 5 (1977), 363-93.
k211. ----------. "Postmodern Hermeneutics and the Act of Reading." R&L 15.3 (1983), 55-84.

k212. Pasternack, Gerhardt. "Interpretation of Methodological Procedure: Methodological Fundaments of a Normed Hermeneutics." Poetics 12.2-3 (1983), 185-205.

k213. Peck, Jeffrey M. "Bibliography of Hermeneutics: Literary and Biblical Interpretation." CCrit 5 (1983), 347-56.

k214. Peeters, L. "Hermeneutics." UES 16.2 (1978), 12-19.

k215. Pellauer, David. "The Significance of the Text in Paul Ricoeur's Hermeneutical Theory," in C. E. Reagan, ed. Studies in the Philosophy of Paul Ricoeur (Athens: Ohio UP, 1979), 97-114.

k216. Poulain, Jacques. "La Quete de l'authenticité: La Fragmentation du vrai ou l'herméneutique cassée." RUO 55.4 (1985), 209-29.

k217. Rantavaara, Ira. "Hermeneutics and Literary Research," in B. Kopeczi and G. M. Vajda, eds. Actes du VIIIe Congres de l'Association Internationale de Littérature Comparée (Stuttgart: Bieber, 1980), 605-09 [discusses Gadamer, Heidegger].

k218. Reagan, Charles E. "Psychoanalysis as Hermeneutics," in C. E. Reagan, ed. Studies in the Philosophy of Paul Ricoeur (Athens: Ohio UP, 1979), 141-61.
k219. ----------. "Hermeneutics and the Semantics of Action." Pre/Text 4.3-4 (1983), 239-55.

k220. Reisinger, Peter. "Uber die Zirkelnatur des Verstehens in der traditionellen Hermeneutik." PJGG 81 (1974), 88-104.

k221. Ricoeur, Paul. History and Truth (Evanston: Northwestern UP, 1965).
k222. ----------. "Le probleme du 'double'-sens comme probleme herméneutique et comme probleme sémantique." CIS 12 (1966), 59-71.

k223. ----------. Freud and Philosophy: An Essay on Interpretation (New Haven: Yale UP, 1970).

k224. ----------. "The Model of the Text: Meaningful Action Considered as a Text." NLH 5 (1973), 91-117.

k225. ----------. "Ethics and Culture: Habermas and Gadamer in Dialogue." Philosophy Today 17 (1973), 153-65.

k226. ----------. "The Hermeneutical Function of Distanciation." Philosophy Today 17 (1973), 129-41.

k227. ----------. "Metaphor and the Main Problem of Hermeneutics." NLH 6 (1974), 95-110.

k228. ----------. The Conflict of Interpretations: Essays in Hermeneutics (Evanston: Northwestern UP, 1974).

k229. ----------. "Phenomenology and Hermeneutics." Nous 9 (1975), 85-102.

k230. ----------. Interpretation Theory: Discourse and the Surplus of Meaning (Ft. Worth: Texas Christian UP, 1976).

k231. ----------. "Expliquer et comprendre: Sur quelques connexions rémarquables entre la théorie du texte, la théorie de l'action et la théorie de l'histoire." RPL 75 (1977), 126-47.

k232. ----------. "The Metaphorical Process as Cognition, Imagination, and Feeling." CritI 5 (1978), 143-59.

k233. ----------. The Rule of Metaphor: Multi-Disciplinary Studies of the Creation of Meaning in Language (Toronto: U of Toronto P, 1978).

k234. ----------. The Philosophy of Paul Ricoeur: An Anthology of His Work (Boston: Beacon P, 1978).

k235. ----------. "Narrative Time." CritI 7 (1980), 169-90.

k236. ----------. "Narrative and Hermeneutics," in J. Fisher, ed. Essays on Aesthetics (Philadelphia: Temple UP, 1981), 149-60.

k237. ----------. Hermeneutics and the Human Sciences: Essays on Language, Action and Interpretation (Cambridge: Cambridge UP; Paris: Editions de la Maison des Sciences de l'Homme, 1981).

k238. ----------. Temps et Récit, 3 vols. (Paris: Seuil, 1983-85) [Time and Narrative, 3 vols. (Chicago: U of Chicago P, 1984-88)].

k239. ----------. "The Text as Dynamic Identity," in M. Valdes and O. Miller, eds. Identity of the Literary Text (Toronto: U of Toronto P, 1985), 175-86.

k240. Riffaterre, Michael. "Hermeneutic Models." PoT 4 (1983), 7-16.

k241. Rogers, Robert. "Science, Psychoanalysis and the Interpretation of Literature." Poetics 13.4-5 (1984), 309-24.

k242. Rorty, Richard. Philosophy and the Mirror of Nature (Princeton: Princeton UP, 1979).

k243. Rosenberg, Rainer. "Literaturgeschichte und Werkinterpretation: Wilhelm Diltheys Verstehenslehre und das Problem einer wissenschaftlichen Hermeneutik." WB 26.1 (1980), 113-42.

k244. Rosenfeld, Alvin H. "The Being of Language and the Language of Being: Heidegger and Modern Poetics." Boundary 4 (1976), 535-53.

k245. Sass, Hans-Martin. Martin Heidegger: Bibliography and Glossary (Bowling Green OH: Philosophy Documentation Center, Bowling Green State U, 1982).

k246. Savile, Anthony. "Historicity and the Hermeneutic Circle." NLH 10 (1978), 49-70.

k247. Schlaffer, Heinz. "Die Enstehung des hermeneutischen Bewusstseins: Eine historische Kritik von Gadamers *Wahrheit und Methode*." LiLi 17 (1975), 62-74.

k248. Schleiermacher, F. E. "The Hermeneutics: Outline of the 1819 Lectures." NLH 10 (1978), 1-16.

k249. Schneidau, Herbert. "For Interpretation." MissR 2.1 (1978), 70-88.

k250. Scott, Nathan A., Jr. "Gadamer's *Truth and Method* ." Boundary 5 (1977), 629-37.

k251. Seung, T. K. Semiotics and Thematics in Hermeneutics (NY: Columbia UP, 1982).
k252. ----------. Structuralism and Hermeneutics (NY: Columbia UP, 1982).

k253. Shapiro, Gary and Alan Sica, eds. Hermeneutics: Questions & Prospects (Amherst: U of Massachusetts P, 1984).

k254. Skinner, Quentin. "Motives, Intentions, and the Interpretation of Texts." NLH 3 (1972), 393-408.
k255. ----------. "Hermeneutics and the Role of History." NLH 7 (1975), 209-32.

k256. Soring, J. "Grenzen der Lesbarkeit: Uber die Kunst des Versagens." BCILA 43 (1986), 189-211.

k257. Spanos, William V. "The Detective and the Boundary: Some Notes on the Postmodern Literary Imagination." Boundary 1 (1972), 147-68.

k258. ----------. "Heidegger, Kierkegaard, and the Hermeneutic Circle:
Towards a Postmodern Theory of Interpretation as Dis-Closure." Boundary
4 (1976), 455-88.

k259. ----------. "Breaking the Circle: Hermeneutics as Dis-Closure."
Boundary 5 (1977), 421-57.

k260. ----------. "Hermeneutics and Memory: Destroying T. S. Eliot's *Four
Quartets*." Genre 11 (1978), 523-73.

k261. ----------, *et al.* Martin Heidegger and the Question of Literature
(Bloomington: Indiana UP, 1979).

k262. ----------. "Retrieving Heidegger's De-Struction." SCE Reports 8
(1980), 30-53.

k263. Sprinker, Michael. "Hermeneutic Hesitation: The Stuttering Text."
Boundary 9 (1980), 217-32.

k264. Stierle, Karlheinz. "Text als Handlung und Text als Werk," in M.
Fuhrmann, H. R. Jauss, and W. Pannenberg, eds. Text und Applikation:
Theologie, Jurisprudenz und Literaturwissenschaft im hermeneutischen
Gesprach (Munich: Fink, 1981), 537-46.

k265. Stout, Jeffrey. "What Is the Meaning of a Text?" NLH 14.1 (1982), 1-
12.

k266. Swearingen, James. "Philosophical Hermeneutics and the Renewal of
Tradition." ECent 22.3 (1981), 195-222.

k267. "Symposium on Hirsch's *Validity in Interpretation* ." Genre 1 (1968),
169-255.

k268. Szondi, Peter. "Introduction to Literary Hermeneutics." NLH 10
(1978), 17-29.

k269. Tatham, Campbell. "High-Altitude Hermeneutics." Diacritics 3.2
(1973), 22-31 [on Palmer].

k270. Thompson, John B. Critical Hermeneutics: A Study in the Thought of
Paul Ricoeur and Jurgen Habermas (Cambridge: Cambridge UP, 1981).

k271. Toulmin, Stephen. "The Construal of Reality: Criticism in Modern
and Postmodern Science." CritI 9.1 (1982), 93-111.

k272. Turk, Horst. Dialektischer Dialog: Literaturwissenschaftliche
Untersuchung zum Problem der Verstandigung (Gottingen: Vandenhoeck,
1975).

k273. Valdes, Mario J. Phenomenological Hermeneutics and the Study of Literature (Toronto: U of Toronto P, 1987).

k274. Van de Pitte, M. M. "Hermeneutics and the 'Crisis' of Literature." BJA 24.2 (1984), 99-112.

k275. Van Rutten, Pierre-M. "Herméneutique et esthétique." SpM 10 (1978), 68-78.

k276. Vasina, Dirk F. "Bibliographie de Paul Ricoeur, compléments (jusqu'a la fin de 1967)." Revue philosophique de Louvain 66 (1968), 85-101.
k277. ----------. "Bibliographie de Paul Ricoeur, compléments (jusqu'a la fin de 1972)." Revue philosophique de Louvain 72 (1974), 156-81.
k278. ----------. "Bibliography of Paul Ricoeur," in C. E. Reagan, ed. Studies in the Philosophy of Paul Ricoeur (Athens: Ohio UP, 1979), 179-94.

k279. Velkley, Richard L. "Gadamer and Kant: The Critique of Modern Aesthetic Consciousness in Truth and Method." IJPP 9.2-3 (1981), 353-64.

k280. Waniek, Erdmann. "Looking and Reading: In Search of a Tertium Comparationis ." BuR 26.1 (1981), 131-38 [discusses Gadamer].

k281. Warnke, Georgia. Gadamer: Hermeneutics, Tradition and Reason (Stanford CA: Stanford UP, 1987).

k282. Watson, Stephen. "Between Truth and Method: Gadamer and the Problem of Justification in Interpretive Practices." UDR 17.1 (1984), 21-31.

k283. Weimar, Klaus. Historische Einleitung zur literaturwissenschaftlichen Hermeneutik (Tubingen: Mohr, 1975).
k284. ----------. Enzyklopadie der Literaturwissenschaft (Munchen: Francke, 1980), §§281-377.

k285. Weinsheimer, Joel C. "'London' and the Fundamental Problem of Hermeneutics." CritI 9 (1982), 303-22.
k286. ----------. Gadamer's Hermeneutics: A Reading of Truth and Method (New Haven: Yale UP, 1985).

k287. Werner, Hans-Georg. "Methodische Probleme wirkungsorientierter Untersuchungen zur Dichtungsgeschichte." WB 25.8 (1979), 14-28.
k288. ----------. "Subjektive Aneignung--objektive Wertung." WB 26.10 (1980), 55-67.

k289. Wilson, Barrie A., *et al*. Interpretation, Meta-Interpretation, and *Oedipus Tyrannus* (Berkeley: Center for Hermeneutical Studies in Hellenistic & Modern Culture, 1980).

k290. Witte, Hans. "Herméneutique symbolique et réunification du réel." CIS 12 (1966), 85-98.

k291. Wolff, Janet. Hermeneutic Philosophy and the Sociology of Art (London: Routledge & Kegan Paul, 1975).

L. Deconstruction, Post-Structuralist Criticism, Post-Deconstructive Criticism

L1. Abel, Lionel. "Jacques Derrida: His *'Difference'* with Metaphysics." Salmagundi 25 (1974), 3-21.

L2. Abrams, M. H. "The Deconstructive Angel." CritI 3 (1977), 425-38.
L3. ----------. "Behaviorism and Deconstruction: A Comment on Morse Peckham's 'The Infinitude of Pluralism.'" CritI 4 (1977), 181-93.
L4. ----------. "How to Do Things With Texts." PR 46 (1979), 566-88.
L5. ----------. "Construing and Deconstructing," in P. Demers, ed. The Creating Word (Edmonton: U of Alberta P, 1986), 30-65.

L6. Adams, Michael Vannoy. "Deconstructive Philosophy and Imaginal Psychology: Comprative Perspectives on Jacques Derrida and James Hillman." Jour of Lit. Crit. 2.1 (1985), 23-39.

L7. Allen, Carolyn J. "Feminist Criticism and Postmodernism," in J. Natoli, ed. Tracing Literary Theory (Urbana: U of Illinois P, 1987), 278-305.

L8. Allison, David. Translator's Preface to J. Derrida, Speech and Phenomena and Other Essays on Husserl's Theory of Signs (Evanston: Northwestern UP, 1973), xxxi-xliii.
L9. ----------. "Derrida and Wittgenstein: Playing the Game." Research in Phenomenology 8 (1978), 93-109.
L10. ----------. *"Destruction/Deconstruction* in the Text of Nietzsche." Boundary 8.1 (1979), 197-222.

L11. Alter, Robert. "The Decline and Fall of Literary Criticism."
Commentary 77.3 (Mar., 1984), 50-56.

L12. Altieri, Charles. "Wittgenstein on Consciousness and Language: A
Challenge to Derridean Literary Theory." MLN 91 (1976), 1397-1423.
L13. ----------. "The Hermeneutics of Literary Indeterminacy: A Dissent
from the New Orthodoxy." NLH 10 (1978), 71-99.

L14. Appiah, Anthony. "Deconstruction and the Philosophy of Language."
Diacritics 16.1 (1986), 49-64 [on Norris].

L15. Arac, Jonathan. "The Criticism of Harold Bloom: Judgment and
History." Centrum 6 (1978), 32-42.
L16. ----------. "The Function of Foucault at the Present Time." Humanities
in Society 3 (1980), 73-86.
L17. ----------. "To Regress from the Rigor of Shelley: Figures of History in
American Deconstructive Criticism." Boundary 8.3 (1980), 241-57.
L18. ----------. "Aesthetics, Rhetoric, History: Reading Nietzsche with
Henry James." Boundary 9.3 (1981), 437-54 [on de Man].
L19. ----------, Wlad Godzich, and Wallace Martin, eds. The Yale Critics:
Deconstruction in America (Minneapolis: U of Minnesota P, 1983) [on
Bloom, Hartman, de Man, Miller].
L20. ----------, ed. Postmodernism and Politics (Minneapolis: U of
Minnesota P, 1986).
L21. ----------. Critical Genealogies: Historical Situations for Postmodern
Literary Studies (NY: Columbia UP, 1987).
L22. ----------, ed. After Foucault (New Brunswick NJ: Rutgers UP, 1988).

L23. Argyros, Alexander. "Daughters of the Desert." Diacritics 10.3
(1980), 27-35 [on Derrida].
L24. ----------. "The Possibility of History." NOR 8.3 (1981), 230-35 [on
Derrida and Foucault].
L25. ----------. "The Residual Difference: Wallace Stevens and American
Deconstruction." NOR 13.1 (1986), 20-31 [Hillis Miller, Riddel].

L26. Atkins, G. Douglas. "J. Hillis Miller, Deconstruction, and the Recovery
of Transcendence." NDEJ 13.1 (1980), 51-63.
L27. ----------. "The Both/and Nature of Deconstruction." CE 42 (1980),
304-05.
L28. ----------. "The Sign as a Structure of Difference: Derridean
Deconstruction and Some of Its Implications," in R. T. DeGeorge, ed.
Semiotic Themes (Lawrence: U of Kansas, 1981), 133-47.
L29. ----------. Reading Deconstruction/Deconstructive Reading (Lexington:
UP of Kentucky, 1983).

L30. ----------. "Partial Stories: Hebraic and Christian Thinking in the Wake of Deconstruction." R&L 15.3 (1983), 7-21.

L31. ----------. "'Count It All Joy': The Affirmative Nature of Deconstruction." HSL 15-16 (1983-84), 120-28.

L32. ----------. "A(fter) D(econstruction): The Relations of Literature and Religion in the Wake of Deconstruction." SLitI 18.1 (1985), 89-100.

L33. ---------- and Michael L. Johnson, eds. Writing and Reading Differently: Deconstruction and the Teaching of Composition and Literature (Lawrence: UP of Kansas, 1985).

L34. ----------. Quests of Difference: Reading Pope's Poems (Lexington: U of Kentucky P, 1986).

L35. Bahti, Timothy. "Ambiguity and Indeterminacy: The Juncture." CL 38.3 (1986), 209-23 [discusses Hartman].

L36. Bandera, Cesareo. "Notes on Derrida, Tombstones, and the Representational Game." SFR 6.2-3 (1982), 311-25.

L37. Barber, Karin. "Yoruba *Oriki* and Deconstructive Criticism." RAL 15.4 (1984), 497-518.

L38. Barney, Richard A. "Deconstructive Criticism: A Selected Bibliography." SCE Reports 8 supp. (1980), 1-54.

L39. ----------. "Uncanny Criticism in the United States," in J. Natoli, ed. Tracing Literary Theory (Urbana: U of Illinois P, 1987), 177-212.

L40. Barnouw, Jeffrey. "Peirce and Derrida: 'Natural Signs' Empiricism versus 'Originary Trace' Deconstruction." PoT 7.1 (1986), 73-94.

L41. Barrow, Craig. "'Deconstruction' and the Self." HS 57 (1983), 6-7.

L42. Barzilai, Shuli and Morton W. Bloomfield. "New Criticism and Deconstructive Criticism; Or, What's New?" NLH 18.1 (1986), 151-69.

L43. Bass, Alan. "'Literature'/ Literature," in R. Macksey, ed. Velocities of Change (Baltimore: Johns Hopkins UP, 1974), 341-53 [on Derrida].

L44. ----------. "The Double Game: An Introduction," in J. H. Smith and W. Kerrigan, eds. Taking Chances: Derrida, Psychoanalysis, and Literature (Baltimore: Johns Hopkins UP, 1984), 66-85.

L45. Bassett, Sharon. "Tristes Critiques: Harold Bloom and the Sorrows of Secular Art." Literature & Psychology 27 (1977), 106-12.

L46. Baudrillard, Jean. The Mirror of Production (St. Louis: Telos P, 1975).

L47. ----------. Oublier Foucault (Paris: Galilée, 1977) ["Forgetting Foucault." Humanities in Society 3 (1980), 87-111].
L48. ----------. For a Critique of the Political Economy of the Sign (St. Louis: Telos, 1981).
L49. ----------. In the Shadow of the Silent Majorities. . . . (NY: Semiotexte(e), 1983).
L50. ----------. Simulations (NY: Semiotext(e), 1983).

L51. Beehler, Michael. T. S. Eliot, Wallace Stevens, and the Discourse of Difference (Baton Rouge: Louisiana State UP, 1986).

L52. Belsey, Catherine. Critical Practice (London: Methuen, 1980).

L53. Benhabib, Seyla. "Epistemologies of Postmodernism: A Rejoinder to Jean-François Lyotard." New German Critique 33 (1985), 103-26.

L54. Bennington, Geoff. "August: Double Justice." Diacritics 14.3 (1984), 64-71 [on Lyotard and J.-L. Thébaud].
L55. ----------. "Lyotard: From Discourse and Figure to Experimentation and Event." Paragraph 6 (1985), 19-27.

L56. Berezdivin, Ruben. "Gloves Inside-Out." Research in Phenomenology 8 (1978), 111-26 [on Derrida].
L57. ----------. "In Stalling Metaphysics: At the Threshold," in J. Sallis, ed. Deconstruction and Philosophy: The Texts of Jacques Derrida (Chicago: U of Chicago P, 1987), 47-59.

L58. Berg, Temma F. "Wrestling with the Deconstructive Angel." Reader 12 (1984), 1-10 [Derrida and reader-response criticism].

L59. Berman, Art. From the New Criticism to Deconstruction: The Reception of Structuralism and Post-Structuralism (Urbana: U of Illinois P, 1988) [chaps. 7-10 on post-structuralism and deconstruction].

L60. Berman, Marshall. Everything That Is Solid Melts Into Air (NY: Simon & Schuster, 1982).

L61. Bernasconi, Robert. "Deconstruction and the Possibility of Ethics," in J. Sallis, ed. Deconstruction and Philosophy: The Texts of Jacques Derrida (Chicago: U of Chicago P, 1987), 122-39.

L62. Bernauer, James and David Rasmussen, eds. The Final Foucault (Cambridge: M.I.T. Press, 1988) [includes comprehensive bibliography, "The Works of Michel Foucault 1954-1984," 118-58].

L63. Bloom, Harold. The Anxiety of Influence: A Theory of Poetry (NY: Oxford UP, 1973).

L64. ----------. A Map of Misreading (NY: Oxford UP, 1975).

L65. ----------. Kabbalah and Criticism (NY: Oxford UP, 1975).

L66. ----------. "The Freshness of Transformation: Emerson's Dialectics of Influence," in D. Levin, ed. Emerson: Prophecy, Metamorphosis, Influence (NY: Columbia UP, 1975), 129-48.

L67. ----------. Figures of Capable Imagination (NY: Seabury, 1976).

L68. ----------. Poetry and Repression: Revisionism from Blake to Stevens (New Haven: Yale UP, 1976).

L69. ----------. Wallace Stevens: The Poems of Our Climate (Ithaca: Cornell UP, 1977).

L70. ----------. "The Breaking of Form," in Deconstruction and Criticism (NY: Seabury P, 1979), 1-37.

L71. ----------. Agon: Towards a Theory of Revisionism (NY: Oxford UP, 1982).

L72. ----------. The Breaking of the Vessels (Chicago: U of Chicago P, 1982).

L73. Bogel, Fredric V. "Deconstructive Criticism: The Logic of Derrida's Difference." Centrum 6 (1978), 50-60.

L74. Boly, John R. "Nihilism Aside: Derrida's Debate Over Intentional Models." P&L 9.2 (1985), 152-65.

L75. Bové, Paul. Destructive Poetics: Heidegger and Modern American Poetry (NY: Columbia UP, 1980).

L76. ----------. "Variations on Authority: Some Deconstructive Transformations of the New Criticism," in J. Arac, W. Godzich, and W. Martin, eds. The Yale Critics: Deconstruction in America (Minneapolis: U of Minnesota P, 1983), 3-19.

L77. ----------. "The Foucault Phenomenon: The Problematics of Style," in G. Deleuze, Foucault (Minneapolis: U of Minnesota P, 1988), vii-xl.

L78. Bowie, Andrew. "Individuality and Différance ." OLR 7.1-2 (1985), 117-30.

L79. Boyne, Roy. "Alcibiades as Hero: Derrida/Nietzsche?" Sub-Stance 28 (1980), 25-36.

L80. Brenkman, John. "Narcissus in the Text." GaR 30 (1976), 293-327.

L81. Brink, André. "Transgressions: A Quantum Approach to Literary Deconstruction." JLSTL 1.3 (1985), 10-26.

L82. Brooker, Peter. "Post-Structuralism, Reading and the Crisis in English," in P. Widdowson, ed. Re-Reading English (London: Methuen, 1982), 61-76.

L83. Brown, P. L. "Epistemology and Method: Althusser, Foucault, Derrida." Research in Phenomenology 8 (1978), 147-62.

L84. Bruns, Gerald L. "Structuralism, Deconstruction, and Hermeneutics." Diacritics 14.1 (1984), 12-23 [on Culler and Gadamer].

L85. Bruss, Elizabeth. Beautiful Theories: The Spectacle of Discourse in Contemporary Criticism (Baltimore: Johns Hopkins UP, 1982).

L86. Brutting, Richard. "Ecriture" und "Texte": Die franzosische Literaturtheorie nach dem Strukturalismus (Bonn: Grundmann, 1976).

L87. Buci-Glucksmann, Christine. "Déconstruction et critique marxiste de la philosophie." L'Arc 54 (1973), 20-32.

L88. Butler, Christopher. Interpretation, Deconstruction and Ideology (London: Oxford UP, 1984).

L89. Cain, William E. The Crisis in Criticism: Theory, Literature and Reform in English Studies (Baltimore: Johns Hopkins UP, 1984).

L90. Campa, Roman de la. "Mainstreaming Poststructuralist and Feminist Thought: Jonathan Culler's Poetics." JMMLA 18.2 (1985), 20-27.

L91. Campbell, Colin. "The Tyranny of the Yale Critics." NY Times Magazine (Feb. 9, 1986), 20 ff.

L92. Cantor, Jay. "On Stanley Cavell." Raritan 1.1 (1981), 48-67 [and deconstruction].

L93. Caputo, John D. "The Economy of Signs in Husserl and Derrida: From Usefulness to Full Employment," in J. Sallis, ed. Deconstruction and Philosophy: The Texts of Jacques Derrida (Chicago: U of Chicago P, 1987), 99-113.
L94. ----------. Radical Hermeneutics: Repetition, Deconstruction, and the Hermeneutic Project (Bloomington: Indiana UP, 1987).

L95. Caraher, Brian G. "Allegories of Reading : Positing a Rhetoric of Romanticism; or, Paul de Man's Critique of Pure Figural Anteriority." Pre/Text 4.1 (1983), 9-51.

L96. ----------. "The Work of Discourse in the Age of Mechanical Reproduction." W&D 2.1 (1984), 7-18 [discusses Benjamin and Foucault].

L97. Carlton, Susan Ruth. "On Authors, Readers, and Phenomenology: Husserlian Intentionality in the Literary Theories of E. D. Hirsch and Jacques Derrida." DAI 45 (1985), 3630A.

L98. Carroll, David. "Freud and the Myth of Origins." NLH 6 (1975), 511-28.
L99. ----------. "Disruptive Discourse and Critical Power: The Conditions of Archaeology and Genealogy." HIS 5.3-4 (1982), 175-200 [discusses Foucault].
L100. ----------. The Subject in Question: The Languages of Theory and the Strategies of Fiction (Chicago: U of Chicago P, 1982).
L101. ----------. "Rephrasing the Political with Kant and Lyotard: From Aesthetic to Political Judgements." Diacriticis 14.3 (1984), 74-88.
L102. ----------. "Institutional Authority vs. Critical Power, or the Uneasy Relations of Psychoanalysis and Literature," in J. H. Smith and W. Kerrigan, eds. Taking Chances: Derrida, Psychoanalysis, and Literature (Baltimore: Johns Hopkins UP, 1984), 107-34.
L103. ----------. "Narrative, Heterogeneity, and the Question of the Political: Bakhtin and Lyotard," in M. Krieger, ed.The Aims of Representation: Subject/ Text/ History (NY: Columbia UP, 1987), 69-106.
L104. ----------. Paraesthetics: Foucault, Lyotard, Derrida (NY& London: Methuen, 1987).

L105. Cascardi, A. J. "Skepticism and Deconstruction." P&L 8.1 (1984), 1-14.

L106. Certeau, Michel de. Heterologies: Discourse on the Other (Minneapolis: U of Minnesota P, 1986) [sec. IV is on Foucault].

L107. Chase, Cynthia. "The Decomposition of the Elephants: Double-Reading Daniel Deronda," PMLA 93 (1978), 215-27.
L108. ----------. "The Accidents of Disfiguration: Limits to Literal and Rhetorical Reading in Book V of The Prelude." SiR 18 (1979), 547-66.
L109. ----------. "Paragon, Perergon: Baudelaire Translates Rousseau." Diacritics 11.2 (1981), 42-51.

L110. Chilton, Paul. "Autonomy and Paradox in Literary Theory." JLS 12.1 (1983), 73-91 [on Culler].

L111. Chnaiderman, Miriam. "Narrating the Narrative: Impasses of Psychoanalysis and Literary Analysis." Dispositio 6 (1981), 165-68 [on Derrida and Lacan].

L112. Clark, Michael. "Putting Humpty Together Again: Essays Toward Integrative Analysis." PoT 3.1 (1982), 159-70.

L113. Clarke, Michael. Michel Foucault: An Annotated Bibliography (NY: Garland, 1983).

L114. Comley, Nancy R. "A Release from Weak Specifications: Liberating the Student Reader," in G. Atkins and M. L. Johnson, eds. Writing and Reading Differently: Deconstruction and the Teaching of Composition and Literature (Lawrence: UP of Kansas, 1985), 129-38.

L115. Conley, Tom. "A Trace of Style," in M. Krupnick, ed. Displacement: Derrida and After (Bloomington: Indiana UP, 1983), 74-92.

L116. Cooper, Barry. Michel Foucault: An Introduction to His Thought (Toronto: Edwin Mellen, 1981).

L117. Corngold, Stanley. "Error in Paul de Man," in J. Arac, W. Godzich, and W. Martin, eds. The Yale Critics: Deconstruction in America (Minneapolis: U of Minnesota P, 1983), 90-108.

L118. Cornwell, Neil. "Roland Barthes: A Man for all *Ecritures* ." EiP 10.1 (1985), 50-65.

L119. Cotrau, Liviu. "Dis-Placing and Re-Placing the Center: The Decentered Discourse." CREL 2 (1985), 100-09.

L120. Cousins, Mark. "The Logic of Deconstruction." OLR 3.2 (1978), 70-77.
L121. ---------- and Athar Hussein. Michel Foucault (London: Macmillan; NY: St. Martin's, 1984).

L122. Crafton, John Michael. "The Death of Man and the Birth of Writing." WGCR 18 (1986), 39-45 [on Derrida and Lacan].

L123. Cressole, Michel. Deleuze (Paris: Universitaires, 1973).

L124. Crowley, Sharon. "On Post-Structuralism and Compositionists." Pre/Text 5.3-4 (1984), 185-95.
L125. ----------. "writing and Writing," in G. Atkins and M. L. Johnson, eds. Writing and Reading Differently: Deconstruction and the Teaching of Composition and Literature (Lawrence: UP of Kansas, 1985), 93-100.

L126. Culler, Jonathan. "Frontiers of Criticism." Yale Review 61 (1971-72), 259-71 [on de Man].

L127. ----------. "Reading and Misreading." Yale Review 65 (1975), 88-95 [on Bloom and Hartman].

L128. ----------. "Jacques Derrida," in J. Sturrock, ed. Structuralism and Since: From Lévi-Strauss to Derrida (NY: Oxford UP, 1979), 154-80.

L129. ----------. "Structuralism and Grammatology." Boundary 8.1 (1979), 75-85.

L130. ----------. "Semiotics and Deconstruction." PoT 1.1-2 (1979), 137-41.

L131. ----------. "Meaning and Convention: Derrida and Austin." NLH 13 (1981), 15-30.

L132. ----------. The Pursuit of Signs: Semiotics, Literature, Deconstruction (London: Routledge & Kegan Paul, 1981).

L133. ----------. On Deconstruction: Theory and Criticism after Structuralism (Ithaca: Cornell UP, 1982).

L134. ----------. "At the Boundaries: Barthes and Derrida," in H. L. Sussman, ed. At the Boundaries (Boston: Northeastern UP, 1983), 23-45.

L135. Cumming, Robert Denoon. "The Odd Couple: Heidegger and Derrida." Review of Metaphysics 34 (1981), 487-521.

L136. Cunningham, Valentine. "Renoving that Bible: That Absolute Text of (Post)Modernism," in F. Gloversmith, ed. The Theory of Reading (Brighton, Sussex: Harvester; Totowa NJ: Barnes & Noble, 1984), 1-51 [discusses Culler, Derrida, J. Hillis Miller].

L137. D'Amico, Robert. "What Is Discourse?" HIS 5.3-4 (1982), 201-12 [on Foucault].

L138. Dasenbrock, Reed Way. "Accounting for the Changing Certainties of Interpretive Communities." MLN 101.5 (1986), 1022-41.

L139. Davidson, Arnold I. "Archaeology, Genealogy, Ethics," in D. C. Hoy, ed. Foucault: A Critical Reader (Oxford: Basil Blackwell, 1986), 221-33.

L140. Davis, Robert Con. "The Case for a Post-Structuralist Mimesis: John Barth and Imitation." AJS 3.3 (1985), 49-72.

L141. ---------- and Ronald Schleifer, eds. Rhetoric and Form: Deconstruction at Yale (Norman: U of Oklahoma P, 1985) [includes Davis' "Error at Yale: Geoffrey Hartman, Psychoanalysis, and Deconstruction," 135-56].

L142. Debicki, Andrew P. "New Criticism and Deconstruction: Two Attitudes in Teaching Poetry," in G. Atkins and M. L. Johnson, eds. Writing and Reading Differently: Deconstruction and the Teaching of Composition and Literature (Lawrence: UP of Kansas, 1985), 169-84.

L143. De Bolla, Peter. "Disfiguring History." <u>Diacritics</u> 16.4 (1986), 49-58 [deconstruction and historical analysis].

L144. Degreef, J. "De la métaphore (a propos de <u>La mythologie blanche</u> de Derrida)." <u>CLLA</u> 3-4 (1971), 45-50.

L145. Deleuze, Gilles. <u>Différence et répétition</u> (Parsi: PUF, 1969).
L146. ----------. <u>Logique du sens</u> (Paris: Minuit, 1969).
L147. ----------. <u>Un Nouvel archiviste</u> (Paris: Fata Morgana, 1972) [on Foucault].
L148. ----------. <u>Proust and Signs</u> (NY: George Braziller, 1972).
L149. ---------- and Félix Guattari. <u>Kafka: Pour une littérature mineure</u> (Paris: Minuit, 1975).
L150. ---------- and Félix Guattari. <u>Rhizome</u> (Paris: Minuit, 1976).
L151. ---------- and C. Barnet. <u>Dialogues</u> (Paris: Flammarion, 1977).
L152. ---------- and Félix Guattari. <u>Anti-Oedipus: Capitalism and Schizophrenia</u> (Minneapolis: U of Minnesota P, 1983).
L153. ----------. <u>Foucault</u> (Paris: Minuit, 1986) [Minneapolis: U of Minnesota P, 1988].

L154. Denham, Robert. "The No-Man's Land of Competing Patterns." <u>CritI</u> 4.1 (1977), 194-202.

L155. "Derrida." <u>OLR</u> 3.2 (1978) [special issue].

L156. Derrida, Jacques. <u>L'Ecriture et difference</u> (Paris: Seuil, 1967) [<u>Writing and Difference</u> (Chicago: U of Chicago P, 1978)].
L157. ----------. <u>La voix et le phénomene</u> (Paris: PUF, 1967) [<u>Speech and Phenomena</u> (Evanston: Northwestern UP, 1972)].
L158. ----------. <u>De la grammatologie</u> (Paris: Minuit, 1967) [<u>Of Grammatology</u> (Baltimore: Johns Hopkins UP, 1976)].
L159. ----------. "The Ends of Man." <u>Philoosphy and Phenomenological Research</u> 30 (1969), 31-57.
L160. ----------. <u>La Dissemination</u> (Paris: Seuil, 1972) [<u>Dissemination</u> (Chicago: U of Chicago P, 1981)].
L161. ----------. <u>Marges de la philosophie</u> (Paris: Minuit, 1972) [<u>Margins of Philosophy</u> (Chicago: U of Chicago P, 1982)].
L162. ----------. <u>Positions</u> (Paris: Minuit, 1972) [<u>Positions</u> (Chicago: U of Chicago P, 1981); interviews].
L163. ----------. "White Mythology: Metaphor in the Text of Philosophy." <u>NLH</u> 6 (1974), 5-74.
L164. ----------. <u>Glas</u> (Paris: Galilée, 1974) [<u>Glas</u> (Lincoln: U of Nebraska P, 1987)].
L165. ----------. "Ou commence et comment finit un corps enseignant," in D. Grisoni, ed. <u>Politiques de la philosophie</u> (Paris: Grasset, 1976), 55-97.

L166. ----------. "Entre crochets." Diagraphe 8 (1976), 97-114 [interview].
L167. ----------. "Ja, ou le faux-bond." Diagraphe 11 (1977), 83-121 [interview].
L168. ----------. "Signature Event Context." Glyph 1 (1977), 172-97.
L169. ----------. "Limited Inc abc." Glyph 2 (1977), 162-254.
L170. ----------. "Fors: the English Words of Nicolas Abraham and Maria Torok." Georgia Rev 31.1 (1977), 64-116.
L171. ----------. Spurs: Nietzsche's Styles (Chicago: U of Chicago P, 1978).
L172. ----------. "The Retrait of Metaphor." Enclitic 2.2 (1978), 5-34.
L173. ----------. La Vérité en peinture (Paris: Flammarion, 1978).
L174. ----------. "Living On: Border-lines," in Deconstruction and Criticism (NY: Seabury P, 1979), 75-176.
L175. ----------. "Scribble (Writing-Power)." YFS 58 (1979), 117-47.
L176. ----------. "The Parergon." October 9 (1979), 3-40.
L177. ----------. La Carte postale de Socrate a Freud et au-dela (Paris: Flammarion, 1980).
L178. ----------. The Archaeology of the Frivolous: Reading Condillac (Pittsburgh: Duquesne UP, 1980).
L179. ----------. "The Law of Genre." CritI 1 (1980), 55-81.
L180. ----------. "TITLE (to be specified)." Sub-Stance 31 (1981), 5-22.
L181. ----------. "Economimesis." Diacritics 11.2 (1981), 3-25.
L182. ----------. "Les Morts de Roland Barthes." Poétique 47 (1981), 269-92.
L183. ----------. "The Principle of Reason: The University in the Eyes of Its Pupils." Diacritics 19 (1983), 3-20.
L184. ----------. "No Apocalypse, Not Now (Full Speed Ahead, Seven Missiles, Seven Missives." Diacritics 14.2 (1984), 20-31.
L185. ----------. "My Chance/*Mes Chances* : A Rendezvous with Some Epicurean Stereophonies," in J. H. Smith and W. Kerrigan, eds. Taking Chances: Derrida, Psychoanalysis, and Literature (Baltimore: Johns Hopkins UP, 1984), 1-32.
L186. ----------. "An Idea of Flaubert: 'Plato's Letter.'" MLN 99 (1984), 748-68.
L187. ----------. Signéponge/Signsponge (NY: Columbia UP, 1984).
L188. ----------. "Of an Apocalyptic Tone Recently Adopted in Philosophy." OLR 6.2 (1984), 3-37.
L189. ----------. Otobiographies: l'enseignement de Nietzsche et la politique du nom propre (Paris: Galilée, 1984) [The Ear of the Other: Otobiography, Transference, Translation: Texts and Discusssions with Jacques Derrida (NY: Schocken, 1986)].
L190. ----------. Le Faculté de juger (Paris: Minuit, 1985).
L191. ----------. Parages (Paris: Galilée, 1986).
L192. ----------. Memoires for Paul de Man (NY: Columbia UP, 1986).
L193. ----------. "The Age of Hegel," Glyph n.s. 1 (1986), 3-43.

L194. ----------. "Shibboleth," in G. Hartman and S. Budick, eds. Midrash and Literature (New Haven: Yale UP, 1986), 307-47.
L195. ----------. "Geschlecht II: Heidegger's Hand," in J. Sallis, ed. Deconstruction and Philosophy: The Texts of Jacques Derrida (Chicago: U of Chicago P, 1987), 161-96.

L196. Descombes, Vincent. Modern French Philosophy (Cambridge: Cambridge UP, 1980).

L197. Desmond, William. "Hegel, Dialectic, and Deconstruction." P&R 18.4 (1985), 244-63.

L198. Detweiler, Robert, ed. Derrida and Biblical Studies (Chico CA: Scholar's P, 1982).

L199. Dews, Peter. "The Nouvelle Philosophie and Foucault." Economy and Society 8.2 (1979), 127-71.
L200. ----------. "The Letter and the Line: Discourse and Its Other in Lyotard." Diacritics 14.3 (1984), 40-49.

L201. Donato, Eugenio. "'Here, Now'/ 'Always, Already': Incidental Remarks on Some Recent Characterizations of the Text." Diacritics 6.3 (1976), 25-29 [on Derrida and Said].
L202. ----------. "The Idioms of the Text : Notes on the Language of Philosophy and the Fictions of Literature." Glyph 2 (1977), 1-13.
L203. ---------- and Edward W. Said. "An Exchange on Deconstruction and History." Boundary 8 (1979), 65-74.
L204. ----------. "Historical Imagination and the Idioms of Criticism." Boundary 8.1 (1979), 39-56.
L205. ----------. "Ending/Closure: On Derrida's Edging of Heidegger." YFS 67 (1984), 3-22.

L206. Donoghue, Denis. "Deconstructing Deconstruction." NY Rev of Books (June 12, 1980), 37-41.
L207. ----------. Ferocious Alphabets (Boston: Little, Brown, 1981) [discusses Bloom, Derrida, de Man].

L208. Doueihi, Milad. "Traps of Representation." Diacritics 14.1 (1984), 66-77.

L209. Dreyfus, Hubert and Paul Rabinow. Michel Foucault: Beyond Structuralism and Hermeneutics, 2nd rev. ed. (Chicago: U of Chicago P, 1983).

L210. ----------. "What Is Maturity? Habermas and Foucault on 'What Is Enlightenment," in D. C. Hoy, ed. Foucault: A Critical Reader (Oxford: Basil Blackwell, 1986), 109-21.

L211. Durand, Regis. "On Conversing: In/On Writing." Sub-Stance 27 (1980), 47-51.

L212. Duyfhuizen, Bernard. "Deconstruction and Feminist Literary Theory." TSWL 3.1-2 (1984), 159-69.
L213. ----------. "Questions of Authority and (Dis)Belief in Literary Theory." NOR 12.3 (1985), 67-74.

L214. Eagleton, Terry. "Marxism and Deconstruction." ConL (1981), 477-88.
L215. ----------. Literary Theory: An Introduction (Minneapolis: U of Minnesota P, 1983) [chap. 4 on "Post-Structuralism"].

L216. Eckhardt, Caroline D. "A Commonsensical Protest Against Deconstruction; or How the Real World at Last Became a Fable." Thought 60 (1985), 310-21.

L217. Ehrmann, Jacques. "Dur le jeu et l'origine, ou il est surtout question de la dissémination de Jacques Derrida." Sub-Stance 7 (1973), 113-23.

L218. Federmayer, Eva. "Beyond Formalism: Problems of Interpretation in Harold Bloom's Antithetical Criticism," in T. Frank, ed. The Origins and Originality of American Culture (Budapest: Akademiai Kiado, 1984), 467-75.

L219. Fekete, John. The Structural Allegory: Reconstructive Encounters with the New French Thought (Manchester: Manchester UP, 1984).

L220. Felperin, Howard. "The Anxiety of Deconstruction." YFS 69 (1985), 254-66.
L221. ----------. Beyond Deconstruction: The Uses and Abuses of Literary Theory (Oxford: Clarendon P, 1985).

L222. Ferguson, Frances C. "Reading Heidegger: Paul de Man and Jacques Derrida." Boundary 4.2 (1976), 593-610.

L223. Finas, Lucette, et al. Ecarts: quatre essais a propos de Jacques Derrida (Paris: Fayard, 1973).

L224. Fischer, Michael. Does Deconstruction Make Any Difference? Poststructuralism and the Defense of Poetry in Modern Criticism (Bloomington: Indiana UP, 1985).

L225. Fischer, Roland. "Deconstructing Reality." Diogenes 129 (1985), 47-62.

L226. Fish, Stanley. "With the Compliments of the Author: Reflections on Austin and Derrida." CritI 8 (1982), 693-721.

L227. Fletcher, Angus. "The Perpetual Error." Diacritics 2.4 (1972), 14-20 [on de Man].

L228. Flores, Ralph. The Rhetoric of Doubtful Authority: Deconstructive Readings of Self-Questioning Narratives, St. Augustine to Faulkner (Ithaca: Cornell UP, 1984).

L229. Foley, Barbara. "The Politics of Deconstruction," in R. C. Davis and R. Schleifer, eds. Rhetoric and Form: Deconstruction at Yale (Norman: U of Oklahoma P, 1985), 113-34.

L230. Foster, Hal, ed. The Anti-Aesthetic (Port Townsend: Bay Press, 1983).
L231. ----------. "(Post)modern Polemics." New German Critique 33 (1984), 67-78.

L232. Foster, Stephen William. "Deconstructing a Text on North Africa: Ricoeur and Post-Structuralism." Pre/Text 4.3-4 (1983), 295-315 [discusses Derrida, Foucault, Ricoeur].

L233. Foucault, Michel. Madness and Civilization (NY: Pantheon, 1965).
L234. ----------. Les mots et les choses: une archéologie des sciences humaines (Paris: Gallimard, 1966) [The Order of Things: An Archaeology of the Human Sciences (NY: Pantheon, 1971)].
L235. ----------. L'archéologie du savoir (Paris: Gallimard, 1969) [The Archaeology of Knowledge (NY: Harper Colophon, 1976)].
L236. ----------. "Qu'est-ce qu'un auteur?" Bulletin de la Société française de Philosophie 63 (1969), 73-104 [trans. in Language, Counter-memory, Practice omits comments by Jacques Lacan, Lucien Goldmann, and others].
L237. ----------. "Monstrosities in Criticism." Diacritics 1.1 (1971), 57-60 and "Foucault Responds 2" Diacritics 1.2 (1971), 60 [replies to essays by George Steiner].
L238. ----------. "History, Discourse and Discontinuity." Salmagundi 20 (1972), 225-48.

L239. ----------. Ceci n'est pas une pipe (Montpellier: Fata Morgana, 1973)
[This Is Not a Pipe (Berkeley: U of California P, 1982)].
L240. ----------. The Birth of the Clinic: An Archaeology of Medical
Perception (NY: Pantheon, 1973).
L241. ----------. "Entretien avec Gilles Deleuze, Félix Guattari." Recherches
13 (Dec. 1973), 27-31, 183-86.
L242. ----------. Surveiller et punir: Naissance de la prison (Paris:
Gallimard, 1975) [Discipline and Punish: The Birth of the Prison (NY:
Pantheon, 1977)].
L243. ----------. "A propos de Marguerite Duras." Cahiers Renaud Barrault
89 (Oct. 1975), 8-22.
L244. ----------. Histoire de la sexualité 1: La volonté de savoir (Paris:
Gallimard, 1976) [The History of Sexuality 1: An Introduction (NY:
Pantheon, 1978)].
L245. ----------. Language, Counter-Memory, Practice: Selected Essays and
Interviews (Ithaca: Cornell UP, 1977).
L246. ----------. Microphysique du pouvoir (Turin: Einaudi, 1978).
L247. ----------. Power/Knowledge: Selected Interviews and Other
Writings, 1972-1977 (NY: Pantheon, 1980).
L248. ----------. "The Subject and Power," afterword to H. Dreyfus and P.
Rabinow, Michel Foucault: Beyond Structuralism and Hermeneutics
(Chicago: U of Chicago P, 1982), 214-32.
L249. ----------. "Nineteenth Century Imaginations." Semiotext(e) 4.2
(1982), 182-90.
L250. ----------. "Structuralism and Post-Structuralism: An Interview with
Michel Foucault." Telos 55 (1983), 195-211.
L251. ----------. Histoire de la sexualité 2: L'usage des plaisirs (Paris:
Gallimard, 1984) [The Use of Pleasure (NY: Pantheon, 1985)].
L252. ----------. Histoire de la sexualité 3: Le souci de soi (Paris: Gallimard,
1984) [The Care of the Self (NY: Pantheon, 1986)].
L253. ----------. "Sexuality and Solitude," in M. Blonsky, ed. On Signs
(Baltimore: Johns Hopkins UP, 1985), 365-72.
L254. ----------. "Of Other Spaces." Diacritics 16.1 (1986), 22-27.
L255. ----------. Death and the Labyrinth: The World of Raymond Roussel
(NY: Doubleday, 1986).
L256. ----------. "Nietzsche, Freud, Marx." Critical Texts 3.2 (Winter,
1986), 1-5.
L257. ----------. Politics, Philosophy, Culture: Interviews and Other
Writings, 1977-1984 (NY: Routledge, 1988).

L258. Frank, Manfred. Das Sagbare und das Unsagbare: Studien zur
neuesten franzosischen Hermeneutik und Texttheorie (Frankfurt: Suhrkamp,
1980).

L259. Fraser, Nancy. "Foucault on Modern Power: Empirical Insights and Normative Confusions." Praxis International 1 (1981), 272-87.

L260. ----------. "The French Derrideans: Politicising Deconstruction or Deconstructing the Political?" NGC 33 (1984), 127-54 [on Lacoue-Labarthe and J.-L. Nancy].

L261. ----------. "Michel Foucault: A 'Young Conservative'?" Ethics 96 (1985), 165-84.

L262. Frow, John. "Foucault and Derrida." Raritan 5.1 (1985), 31-42.

L263. Gans, Eric. "Vers un principe d'indétermination en critique littéraire." RevR 9 (1974), 188-99.

L264. ----------. "Differences." MLN 96.4 (1981), 792-808 [on Derrida and René Girard].

L265. Garver, Newton. "Preface," in J. Derrida, Speech and Phenomena (Evanston: Northwestern UP, 1973), ix-xxix [Derrida and Wittgenstein].

L266. ----------. "Derrida on Rousseau on Writing." Journal of Philosophy 74.11 (1977), 663-73.

L267. Gasché, Rodolphe. "The Scene of Writing: A Deferred Outset." Glyph 1 (1977), 150-71.

L268. ----------. "Deconstruction as Criticism." Glyph 6 (1979), 177-215.

L269. ----------. "Unscrambling Positions: On Gerald Graff's Critique of Deconstruction." MLN 96.5 (1981), 1015-34.

L270. ----------. "'Setzung' und 'Ubersetzung': Notes on Paul de Man." Diacritics 11.4 (1981), 36-57.

L271. ----------. "Joining the Text: From Heidegger to Derrida," in J. Arac, W. Godzich, and W. Martin, eds. The Yale Critics: Deconstruction in America (Minneapolis: U of Minnesota P, 1983), 156-75.

L272. ----------. The Tain of the Mirror: Derrida and the Philosophy of Reflection (Cambridge MA: Harvard UP, 1986).

L273. ----------. "Infrastructures and Systematicity," in J. Sallis, ed. Deconstruction and Philosophy: The Texts of Jacques Derrida (Chicago: U of Chicago P, 1987), 3-20.

L274. Gavin, William J. "James and Deconstruction: What Difference Does Différance Make?" Soundings 68.4 (1985), 537-59.

L275. Gearhart, Suzanne. "Philosophy before Literature: Deconstruction, Historicity, and the Work of Paul de Man." Diacritics 13.4 (1983), 63-81.

L276. Gelley, Alexander. "Form as Force." Diacritics 2.1 (1972), 9-13 [on Derrida].

L277. Giddens, Anthony. "Action, Subjectivity, and the Constitution of Meaning," in M. Krieger, ed.The Aims of Representation: Subject/ Text/ History (NY: Columbia UP, 1987), 159-74.

L278. Girard, René. Deceit, Desire, and the Novel: The Self and Other in Literary Structure (Baltimore: Johns Hopkins UP, 1965).
L279. ----------. "Lévi-Strauss, Frye, Derrida, and Shakespeare Criticism." Diacritics 3.3 (1973), 34-38.
L280. ----------. Critique dans le souterrain (Lausanne: L'Age d'Homme, 1976) [includes discussion of Deleuze].
L281. ----------. Violence and the Sacred (Baltimore: Johns Hopkins UP, 1977).
L282. ----------. "To Double Business Bound": Essays in Literature, Mimesis, and Anthropology (Baltimore: Johns Hopkins UP, 1978).

L283. Godzich, Wlad. "Harold Bloom as Rhetorician." Centrum 6 (1978), 43-49.
L284. ----------. "The Domestication of Derrida," in J. Arac, W. Godzich, and W. Martin, eds. The Yale Critics: Deconstruction in America (Minneapolis: U of Minnesota P, 1983), 20-40.

L285. Goldberg, Jonathan. "Deconstruction as/of Politics." MLN 96.5 (1981), 1106-12.

L286. Goldstein, Philip. "The Politics of Literary Criticism: An Introduction to Neo-Marxism." DAI 46 (1985), 695A.

L287. Goodheart, Eugene. "Literature as a Game." TriQ 52 (1981), 134-49.
L288. ----------. The Skeptic Disposition in Contemporary Criticism (Princeton: Princeton UP, 1984) [Derrida, Fish, de Man].

L289. Gordon, David J. "The Critic as Co-Creator." SR 90.4 (1982), 525-40 [on Derrida, Hartman].

L290. Gould, Eric. "Deconstructionism and Its Discontents." DQ 15.2 (1980), 90-106.

L291. Graff, Gerald. "Fear and Trembling at Yale." ASch 46 (1977), 467-78.
L292. ----------. Literature Against Itself (Chicago: U of Chicago P, 1979).
L293. ----------. "Deconstruction as Dogma, or, 'Come Back to the Raft Ag'in, Strether Honey!" GaR 34 (1980), 404-21.
L294. ----------. "Politics, Language, Deconstruction, Lies, and the Reflexive Fallacy: A Rejoinder to W. J. T. Mitchell." Salmagundi 47-48 (1980), 78-94.

L295. ----------. "Who Killed Criticism?" American Scholar 49 (1980), 337-55.

L296. ----------. Professing Literature: An Institutional History (Chicago: U of Chicago P, 1987).

L297. Granel, Gérard. "Jacques Derrida et la rature de l'origine." Critique 246 (1967), 887-905.

L298. Greenblatt, Stephen. "Capitalist Culture and the Circulatory System," in M. Krieger, ed.The Aims of Representation: Subject/ Text/ History (NY: Columbia UP, 1987), 257-73.

L299. Greisch, Jean, et al. La Crise contemporaine: Du modernisme a la crise des herméneutiques (Paris: Beauchesne, 1973).
L300. ----------. Herméneutique et grammatologie (Paris: CNRS, 1977).

L301. Grene, Marjorie. "Life, Death, and Language: Some Thoughts on Wittgenstein and Derrida." Partisan Review 43 (1976), 265-79.

L302. Gress, David. "Michel Foucault." NewC 4 (April 1986), 19-33.

L303. Guédez, Annie. Foucault (Paris: Universitaires, 1972).

L304. Guedon, Jean-Claude. "Michel Foucault: The Knowledge of Power and the Power of Knowledge." Bull. of the History of Medicine 51 (1977), 245-77.

L305. Habermas, Jurgen. "Taking Aim at the Heart of the Present," in D. C. Hoy, ed. Foucault: A Critical Reader (Oxford: Basil Blackwell, 1986), 103-08.

L306. Hacking, Ian. "The Archaeology of Foucault" and "Self-Improvement," in D. C. Hoy, ed. Foucault: A Critical Reader (Oxford: Basil Blackwell, 1986), 27-40, 235-40.

L307. Hagstrum, Jean H. "Samuel Johnson Among the Deconstructionists." GaR 39.3 (1985), 537-47.

L308. Hall, Robert A., Jr. "Deconstructing Derrida on Language," in Tra linguistica storica e linguistica generale (Pisa: Pacini, 1985), 107-16.

L309. Hamon, Philippe. "Texte littéraire et métalangage." Poétique 31 (1977), 261-84.

L310. Handelman, Susan A. The Slayers of Moses: The Emergence of Rabbinic Interpretation in Modern Literary Theory (Albany: State U of NY P, 1982) [discusses Bloom, Derrida, Lacan].

L311. Hans, James S. "Derrida and Freeplay." MLN 94 (1979), 809-26.

L312. Harari, Josué V., ed. Textual Strategies: Perspectives in Post-Structuralist Criticism (Ithaca: Cornell UP, 1979) [includes Harari's "Critical Factions/ Critical Fictions," 17-72].

L313. Harland, Richard. Superstructuralism: The Philosophy of Structuralism and Post-Structuralism (London & NY: Methuen, 1987).

L314. Harrison, Bernard. "Deconstructing Derrida." CCrit 7 (1985), 3-24.

L315. Hart, Kevin. "Maps of Deconstruction." Meanjin 45.1 (1986), 107-16.

L316. Hartman, Geoffrey H. "War in Heaven." Diacritics 3.1 (1973), 26-32 [on Bloom].
L317. ----------. The Fate of Reading and Other Essays (Chicago: U of Chicago P, 1975).
L318. ----------. "Hermeneutic Hesitation: A Dialogue Between Geoffrey Hartman and Julian Moynahan." Novel 12 (1979), 101-12.
L319. ----------. "Words, Wish, Worth: Wordsworth," in Deconstruction and Criticism (NY: Seabury, 1979), 177-216.
L320. ----------. Criticism in the Wilderness: The Study of Literature Today (New Haven: Yale UP, 1980).
L321. ----------. Saving the Text: Literature, Derrida, Philosophy (Baltimore: Johns Hopkins UP, 1981).
L322. ----------. "Tea and Totality: The Demand of Theory on Critical Style," in G. S. Jay and D. L. Miller, eds. After Strange Texts: The Role of Theory in the Study of Literature (University AL: U of Alabama P, 1985), 29-45.
L323. ----------. "Understanding Criticism," in G. Atkins and M. L. Johnson, eds. Writing and Reading Differently: Deconstruction and the Teaching of Composition and Literature (Lawrence: UP of Kansas, 1985), 149-68.

L324. Harvey, Irene. "Derrida and the Concept of Metaphysics." Research in Phenomenology 13 (1983), 113-48.
L325. ----------. Derrida and the Economy of Différance (Bloomington: Indiana UP, 1986).
L326. ----------. "Doubling the Space of Existence: Exemplarity in Derrida--the Case of Rousseau," in J. Sallis, ed. Deconstruction and Philosophy: The Texts of Jacques Derrida (Chicago: U of Chicago P, 1987), 60-70.

L327. ----------. "The Wellsprings of Deconstruction," in J. Natoli, ed. Tracing Literary Theory (Urbana: U of Illinois P, 1987), 127-47.

L328. Harwood, John. "From 'The Annotated Gospel According to Jacques.'" English 34 (1985), 44-50 [on Derrida].

L329. Hauge, Hans. "The Reception of Recent Continental Ideas in the United States," in D. E. Nye and C. K. Thomsen, eds. American Studies in Transition (Odense: Odense UP, 1985), 13-28.

L330. Hefner, R. W. "The Tel Quel Ideology: Material Practice upon Material Practice." Sub-Stance 8 (1974), 127-38.

L331. Henning, E. M. "Foucault and Derrida: Archaeology and Deconstruction." SFR 5.2 (1981), 247-64.

L332. Henricksen, Bruce, ed. "The Post-Structuralist Issue." NOR 8.3 (1981) [special issue].

L333. Herring, Henry D. "Constructivist Interpretation: An Alternative to Deconstruction." BuR 29.2 (1985), 32-46.

L334. Heyndels, Ralph. "Intertexte, institution, pédagogie." Neohelicon 10.1 (1983), 301-09.

L335. Hobson, Marian. "Deconstruction, Empiricism, and the Postal Services." FS 36.3 (1982), 290-314 [on Derrida].

L336. Holub, Robert C. "Leftist Recreation: The Politicizing of Deconstruction." Enclitic 7.1 (1983), 62-65.
L337. ----------. "Counter-Epistemology and Marxist Deconstruction: A Reply to Christopher Norris." SoRA 18.2 (1985), 206-14.
L338. ----------. "Trends in Literary Criticism: Remembering Foucault." GQ 58.2 (1985), 238-56.

L339. Holland, Eugene W. "Poststructuralism in the United States: The Supplement of Complacency." NOR 10.2-3 (1983), 48-53 [on de Man].

L340. Horstmann, Ulrich. "The Over-Reader: Harold Bloom's Neo-Darwinian Revisionism." Poetics 12.2-3 (1983), 139-49.
L341. ----------. "Parakritik und Dekonstruktion: Der amerikanische Post-Strukturalismus." ArAA 8.2 (1983), 145-58.

L342. Horton, Susan R. "Reader? Response? Text? Self?" Reader 12 (1984), 11-20.

L343. Hoy, David Couzens. The Critical Circle: Literature and History in Contemporary Hermeneutics (Berkeley: U of California P, 1978).
L344. ----------. "Forgetting the Text: Derrida's Critique of Heidegger." Boundary 8.1 (1979), 223-35.
L345. ----------. "Philosophy as Rigorous Philology? Nietzsche and Poststructuralism." NYLF 8-9 (1981), 171-85.
L346. ----------, ed. Foucault: A Critical Reader (Oxford: Basil Blackwell, 1986).
L347. ----------. "Power, Repression, Progress: Foucault, Lukes, and the Frankfurt School," in D. C. Hoy, ed. Foucault: A Critical Reader (Oxford: Basil Blackwell, 1986), 123-47.

L348. Hughes, Daniel. "Geoffrey Hartman, Geoffrey Hartman." MLN 96.5 (1981), 1134-48.

L349. Huyssen, Andreas. "Mapping the Postmodern." New German Critique 33 (1984), 5-52.

L350. Hyman, Lawrence W. "Indeterminacy in Literary Criticism." Soundings 59 (1976), 345-56.

L351. Iser, Wolfgang. "Representation: A Performative Act," in M. Krieger, ed.The Aims of Representation: Subject/ Text/ History (NY: Columbia UP, 1987), 217-34.

L352. Jacob, André. Introduction a la philosophie du langage (Paris: Gallimard, 1976) [chap. 12: "De la socio-analyse a la grammatologie"].

L353. Jacobs, Carol. The Dissimulating Harmony: The Image of Interpretation in Nietzsche, Rilke, Artaud, and Benjamin (Baltimore: Johns Hopkins UP, 1978).

L354. "Jacques Derrida." L'Arc 54 (1973) [special issue].

L355. Jay, Gregory S. "Going After New Critics: Literature, History, Deconstruction." NOR 8.3 (1981), 251-64 [on Lentricchia and de Man].
L356. ---------- and David L. Miller, eds. After Strange Texts: The Role of Theory in the Study of Literature (University: U of Alabama P, 1985).

L357. Jay, Martin. Marxism and Totality: The Adventures of a Concept from Lukacs to Habermas (Berkeley: U of California P, 1984) ["Epilogue: The Challenge of Post-Structuralism," 510-37].
L358. ----------. "In the Empire of the Gaze: Foucault and the Denigration of Vision in Twentieth-Century French Thought," in D. C. Hoy, ed. Foucault: A Critical Reader (Oxford: Basil Blackwell, 1986), 175-204.

L359. "Jean-François Lyotard." Diacritics 14.3 (1984) [special issue].

L360. Johnson, Barbara. The Critical Difference: Essays in the Contemporary Rhetoric of Reading (Baltimore: Johns Hopkins UP, 1980).
L361. ----------. "Rigorous Unreliability." CritI 11.2 (1984), 278-85 [on de Man].
L362. ----------. "Gender Theory and the Yale School," in R. C. Davis and R. Schleifer, eds. Rhetoric and Form: Deconstruction at Yale (Norman: U of Oklahoma P, 1985), 101-12.
L363. ----------, Louis Mackey, and J. Hillis Miller. "Marxism and Deconstruction: Symposium at the Conference of Contemporary Genre Theory and the Yale School 1 June 1984," in R. C. Davis and R. Schleifer, eds. Rhetoric and Form: Deconstruction at Yale (Norman: U of Oklahoma P, 1985), 75-97.
L364. ----------. "Teaching Deconstructively," in G. Atkins and M. L. Johnson, eds. Writing and Reading Differently: Deconstruction and the Teaching of Composition and Literature (Lawrence: UP of Kansas, 1985), 140-48.
L365. ----------. A World of Difference (Baltimore: Johns Hopkins UP, 1987).

L366. Jones, Steven Jeffrey. "Dispersing Circles: Textualism, the Practices of Criticism, and the Horizons Left Behind." W&D 2.1 (1984), 65-92 [Derrida and Gadamer].

L367. Joseph, Terri Brint. "Murray Krieger as Pre- and Post-Deconstructionist." NOR 12.4 (1985), 18-26.

L368. Juhl, P. D. "Playing with Texts: Can Deconstruction Account for Critical Practice?" in J. Hawthorn, ed. Criticism and Critical Theory (London: Arnold, 1984), 58-71.

L369. Kaufer, David and Gary Waller. "To Write Is To Read Is To Write, Right?" in G. Atkins and M. L. Johnson, eds. Writing and Reading Differently: Deconstruction and the Teaching of Composition and Literature (Lawrence: UP of Kansas, 1985), 16-26.

L370. Keefer, Michael H. "Deconstruction and the Gnostics." UTQ 55.1 (1985), 74-93.

L371. Keenan, Paul. "Bibliography of Texts by Paul de Man." YFS 69 (1985), 315-22.

L372. Kendrick, Walter. "Confessions of a Deconstructor." BRev 11.3 (1986), 5-6, 25-26.

L373. Kennedy, Alan. "Deconstruction Meets the Departments of Englit." DR 64.2 (1984), 452-71.

L374. Kinneavy, James L. "Deconstructing the Rhetoric/Poetic Distinction: The Platonizing of Rhetoric and Literature." Dieciocho 8.1 (1985), 70-79 [on Derrida].

L375. Klein, Richard. "Prolegomenon to Derrida." Diacritics 2.4 (1972), 19-34.
L376. ----------. "The Blindness of Hyperboles: The Ellipses of Insight." Diacritics 3.2 (1974), 33-44.
L377. ----------. "Kant's Sunshine." Diacritics 11 (1981), 26-41.

L378. Knapp, Peggy. "Repairing the Ruins." ADEB 72 (1982), 18-22.

L379. Koelb, Clayton and Virgil Lokke, eds. The Current in Criticism: Essays on the Present and Future of Literary Theory (West Lafayette IN: Purdue UP, 1987).

L380. Kofman, Sarah. Lectures de Derrida (Paris: Galilée, 1984).

L381. Konigsberg, Ira, ed. American Criticism in the Post-Structuralist Age (Ann Arbor: U of Michigan P, 1981).

L382. Krell, David Farrell. "The Perfect Future: A Note on Heidegger and Derrida," in J. Sallis, ed. Deconstruction and Philosophy: The Texts of Jacques Derrida (Chicago: U of Chicago P, 1987), 114-21.

L383. Kremer-Marietti, Angele. Foucault et l'archéologie du savoir (Paris: Seghers, 1974).

L384. Krieger, Murray. Theory of Criticism (Baltimore: Johns Hopkins UP, 1976).
L385. ----------. Poetic Presence and Illusion (Baltimore: Johns Hopkins UP, 1979).
L386. ----------. "An Apology for Poetics," in I. Konigsberg, ed. American Criticism in the Post-Structuralist Age (Ann Arbor: U of Michigan P, 1981), 87-101.
L387. ----------. "In the Wake of Morality: The Thematic Underside of Recent Theory." NLH 15.1 (1983), 119-36.
L388. ----------. "Post-New-Critical Fashions in Theory." IJAS 14.2 (1984), 189-206.
L389. ----------. "Literature vs. Ecriture " Constructions and Deconstructions in Recent Critical Theory," in V. A. Kramer, ed. American Critics at Work (Troy NY: Whitston, 1984), 27-48.

L390. ----------, ed. The Aims of Representation: Subject/Text/History (NY: Columbia UP, 1987) [includes Krieger's essay, "The Literary, the Textual, the Social," 1-22].

L391. Krupnick, Mark, ed. Displacement: Derrida and After (Bloomington: Indiana UP, 1983).

L392. LaCapra, Dominick. Rethinking Intellectual History: Texts, Contexts, Language (Ithaca: Cornell UP, 1983) [discusses Bakhtin, Derrida, Foucault, Lacan].
L393. ----------. "Criticism Today," in M. Krieger, ed. The Aims of Representation: Subject/ Text/ History (NY: Columbia UP, 1987), 235-56.

L394. Lacoue-Labarthe, Philippe and Jean-Luc Nancy. Le Titre de la lettre (Paris: Galilée, 1973) [on Lacan].
L395. ----------. Mimesis: Desarticulations (Paris: Flammarion, 1975).
L396. ---------- and Jean-Luc Nancy. L'Absolu littéraire: théorie de la littérature du romantisme allemand (Paris: Seuil, 1978).
L397. ----------. Le sujet de la philosophie (Paris: Flammarion, 1979).
L398. ---------- and Jean-Luc Nancy, eds. Les Fins de l'homme: A partir du travail de Jacques Derrida (Paris: Galilée, 1981).
L399. ----------. "Talks." Diacritics 14.3 (1984), 24-37 [on Lyotard].
L400. ----------. L'Imitation des modernes (Paris: Galilée, 1986).

L401. Lamizet, Bernard and Frédéric Nef. "Entrave double: le glas et la chute (sur Glas de J. Derrida)." Gramma 2 (1975), 129-50.

L402. Lang, Candace. "Aberrance in Criticism?" Sub-Stance 41 (1983), 3-16 [Barthes, Derrida].

L403. Langellier, Kristin M. "Doing Deconstruction: Sexuality and Interpretation." LPer 4.1 (1983), 45-50.

L404. Laruelle, François. "Le Texte quatrieme." L'Arc 54 (1973), 38-45 [on Derrida].
L405. ----------. "Le Style di-phallique de Jacques Derrida." Critique 31 (1975), 320-29.
L406. ----------. "La Scene du vomi ou comment ça se détraque dans le théorie." Critique 32 (1976), 265-79.
L407. ----------. Machines textuelles: Déconstruction et libido d'écriture (Paris: Seuil, 1976).

L408. Latimer, Dan. "A Yale Primer, or: Paul de Man in Other Words." NOR 10.4 (1983), 71-80.

L409. Leavey, John P., Jr. "Derrida and Dante: Différance and the Eagle in the Sphere of Jupiter." MLN 91.1 (1976), 60-68.

L410. ---------- and David B. Allison. "A Derrida Bibliography." Research in Phenomenology 8 (1978), 145-60.

L411. ----------. "Four Protocols: Derrida, His Deconstruction." Semeia 23 (1982), 42-57.

L412. ----------. "Jacques Derrida's Glas : A Translated Selection and Some Comments on an Absent Colossus." ClioI 11.4 (1982), 327-37.

L413. ----------. "Destinerrance: The Apotropocalyptics of Translation," in J. Sallis, ed. Deconstruction and Philosophy: The Texts of Jacques Derrida (Chicago: U of Chicago P, 1987), 33-43.

L414. ----------. Glossary (Lincoln: U of Nebraska P, 1987) [on Derrida's Glas].

L415. Lecercle, J. L. Philosophy through the Looking-Glass (London: Hutchinson, 1985) [on Deleuze].

L416. Leitch, Vincent. "The Lateral Dance: The Deconstructive Criticism of J. Hillis Miller." CritI 6 (1980), 593-607.

L417. ----------. Deconstructive Criticism: An Advanced Introduction (NY: Columbia UP, 1983).

L418. ----------. "The Book of Deconstructive Criticism," in V. A. Kramer, ed. American Critics at Work (Troy NY: Whitston, 1984), 111-42.

L419. ----------. "Derrida's Assault on the Institution of Style." BuR 29.2 (1985), 17-31.

L420. ----------. "Deconstruction and Pedagogy," in G. Atkins and M. L. Johnson, eds. Writing and Reading Differently: Deconstruction and the Teaching of Composition and Literature (Lawrence: UP of Kansas, 1985), 16-26.

L421. Lemert, Charles C. and Garth Gillan. Michel Foucault: Social Theory and Transgression (NY: Columbia UP, 1982).

L422. Lentriccia, Frank. After the New Criticism (Chicago: U of Chicago P, 1980) [esp. "History or the Abyss: Poststructuralism," 156-210].

L423. ----------. Criticism and Social Change (Chicago: U of Chicago P, 1983).

L424. Lepick, Julie Ann. "Jacques Derrida at the Limits." NOR 8.3 (1981), 225-30.

L425. Lévesque, Claude. L'Etrangeté du texte: Essais sur Nietzsche, Freud, Blanchot et Derrida (Montreal: VLB, 1976).

L426. Lewis, Clayton W. "Identifications and Divisions: Kenneth Burke and the Yale Critics." SoR 22.1 (1986), 93-102.

L427. Lewis, Philip. "The Post-Structuralist Condition." Diacritics 12.1 (1982), 2-24.

L428. Lindsay, Cecile. "Experiments in Postmodern Dialogue." Diacritics 14.3 (1984), 52-62 [on Lyotard and J.-L. Thébaud].

L429. Lipking, Lawrence I. "The Practice of Theory." ADEB 76 (1983), 22-29.

L430. Llewelyn, John. Derrida on the Threshold of Sense (London: Macmillan, 1986).
L431. ----------. "A Point of Almost Absolue Proximity to Hegel," in J. Sallis, ed. Deconstruction and Philosophy: The Texts of Jacques Derrida (Chicago: U of Chicago P, 1987), 87-95.

L432. Logan, Marie-Rose. "Deconstruction: Beyond and Back." Boundary 8.1 (1979), 57-63 [on Donato].

L433. Loselle, Andrea. "Freud/Derrida as Fort/Da and the Repetitive Eponym." MLN 97.5 (1982), 1180-85.

L434. Lyotard, Jean-François. Discours, figure (Paris: Klincksieck, 1971).
L435. ----------. Dérive a partie de Marx et Freud (Paris: Union Générale, 1973).
L436. ----------. Economie libidinale (Paris: Minuit, 1974).
L437. ----------. "Analyzing Speculative Discourse as Language Game." OLR 4 (1981), 59-67.
L438. ----------. The Post-Modern Condition: A Report on Knowledge (Minneapolis: U of Minnesota P, 1983).
L439. ----------. "The Différend , the Referent and the Proper Name." Diacritics 14.3 (1984), 4-14.
L440. ---------- and Jean-Loup Thébaud. Just Gaming (Minneapolis: U of Minnesota P, 1986).
L441. ----------. "Judiciousness in Dispute, or Kant after Marx," in M. Krieger, ed.The Aims of Representation: Subject/ Text/ History (NY: Columbia UP, 1987), 23-68.

L442. Macann, Christopher. "Jacques Derrida's Theory of Writing and the Concept of Trace." Journal of the British Society for Phenomenology 3.2 (1972),197-200.

L443. MacCannell, Juliet Flower. "Portrait: de Man," in R. C. Davis and R. Schleifer, eds. Rhetoric and Form: Deconstruction at Yale (Norman: U of Oklahoma P, 1985), 51-74.

L444. Machin, Richard and Christopher Norris, eds. Post-Structuralist Readings of English Poetry (Cambridge: Cambridge UP, 1987).

L445. Macksey, Richard and Eugenio Donato, eds. The Structuralist Controversy: The Languages of Criticism and the Sciences of Man, 2nd ed. (Baltimore: Johns Hopkins UP, 1972).
L446. ----------, ed. "The World as Text: Nonliterary Genres." Genre 16.4 (1983) [special issue].

L447. Magliola, Robert. Derrida on the Mend (West Lafeyette IN: Purdue UP, 1984).

L448. Major-Poetzl, Pamela. Michel Foucault's Archaeology of Western Culture: Toward a New Sscience of History (Chapel Hill: U of North Carolina P, 1983).

L449. Malmberg, Bertil. "Derrida et sémiologie: Quelques notes marginales." Semiotica 11.2 (1974), 189-99.

L550. Man, Paul de. [note: the U of Nebraska P will publish a collection of de Man's wartime journalism along with a separate collection of responses to this discovery of de Man's work for a collaborationist journal, the connections between theory and politics, etc.].
L551. ----------. Allegories of Reading: Figural Language in Rousseau, Nietzsche, Rilke, and Proust (New Haven: Yale UP, 1979).
L552. ----------. Blindness and Insight: Essays in the Rhetoric of Contemporary Criticism, 2nd rev. ed. (Minneapolis: U of Minnesota P; London: Methuen, 1983).
L553. ----------. The Rhetoric of Romanticism (NY: Columbia UP, 1984).
L554. ----------. The Resistance to Theory (Minneapolis: U of Minnesota P, 1986).

L555. Mandel, Ross. "Deconstruction and Presence: An Introduction to the Writings of Jacques Derrida." DAI 46 (1985), 719A.

L556. Markley, Robert. "*Tristram Shandy* and 'Narrative Middles': Hillis Miller and the Style of Deconstructive Criticism," in R. C. Davis and R. Schleifer, eds. Rhetoric and Form: Deconstruction at Yale (Norman: U of Oklahoma P, 1985), 179-90.

L557. Marshall, Donald G. "History, Theory, and Influence: Yale Critics as Readers of Maurice Blanchot," in J. Arac, W. Godzich, and W. Martin, eds. The Yale Critics: Deconstruction in America (Minneapolis: U of Minnesota P, 1983), 135-55.

L558. Martin, Wallace. "Literary Critics and Their Discontents: A Response to Geoffrey Hartman." CritI 4 (1977), 397-406.

L559. McDonald, Christie V. "Jacques Derrida's Reading of Rouuseau." ECent 20 (1979), 82-95.
L560. ----------. "Choreographies." Diacritics 12.2 (1982), 66-76 [interview with Derrida concerning feminism].

L561. McDonald, David. "The Trace of Absence: A Derridean Analysis of Oedipus Rex." TJ 31 (1979), 147-61.
L562. ----------, ed. "Deconstructions: Corneille and Moliere." TJ 34.4 (1982) [special issue].

L563. McGraw, Betty R. "(De)Constructing Consciousness: The 'Subject' in Phenomenology, Structuralism, and 'Left Bank Semiotics.'" Research Studies 45.4 (1977), 224-35.

L564. McKenna, Andrew J. "History of the Ear: Ideology and Poetic Deconstruction." Centrum 3 (1975), 65-79.

L565. Megill, Allan. "Foucault, Structuralism, and the End of History." Journal of Modern History 51 (1979), 451-503.
L566. ----------. Prophets of Extremity: Nietzsche, Heidegger, Foucault, Derrida (Berkeley: U of California P, 1985).

L567. Mehlman, Jeffrey. "Orphée scripteur: Blanchot, Rilke, Derrida." Poétique 20 (1974), 458-82.
L568. ----------. "Rose de Rivoli : Politics and Deconstruction." MLN 91 (1976), 1061-72.

L569. Melville, Stephen. Philosophy Beside Itself: On Deconstruction and Modernism (Minneapolis: U of Minnesota P, 1986).

L570. Merod, Jim. "On the Use of Bookshelves: Deconstruction and the Politics of Writing," in J. H. Smith, ed. Brandeis Essays in Literature (Waltham MA: Dept. of Eng. & American Lit., Brandeis U, 1983), 149-71.

L571. Merquior, J. G. Foucault (London: Fontana, 1985).

L572. Merrell, Floyd. Deconstruction Reframed (West Lafayette IN: Purdue UP, 1985).

L573. Meschonnic, Henri. "L'Ecriture de Derrida." Les Cahiers du Chemin 24 (1975), 137-80.

L574. Miel, Jan. "Ideas or Epistemes: Hazard versus Foucault." YFS 49 (1973), 231-45.

L575. Miller, J. Hillis. Thomas Hardy: Distance and Desire (Cambridge: Harvard UP, 1970).
L576. ----------. "The Geneva School: The Criticism of Marcel Raymond, Albert Beguin, Georges Poulet, Jean Rousset, Jean-Pierre Richard, and Jean Starobinski," in J. K. Simon, ed. Modern French Criticism (Chicago: U of Chicago P, 1972), 277-310.
L577. ----------. "Tradition and Difference." Diacritics 2.4 (1972), 6-13.
L578. ----------. "Narrative and History." ELH 41 (1974), 455-73.
L579. ----------. "Deconstructing the Deconstructors." Diacritics 5.2 (1975), 24-31.
L580. ----------. "Optic and Semiotic in Middlemarch," in J. H. Buckley, ed. The Worlds of Victorian Fiction (Cambridge: Harvard UP, 1975), 125-45.
L581. ----------. "Beginning with a Text." Diacritics 6 (1976), 2-7.
L582. ----------. "Stevens' Rock and Criticism as Cure." GaR 30 (1976), 5-31, 330-48.
L583. ----------. "Narrative Middles: A Preliminary Outline." Genre 11 (1978), 375-87.
L584. ----------. "The Critic as Host," in H. Bloom, et al, Deconstruction and Criticism (NY: Seabury P, 1979), 217-53.
L585. ----------. "A 'Buchstabliches' Reading of the Elective Affinities." Glyph 6 (1979), 1-23.
L586. ----------. "The Function of Rhetorical Study at the Present Time." ADEB 62 (1979), 10-18.
L587. ----------. "On Edge: The Crossways of Contemporary Criticism." Bulletin of the American Academy of Arts and Sciences 32.4 (1979), 13-32.
L588. ----------. "The Figure in the Carpet." PoT 1.3 (1980), 107-18.
L589. ----------. "A Guest in the House." PoT 2 (1980-81), 189-91.
L590. ----------. "Theory and Practice: Response to Vincent Leitch." CritI 6 (1980), 609-14.
L591. ----------. "The Ethics of Reading: Vast Gaps and Parting Hours," in I. Konigsberg, ed. American Criticism in the Post-Structuralist Age (Ann Arbor: U of Michigan P, 1981), 19-41.
L592. ----------. "The Disarticulation of the Self in Nietzsche." The Monist 64 (1981), 247-61.
L593. ----------. Fiction and Repetition: Seven English Novels (Cambridge: Harvard UP, 1982).

L594. ----------. "Composition and Decomposition," in W. B. Horner, ed. Composition and Literature: Bridging the Gap (Chicago: U of Chicago P, 1983), 40-57.

L595. ----------. "Thomas Hardy, Jacques Derrida, and the 'Dislocation of Souls,'" in J. H. Smith and W. Kerrigan, eds. Taking Chances: Derrida, Psychoanalysis, and Literature (Baltimore: Johns Hopkins UP, 1984), 135-45.

L596. ----------. "The Search for Grounds in Literary Study," in R. C. Davis and R. Schleifer, eds. Rhetoric and Form: Deconstruction at Yale (Norman: U of Oklahoma P, 1985), 19-36.

L597. ----------. "The Two Rhetorics: George Eliot's Bestiary," in G. Atkins and M. L. Johnson, eds. Writing and Reading Differently: Deconstruction and the Teaching of Composition and Literature (Lawrence: UP of Kansas, 1985),101-14.

L598. Miller, Susan Hawkins. "The Endless Calculus of Critical Language." DQ 16.4 (1982), 57-74 [on J. Hillis Miller].

L599. Minister, Kristina. "Doing Deconstruction: The Extra-Institutional Performance of Literature." LPer 4.1 (1983), 51-54.

L600. Mitchell, Sollace. "Post-Structuralism, Empiricism, and Interpretation," in S. Mitchell and M. Rosen, eds. The Need for Interpretation (London: Athlone; Totowa NJ: Humanities P, 1983), 54-89.

L601. Mitchell, W. J. T. "Intellectual Politics and the Malaise of the Seventies." Salmagundi 47-48 (1980), 67-77 [see Graff].

L602. Morris, Meaghan and Paul Patton, eds. Michel Foucault: Power, Truth, Strategy (Sydney: Feral P, 1979).

L603. Morris, Wesley. "The Irrepressible Real: Jacques Lacan and Poststructuralism," in I. Konigsberg, ed. American Criticism in the Post-Structuralist Age (Ann Arbor: U of Michigan P, 1981), 116-34.

L604. Moynihan, Robert. "Interview with Geoffrey Hartman. . . ." Boundary 9.1 (1980), 191-25.

L605. ----------. "Interview with J. Hillis Miller. . . ." Criticism 24.2 (1982), 99-125.

L606. Muller, Harro. "Kleist, Paul de Man und Deconstruction: Argumentative Nach-Stellungen." Merkur 40.2 (1986), 108-15.

L607. Mulligan, Kevin. "Inscriptions and Speaking's Place: Derrida and Wittgenstein." OLR 3.2 (1978), 62-67.

L608. Murphy, John J. "Deconstruction and the Subversion of 'Affirmative Culture.'" NOR 13.2 (1986), 90-97 [politics].

L609. Murray, Timothy. "What's Happening?" Diacritics 14.3 (1984), 100-10 [on Lyotard].

L610. Neel, Jasper. Plato, Derrida, and Writing (Carbondale: Southern Illinois UP, 1988).

L611. Nelson, Robert J. "*Seeing* through Words, Seeing *through* Words, Seeing through Words, Seeing Word (as) Through." GaR 35.3 (1981), 661-72.

L612. Nevo, Ruth. "*The Waste Land* : The Ur-Text of Deconstruction." NLH 13.3 (1982), 453-61.

L613. Norris, Christopher. "Deconstruction and the Limits of Sense." EIC 30 (1980), 281-92.
L614. ----------. "Derrida at Yale: The 'Deconstructive Moment' in Modernist Poetics." P&L 4 (1980), 242-56.
L615. ----------. "Harold Bloom: A Poetics of Reconstruction." BJA 20 (1980), 67-76.
L616. ----------. "Wrestling with Deconstructors." CritQ 22.1 (1980), 57-62.
L617. ----------. "Between Marx and Nietzsche: The Prospects for Critical Theory." JLS 10.2 (1981), 104-15.
L618. ----------. Deconstruction: Theory and Practice (London: Methuen, 1982).
L619. ----------. The Deconstructive Turn: Essays in the Rhetoric of Philosophy (London: Methuen, 1983).
L620. ----------. "Deconstruction, Naming and Necessity: Some Logical Options." JLS 13.3 (1984), 159-80.
L621. ----------. "Justified Margins." SHR 18.4 (1984), 289-98.
L622. ----------. "On Marxist Deconstruction: Prospects and Problems." SoRA 17 (1984), 203-11.
L623. ----------. The Contest of Faculties: Philosophy and Theory After Deconstruction (London: Methuen, 1985).
L624. ----------. "Some Versions of Rhetoric: Empson and de Man," in R. C. Davis and R. Schleifer, eds. Rhetoric and Form: Deconstruction at Yale (Norman: U of Oklahoma P, 1985), 191-214.
L625. ----------. "On Paul de Man's *The Rhetoric of Romanticism*." SHR 20.1 (1986), 53-69.
L626. ----------. "On Derrida's "Apocalyptic Tone': Textual Politics and the Principle of Reason." SoRA 19.1 (1986), 13-30.

L627. ----------. "Deconstruction Against Itself: Derrida and Nietzsche." Diacritics 16.4 (1986), 61-69.
L628. ----------. Derrida (Cambridge MA: Harvard UP, 1987).

L629. Northam, Paul. "Heuristics and Beyond: Deconstruction/Inspiration and the Teaching of Writing Invention," in G. Atkins and M. L. Johnson, eds. Writing and Reading Differently: Deconstruction and the Teaching of Composition and Literature (Lawrence: UP of Kansas, 1985), 115-28.

L630. O'Hara, Daniel. "The Ideology of Romance: Two Recent Critical Cases." ConL 23.4 (1982), 381-89 [on Hartman and Jameson].
L631. ----------. "The Genius of Irony: Nietzsche in Bloom," in J. Arac, W. Godzich, and W. Martin, eds. The Yale Critics: Deconstruction in America (Minneapolis: U of Minnesota P, 1983), 109-32.
L632. ----------. "The Approximations of Romance: Paul Ricoeur and the Ironic Style of Postmodern Criticism," in W. Cain, ed. Philosophical Approaches to Literature (Lewisburg: Bucknell UP, 1984), 183-201 [Derrida and Ricoeur].
L633. ----------. "Revisionary Madness: The Prospects of American Literary Theory at the Present Time," in W. J. T. Mitchell, ed. Against Theory: Literary Studies and the New Pragmatism (Chicago: U of Chicago P, 1985), 31-47.
L634. ----------. The Romance of Interpretation: Visionary Criticism from Pater to de Man (NY: Columbia UP, 1985).

L635. O'Kane, John. "Marxism, Deconstruction, and Ideology: Notes Toward an Articulation." NGC 33 (1984), 219-47.

L636. Okhamafe, E. Imafedia. "The 'Politics' of Pharmakon ." DAI 45 (1985), 2136A [on Derrida and Nietzsche].

L637. Orr, Leonard, ed. De-Structing the Novel: Essays in Applied Postmodern Hermeneutics (Troy NY: Whitston, 1982) [includes "Checklist of Books and Articles of Importance to 'Postmodern' Critical Approaches," 223-61].
L638. ----------. "The Post-Turn Turn: Derrida, Gadamer, and the Remystification of Language." Journal of Literary Criticism 1.2 (1984), 23-35.
L639. ----------, ed. Yeats and Postmodernism (Syracuse: Syracuse UP, forthcoming) [includes Orr's introduction, "Yeats and Post-Structuralist Criticism"].

L640. Parker, Andrew. "Of Politics and Limits: Derrida Re-Marx." SCE Reports 8 (1980), 83-104.

L641. ----------. "'Taking Sides' (on History): Derrida Re-Marx." <u>Diacritics</u> 11.4 (1981), 57-73 [Derrida, Foucault, Marxism].
L642. ----------. "Between Dialectics and Deconstruction: Derrida and the Reading of Marx," in G. S. Jay and D. L. Miller, eds. <u>After Strange Texts: The Role of Theory in the Study of Literature</u> (University: U of Alabama P, 1985), 146-68.

L643. Parret, Herman. "Grammatology and Linguistics: A Note on Derrida's Interpretation of Linguistic Theories." <u>Poetics</u> 4.1 (1975), 107-27.

L644. Pease, Donald. "J. Hillis Miller: The Other Victorian at Yale," in J. Arac, W. Godzich, and W. Martin, eds. <u>The Yale Critics: Deconstruction in America</u> (Minneapolis: U of Minnesota P, 1983), 66-89.

L645. Pechey, Graham. "Bakhtin, Marxism, and Post-Structuralism," in F. Barker, et al, eds. <u>The Politics of Theory</u> (Colchester: U of Esex, 1983), 234-37.

L646. Pecora, Vincent. "Deleuze's Nietzsche and Post-Structuralist Thought." <u>Sub-Stance</u> 14.3 (1986), 34-50.

L647. Poole, Roger. "The Yale School as a Theological Enterprise." <u>RMS</u> 27 (1983), 1-29.

L648. Poster, Mark. <u>Foucault, Marxism and History</u> (Cambridge: Polity, 1984).
L649. ----------. "Foucault and the Tyranny of Greece," in D. C. Hoy, ed. <u>Foucault: A Critical Reader</u> (Oxford: Basil Blackwell, 1986), 205-20.
L650. ----------. "Foucault, Post-Structuralism, and the Mode of Information," in M. Krieger, ed.<u>The Aims of Representation: Subject/ Text/ History</u> (NY: Columbia UP, 1987), 107-30.

L651. Pressler, Charles A. "Redoubled: The Bridging of Derrida and Heidegger." <u>HumanS</u> 7.3-4 (1984), 325-42.

L652. Pritchard, William H. "The Hermeneutical Mafia or, After Strange Gods at Yale." <u>HudR</u> 28 (1975), 601-10.

L653. Rabinow, Peter, ed. <u>The Foucault Reader</u> (NY: Pantheon, 1984).

L654. Racevskis, Karlis. <u>Michel Foucault and the Subversion of the Intellect</u> (Ithaca: Cornell UP, 1983).

L655. Raina, Badri N. <u>Dickens and the Dialectic of Growth</u> (Madison: U of Wisconsin P, 1986).

L656. Rajan, Gita. "Bibliography: Hartman, de Man, Miller," in R. C. Davis and R. Schleifer, eds. Rhetoric and Form: Deconstruction at Yale (Norman: U of Oklahoma P, 1985), 239-51.

L657. Rajan, Tilottama. "Displacing Post-Structuralism: Romantic Studies after Paul de Man." SIR 24.4 (1985), 451-74.

L658. Rajchman, John. Michel Foucault: The Freedom of Philosophy (NY: Columbia UP, 1985).

L659. Rapaport, Herman. "On Recuperating Derrida." NOR 8.3 (1981), 238-40.
L660. ----------. "Geoffrey Hartman and the Spell of Sounds," in R. C. Davis and R. Schleifer, eds. Rhetoric and Form: Deconstruction at Yale (Norman: U of Oklahoma P, 1985), 159-77.

L661. Raschke, Carl A. "Harlequins and Beggars: Deconstruction and the Face of Fashionable Nihilism." DQ 19.4 (1985), 118-26.

L662. Raval, Suresh. Metacriticism (Athens: U of Georgia P, 1981) ["Deconstruction and Criticism," 188-238].

L663. Ray, William. Literary Meaning from Phenomenology to Deconstruction (Oxford: Basil Blackwell, 1984) [esp. chap. 11: "From Structuralism to Post-Structuralism--Derrida's Strategy"].

L664. Reed, Walter L. "Deconstruction and Tradition." SNNTS 14.4 (1982), 377-83.

L665. Reeves, Charles Eric. "Deconstruction, Language, Motive, Rortian Pragmatism and the Uses of 'Literature.'" JAAC 44.4 (1986), 351-56.

L666. Rey, Jean-Michel. L'Enjeu des signes: Lecture de Nietzsche (Paris: Seuil, 1965).
L667. ----------. "La Scene du texte." Critique 25 (1969), 1059-73.
L668. ----------. Parcours de Freud: Economie et discours (Paris: Galilée, 1974).

L669. Riddel, Joseph. The Inverted Bell: Modernism and the Counter Poetics of William Carlos Williams (Baton Rouge: Louisiana State UP, 1974).
L670. ----------. "A Miller's Tale." Diacritics 5.3 (1975), 56-65.
L671. ----------. "From Heidegger to Derrida to Chance: Doubling and (Poetic) Language." Boundary 4.2 (1976), 571-92.

L672. ----------. "Decentering the Image: The 'Project' of 'American' Poetics?" in J. Harari, ed. Textual Strategies: Perspectives in Post-Structuralist Criticism (Ithaca: Cornell UP, 1979), 322-58.

L673. ----------. "Re-Doubling the Commentary." ConL 20 (1979), 237-50 [on Derrida and Foucault].

L674. ----------. "Juda Becomes New Haven." Diacritics 10.2 (1980), 17-34 [on Bloom].

L675. ----------. "'Keep Your Pecker Up'--*Paterson Five* and the Question of Metapoetry." Glyph 8 (1981), 203-31.

L676. ----------. "The Climate of Our Poems." WSJour 7.3-4 (1983), 59-75 [Bloom and Lentricchia].

L677. ----------. "Coup de Man; Or, The Uses and Abuses of Semiotics." Cultural Critique 4 (1986), 81-109 [discusses de Man, Lyotard].

L678. Riffaterre, Michael. "Syllepsis." CritI 6 (1980), 625-38 [on Derrida's *Glas*].

L679. Rimmon-Kenan, Shlomith. "Deconstructive Reflection on Deconstruction: In Reply to Hillis Miller." PoT 2 (1980-81), 185-88.

L680. Robertson, M. J. "In the Dresden Gallery: Heidegger, Derrida, and Anaximander." QFG 3 (1984), 235-50.

L681. Rorty, Richard. "Derrida on Language, Being, and Abnormal Philosophy." Journal of Philosophy 74.11 (1977), 673-81.

L682. ----------. Philosophy and the Mirror of Nature (Princeton: Princeton UP, 1979).

L683. ----------. "Philosophy as a Kind of Writing," in Consequences of Pragmatism (Minneapolis: U of Minnesota P, 1982), 89-109 [on Derrida].

L684. ----------. "Deconstruction and Circumvention." CritI 11.1 (1984), 1-23.

L685. ----------. "Habermas and Lyotard on Postmodernity," in R. J. Bernstein, ed. Habermas and Modernity (Cambridge: MIT P, 1985), 161-75.

L686. ----------. "Foucault and Epistemology," in D. C. Hoy, ed. Foucault: A Critical Reader (Oxford: Basil Blackwell, 1986), 41-49.

L687. Rose, Gillian. Dialectic of Nihilism (Oxford: Blackwell, 1984).

L688. Rosen, Stanley. "*Of Grammatology* ." P&R 15.1 (1982), 66-70 [on Derrida].

L689. Rosenfeld, Alvin. "'Armed for War': Notes on the Antithetical Criticism of Harold Bloom." Southern Rev 13 (1977), 554-66.

L690. Rosso, Stephano. "An Interview with Paul de Man." CritI 12.4 (1986), 788-95.

L691. Roudiez, Leon S. "Twelve Points from *Tel Quel*." ECr 14 (1974), 291-303.

L692. Rousseau, G. S. "Whose Enlightenment? Not Man's: The Case of Michel Foucault." Eighteenth-Century Studies 6 (1972-73), 238-56.

L693. Rowe, John Carlos. "Surplus Economies: Deconstruction, Ideology and the Humanities," in M. Krieger, ed.The Aims of Representation: Subject/ Text/ History (NY: Columbia UP, 1987), 131-58.

L694. Royle, Nick. "Nor Is Deconstruction." OLR 5.1-2 (1982), 170-77 [on C. Norris].

L695. Ryan, Michael. "Self-De(con)struction." Diacritics 6.1 (1976), 34-41.
L696. ----------. "New French Theory in *New German Critique*." NGC 22 (1981), 145-61 [Derrida, Lacan].
L697. ----------. Marxism and Deconstruction: A Critical Articulation (Baltimore: Johns Hopkins UP, 1982).
L698. ----------. "Deconstruction and Social Theory: The Case of Liberalism," in M. Krupnick, ed. Displacement: Derrida and After (Bloomington: Indiana UP, 1983), 154-68.

L699. Sabo, Kathy and Greg Marc Nielsen. "Critique dialogique et postmodernisme." EF 20.1 (1984), 75-85 [on Bakhtin].

L700. Said, Edward. Beginnings: Intention and Method (NY: Basic Books, 1975).
L701. ----------. "The Problem of Textuality: Two Exemplary Positions." CritI 4 (1978), 673-714 [Derrida, Foucault].
L702. ----------. Orientalism (NY: Pantheon, 1978).
L703. ----------. The World, the Text and the Critic (Cambridge MA: Harvard UP, 1984).
L704. ----------. "Foucault and the Imagination of Power," in D. C. Hoy, ed. Foucault: A Critical Reader (Oxford: Basil Blackwell, 1986), 149-55.

L705. Sallis, John, ed. Deconstruction and Philosophy: The Texts of Jacques Derrida (Chicago: U of Chicago P, 1987).

L706. Saunders, Ian. "Criticism and the Object of Explnation: Paul de Man's Trope of Interruption." SoRA 18.1 (1985), 49-64.

L707. Scheer, Steven C. "Unfixing 'The Fixation of Belief': Can Peirce Be Deconstructed?" in J. Deely, ed. Semiotics 1984 (Lanham MD: UP of America, 1985), 333-40.

L708. Schleifer, Ronald. "The Anxiety of Allegory: De Man, Greimas, and the Problem of Referentiality," in R. C. Davis and R. Schleifer, eds. Rhetoric and Form: Deconstruction at Yale (Norman: U of Oklahoma P, 1985), 215-37.

L709. Schneidau, Herbert N. "The Word against the Word: Derrida on Textuality." Semeia 23 (1982), 5-28.

L710. Scholes, Robert. Textual Power: Literary Theory and the Teaching of English (New Haven: Yale UP, 1985).

L711. Searle, John. "Reiterating the Differences." Glyph 1 (1977), 198-208 [on Derrida].

L712. Seeley, David. "Poststructuralist Criticism and Biblical History," in R. Detweiler, ed. Art/Literature/Religion: Life on the Borders (Chico CA: Scholars, 1983), 157-71.

L713. Seem, Mark D. "Liberation of Difference: Toward a Theory of Antiliterature." NLH 5.1 (1973), 121-34.

L714. Selden, Raman. A Reader's Guide to Contemporary Literary Theory (Lexington: UP of Kentucky, 1985) [chap. 4 on deconstruction and post-structuralism].

L715. Seltzer, Mark. "Reading Foucault: Cells, Corridors, Novels." Diacritics 14.1 (1984), 78-89.

L716. Sercello, Guy. "The Poetry of Theory: Reflections on After the New Criticism ." JAAC 42.4 (1984), 388-96 [on Lentricchia].

L717. Serio, John N., ed. "Stevens and Postmodern Criticism." WSJour 7.3-4 (1983) [special issue].

L718. Serres, Michel. Hermes, 4 vols. (Paris: Minuit, 1968-77).
L719. ----------. Le Parasite (Paris: Grasset, 1980).

L720. Sheridan, Alan. Michel Foucault: The Will to Truth (London: Tavistock, 1980).

L721. Shusterman, Richard. "Deconstruction and Analysis: Confrontation and Convergence." BJA 26.4 (1986), 311-27.

L722. Siebers, Tobin. "Ethics in the Age of Rousseau: From Lévi-Strauss to Derrida." MLN 100.4 (1985), 758-69.
L723. ----------. "Language, Violence, and the Sacred: A Polemical Survey of Critical Theories," in To Honor René Girard (Saratoga CA: Anma Libri, 1986), 203-19 [discusses Derrida, Foucault, Girard, Hillis Miller].
L724. ----------. "Paul de Man and the Rhetoric of Selfhood." NOR 13.1 (1986), 5-9.

L725. Silverman, Hugh J. "Self-Decentering: Derrida Incorporated." Research in Phenomenology 8 (1978), 673-714.
L726. ---------- and Don Ihde, eds. Hermeneutics and Deconstruction (Albany: State U of NY P, 1985).
L727. ----------. "Philosophy Has Its Reasons. . . ," in J. Sallis, ed. Deconstruction and Philosophy: The Texts of Jacques Derrida (Chicago: U of Chicago P, 1987), 21-32.

L728. Sim, Stuart. "De-Composing in Bad Faith: Its Cause and Cure." CritQ 24.4 (1982), 25-36.

L729. Singer, Alan. "Desire's Desire: Toward an Historical Formalism." Enclitic 8.1-2 (1984), 57-67 [discusses Jameson and Althusser].

L730. Smart, Barry. Foucault, Marxism and Critique (London: Routledge & Kegan Paul, 1983).

L731. Smith, F. Joseph. "Jacques Derrida's Husserl Interpretation." Philosophy Today 9 (1967), 106-23.

L732. Smith, Joseph H. and William Kerrigan, eds. Taking Chances: Derrida, Psychoanalysis, and Literature (Baltimore: Johns Hopkins UP, 1984).

L733. Spanos, William V., Paul Bové, and Daniel O'Hara, eds. The Question of Textuality: Strategies of Reading in Contemporary American Criticism (Bloomington: Indiana UP, 1982).

L734. Spivak, Gayatri Chakravorty. "Translator's Preface" to Derrida, Of Grammatology (Baltimore: Johns Hopkins UP, 1976).
L735. ----------. "Glas-Piece: A Compte Rendu ." Diacritics 7.3 (1977), 22-43.
L736. ----------. "Revolutions that as Yet Have No Model: Derrida's 'Limited Inc.'" Diacritics 10 (1980), 29-49.

L737. ----------. "Displacement and the Discourse of Woman," in M. Krupnick, ed. Displacement: Derrida and After (Bloomington: Indiana UP, 1983), 169-95.
L738. ----------. "Love Me, Love My Ombre, Elle." Diacritics 14.4 (1984), 19-36 [Derrida and feminism].
L739. ----------. "Reading the World: Literary Studies in the 1980s," in G. Atkins and M. L. Johnson, eds. Writing and Reading Differently: Deconstruction and the Teaching of Composition and Literature (Lawrence: UP of Kansas, 1985), 27-37.

L740. Sprinker, Michael. "Criticism as Reaction." Diacritics 10.3 (1980), 2-14 [on Graff].
L741. ----------. "The Use and Abuse of Foucault." Humanities in Society 3 (1980), 1-20.
L742. ----------. "Textual Politics: Foucault and Derrida." Boundary 8.3 (1980), 75-98.
L743. ----------. "Aesthetic Criticism: Geoffrey Hartman," in J. Arac, W. Godzich, and W. Martin, eds. The Yale Critics: Deconstruction in America (Minneapolis: U of Minnesota P, 1983), 43-65.

L744. Staten, Henry. Wittgenstein and Derrida (Lincoln: U of Nebraska P, 1984).

L745. Steiner, George. "The Mandarin of the Hour--Michel Foucault." NY Times Book Review (Feb. 28, 1971), 8, 23-31.
L746. ----------. "Steiner Responds to Foucault." Diacritics 1.2 (1971), 59.

L747. Stempel, Daniel. "History and Postmodern Literary Theory," in J. Natoli, ed. Tracing Literary Theory (Urbana: U of Illinois P, 1987), 80-104.

L748. Stern, Carol Simpson. "Deconstruction and the Phenomenological Alternative." LPer 4.1 (1983), 41-44.

L749. Stivale, Charles J. "Gilles Deleuze and Félix Guattari: Schizoanalysis & Literary Discourse." SubStance 29 (1981), 51-55.

L750. Sussman, Henry. "The Deconstructor as Politician: Melville's Confidence-Man." Glyph 4 (1978), 32-56.
L751. ----------. Franz Kafka: Geometrician of Metaphor (Madison WI: Coda P, 1979).

L752. Swiggart, Peter. "Criticism and the New Poetics," in J. H. Smith, ed. Brandeis Essays in Literature (Waltham MA: Dept. of Eng. & American Lit., Brandeis U, 1983), 173-201 [discusses de Man and Stanley Fish].

L753. Taft-Kaufman, Jill. "Deconstructing the Text: Performance Implications." LPer 4.1 (1983), 55-59.

L754. Tallack, Douglas. "Deconstruction: Henry James, *In the Cage,*" in D. Tallack, ed. Literary Theory at Work: Three Texts (Totowa NJ: Barnes & Noble, 1987), 159-80.

L755. Tanner, Stephen L. "Joyce and Modern Critical Theory." ArQ 40.3 (1984), 269-79.

L756. Taylor, Charles and William Connolly. "Michel Foucault: An Exchange." Political Theory 13 (1985), 365-86.
L757. ----------. "Foucault on Freedom and Truth," in D. C. Hoy, ed. Foucault: A Critical Reader (Oxford: Basil Blackwell, 1986), 69-102.

L758. Taylor, Jacqueline. "Performance Centered Research: Post-Structuralist Implications." LPer 4.1 (1983), 37-40.

L759. Taylor, Mark C. "Deconstruction: What's the Difference?" Soundings 66.4 (1983), 387-403.
L760. ----------, ed. Deconstruction in Context: Literature and Philosophy (Chicago: U of Chicago P, 1986).

L761. Teets, Bruce E. "Ruminations on Joseph Conrad and Post-Structuralism: A Common Ground." Conradian 8.1 (1983), 10-21.

L762. Terdiman, Richard. "Deconstruction/Mediation: A Dialectical Critique of 'Derrideanism.'" MinnR 19 (1982), 103-11.

L763. Thompson, Michael. Rubbish Theory: The Creation and Destruction of Value (Oxford: Oxford UP, 1979).

L764. Tompkins, Jane. "Graff Against Himself." MLN 96.5 (1981), 1091-96.

L765. Ulmer, Gregory L. "Jacques Derrida and Paul de Man on/in Rousseau's Faults." ECent 20 (1979), 164-81.
L766. ----------. "The Post-Age." Diacritics 11.3 (1981), 39-56 [on Derrida].
L767. ----------. "Of a Parodic Tone Recently Adopted in Criticism." NLH (1982), 543-59.
L768. ----------. "Op Writing: Derrida's Solicitation of Theoria," in M. Krupnick, ed. Displacement: Derrida and After (Bloomington: Indiana UP, 1983), 29-58.

L769. ----------. Applied Grammatology: Post(e)-pedagogy from Jacques Derrida to Joseph Beuys (Baltimore: Johns Hopkins UP, 1985).
L770. ----------. "Textshop for Post(e)pedagogy," in G. Atkins and M. L. Johnson, eds. Writing and Reading Differently: Deconstruction and the Teaching of Composition and Literature (Lawrence: UP of Kansas, 1985), 38-64.

L771. Van Den Abbeele, Georges. "Up Against the *Wall* : The Stage of Judgment." Diacritics 14.3 (1984), 90-98 [on Lyotard].

L772. Vander Weele, Michael. "History, Irony and the Heavenly Phoenix of Interpretation." R&L 17.1 (1985), 25-45 [discusses G. Bruns and G. Hartman].

L773. Verdicchio, Massimo. "A Reader Like Phaedrus." Diacritics 14.1 (1984), 24-35 [on Culler, Derrida, de Man, Plato].

L774. Waite, Geoffrey. "Nietzsche and Deconstruction: The Politics of 'The Question of Style.'" BMMLA 16.1 (1983), 70-86.

L775. Waller, Gary F. "Deconstruction and Renaissance Literature." Assays 2 (1982), 69-93.
L776. ----------. "Working within the Paradigm Shift: Poststructuralism and the College Curriculum." ADEB 81 (1985), 6-12.
L777. ----------. "Writing the Languages Writing Us." DQ 20.1 (1985), 126-34 [on Foucault].

L778. Walzer, Michael. "The Politics of Michel Foucault," in D. C. Hoy, ed. Foucault: A Critical Reader (Oxford: Basil Blackwell, 1986), 51-68.

L779. Wartenberg, Thomas. "Foucault's Archaeological Method." Philosophical Forum 15 (1984), 345-64.

L780. Watson, Stephen. "Regulations: Kant and Derrida at the End of Metaphysics," in J. Sallis, ed. Deconstruction and Philosophy: The Texts of Jacques Derrida (Chicago: U of Chicago P, 1987), 71-86.

L781. Weber, Samuel. "The Sideshow, or: Remarks on a Canny Moment." MLN 88 (1973), 1102-33.
L782. ----------. "Saussure and the Apparition of Language." MLN 91 (1976), 913-38.
L783. ----------. "It." Glyph 4 (1978), 1-29 [on Derrida and Freud].
L784. ----------. "A Stroke of Luck." Enclitic 6.2 (1982), 29-31 [Derrida and Saussure].

L785. ----------. Institution and Interpretation (Minneapolis: U of Minnesota P, 1987).

L786. Weedon, Chris. Feminist Practice and Poststructuralist Theory (Oxford: Blackwell, 1987).

L787. Weimann, Robert. "Mimesis und die Burge der Reprasentation: Der Poststrukturalismus und das Produktions-problem in fiktiven Texten." WB 31.7 (1985), 1061-99 [discusses Derrida, Foucault, Girard].
L788. ----------. "History, Appropriation, and the Uses of Representation in Modern Narrative," in M. Krieger, ed.The Aims of Representation: Subject/ Text/ History (NY: Columbia UP, 1987), 175-215.

L789. Wellek, René. "Destroying Literary Studies." NewC 2.4 (1983), 1-8.

L790. Wesling, Donald. "Difficulties of the Bardic: Literature and the Human Voice." CritI 8.1 (1981), 69-81 [discusses Derrida].

L791. White, Hayden. "Foucault Decoded: Notes from Underground." History and Theory 12 (1973), 23-54.
L792. ----------. Tropics of Discourse (Baltimore: Johns Hokpins UP, 1978).
L793. ----------. "Michel Foucault," in J. Sturrock, ed. Structuralism and Since: From Lévi-Strauss to Derrida (Oxford & NY: Oxford UP, 1979), 81-115.

L794. Williams, William Frederick. "The Possibility of the Existence of Literature from a Poststructuralist Perspective: A Metacritical Examination of Textuality through Categorical Deconstruction." DAI 45 (1985), 2864A.

L795. Wills, David. "Prosthesis: An Introduction to Textual Artifice." SoRA 17.1 (1984), 59-67.

L796. Winders, James A. "Foucault and Marx: A Critical Articulation of Two Theoretical Treatments." NOR 11.3-4 (1984), 134-48.
L797. ----------. "Poststructuralist Theory, Praxis, and the Intellectual." ConL 27.1 (1986), 73-84.

L798. Winterowd, W. Ross. "Post-Structuralism and Composition." Pre/Text 4.1 (1983), 79-92.

L799. Wood, David. "An Introduction to Derrida." Radical Philosophy 21 (1979), 18-28.
L800. ----------. "Derrida and the Pardoxes of Reflection." Journal of the British Society for Phenomenology 11.3 (1980), 225-36.

L801. ----------. "Style and Strategy at the Limits of Philosophy: Heidegger and Derrida." Monist 63.4 (1980), 494-511.
L802. ----------, ed. Derrida and Différance (Coventry: Parousia P, 1985).
L803. ----------. "Following Derrida," in J. Sallis, ed. Deconstruction and Philosophy: The Texts of Jacques Derrida (Chicago: U of Chicago P, 1987), 143-60.

L804. Wordsworth, Ann. "Derrida and Criticism." OLR 3.2 (1978), 47-52.
L805. ----------. "Household Words: Alterity, the Unconscious and the Text." OLR 5.1-2 (1982), 80-92.

L806. Wright, Iain. "'What Matter Who's Speaking?' Beckett, the Authorial Subject and Contemporary Critical Theory." SoRA 16.1 (1983), 5-30.
L807. ----------. "History, Hermeneutics, Deconstruction," in J. Hawthorn, ed. Criticism and Critical Theory (London: Edward Arnold, 1984), 83-96.

L808. Young, Robert, ed. Untying the Text: A Post-Structuralist Reader (Boston: Routledge & Kegan Paul, 1981).
L809. ----------. "Post-Structuralism: The End of Theory." OLR 5.1-2 (1982), 3-15.

L810. Zhang, Longxi. "The Tao and the Logos : Notes on Derrida's Critique of Logocentrism." CritI 11.3 (1985), 385-98.

M. Classified Index of Subjects and Major Theorists

The divisions of this index parallel the sections of the Classified Bibliography. The sections are as follows:

A. Structuralism
B. Semiotics
C. Narratology
D. Psychological Criticism
E. Sociological Criticism
F. Marxist Criticism
G. Feminist Criticism
H. Reader-Response Criticism
I. Reception Aesthetics
J. Phenomenological Criticism
K. Hermeneutics
L. Deconstruction and Post-Structuralism

Following these section-by-section indexes, there is a general cumulative index, the General Index which includes all of the headings from all of the section indexes as well as cross-references by section letter. The section indexes include item numbers; the general index does not include item numbers since it refers to the separate indexes. Italicized item numbers in name entries refer to works by that theorist while the other items comment on the theorist. Since the sections of the Classified Bibliography are arranged alphabetically by author, the section indexes do not index the authors (except for major theorists). However, a final Author Index provides access to all entries in all sections of the bibliography.

A. STRUCTURALISM

Althusser, Louis: a85, a161

Anglo-American criticism and structuralism: a8, a38, a182

anthologies: a6, a12, a99, a120, a125, a165, a179, a197, a218, a222, a239, a249, a301, a306, a395

applications: African poetics, a5; American literature, a304; British literature, a242; French literature, a17, a18, a26, a28, a31, a32, a53, a54; medieval literature, a118, a414

B. SEMIOTICS

German and Austrian semiotics: b133, b205, b207

Girard, René: b238

glossaries and dictionaries: b79, b138, b259, b331

Greece, semiotics in: b35

Greimas, A.-J.: b5, b42, *b135-38,* b204, b312
hermeneutics and semiotics: b256, b277, b339

histories of semiotics: b72, b81, b101, b165, b393

Hjelmslev, Louis: b381
66, b84-85, b89-92, b103, b115-16, b127, b142, b144, b146, b150, b152,
b154, b173-76, b178, b221, b232, b239-41, b243, b247-49, b269, b272,
b273, b294, b319-20, b322-28, b330-32, b337-38, b352, b354, b368-69,
b372, b375, b379-80, b394-95, b401

Israeli semiotics: b181

Italy, semiotics in: b31, b59, b250

Jakobson, Roman: b82, b93, b157, *b162-70,* b179, b200, b242, b313, b391

Japan, semiotics in: b378

Kristeva, Julia: b2, *b192-99,* b404

Leibniz, G. W.: b70-71

linguistics and semiotics: b1, b6, b13-14, b27-28, b57, b135, b138, b147,
b162, b164, b167-70, n185, b187-88, b246, b257, b267-68, b288, b343,
b355

Lotman, Juri: b82, b200-02, *b210-19,* b226, b230, b235, b253, b291, b345-
47, b374

medieval semiotics: b41, b53-54, b102, b148, b299

Mexico, semiotics in: b172

Morris, Charles: b50, b79, b99-100, b108, *b245,* b284, b306, b357

Mukarovsky, Jan: b82, *b251,* b357

Venezuela, semiotics in: b237

C. NARRATOLOGY

allusions: c45, c273, c275, c427

ambiguity: c488, c491

anthologies: c233, c247, c374, c383, c389, c543, c546

applications: American narratives, c38, c363, c398, c486, c488-89; British narratives, c78, c89, c282, c307, c348, c373, c379, c392, c404, c491, c590; Czech narratives, c152, c159; French narratives, c14, c287, c535, c540; medieval narrative, c8, c163, c597; Russian narratives, c10, c16, c19, c263, c387, c426, c520, c591; children's literature: c268-69, c324-25; postmodern novels: c367, c402

Bakhtin, Mikhail: c10-c11, *c14-20,* c48-50, c62, 87-88, c111, c131-32, c162, c182, c185, c231-32, c256, c272, c278, c280, c305, c312, c320, c345-36, c387-88, c392, c425-26, c439-40, c537, c567, c571, c579, c591-92

Bal, Mieke: *c21-30,* c47, c79

Barthes, Roland: c230, c486

bibliographies: c360, c405

Booth, Wayne: c13, c49, *c59-60*

characters, characterization: c4-c5, c67, c99, c107, c110, c149, c189, c194, c235, c244, c257, c351, c353, c359, c363, c514, c549, c579, c590, c605

Chatman, Seymour: c48, *c99-108,* c350, c544

closure: c267, c295, c372, c574

conventions: c73, c422

deconstruction and narrative theory: c108, c138-39, c592

description: c22, c26, c41, c53-54, c90, c134-36, c227, c242-43, c277, c301-02, c482 discourse analysis: c40

embedded narratives, narrative frames: c24, c46, c91, c512

feminist theory and narrative: c140, c322

fictionality and referent: c245, c248, c265, c319, c332-33, c357-58, c362, c415, c417-20, c500, c593, c595

focalization: c25, c27, c38, c79, c150, c321, c335, c340, c501, c504, c577, c585

free indirect discourse >> speech

Freud, Sigmund: c81

general theories of fiction: c1-c3, c6, c23, c39, c56, c82, c89, c94, c114, c161, c166-67, c186, c196, c211, c213-14, c216, c234, c249, c258, c261, c279, c354, c357, c431, c438, c462-64, c469-71, c477, c490, c503, c513, c534, c542, c562, c575, c594, c598, c601-04, c606

Genette, Gérard: c12, c30, c38, c47, c78, c100, c109, c115-16, *c197-205,* c230, c432-33, c487, c540, c572, c576, c581
glossaries and dictionaries: c223, c405, c459

Greimas, A.-J.: c7, c61, *c217-225,* c228-29, c251, c408, c410-12, c479, c519

Hamon, Philippe: *c235-44*

ideological criticism and narrative: c37, c87-88, c284, c320, c324, c537-39, c565

interior monologue: c51, c184

intertextuality: c76, c128-29, c188, c286, c334, c380, c384, c386, c483-84, c506, c561

introductions and methodological surveys: c12, c29-30, c58, c60, c66, c68-71, c80, c83-84, c86, c102-03, c105-06, c108, c122-25, c178, c180, c195, c212, c226, c236, c238, c241, c246, c252, c259-60, c289, c291, c295-99, c303-04, c323, c327, c329, c336, c343-44, c357, c360-61, c367, c390-91, c393, c421, c424, c442-61, c492, c521-26, c528, c531-32, c552, c554, c560, c568-69, c599, c600

repetition: c9, c43, c63, c97-98, c112, c376-77, c379, c468, c490, c540, c564

representation and realism: c5, c31-35, c175-76, c192, c309, c319, c328, c330, c394, c396, c437, c504, c535, c557, c584

Ricardou, Jean: *c472-76*

Ricoeur, Paul: *c477-80*

Riffaterre, Michael: c55, c278, *c482-85*

semiotics of narrative: c39, c57, c85, c93, c117, c120-21, c124, c170-72, c174, c179, c227, c251, c263-65, c285, c303-04, c355, c403-06, c408, c410, c412, c429, c467-68, c485, c530, c588
space in fiction: c127, c164, c250, c258, c266, c277, c283, c300, c347, c370, c406, c496, c543, c556, c558, c607

speech (represented speech, direct and indirect): c20, c31-34, c148, c253, c255, c364, c409, c494, c533, c533, c559, c563, c573

Stanzel, Franz: c75, c115, c327, *c547-51*, c596

style: c74, c113, c160, c578, c597

text grammars: c40, c141-47, c190-91, c206-10, c228-29, c262, c279, c282, c395, c401, c413, c421, c430, c481, c507, c550, c587-89

time in fiction: c77, c100, c156, c164-65, c270, c371, c400, c478, c480, c499, c505, c531, c555-56, c558, c570, c576

Todorov, Tzvetan: c12, c96, *c571*

verisimilitude: c73, c104, c399

voice: c10

D. PSYCHOLOGICAL CRITICISM

Adlerian theory: d359

feminism and psychoanalytic approaches: d60, d109, d201, d229-31, d241-44, d248, d252-53, d372, d375, d381-82, d543, d559, d564, d603, d613, d643, d653, d665, d671, d673, d677, d740, d777-78

Foucault, Michel: d220

Freud, Sigmund: d4, d13, d17, d22, d24, d26, d28-29, d33, d51, d54, d56, d58, d61, d62, d64, d73-74, d84-85, d88, d95, d97, d98, d108, d113, d123-24, d141, d145, d169, d192, d209, d223, d256-57, d275, d285, d287-88, d316, d323-25, d355, d365-67, d381, d400, d411-12, d435, d455, d460, d475, d483, d487-92, d498-99, d505-08, d522, d531, d536, d542, d550, d560-61, d622, d627-28, d635, d643, d651, d656, d661, d670, d710-12, d748-49, d757, d761. d763-66, d772, d775, d779

Fromm, Erich: d668

Gestalt theory: d228

Girard, René: d179, *d266-71*
glossaries and dictionaries: d457-58

Greimas, A.-J.: d678

Guattari, Félix >> Deleuze, Gilles

Heidegger, Martin: d93

hermeneutics: d651

histories of psychoanalytic approaches: d84-86, d200, d214, d220, d256-57, d325, d480, d522, d526, d550, d634, d654, d656, d711-12, d780, d786

Holland, Norman: d165, *d331-52,* d383, d546

Horney, Karen: d82, d582, d625

ideological criticism and psychoanalysis: d117-19, d183, d235-36, d370-73

intertextuality: d638

introductions and methodological surveys: d2, d5, d8-9, d14, d30-31, d36, d38, d45-46, d48, d62, d65, d67-69, d77-78, d80, d89-91, d93, d101, d110, d114-15, d125, d135-39, d151, d161-65, d178, d183-87, d197, d203-04, d206-07, d212-213, d221-22, d225-26, d228. d232, d234, d262-65, d273-

74, d276-77, d291-92, d296-300, d304, d309, d317-19, d331-32, d335, d338-39, d342-43, d351, d357, d360, d362, d384, d386, d388, d393, d395, d417, d429, d431, d454, d464, d467-70, d477-79, d501, d510, d518, d519, d534-35, d550, d551, d565-66, d568-70, d572, d574-79, d584-86, d589-91, d596, d599, d605-06, d626, d636-37, d639-41, d644, d646-48, d663, d669-70, d674, d688-89, d691, d698, d703-07, d721, d723-25, d727-28, d731-32, d734, d736, d737, d739, d742, d745-46, d758-60, d762, d774, d780-81, d788-91, d793, d795

Irigaray, Luce: d82, d241, *d363-64*

Jung, Carl, and Jungian approaches: d3, d49, d94, d124, d129, d176, d225, d356, *d379,* d397, d402-08, d430, d573, d600, d603, d629, d652, d709

Klein, Melanie: d79, d301

Kohut, Heinz: d413-16

Kristeva, Julia: d7, d401, *d419-26*

Lacan, Jacques, and Lacanian criticism: d4, d7, d12, d13, d19-21, d29, d34, d51, d63-64, d81-82, d96-97, d108, d116, d120-21, d127-28, d131, d142-44, d166, d170, d173, d180-82, d199-200, d201-08, d211, d215, d223, d227, d232, d235-36, d239-48, d254-55, d261, d285, d307-08, d310, d316, d325, d328, d353-55, d358, d361, d368, d370-71, d372, d380, d381, d387, d418, d433, *d436-54,* d456, d457-59, d463, d466-69, d471, d473, d483, d492-94, d496, d503-04, d511, d526, d529-30, d532, d534-35, d538-39, d541, d543, d553-59, d571, d580, d607-09, d612-15, d617, d621-22, d630-33, d640, d649, d653-59, d678-79, 681-84, d686-87, d692, d697, d699, d702, d708, d716, d718, d722, d744, d750-52, d756-57, d765, d772-73, d785, d794

Laing, R. D.: d272

language and psychoanalytic criticism: d33, d72, d79, d107, d146-50, d186, d190, d326-27, d353, d358, d361, d399, d480, d496, d491-92, d497, d556-57, d612, d621, d627, d630, d637, d645, d662, d675, d686-87, d743, d771, d774

Lévi-Strauss, Claude: d85, d526-27

Lyotard, Jean-François: *d486-91*

narrative and psychoanalysis: d73-77, d95, d104, d143-44, d182, d308, d486, d493, d496-97, d676, d678, d678-79, d694, d713, d740, d755

E. SOCIOLOGICAL CRITICISM

Gramsci, Antonio: e22

hermeneutics and sociological criticism: e96

histories of sociological criticism, historical surveys: e12, e122, e141

ideological criticism: e2, e42, e64-65, e100, e219

introductions and methodological surveys: e1, e3, e8-9, e13-19, e23, e28, e31-35, e38, e40, e44-50, e53-62, e66-71, e74-76, e85-87, e91-94, e97, e99, e101-04, e109-17, e120, e123, e128-29, e131-32, e134, e136, e137, e142-44, e151, e154-56, e159-68, e171-73, e175-83, e186-93, e196-201, e203-04, e206, e208-10, e213-15, e218-22

Jameson, Fredric: e107

Kristeva, Julia: e2

Lukacs, Gyorgy: e153

Macherey, Pierre: e135
Marxist criticism and sociological criticism: e21, e43, e79, e207

novel and sociological criticism: e5, e82, e98, e118, e107, e125, e194, e202, e216

psychoanalysis and sociological criticism: e88

readers, sociological studies of reading: e6, e7, e51, e52, e126-27, e135, e139, e211

Ricoeur, Paul: e138

Russian sociological criticism: e30, e106, e207

semiotics: e208

Williams, Raymond: *e73*

F. MARXIST CRITICISM

Adorno, Theodor: *f5-11,* f97, f105, f234, f269, f316, f318, f334, f342, f350, f352, f374, f384, f405, f433-34, f474, f503, f509, f521, f563, f587, f610, f618-19, f678, f695, f702-03, f722, f749, f757, f760, f769, f773

Plekhanov, George: f42, f652

politics and literature: f14, f29, f49, f70, f73, f78, f85, f87, f107, f109, f134-35, f212-13, f221, f276, f278-79, f550, f553-54, f566, f594, f609, f642-44, f710, f751

postmodernism, poststructuralism: f16-18, f106, f172, f175, f509, f722

realism: f76, f147, f224, f288, f361, f422, f432, f511, f544, f546, f688

Said, Edward: *f599-601*

Sartre, Jean-Paul: f318, f555, *f609,* f648

socialist realism: f67, f76, f100, f247-48, f272, f280, f286, f315, f341, f370-71, f409-10, f448-50, f462, f480-82, f497-98, f528, f532, f556, f611, f621, f632, f638

Soviet Marxist criticism: f100, f149, f157, f186, f192, f195, f222, f315, f345, f369, f375, f417, f465, f552, f571, f628-29, f649, f750

structuralism and Marxism: f225, f230-31, f271, f354, f471, f637, f774-77

Thompson, E. P.: f209

Trotsky, Leon: f616, f630
United States, Marxist and political criticism in: f48, f120-21, f201, f262

Williams, Raymond: f34, f71, f137, *f243,* f283, f294-95, f535, f540, f631, f709, *f736-48*

G. FEMINIST CRITICISM

anthologies: g1-g2, g6, g18, g40, g42, g77, g79, g81, g136, g137, g142, g154, g158, g189, g200, g207, g222, g224, g253-54, g270, g290, g374, g376, g378-79, g391, g394-95, g409, g411, g413

applications: African literature, g44; American literature, g22, g27, g30, g48, g84, g111, g120, g169, g204, g220, g223, g230, g249, g305, g311, g328, g397, g400, g401; British and Irish literature, g3, g8, g10-11, g17, g20, g24-26, g30, g32, g34, g37, g50, g54, g92, g94, g115, g121, g135-36, g141-42, g151, g153, g165, g167, g169-71, g189-90, g197, g208, g213, g223, g248, g259, g261, g264, g266, g277, g294, g300, g302, g305, g319, g321, g330, g346, g351, g359, g369, g374, g376, g386, g388, g412; French

H. READER-RESPONSE CRITICISM

feminist criticism: h59, h115-17, h127-30, h141, h359, h366, h373

Fish, Stanley: h7, h25, h54, h56, h65, h90, h98, h114, *h118-25,* h151, h169, h179, h195, h197, h201, h221, h236, h241, h283, h306, h323, h329-30, h332, h334, h363, h385, h401, h414

gender studies and reader response: h42, h83, h93, h127-30, h165, h253, h288, h309, h367

Gramsci, Antonio: h145

hermeneutics: h234, h237

Hirsch, E. D.: h221

historical studies of readers: h13-14, h16, h74, h153

Holland, Norman: h56, h66, h114, h141, h143, *h166-78,* h183, h242, h382, h406

Ingarden, Roman: h40, h51

intertextuality: h338

introductions and methodological surveys: h3, h5, h8-9, h15-17, h19-22, h28, h31-39, h41, h46, h53, h60-61, h63, h66, h69, h78-79, h81, h87-89. h91, h94-95, h98, h100, h105-07, h109, h111, h113, h122, h124, h125, h131, h136-37, h146-47, h149, h152, h154, h156, h160, h163, h166, h170-77, h181, h182, h184, h186-89, h191-93, h203, h205-06, h209, h211, h213, h214, h216, h219, h222-24, h226-28, h230, h232, h238-40, h243, h247, h248, h256, h258-59, h265-68, h270-71, h273-75, h277-80, h287, h289-90, h296, h302-05, h307-08, h310-13, h315, h319, h320-21, h325, h331, h333, h336, h341-42, h344-54, h356-58, h365, h368-72, h376-77, h381, h384, h386-88, h392-93, h398-400, h403-05, h407, h409-11

Iser, Wolfgang: h8, h40, h44, h51, h56, h123, h164, *h185-95,* h202, h220, h229, h276, h322, h343, h362, h378, h385, h411

Jauss, Hans Robert: *h197*

Juhl, P. D.: h25, *h201*

lesbian feminist criticism and reader response: h204

linguistics and reader response: h133-35, h150, h158, h218, h379

Lotman, Juri: h222

narrative theory and reader response: h43, h45, h63, h76, h132, h142, h185, h190, h218, h269-70, h291, h298-99, h301, h340

phenomenological approaches and reader response: h127, h140, h186, h293-94, h324

Prince, Gerald: h291, h296, *h298-301*, h322, h411

psychoanalysis and reader-response criticism: h1, h27, h114, h141, h144, h159, h162, h239, h409

realism: h82, h239

reception theory and reader response: h61, h149, h361

reflexivity and reader response: h63, h92, h269

rhetorical analysis and reader response: h12, h17, h70, h72-73, h199, h412

Riffaterre, Michael: *h337-42*

Said, Edward: *h356*

semiotics and reader response: h110-12, h339

sociology of reading: h80, h102, h104, h139, h217

speech act theory and reader response: h236, h295
structuralism and reader response: h213, h251, h259

I. RECEPTION AESTHETICS

Adorno, Theodor: i100

anthologies: i2-3, i33-34, i40, i49, i51, i60, i62, i82, i101, i108-09, i112, i114-15, i145, i153-54, i158

applications: British and Irish literature, i14; French, i13-14, i117; German literature, i8, i10, i15, i26, i28, i32, i35, i35, i39, i71, i76-77, i80, i92, i99, i101, i104, i107-08, i116, i123, i129, i147; German philosophy, i48, i100; Spanish and South American literature, i150; ancient literature, g126; the comic, i109; the novel, i72, i82, i140, i142, i152; poetry, i88

J. PHENOMENOLOGICAL CRITICISM

repetition: k158, k166

Ricoeur, Paul: k28-29, k57, k90, k140, k157, k165-66, k189, k199, k215, k218-19, *k221-39,* k270, k276-78

Rorty, Richard: k43, *k242*

Schlegel, Friedrich: k170

Schleiermacher, Friedrich: k2, k66, k209, *k248*

semiotics and hermeneutics: k170, k251

structuralism and hermeneutics: k130, k252

Szondi, Peter: k2, k27, k68, k95, k97, k113, k200, *k268*

tradition: k37, k91, k159, k266

L. DECONSTRUCTION AND POST-STRUCTURALIST CRITICISM

Abrams, M. H.: *L2-5*

Althusser, Louis: L83, L729

anthologies: L19-20, L22, L33, L141, L312, L356, L379, L381, L390, L445-46, L637, L726, L732-33, L760, L808

applications: African literature, L37; American literature, L25, L51, L66, L67-69, L75, L140, L228, L274, L582, L612, L669, L672, L675, L717, L750, L754; British and Irish literature, L29, L34, L67-68, L107-08, L319, L444, L556, L575, L580, L593, L595, L597, L637, L639, L655, L755, L761, L809; French literature, L109, L148, L243, L255, L353, L551, L559, L562, L567; German literature, L49, L353, L567, L585, L751; various, L228, L278, L281-82; ancient literature, L561

Bakhtin, Mikhail: L103, L392, L645, L699

Barthes, Roland: L118, L134, L182, L402
Baudrillard, Jean: *L46-50*

Benjamin, Walter: L96

bibliographies: L38, L62, L113, L371, L410, L637, L656

Bloom, Harold: L15, L19, L45, *L63-72,* L127, L207, L218, L283, L310, L316, L340, L615, L631, L674, L676, L689

Culler, Jonathan: L84, L90, L110, *L126-34,* L136, L773

Deleuze, Gilles: L77, L123, *L145-53,* L241, L280, L415, L646, L749

Derrida, Jacques: L1-L2, L6, L8-10, L23-24, L36, L40, L43, L56-58, L61, L73-74, L83, L93-94, L97, L102, L104, L111, L122, L128, L131, L134-36, L144, L155, *L156-95,* L198, L201, L205, L207, L217, L222-23, L226, L232, L262, L264, L265-66, L271-72, L279, L284, L297, L301, L308, L310-11, L314, L321, L324-26, L328, L331, L335, L344, L354, L360, L365-66, L374-76, L380, L382, L391-92, L398, L401-02, L404-07, L409-14, L419, L424-25, L430-31, L433, L442, L447, L449, L552, L555, L559-60, L566-67, L573, L595, L607, L610, L614, L618-19, L626-28, L632, L636, L638, L640-43, L651, L659, L663, L671, L673, L678, L680-81, L683, L688, L696, L701, L705, L709, L711, L722-23, L725, L727, L731-32, L734-38, L742, L744, L765-69, L773, L780, L783-84, L787, L790, L799-804, L810

Eagleton, Terry: *L214-15*

feminism and deconstruction: L7, L90, L212, L362, L365, L560, L737-39, L786

Fish, Stanley: *L226,* L288, L752

Foucault, Michel: L16, L22, L24, L47, L62, L77, L83, L96, L99, L104, L106, L113, L116, L121, L137, L139, L147, L153, L199, L209-10, L232, *L233-57,* L259, L261-62, L302-06, L331, L338, L346-47, L358, L383, L392, L421, L448, L565-66, L571, L574, L602, L641, L648-50, L653-54, L658, L673, L686, L692, L701, L704, L715, L720, L723, L730, L741-42, L745-46, L756-57, L777-79, L787, L791-93, L796

Freud, Sigmund: L98, L177, L256, L425, L433, L435, L668, L781, L783

Frye, Northrop: L279

Gadamer, Hans-Georg: L84, L366, L638

Girard, René: L264, *L278-82,* L723, L787

Graff, Gerald: L269, *L291-96,* L601, L740, L764

N. General Index

[This index excludes the listings of anthologies, applications, bibliographies, and introductions and methodological surveys, since these categories appear in all of the section-by-section bibliographies.]

O. Author Index

Aaron, Daniel: f1
Aarsleff, Hans: f2
Abdulla, Adnan K.: d1
Abel, Elizabeth: g1-2
Abel, Emily: g2
Abel, Lionel: a1, L1
Abicht, Ludo: f3
Abrams, M. H.: L2-5
Ackerman, James S.: e1
Ackerman, Robert: a2
Adamowski, T. H.: j1
Adams, Jean-Michel: b1, c1-3
Adams, Michael Vannoy: L6
Adelman, Janet: g3
Adereth, Maxwell: f4
Adler, Gunter: i1
Adorno, Theodor W.: f5-11
Adriaens, Mark: b2, e2
Agosti, Stefano: d2
Albanese, Ralph: e3
Alberes, R.-M.: a3
Albrecht, Milton C.: e4
Alcorn, Marshall W., Jr.: h1
Aler, Jean: k1
Alexander, Anne: d3
Alexander, Ian W.: j2
Alexander, Meena: j3
Alexandrescu, Sorin: c4
Allen, Carolyn: g4, L7
Allen, Douglas: j4
Allison, David: L8-10
Altenhofer, Norbert: k2
Alter, Jean: e5, f12
Alter, Robert: L11
Althaus, Horst: e6
Althusser, Louis: d4
Altick, Richard: e7, L12-13
Altieri, Charles: k3
Amacher, Richard: i2
Amalric, Jean-Claude: d5
Ames, Sanford: a4
Amigone, Grace Ritz: h2
Amossy, Ruth: c5, h3

About the Author

LEONARD ORR is Assistant Professor of English at the University of Notre Dame. He is the author of *Semiotic and Structuralist Analyses of Fiction* and *Problems and Poetics of the Nonaristotelian Novel,* and he has edited *Yeats and Postmodernism* and *De-Structing the Novel: Essays in Applied Postmodern Hermeneutics.* Orr is currently completing *A Dictionary of Critical Theory* and *A Handbook of Critical Theory,* both to be published by Greenwood Press, and he is editing *Critical Essays on Samuel Taylor Coleridge.* He has written numerous articles published in *Modern Fiction Studies, The Journal of Narrative Technique, SubStance, Neophilologus, College English,* and other journals.